Fodor's 2009

D0928674

PUERTO VALLARTA

By Jane Onstott

Where to Stay and Eat
for All Budgets

Must-See Sights
and Local Secrets

Ratings You Can Trust

Fodor's Travel Publications   New York, Toronto, London, Sydney, Auckland
www.fodors.com

FODOR'S PUERTO VALLARTA 2009
By: Jane Onstott

Editor: Laura Kidder

Editorial Production: Astrid deRidder
Maps & Illustrations: David Lindroth, cartographer, with additional cartography
provided by Henry Columb, Mark Stroud, and Ali Baird, Moon Street Cartography;
Bob Blake, Rebecca Baer, *map editors;* William Wu, *information graphics*
Design: Fabrizio LaRocca, *creative director;* Guido Caroti, Siobhan O'Hare, *art directors;*
Tina Malaney, Chie Ushio, Ann McBride, Jessica Walsh, *designers;* Melanie Marin,
senior picture editor; Moon Sun Kim, *cover designer*
Cover Photo: Tequila, Jalisco: Patrick Frilet/hemis.fr
Production/Manufacturing: Matt Struble

COPYRIGHT

ISBN 978–1–4000–1959–5

ISSN 1558–8718

SPECIAL SALES

This book is available at special discounts for bulk purchases for sales promotions or
premiums. Special editions, including personalized covers, excerpts of existing books,
and corporate imprints, can be created in large quantities for special needs. For more
information, write to Special Markets/Premium Sales, 1745 Broadway, MD 6-2, New
York, New York 10019, or e-mail specialmarkets@randomhouse.com.

AN IMPORTANT TIP & AN INVITATION

Although all prices, opening times, and other details in this book are based on information supplied to us at press time, changes occur all the time in the travel world, and
Fodor's cannot accept responsibility for facts that become outdated or for inadvertent
errors or omissions. So **always confirm information when it matters,** especially if you're
making a detour to visit a specific place. Your experiences—positive and negative—
matter to us. If we have missed or misstated something, **please write to us.** We follow
up on all suggestions. Contact the Puerto Vallarta editor at editors@fodors.com or c/o
Fodor's at 1745 Broadway, New York, NY 10019.

PRINTED IN THE UNITED STATES OF AMERICA

10 9 8 7 6 5 4 3 2 1

Be a Fodor's Correspondent

Your opinion matters. It matters to us. It matters to your fellow Fodor's travelers, too. And we'd like to hear it. In fact, we need to hear it.

When you share your experiences and opinions, you become an active member of the Fodor's community. That means we'll not only use your feedback to make our books better, but we'll publish your names and comments whenever possible. Throughout our guides, look for "Word of Mouth," excerpts of your unvarnished feedback.

Here's how you can help improve Fodor's for all of us.

Tell us when we're right. We rely on local writers to give you an insider's perspective. But our writers and staff editors—who are the best in the business—depend on you. Your positive feedback is a vote to renew our recommendations for the next edition.

Tell us when we're wrong. We're proud that we update most of our guides every year. But we're not perfect. Things change. Hotels cut services. Museums change hours. Charming cafés lose charm. If our writer didn't quite capture the essence of a place, tell us how you'd do it differently. If any of our descriptions are inaccurate or inadequate, we'll incorporate your changes in the next edition and will correct factual errors at fodors.com immediately.

Tell us what to include. You probably have had fantastic travel experiences that aren't yet in Fodor's. Why not share them with a community of like-minded travelers? Maybe you chanced upon a beach or bistro or B&B that you don't want to keep to yourself. Tell us why we should include it. And share your discoveries and experiences with everyone directly at fodors.com. Your input may lead us to add a new listing or highlight a place we cover with a "Highly Recommended" star or with our highest rating, "Fodor's Choice."

Give us your opinion instantly at our feedback center at www.fodors.com/feedback. You may also e-mail editors@fodors.com with the subject line "Puerto Vallarta Editor." Or send your nominations, comments, and complaints by mail to Puerto Vallarta Editor, Fodor's, 1745 Broadway, New York, NY 10019.

You and travelers like you are the heart of the Fodor's community. Make our community richer by sharing your experiences. Be a Fodor's correspondent.

Happy traveling!

Tim Jarrell, Publisher

CONTENTS

MAPS

PUERTO VALLARTA IN FOCUS

ABOUT THIS BOOK

Our Ratings

Sometimes you find terrific travel experiences and sometimes they just find you. But usually the burden is on you to select the right combination of experiences. That's where our ratings come in.

As travelers we've all discovered a place so wonderful that its worthiness is obvious. And sometimes that place is so experiential that superlatives don't do it justice: you just have to be there to know. These sights, properties, and experiences get our highest rating, **Fodor's Choice**, indicated by orange stars throughout this book.

Black stars highlight sights and properties we deem **Highly Recommended**, places that our writers, editors, and readers praise again and again for consistency and excellence.

By default, there's another category: any place we include in this book is by definition worth your time, unless we say otherwise. And we will.

Disagree with any of our choices? Care to nominate a place or suggest that we rate one more highly? Visit our feedback center at fodors. com.

Budget Well

Hotel and restaurant price categories from ¢ to $$$$ are defined in the opening pages of chapters 15 and 16. For attractions, we always give standard adult admission fees; reductions are usually available for children, students, and senior citizens. Want to pay with plastic? **AE, D, DC, MC, V** following restaurant and hotel listings indicate if American Express, Discover, Diners Club, MasterCard, and Visa are accepted.

Restaurants

Unless we state otherwise, restaurants are open for lunch and dinner daily. We mention dress only when there's a specific requirement and reservations only when they're essential or not accepted—it's always best to book ahead.

Hotels

Hotels have private bath, phone, TV, and air-conditioning and operate on the European Plan (aka EP, meaning without meals), unless we specify that they use the Continental Plan (CP, with a Continental breakfast), Breakfast Plan (BP, with a full breakfast), or Modified American Plan (MAP, with breakfast and dinner) or are all-inclusive (AI, including all meals and most activities). We always list facilities but not whether you'll be charged an extra fee to use them, so when pricing accommodations, find out what's included.

Many Listings

★	Fodor's Choice
★	Highly recommended
✉	Physical address
✛	Directions
ᨏ	Mailing address
☎	Telephone
📠	Fax
⊕	On the Web
✍	E-mail
🎫	Admission fee
☉	Open/closed times
Ⓜ	Metro stations
⊟	Credit cards

Hotels & Restaurants

☷	Hotel
🛏	Number of rooms
⚴	Facilities
ⅰⓄⅰ	Meal plans
✕	Restaurant
⚑	Reservations
↘	Smoking
ᵷ	BYOB
✕☷	Hotel with restaurant that warrants a visit

Outdoors

⅄	Golf
⚠	Camping

Other

☾	Family-friendly
⇨	See also
✉	Branch address
☞	Take note

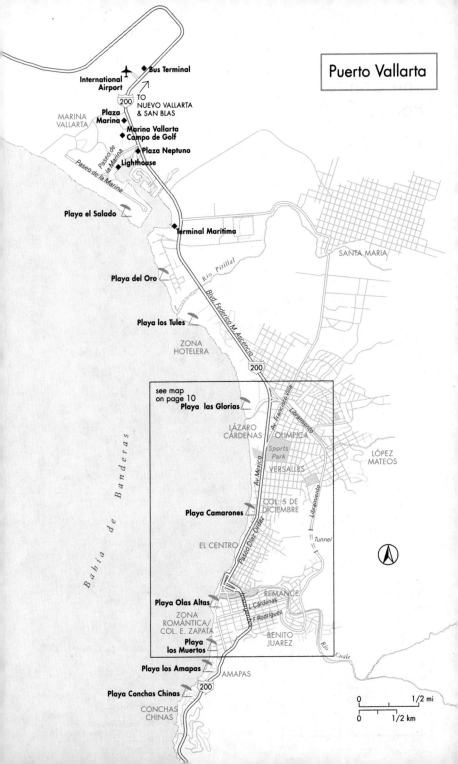

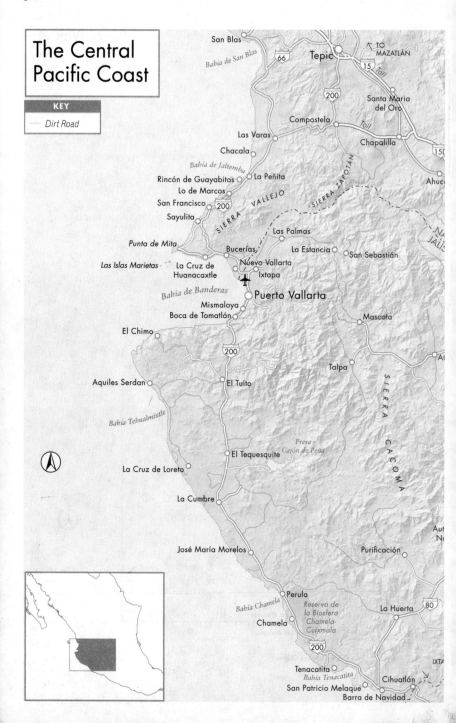

The Central Pacific Coast

KEY
- - - - - Dirt Road

San Blas
Bahía de San Blas
66
Tepic
TO MAZATLÁN
15 Toll
200
Santa María del Oro
Compostela
Toll
Las Varas
Chapalilla
Chacala
150
Bahía de Jaltemba
La Peñita
Rincón de Guayabitos
Lo de Marcos
San Francisco
200
Sayulita
SIERRA ZAPOTÁN
Ahuc
SIERRA VALLEJO
Las Palmas
Punta de Mita
Bucerías
La Estancia
San Sebastián
NA JALIS
Las Islas Marietas
La Cruz de Huanacaxtle
Nuevo Vallarta
Ixtapa
Bahía de Banderas
Puerto Vallarta
Mismaloya
Boca de Tomatlán
Mascota
El Chimo
200
Talpa
SIERRA CACOMA
Aquiles Serdan
El Tuito
Bahía Tehualmixtle
Presa Cañón de Peña
El Tequesquite
La Cruz de Loreto
La Cumbre
Aut N
José María Morelos
Purificación
Perula
Bahía Chamela
Reserva de la Biosfera Chamela-Cuixmala
La Huerta
80
Chamela
200
Tenacatita
Bahía Tenacatita
IXTA
San Patricio Melaque
Cihuatlán
Barra de Navidad

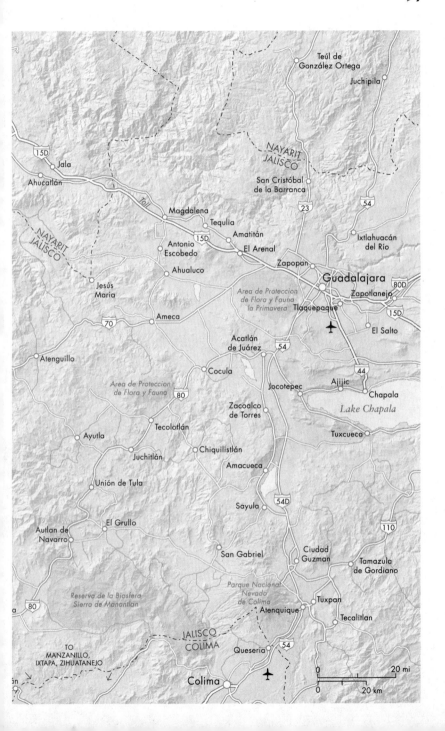

Teúl de
González Ortega

Juchipila

15D
Jala

Ahucatlán

NAYARIT
JALISCO

San Cristóbal
de la Barranca

23

54

Toll

Magdalena

Tequlia

Amatitán

Antonio
Escobedo

15D

El Arenal

Ixtlahuacán
del Río

NAYARIT
JALISCO

Ahualuco

Zapopan

Guadalajara

80D

Jesús
Maria

Area de Proteccion
de Flora y Fauna
la Primavera

Zapotlanejo

Tlaquepaque

15D

Ameca

70

Acatlán
de Juárez

54

El Salto

Atenguillo

Cocula

44

Area de Proteccion
de Flora y Fauna

80

Jocotepec

Ajijic

Chapala

Zacoalco
de Torres

Lake Chapala

Ayutla

Tecolotlán

Chiquilistlán

Tuxcueca

Juchitlán

Amacueca

Unión de Tula

Sayula

54D

110

Autlan de
Navarro

El Grullo

San Gabriel

Ciudad
Guzman

Tamazula
de Gordiano

80

Reserva de la Biosfera
Sierra de Manantlan

Parque Nacional
Nevado
de Colima

Tuxpan

Atenquique

Tecalitlan

JALISCO
COLIMA

TO
MANZANILLO,
IXTAPA, ZIHUATANEJO

Queseria

54

0   20 mi

Colima

0   20 km

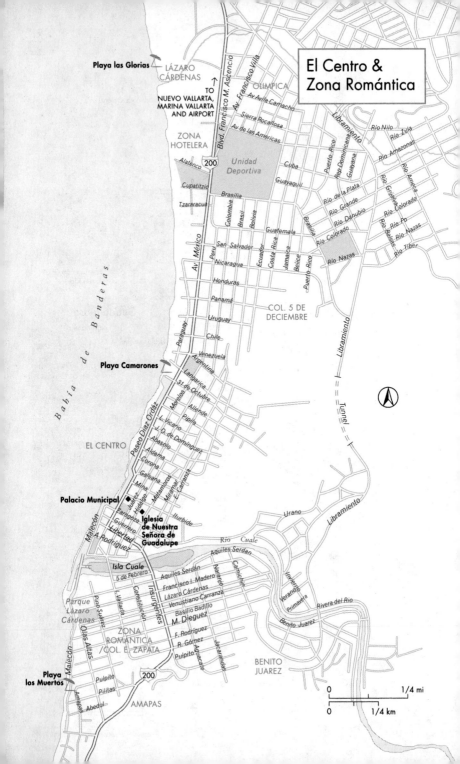

Experience
Puerto Vallarta

Looking out over downtown and the Bay of Banderas

WORD OF MOUTH

"While it's true the beaches/water are nicer on the Caribbean side, that's not the draw of Vallarta for those of us who love it dearly. It's about the Old Town, the welcoming local people, the lush jungles and mountains surrounding the Bay of Banderas, being part of a 'real' working city, etc. While there are ruins on the Yucatan peninsula, I would not agree that that means there is 'more to do' there. Plenty to see and do in Puerto Vallarta, into the mountains, and both north and south along the coastline."

—suze

WELCOME TO PUERTO VALLARTA

TOP REASONS TO GO

★ **Legendary restaurants:** Eat barbecued snapper with your feet in the sand or chateaubriand with a killer ocean view.

★ **Adventure and indulgence:** Ride a horse, mountain bike or go four-wheeling into the mountains, dive into the sea, and relax at an elegant spa—all in one day.

★ **Natural beauty:** Enjoy the physical beauty of Pacific Mexico's prettiest resort town, where cobblestone streets disappear into emerald green hills with the big, sparkling bay below.

★ **Authentic art:** PV's artists and artisans—from Huichol Indians to expats—produce a huge diversity of exceptional folk treasures and fine art.

★ **Diverse nightlife:** Whether you're old, young, gay, straight, mild, or wild, PV's casual and unpretentious party scene has something to entice you after dark.

1 Old Vallarta. Rising abruptly from the sea are the hilly cobblestoned streets of El Centro (Downtown), lined with white-washed homes and shops. South of the Cuale River, the Zona Romántica (Romantic Zone, in Col. E. Zapata) has PV's highest density of restaurants and shops.

2 North of Downtown. Facing a busy avenue, the Zona Hotelera Norte (Northern Hotel Zone) has malls, businesses, and high-rise hotels. The shopping centers and deluxe hotels of Marina Vallarta are sandwiched between a golf course and the city's main marina.

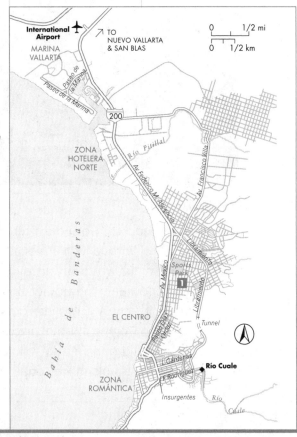

3 Nuevo Vallarta. The southernmost spot in Nayarit State, this planned resort is ideal if you want all-inclusive hotels. It has few restaurants and shops outside the Paradise Plaza mall.

4 The Southern Nayarit Coast. Exclusive Punta de Mita is dominated by the Four Seasons. Sayulita, San Francisco, and La Cruz de Huanacaxtle attract visitors with their small-town charm. Lovely, un-touristy beaches like Playa Chacala complete the picture.

5 South of Puerto Vallarta. To Mismaloya, the hotels of the Zona Hotelera Sur hug the beach or overlook it from cliffside aeries. Between La Cruz de Loreto and the Colima State border, the Costalegre is a mixture of luxury resorts and earthy seaside hamlets.

Dreams Hotel, Puerto Vallarta, Jalisco, Mexico

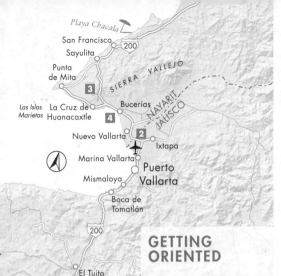

Playa Chacala

San Francisco
Sayulita
200
Punta de Mita
SIERRA VALLEJO
3
Las Islas Marietas
La Cruz de Huanacaxtle
Bucerías
4
NAYARIT
JALISCO
Nuevo Vallarta
2
Ixtapa
Marina Vallarta
Puerto Vallarta
Mismaloya
Boca de Tomatlán
200
El Tuito

La Cruz de Loreto
El Tequesquite

La Cumbre

5

José María Morelos
200

Bahía de Banderas

Bahía Chamela
Perula

Reserva de la Biosfera Chamela-Cuixmala
Chamela

Tenacatita
Bahía Tenacatita
San Patricio Melaque
Barra de Navidad

GETTING ORIENTED

The original town, Old Vallarta, sits at the center of 42-km (26-mi) Bahía de Banderas, Mexico's largest bay, in Jalisco State. From here, the Sierra Madre foothills dive into the sea. Mountain-fed rivers nourish tropical deciduous forests as far north as San Blas, in Nayarit State. South of PV the hills recede from the coast and the drier tropical thorn forest predominates south to Barra de Navidad.

0   10 mi
0   10 km

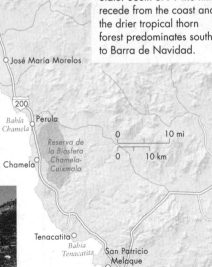

TOP EXPERIENCES

The Malecón

Nighttime is the right time for strolling PV's famous malecón. Bring your camera to photograph the seawalk's whimsical statues at sunset. Sip a cool drink, buy a caramel-topped crêpe from a vendor, or eat at a restaurant across the street. At the end of your eight-block promenade, take in the near-nightly free evening entertainment—be it a brass band or outdoor dance at the town square or a magician or mime at adjoining Los Arcos outdoor amphitheater, overlooking the sea.

Canopy Tours

Zinging through the treetops makes even a timid traveler feel like a superhero. Canopy tours are action-packed rides, where, fastened to a zip line high off the ground, you fly from tree to tree. Blue sky above, ribbons of river below, and in between: a forest of treetops and a healthy shot of adrenaline. The most highly praised area operators are El Edén and Canopy Tour Los Veranos, both south of PV near Mismaloya.

In, On, Under and Above the Water

Spend a day on the bay. Dive the varied landscape of Las Marietas Islands, angle for giant billfish, or soar above the scene in a colorful parasail. Look for orcas or humpbacks in winter and dolphins year-round. Swim, snorkel, or learn to surf or sail. Perhaps just build a sandcastle with your kids.

What You Want & Where To Get It

	PEACE & QUIET	LUXURY DIGS	NATURAL BEAUTY	KNOWN FOR RESTAURANTS	SHOPPING	LOTS OF SPORTS	LOW ON TOURISTS
Old Vallarta			✔	✔	✔	✔	
Nuevo Vallarta	✔	✔				✔	
Bucerías	✔			✔			✔
Punta de Mita	✔	✔	✔				
Zona Hotelera Sur	✔	✔	✔				
Costalegre	✔	✔	✔				✔
Barra/Melaque	✔		✔				✔
Rincón de Guayabitos			✔				
Zona Hotelera Norte		✔				✔	
Marina Vallarta	✔	✔				✔	

This table reflects the atmosphere in high season. In low season, most beaches are uncrowded, activities may decrease, and some shops and restaurants close.

Late Nights, Latino Style

Much of Vallarta is geared to the gringo palate, however, there's plenty of authentic spice for those who crave it. Stray a bit from the tourist scene for a mojito—Cuba's version of the mint julep—at La Bodeguita del Medio, on the malecón. Dine on roast pork, black beans, and fried plantains before heading for the dance floor at around 9, when the house band comes to life. Wednesday through Friday, take a taxi to J.B. Dance Club, in the hotel zone, for $2 dance lessons at 9:30. Otherwise hang at La Bodeguita until around 11, when the Mexican and Latino crowds start to arrive at J.B. for a late night of cumbia, salsa, and hot merengue.

Sensational Sunsets

After a day of activity, you deserve some R, R, and R: rest, relaxation, and rewarding views. Sip a fancy cocktail with a live music accompaniment at busy Los Muertos Beach or indulge in dessert from the crow's nest at Bucerías's The Bar Above. For the most dramatic views from high above the sea head to Barcelona Tapas, Vista Guayabitos, Las Carmelitas, or Le Kliff (⇨ chapter 3). All of them serve dinner and drinks.

20 Minutes to a More Elevated You

Get away from the gringo trail 4,000 feet above sea level in the mountain towns west of PV. Admire the elegant simplicity of tiny San Sebastián; in Talpa, visit the diminutive Virgin of Talpa statue, revered throughout Mexico for petitions granted. Buy keepsakes and mountain-grown coffee in small shops around the square. Or fly to Mascota, where you can sample homemade raicilla—second cousin of tequila. Hike into tapestry hills and deep green valleys where, on a good day, you can spy Puerto Vallarta and a ribbon of the Pacific far below.

> ### WORD OF MOUTH
>
> "Don't Miss:
>
> ■ Every sunset.
>
> ■ Eating out at all the great restaurants. Don't stay in the hotel even if it is all-inclusive. There are too many great places to go.
>
> ■ A visit up the coast to Punta Mita
>
> ■ Bus rides in town
>
> ■ Getting to know the local people"
>
> —Anne-Marie

TOP EXPERIENCES

People and Culture

Despite its population of more than 200,000, Puerto Vallarta feels—and thinks—like a small town. People know their neighbors; school chums run the city and the corner taco stand. Although the majority of *vallartenses* (residents of Puerto Vallarta) are far from wealthy—most are middle class, and securely employed—few of the alms-seekers downtown are locals.

Vallartenses value nice things, but much less so than sharing and socializing with family and friends. In her book *The Magic of Puerto Vallarta,* Venezuelan Marilú Suárez-Murias aptly describes Puerto Vallartans as "free, proud, simple, noble, friendly, kind, and never in a hurry."

Like many others from around the world, Ms. Suárez-Murias visited in the 1980s and opted to stay. Vallarta has one of the largest English-speaking expat communities in Mexico consisting of Americans and Canadians especially. Expats tend to settle in Old Vallarta or the condos and private homes climbing the ocean-facing hills south of town. Small towns like Sayulita, north of PV, are also increasingly popular.

The Hotel Scene

Choosing where to stay may be half of the equation to having a fabulous vacation. Unfortunately, it's not an easy task since Puerto Vallarta has something for every budget and personality, from cliff-side condos with stairs winding down to the sea to classy little cottages surrounded by nature trails. *Gran turismo* (beyond five-star) hotels and resorts are found up and down the coast; think beachside villa with a private plunge pool. Some of those on the prettiest beaches are in Punta de Mita and the Costalegre, but you'll find them also in the south hotel zone and Nuevo Vallarta, which has mainly all-inclusive hotels. Southern Nayarit State, north of PV, has a sprinkling of small hotels, guesthouses, private rentals, and bed-and-breakfasts, many of them popular with honeymooners, families, and anyone looking for more intimate digs away from large crowds.

The Food Scene

First-time travelers come for the sun and sea, but it's PV's wonderful restaurants that create legions of long-term fans. Only a generation ago, much of the best, locally caught fish was shipped to Guadalajara; Vallartans had to buy it back frozen, or overstock and freeze fresh catches for future meals. Likewise, a variety of vegetables was hard to find. But as the destination has grown in popularity and dozens of excellent chefs have opened restaurants, the culinary outlook has improved exponentially. Now those who know where to look can shop locally for designer greens, baby eggplant, and an increasingly sophisticated range of ingredients.

PV's level of culinary chic is reflected in November's International Gourmet Festival, when dozens of guest chefs bring new recipes and ideas from around the globe.

It's not just foreigners and Cordon Bleu–trained chefs, however, that keep the foodies fat and happy. Seaside family-owned eateries grill fish right off the boat, and tiny city cafés have great eats at bargain prices. And a number of streetside stalls are as hygienic as five-star-hotel restaurants.

The Overall Vibe

Mexico's second-most-visited resort after Cancún, Puerto Vallarta is, without a doubt, "touristy." From the clean streets to the English-speaking personnel and menus, business owners and tourism officials aim to help you feel at home. But you won't feel like a cipher or, worse, a bothersome intruder. Cancún didn't exist before the 1970s, and employees and business owners are imported from elsewhere. In contrast, the majority of Puerto Vallarta's tour companies, restaurants, and hotels are run by local people—proud of their city and happy to have you. Happy, because tourism is PV's only real industry. And though plenty of twentysomethings party all night at Señor Frogs or Carlos O'Briens, this is not a spring-break destination. A sense of decorum and pride in the city keeps things reasonably restrained.

Thinking Outside the Bay

As numerous as the activities in and around Puerto Vallarta and Banderas Bay are the opportunities beyond its boundaries. Vallarta Adventures and smaller tour operators make things easy with day trips to the mountains, Guadalajara, San Blas, and La Tovara estuaries. While tour companies can design individual, overnight tours, most folks heading north or south of Banderas Bay rent a car (or hop on a bus) and go on their own. But there's plenty to keep you busy in and around Puerto Vallarta, so if your time is limited, establishing a base of operations there is usually the least hassle-free way to explore.

A Brief History

Except for small coastal settlements that subsisted on fishing and a small enterprise importing salt (used to separate silver from stone), the first European and mestizo settlers in the region were miners and mine owners far from the coast, in the mineral-laced Sierra Madre. When mining petered out in the early 20th century, many families moved to the band of rich farmland near the coast around present-day Puerto Vallarta. Tourism along the gorgeous 42-km (26-mi) Bahía Banderas (Bay of Flags), really took off in the '50s and '60s, when a Mexican newsreel showed off its natural beauty and famous lovers Elizabeth Taylor and Richard Burton brought the paparazzi during the filming of *The Night of the Iguana,* in 1963.

GREAT ITINERARIES

Each of these fills one day. Together they touch on some of PV's most quintessential experiences, from shopping to getting outdoors for adventure tours or golfing, or just relaxing at the best beaches and spas.

Romancing the Zone

Head south of downtown to the **Zona Romántica** for a day of excellent shopping and dining. Stop at Isla del Río Cuale for trinkets and T-shirts; have an island breakfast overlooking the stream at the River Cafe or an excellent lunch at Le Bistro, where the romantic, neo-Continental decor and monumental architecture produce a flood of endorphins.

■ TIP➔ **Most of the stores in the neighborhood will either ship your oversized prizes for you or expertly pack them and recommend reputable shipping companies.**

Crossing the pedestrian bridge nearest the bay, drop nonshoppers at **Los Muertos Beach.** They can watch the fishermen on the small pier, lie in the sun, sit in the shade with a good book, or walk south to the rocky coves of **Conchas Chinas Beach,** which is good for snorkeling when the water is calm. Meanwhile, the shoppers head to **Calle Basilio Badillo** and surrounding streets for folk art, housewares, antiques, clothing, and accessories. End the day back at Los Muertos with dinner, drinks, and live music.

■ TIP➔ **Some of the musicians at beachfront restaurants work for the restaurant, others are freelancers. If a roving musician (or six) ask what you'd like to hear, ask the price of a song.**

A Different Resort Scene

If you've got wheels, explore a different sort of beach resort. After breakfast, grab beach togs, sunscreen, and other essentials for a day at the beach and head north. Those with a sweet tooth might make a pit stop at Pie in the Sky, with excellent pie, chocolate, and other sugar fixes. About an hour north of PV, join Mexican families on the beach at **Rincón de Guayabitos,** on attractive Jaltemba Bay. Play in the mild surf; walk the pretty, long beach; or take a ride in a glass-bottom boat to **El Islote,** an islet with a small restaurant and snorkeling opportunities. Vendors on the sand sell grilled fish and chilled coconuts and watermelon from their brightly colored stands. On the way back south, stop in the small town of **San Francisco,** aka San Pancho, for dinner. You can't go wrong at La Ola Rica, Gallo's Pizzeria, or the more sophisticated Cafe del Mar (brush the sand off your feet for that one). In high season and especially on weekend evenings, one of the three will probably have live music, especially Gallo's.

■ TIP➔ **Take a water taxi out for a look at El Islote island, where with luck you might spot a whale between December and March.**

Head for the Hills

For an unforgettable experience (at least for a few days, until your thigh muscles recover), take a horse-riding expedition (⇨ *Chapter 7*) into Vallarta's verdant tropical forest. Rancho Charro and Rancho Ojo de Agua have full-day excursions; the former offers multiday excursions as well, including tours to the former silver-mining towns of Mascota and San Sebastián. For those who prefer motorized horsepower, Wild Vallarta runs full-day ATV tours to San Sebastián.

■TIP→ Full-day and overnight trips provide food and refreshments, but if possible bring a day pack with things to make yourself comfortable: bottled water, tissues or handkerchief, bandanna, and plenty of sunblock. Don't pack it so full that it's unpleasantly heavy, however. Wear a hat.

A Day of Golf and Steam

Puerto Vallarta is one of Mexico's best golfing destinations (⇨ Chapter 7). And what better way to top off a day of play than with a steam, soak, and massage? At the southern end of the Costalegre, Tamarindo and Grand Bay Isla Navidad have courses (18 great holes and three 9-hole courses, respectively) and very good spas. Above PV, the Four Seasons has 19 holes of good golfing (the optional 19th on its own little island) and an excellent spa, but the latter is for guests only and nonguests rarely get desirable tee-times. In between these extremes are less-exclusive but still great courses. The closest spas to the greens of Marina Vallarta and the Vista Vallarta are those at the Westin Regina and the CasaMagna Marriott, which has gorgeous new facilities. The El Tigre course is associated with the Paradise Village resort, but this moderately priced spa is open also to those who golf at Mayan Palace, just up the road and at Flamingos, at the far northern edge of Nuevo Vallarta.

■TIP→ Ask your concierge (or look online) to find out how far ahead you can reserve, and then try for the earliest possible tee time to beat the heat. If the course you choose doesn't have a club pool, you can have lunch and hang at the pool at the resorts suggested above, or get a massage, facial, or other treatment (always reserve ahead).

Downtown Exploration

Puerto Vallarta hasn't much at all in the way of museums, but with a little legwork, you can get a bit of culture. Learn about the area's first inhabitants at the tiny but tidy **Museo Arqueológico** (closed Sunday), with info in English. From the museum, you can head downtown along the newest section of the **malecón,** which now crosses the river. About four blocks north, check out the action in the main plaza and Los Arcos amphitheater. At the **Iglesia de Nuestra Señora de Guadalupe,** you can pay your respects to the patron saint of the city (and the country). Taking a stroll farther north along the malecón is like walking through a sculpture garden: look for the statue of a boy riding a sea horse (it's become PV's trademark), and La Nostalgia, a statue of a seated couple, by noted PV artist Ramiz Barquet. Three figures climb a ladder extending into the air in Sergio Bustamante's In Search of Reason. One of the most elaborate sculptures is by Alejandro Colunga. Rotunda del Mar has more than a dozen fantastic figures—some with strange, alien appendages—seated on chairs and pedestals of varying heights.

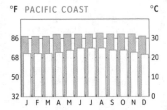

WHEN TO GO

The beach resorts are the most crowded and expensive December through Easter, especially the Christmas/New Year's holiday and the weeks before and after Easter. Despite the humidity, upper-class Mexican families book resort hotels during July and August school vacations while the masses rent bungalows in the smaller beach towns and camp out on popular beaches. Mexicans also travel over extended national holiday weekends, called *puentes* (bridges).

Holy days and cultural festivals play a big role in Mexican life. If you plan to travel during a major national event, reserve lodgings and transportation well in advance. November brings the PV Film Festival of the Americas and International Gourmet Festival.

Climate

On the same latitude as the Hawaiian Islands, Puerto Vallarta is tropical, and can be visited any time of year. Mid-June through mid-October is the rainy season; afternoon showers clear the air and temporarily reduce humidity. Rainy season temperatures are often in the 80s and 90s Fahrenheit (20s and 30s Celsius) and feel hotter due to high humidity. November through May is the dry season. Summer means bathtub-like ocean temperatures, the best diving and snorkeling conditions, and the most surfable waves. December through March brings the coolest temperatures: daytime temps still reach the 80s but at night drop to the 50s or 60s. May, June, August, and September are the hottest months. The proximity of tall mountains to the coast increases humidity: from Puerto Vallarta north to San Blas there's jungly terrain (officially, tropical decidu-ous forest). South of PV, the mountains recede from the coast, making that area's thorn-forest ecosystem drier.

Forecasts **U.S. National Weather Service** (⊕ *weather.noaa.gov/weather/current/ MMPR. html*). **The Weather Channel** (⊕*www. weather.com*).

°F   PACIFIC COAST   °C

Month	J	F	M	A	M	J	J	A	S	O	N	D

Where to Stay

Massage pavillion at El Tamarindo Golf Resort

WORD OF MOUTH

"[For our first trip to PV], we chose the Playa Los Arcos due to the location and convenience to get to the malecón, restaurants, and bars. We were advised numerous times not to go "All-Inclusive" (AI) in PV since there are so many great restaurants and bars. However, [there's something to be said for] AI—especially the convenience and affordability."

—KVR

WHERE TO STAY PLANNER

When to Go

High season is November through April, but if you don't mind afternoon rain showers and a lot of humidity, late June through October is a great time to visit for lower-priced lodgings (up to 40%) and rental cars and smaller crowds.

By August the entire coast and inland forests are green and bursting with blooms. Afternoon rains clean the streets and houses; waterfalls and rivers outside of town spring into action. On the downside, many restaurants and some other businesses close shop in the hottest months, August and September, and performances and nightlife slack off.

■TIP➔**Overbooking is a common practice. To protect yourself, get a confirmation in writing, via fax or e-mail.**

Parking Blues

Very few downtown Puerto Vallarta hotels have parking. Old town parking has always been problematic, but new pay lots at Parque Hidalgo and Parque Lázaro Cárdenas now provide some relief. Most of the condos in the Zona Hotelera Sur have parking, but not necessarily one space per apartment. Virtually all of the hotels outside the city center have free parking for guests.

Choosing a Hotel

If you want to walk everywhere, **Old Vallarta** (downtown, which includes El Centro and the Romantic Zone) is the place to be. El Centro's hilly streets provide excellent views and aerobic workouts. South of the Cuale River, the Romantic Zone has even more shops, restaurants, and Los Muertos Beach—and no hills. Most hotels here are inexpensive to moderate.

South of town, the **Zona Hotelera Sur** has many condos as well as luxury and a few moderately priced hotels—most with dramatic ocean views. Downtown is a short cab or bus ride away. The beaches and views aren't as appealing in the **Zona Hotelera Norte.** The long stretch of mid-range and higher-end chains is interspersed with malls and mega–grocery stores. **Marina Vallarta,** with its luxury hotels, is close to golf courses and is a good place for biking and strolling.

Nuevo Vallarta is a planned resort on a long, sandy beach about 12 miles north of downtown PV—about 40 minutes by car or bus when traffic complicates things. This is a good place to stay if you're content to stay put and enjoy your all-inclusive, high-rise hotel. Bucerías and the towns of **southern Nayarit** (north of PV) call to adventurous souls. Several hours south of Vallarta, the **Costalegre** is a place of extremes. High-priced hotels on gorgeous beaches attract celebs and honeymooners, while small towns like Barra de Navidad have modest digs and a more authentically Mexican experience—and nice beaches, too.

Gran Turismo

The government categorizes hotels as gran turismo (five-star-plus), of which only about 30 are chosen nationwide each year in addition to those; five-star to one-star. Note that hotels might lose out on a higher rating only because they lack an amenity like air conditioning (which isn't always needed if there are good breezes).

Lodging Alternatives

APARTMENTS & VILLAS

When shared by two couples, a spacious villa can save you a bundle on upscale lodging and on meals. Villas often come with stereo systems, DVD players, a pool, maid service, and air conditioning. Prices range from $100 to $1,000 per night, with 20% discounts off-season.

At Home Abroad ☎ 212/421–9165 ⊕ www.athome-abroadinc.com. **Cochran Real Estate** ☎ 322/228–0419 in PV, 800/603–2959 in U.S. ⊕ www.buyeragentmexico.com. **Hideaways International** ☎ 603/430–4433, 800/843–4433 in U.S. ⊕ www.hideaways.com. **Pacific Mexico Real Estate** ☎ 329/298–1644 in Bucerías ⊕ www.pacific mexicorealestate.com. **Villas and Apartments Abroad** ☎ 212/213–6435, 800/433–3020 in U.S. ⊕ www.vaanyc.com. **Villas International** ☎ 415/499–9490, 800/221–2260 in U.S. ⊕ www.villasintl.com.

BOUTIQUE HOTELS

México Boutique Hotels (☎ 322/221–2277 or 01800/508–7923 in Mexico, 800/728–9098 in the U.S. or Canada ⊕ www.mexicoboutiquehotels.com) is a private company that represents 45 intimate and unique properties—most with fewer than 50 rooms—selected for their setting, cuisine, service, and overall allure. Each is inspected annually.

CHAIN HOTELS

Tried-and-true chains may have excellent rates, and can be good last-minute options. **Holiday Inn** ☎ 800/465–4329 in U.S. ⊕ www.holiday-inn.com. **Inter-Continental** ☎ 888/424–6835 in U.S. ⊕ www.ichotelsgroup.com. **Marriott** ☎ 888/236–2427 ⊕ www.marriott.com. **Sheraton** ☎ 800/325–3535 in U.S. ⊕ www.starwood.com/sheraton. **Westin** ☎ 800/937–8461 ⊕ www.starwoodhotels.com.

LODGING PRICE CATEGORIES

¢	$	$$	$$$	$$$$
Hotels				
under $50	$50–$75	$75–$150	$150–$250	over $250

For a standard room, generally excluding taxes and service charges.

Meal Plans

EP: European Plan; without meals

CP: Continental Plan; continental breakfast

BP: Breakfast Plan; full breakfast

MAP: Modified American Plan; breakfast and dinner

FAP: Full American Plan; breakfast, lunch, and dinner

AI: All-Inclusive; including all meals, drinks, and most activities

Pricing

We give high-season prices before meals or other amenities. Low-season rates usually drop 20%–30%. We always list the available facilities, but we don't specify whether they cost extra.

Less expensive hotels include tax in the quote. Most higher-priced resorts add 17% tax on top of the quoted rate; some add a 5%–10% service charge. Moderately priced hotels swing both ways. You might be charged extra for paying with a credit card. Tax and/or tips are often included with all-inclusive plans, making a $$$$ property affordable.

An all-inclusive (AI) might make you reluctant to spend money elsewhere. So you don't miss out on area restaurants and activities, stay at more modest digs for part of your trip, and go AI for a day or two. Many AI hotels have day passes ($50–$75).

PUERTO VALLARTA

ZONA ROMÁNTICA

¢ ▦ **Ana Liz.** Those who prefer to spend their vacation cash on eating out and shopping might consider this clean, bright, motel-like budget hotel a few blocks south of the Cuale River, behind Cine Bahía. Two floors of rooms face each other across an outdoor corridor and have tiny bathrooms but comfortable beds. Ask for a room away from the noisy street; don't ask to use the lobby phone—it's not allowed. Small TVs (local channels only) are available for about $3 a day; a deposit is required for a towel. Small-time businesspeople and backpacking Europeans stay at this extremely plain place when they come to town; they're likely drawn by the substantial discounts for monthly stays. **Pros:** Best bargain in town for dedicated budget travelers; walking distance to beach, PV eateries and mini-grocery stores; near Internet cafés and taco stands. **Cons:** Zero frills, fee TV with local channels only. ✉ *Francisco I. Madero 429, Col. E. Zapata* ☎ *322/222–1757* ☞ *23 rooms* ♿ *In-room: no a/c (some), no phone. In hotel: no elevator* ⊟ *No credit cards* ⦿*EP.*

$$ ▦ **Casa Andrea.** One- and two-bedroom apartments in this spiffy property are truly homey. Each has a different floor plan—some have larger kitchens but all of them are fully equipped. All have air-conditioning, ceiling fans, plus dark-wood beams that contrast with white ceilings and walls. Use the hotel's computers to check your e-mail, or curl up with a book or watch a video in the library. Coffee and pastries are served each morning on the garden patio, where guests (many of them return visitors) sit and chat. The location, a few blocks from Los Arcos and the malecón, is a real plus. With some exceptions, high-season bookings are by the week. Expect some homely but sweet rescued dogs to be wandering about. **Pros:** Free Wi-Fi, great location in Zona Romantica, homey feel, good value. **Cons:** Often fully booked, no credit cards accepted. ✉ *Calle Francisca Rodríguez 174, Col. E. Zapata* ☎ *322/222–1213* ⊕ *www.casa-andrea.com* ☞ *11 apartments* ♿ *In-room: no phone, kitchen, no TV, Wi-Fi. In-hotel: bar, pool, gym, no elevator, laundry facilities, public Internet* ⊟ *No credit cards* ⦿*CP.*

$ ▦ **Eloísa.** Despite being a block from the beach, this hotel has more of a downtown feel, and sits on pretty Lázaro Cárdenas Park. Rooms are generally plain but clean, and there's a great city-and-mountain view from the rooftop, which has a pool and party area. Studios have small kitchenettes in one corner; suites have larger kitchens, separate bedroom, and two quiet air-conditioners. Units with great views (#511–514) cost the same as those without, so ask for one *con vista panorámica* (with a panoramic view). **Pros:** Snug studios overlook park, large pool on roof. **Cons:** No parking, mainly older a/c units. ✉ *Lázaro Cárdenas 179, Col. E. Zapata* ☎ *322/222–6465 or 322/222–0286* ⊕ *www.hoteleloisa.com* ☞ *60 rooms, 6 studios, 8 suites* ♿ *In-room: no phone, kitchen (some), refrigerator (some). In-hotel: restaurant, bar, pools* ⊟ *MC, V* ⦿*EP.*

$-$$ 🖼**Gaviota Vallarta.** Simple rooms in this six-story low-rise have some-what battered colonial-style furnishings; some have tiny balconies but only a few on the top floors have a partial ocean view. The small fig-ure-8 pool in the middle of the courtyard is exposed, but still refreshes. Choose air-conditioning or fan, cable TV or no, and a fridge if you like; room costs vary according to these choices. ■**TIP→ Don't bother with the two-bedroom apartments; they are poorly designed and not worth $150 a night.** **Pros:** Moderately priced rooms a block from the beach, free parking, inexpensive Internet salon. **Cons:** Poor pool placement, unattractive furnishings. ✉*Francisco I. Madero 176, Col. E. Zapata* ☎*322/222–1500* ⊕*www.hotelgaviota.com* 📞*84 rooms* ♿*In-room: no phone, kitchenette (some), refrigerator (some). In-hotel: restaurant, bar, pool, parking (no fee)* ▤*MC, V* ⫶⊙⫶*EP.*

$$ 🖼**Playa Los Arcos.** This hotel is attractive because of its location: right on the beach and in the midst of Zona Romántica's restaurants, bars, and shops. Though the price is right, both service and quality have slipped in recent years: Still, yellow trumpet vines and lacy palms draped in tiny white lights enliven the pool and the bar-restaurant, which has music nightly and a Mexican fiesta on Saturday evening. If you're willing to cross the street, you can get a better deal at Los Arcos Suites, which has larger yet cheaper rooms with kitchenettes; some have balconies, too. **Pros:** Great Zona Romántica location, nightly entertain-ment with theme-cuisine buffet. **Cons:** Small bathrooms, tired furnish-ings, tour group noise in high season. ✉*Av. Olas Altas 380, Col. E. Zapata* ☎*322/222–0583, 800/648–2403 in U.S., 888/729–9590 in Canada, 01800/327–7700 toll-free in Mexico* ⊕*www.playalosarcos. com* 📞*158 rooms, 13 suites* ♿*In-room: safe (some), kitchen (some). In-hotel: restaurant, bar, pool, beachfront, parking (no fee), no-smok-ing rooms* ▤*MC, V* ⫶⊙⫶*AI, EP.*

$ 🖼**Posada de Roger.** If you hang around the pool or the small shared balcony overlooking the street and the bay beyond, it's not hard to get to know the other guests—many of them savvy budget travelers from Europe and Canada. A shared, open-air kitchen on the fourth floor has a great view, too. Rooms are spare and vaultlike—some have scruffy features—and security on the first floor isn't what it should be. But the showers are hot, and the beds comfortable (if you like a very firm mat-tress). Freddy's Tucan, the indoor-outdoor bar-restaurant (no dinner; $) is popular with locals—mainly for breakfast. The hotel is in a prime part of the Zona Romántica known for its restaurants and shops; Playa los Muertos is a few blocks away. **Pros:** Good Zona Romántica loca-tion, tinkling fountain and quiet courtyard, good bar/restaurant next door. **Cons:** Room safes at front desk; many rooms cramped. ✉*Calle Basilio Badillo 237, Col. E. Zapata* ☎*322/222–0836 or 322/222–0639* ⊕*www.hotelposadaderoger.com* 📞*47 rooms* ♿*In-hotel: restaurant, bar, pool, no elevator* ▤*AE, MC, V* ⫶⊙⫶*EP.*

$$ 🖼**Tropicana.** This is a well-groomed, bright white hotel at the south end of Playa Los Muertos for a reasonable price. Save $15 a night by booking a standard rather than superior room; except for the size of the TV, they're almost the same. Each has several different areas for sitting or playing cards, but the beds are hard. Suites have no separate

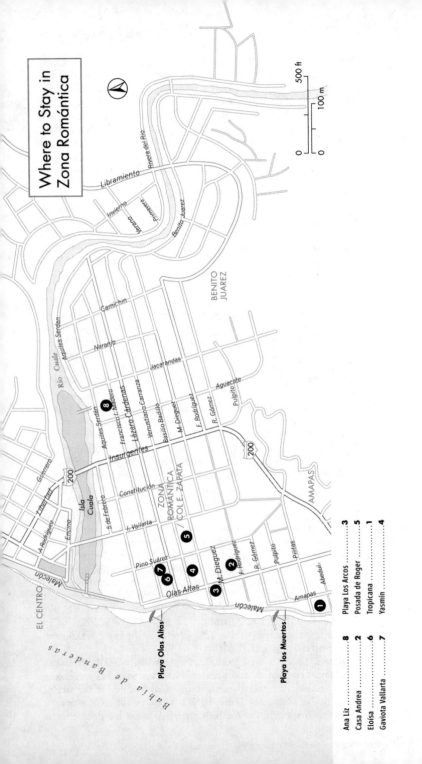

Where to Stay in Zona Romántica

Playa de Banderas

EL CENTRO

Playa Olas Altas

Playa los Muertos

BENITO JUAREZ

ZONA ROMÁNTICA
COL E. ZAPATA

AMAPAS

Ana Liz **8**	Playa Los Arcos **3**
Casa Andrea **2**	Posada de Roger **5**
Eloísa **6**	Tropicana **1**
Gaviota Vallarta **7**	Yasmín **4**

0 — 500 ft
0 — 100 m

living area, but are larger than other rooms and each has a four-burner stove, blender, and fridge. Room views vary, and so do amenities (e.g., some rooms have larger beds than others, some rooms have TV and some don't, and so on). Ask to change rooms if the one you're given doesn't suit you. **Pros:** Great beach views and access, great Zona Romántica location, nice pool and

> **MONEY CAN'T BUY HAPPINESS**
>
> Not all Los Arcos's guests are budget travelers: some better-heeled guests stay here for the easy-going ambience and the location on the beach near Zona Romántica restaurants, bars, and shops.

landscaping. **Cons:** No bathtubs; no Internet access; wristbands required for all guests; elevator, furnishings and paint need upgrading. ⊠*Calle Amapas 214, Col. E. Zapata* 🕾*322/226-9696* ⬳*148 rooms, 12 suites* ⌂*In room: no TV (some). In-hotel: restaurant, bar, pool, beachfront, parking (no fee)* ▭*MC, V* ⑩*EP.*

¢   🕾**Yasmín.** Two-story and L-shaped, this budget baby has no pool, but it's just a block from the beach and joined at the hip to Café de Olla (⇨*Chapter 3*), the extremely popular Mexican restaurant. Small, ho-hum rooms have low ceilings, firm beds, and open closets but also floor fans and cable TV: not a bad deal for the price. About six bucks more buys you an a/c. **Pros:** Very inexpensive; close to Zona Romántica action; pleasant courtyard garden with café, tables, and chaise lounges. **Cons:** Dark rooms, low ceilings, no pool. ⊠*Calle Basilio Badillo, Col. E. Zapata* 🕾*322/222–0087* ⬳*27 rooms* ⌂*In-room: no phone. In-hotel: no elevator* ▭*No credit cards* ⑩*EP.*

EL CENTRO & ENVIRONS

$$$ 🕾**Buenaventura Grand Hotel & Spa.** The location is ideal: on downtown's northern edge, just a few blocks from the malecón, shops, hotels, and restaurants. The beach has gentle waves, but with brown sand and rocks, it's not the prettiest beach and attracts few bathers. There's a lively pool scene; the adults-only area facing the sea, always crowded, is a big part of the draw. Rooms were redecorated in 2007, and are now cheerful, with bright striped textiles and framed tropical prints. Ocean-facing balconies are tiny, and if you sit, you can't see a thing. Still, the sum of the whole makes up for any deficiencies, and the all-inclusive rate is a good deal, especially for families. **Pros:** 24-hour business center and room service, great place to socialize, five-minute walk to the malecón and downtown. **Cons:** Recent renovation brought along a price hike, balconies are small. ⊠*Av. México 1301, Col. 5 de Diciembre* 🕾*322/226–7000 or 888/859–9439 in U.S. and Canada* ⊕*www.hotelbuenaventura.com.mx* ⬳*216 rooms, 18 suites* ⌂*In-room: Wi-Fi. In hotel: 5 restaurants, room service, bars, pools, spa, beachfront, concierge, laundry service, public Internet, public Wi-Fi.* ▭*AE, MC, V* ⑩*AI, EP.*

$–$$ 🕾**Casa Dulce Vida.** Hidden four blocks off the busy malecón, this '60s-era villa has apartments of various sizes filled with modern Mexican art and comfortable, if well-worn, furniture. All apartments have well-

PUERTO VALLARTA HOTELS AT A GLANCE

HOTEL	Worth Noting	Cost	Rooms	Restaurants	On the Beach	Dive Shop	Pools	Spa	Golf Course	Tennis Courts	Health Club/Gym	Children's Program	Location
Puerto Vallarta													
Ana Liz	Barebones; great location	$26	23	3									Col. E. Zapata
Barceló	all suites; lots to do	$293	304	5	yes	yes	4	yes	1	yes		4–9	Mismaloya
Buenaventura	ideal location	$166	234		yes		2	yes		yes			Col. 5 de Diciembre
Casa Andrea	homey apartments	$700/week	11	1			1						Col. E. Zapata
Casa Dulce Vida	spacious apartments	$70–$125	7				1						Centro
Casa Iguana All Suites	all suites; full kitchens	$71	52	1			1						Mismaloya
CasaMagna Marriott	something for everyone	$289	433	4	yes		2	yes	2*	yes		4–12	Marina Vallarta
Los Cuatro Vientos	Old PV spirit; good restaurant	$59–$69	14	1			1						Centro
Dreams	elaborate theme nights	$500	337	5	yes		3	yes	2	yes		4–17	Zona Hotelera Sur
Eloísa	request a free view	$61–$73	74	1			2						Col. E. Zapata
Fiesta Americana	amazing palapa	$270	291	3	yes		1	yes		yes		4–12	Zona Hotelera Norte
Gaviota Vallarta	a block from the beach	$64–$92	84	1	yes		1						Col. E. Zapata
Hacienda San Angel	only $$$$$ downtown; elegant	$310–$495	16	1			3						Col. El Cerro
Majahuitas	romantic, isolated casitas	$375	8	1	yes								Cabo Corrientes Norte
El Pescador	modest Mexican favorite	$97	103	1			1						Col. 5 de Diciembre
Playa Conchas Chinas	great beach	$102–$114	23	1	yes		1						Conchas Chinas
Playa Los Arcos	fab location w/rates to match	$145	171	1	yes		1						Col. E. Zapata
Posada de Roger	downtown; varied crowd	$65	47	1			1						Col. E. Zapata
Presidente InterContinental	secluded cove	$185	120	3	yes		1	yes	1	yes		4–12	Mismaloya
Quinta María Cortez	warm staff; lots of soul	$120–$240	10	1	yes		1						Conchas Chinas
Río	24-hour computer room	$68	47	1			1						Centro
Rosita	north end of Malecón	$87–$99	115	1	yes		1						Col. 5 de Diciembre
Sheraton Buganvilias	large but reliable	$240	600	3	yes		2	yes	2	yes		4–12	Zona Hotelera Norte
Sol Meliá Puerto Vallarta	great for younger kids	$350	221	6	yes		1		2	yes		inf–13	Marina Vallarta

HOTEL	Worth Noting	Cost	Rooms	Restaurants	On the Beach	Dive Shop	Pools	Spa	Golf Course	Tennis Courts	Health Club/Gym	Children's Program	Location
Tropicana	modest beachfront digs	$94	160	1	yes		1						Col. E. Zapata
Velas Vallarta	all suites; lots of comforts	$390	339	2	yes		2	yes	3	yes		6–12	Marina Vallarta
Westin Resort & Spa	great architecture	$249–$269	280	2	yes		3	yes	3	yes		inf-12	Marina Vallarta
Yasmín	budget rooms w/ cable	$48	27										Col. E. Zapata
North of Puerto Vallarta													
Bungalows Los Picos	fills with families and snowbirds	$62	56	1	yes								Bucerías (Playa del Beso)
Casa de Mita	excellent eats included	$415–$615	8	1			1						Punta de Mita, Playa Careyeros
Costa Azul	lots of sports and activities	$140	27	1	yes		1						Fracc. Costa Azul, San Francisco
Decameron	bargain all inclusive	$132	620	7	yes		4		3				Bucerías
Four Seasons Resort	excellent spa, golf	$590	168	3	yes		3	yes	4	yes		5-12	Punta de Mita
Grand Velas	sleek majesty	$1,100	269	4	yes		4	yes	1	yes		4-12	Nuevo Vallarta
Marco's Place Villas	basic but comfortable	$62	18	1			1						Bucerías
Marival	lots to do	$368	490	6	yes		4	yes	4	yes		4-17	Nuevo Vallarta
Palmeras	bright, cheerful rooms	$35–$85	21	4			1						Bucerías
Royal Paradise Village	great for families	$153–$239	490	4	yes		2	yes	7	yes		4-11	Nuevo Vallarta
Villa Amor	terrific views	$110–$180	32	1									Sayulita
Villa Bella	tranquil	$100–$250	7	1			1						La Cruz de Huanacaxtle
Villas Buena Vida	good swimming beach	$81	45	1	yes		2						Rincón de Guayabitos
Villa Varadero	great Nuevo Vallarta value	$64	58	1	yes		1						Nuevo Vallarta

equipped kitchens—again, we're not talking sparkly here (some fridges have rusty faces), but everything works. A few rooms have ocean-view terraces; the largest has three bedrooms, two baths, and a separate dining room. There's a red-tile pool and tropical gardens. In high season the property only accepts weeklong bookings. **Pros:** Home-away-from-home feel, great value, lush landscaping and ocean breezes, friendly staff helps book tours. **Cons:** Booked for weeks and months at a time in high season, some rooms better than others. ⊠ *Calle Aldama 295, El Centro* ☎ *322/222–1008* ⊕ *www.dulcevida.com* ➳ *7 suites* ⌂ *In-room: no a/c (some), no phone (some), safe (some), kitchen, refrigerators, no TV, Wi-Fi (some). In-hotel: pool, no elevator, public Wi-Fi* ⊟ *V* ⦿ *EP.*

$ ⊞ **Los Cuatro Vientos.** Gloria Whiting has owned this Old Vallarta original, which opened in 1955, for about 25 years, and some guests have been coming forever. That explains why most of the guests and staff seem like old friends. The Chez Elena *restaurant*, the unadorned rooftop bar, and the best rooms have nice views of the bay and of the city's red rooftops. Come to rub shoulders with Europeans and others who appreciate a bargain and a bit of history. Rooms are plain and without amenities, yet the traditional brick ceilings give a homey feel. **Pros:** Downtown location overlooking the bay; deep, grottolike pool; free Wi-Fi. **Cons:** Short but steep walk or drive from downtown; no lounge area around pool; no a/c. ⊠ *Calle Matamoros 520, El Centro* ☎ *322/222–0161* ⊕ *www.cuatrovientos.com* ➳ *14 rooms* ⌂ *In-room: Wi-Fi (some), no a/c, no phone, no TV. In-hotel: restaurant, room service, bar, pool, no elevator* ⊟ *MC, V* ⦿ *CP (high season only).*

$$$$ ⊞ **Fiesta Americana.** The dramatically designed terra-cotta building rises above a deep-blue pool that flows under bridges and beside palm oases; a seven-story palapa (which provides natural air-conditioning) covers the elegant lobby—paved in patterned tile and stone—and a large round bar. The ocean-view rooms have a modern pink and terra-cotta color scheme, beige marble floors, balconies, and tile baths with powerful showers. The beach is small, but bustles with activity and equipment rentals, and the breakwater forms a sheltered nook that's nice for swimming. It's about halfway between the Marina Vallarta complex and Downtown PV. **Pros:** Across from Plaza Caracol, with its shops, grocery store, and cineplex; lots of onsite shops; AAA discount. **Cons:** No ocean view from second and third floors, the hotel is a cab or bus ride from most shops and restaurants. ⊠ *Blvd. Federico M. Ascencio, Km 2.5, Zona Hotelera Norte* ☎ *322/226–2100, 800/343–7821 in U.S.* ⊕ *www.fiestaamericana.com* ➳ *288 rooms, 3 suites* ⌂ *In-room: safe, refrigerator, dial-up, Wi-Fi. In-hotel: 3 restaurants, room service, spa, bars, pool, gym, beachfront, concierge, children's programs (ages 4–12), laundry service, public Wi-Fi, parking (no fee), no-smoking rooms* ⊟ *AE, DC, MC, V* ⦿ *EP.*

$$$$
★ ⊞ **Hacienda San Angel.** Each room is unique and elegant at this boutique hotel in the hills six blocks above the malecón. Public spaces also exude wealth and privilege: 16th- through 19th-century antiques are placed throughout, water pours from fonts into Talavera tile–lined basins, mammoth tables grace open dining areas. The Celestial Room has a wondrous

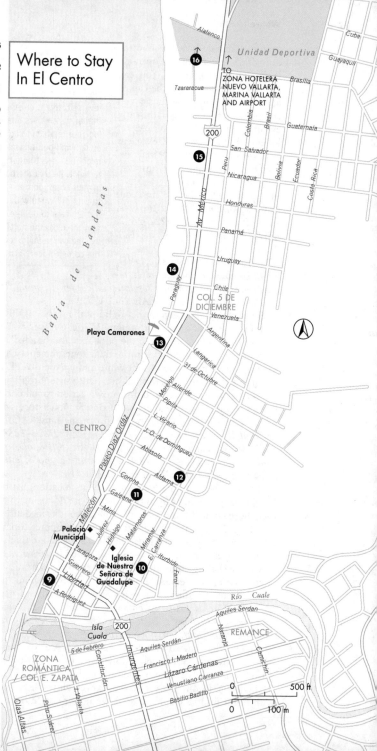

Where to Stay In El Centro

view of Bahía de Banderas and the cathedral's tower from its open-air, thatch-roof living room. You can call or e-mail Canada or the United States for free; enjoy live music with complimentary cocktails in the early evening. **Pros:** The only elegant lodging in downtown PV, excellent bay views, reasonably priced airport transfers. **Cons:** Scary drive up congested cobblestone streets, short but steep walk from the malecón. ⊠*Calle Miramar 336, at Iturbide, Col. El Cerro* ☎*322/222–2692, 877/815--6594 toll-free in U.S.* ⊕*www.haciendasanangel.com* 🛏*16 rooms* ⚿*In-room: safe, DVD, VCR. In-hotel: restaurant, pools, no elevator, concierge, laundry service, public Internet, public Wi-fi, airport shuttle, no kids under 16* ⊟*AE, MC, V* ⎮○⎮*CP.*

> ### CAN I DRINK THE WATER?
>
> Most of the fancier hotels have reverse osmosis or other water filtration systems. It's fine for brushing your teeth, but play it safe by drinking bottled water (there might be leaks that let groundwater in). Note that the bottled water in your hotel room may be added to your bill when you leave, even if it appears to be free. It seems that the nicer the hotel, the costlier the water. Buy a few bottles at the corner grocery instead.

$$ 🏨**El Pescador.** Fall asleep to the sound of the waves at this modest yet cheerful hotel that's a favorite among Mexican travelers. Balconies are narrow but provide a view of the pool area and beach. The latter has sand but also fist-size rocks in the tidal zone; the curvy, medium-size pool is a nice alternative. Bright white and inexpensive, El Pescador is about five blocks north of the malecón (and a sister property, Hotel Rosita). **Pros:** Near malecón and downtown action; small parking garage; live music during weekend brunch. **Cons:** Summer storms deliver rocks on the narrow, brown-sand beach; no ceiling fans. ⊠*Calle Paraguay 1117 at Uruguay, Col. 5 de Diciembre* ☎*322/222–1884, 888/242–9587 in Canada, 877/813–6712 in U.S.* ⊕*www.hotelpescador. com* 🛏*103 rooms* ⚿*In-hotel: restaurant, bar, pool, laundry service, public Internet, public Wi-Fi* ⊟*MC, V* ⎮○⎮*EP.*

$ 🏨**Río.** This budget hotel get points for its location just north of Isla Río Cuale, two blocks from both the beach and the main plaza. It gets even more points for the cheerful, well-air-conditioned little restaurant-bar serving Mexican specials, and for the computer room with many stations, open 24 hours a day. On the downside are uninspired, older furnishings in some of the rooms, and rusted fridges in some "suites," which are slightly larger than standard rooms and have sinks and free microwaves upon request. **Pros:** Friendly staff, 24-hour Internet, near beach. **Cons:** Smallish, non-private pool; furnishings need upgrade. ⊠*Calle Morelos 170, El Centro* ☎*322/222–0366* ⊕*www.hotelrio. com.mx* 🛏*47 rooms* ⚿*In-room: kitchen (some), refrigerator (some). In-hotel: restaurant, bar, pool, public Internet* ⊟*MC, V* ⎮○⎮*EP.*

$$ 🏨**Rosita.** What started as a sleepy 12-room hostelry—one of PV's very first—is now a busy 115-room downtown hotel. It's still a viable budget option, mainly recommended for its location on the north end of the malecón. Rooms are very basic; expect white-tile floors and fabrics with floral prints. The cheapest have no air-conditioning. Request a

TENNIS, ANYONE?

Public tennis courts are few and far between in Vallarta, although most hotels have courts for guests.

Of the public tennis complexes, **Club de Tenis Canto del Sol** (⊠ *Hotel Canto del Sol, Local 18, Planta Baja, Zona Comercial Zona Hotelera* 🕾 *322/226–0123*) is the largest, with four clay and four asphalt courts; all but two are lighted. Private lessons are $33 per hour, including racquet; court rental is $14 per hour, $22 per hour for night play.

Club hours are 7 AM to 10 PM (7–5 on Sunday); fees give you access to showers, lockers, and steam room. The **Holiday Inn** (⊠ *Blvd. Federico Medina Ascencio, Km. 3.5 Zona Hotelera Norte* 🕾 *322/226–1700*) has two asphalt courts rented out at $5 per hour ($10 if you need to rent the racquets and balls as well), and $10 per hour at night. Hours are 9 AM–5 PM (2 PM ON SATURDAY); but you can usually make arrangements to stay later. A pro gives lessons. Reservations are essential.

room facing the water, as much for the view as for the natural light; rooms facing the street are dark, making them feel cramped. **Pros:** Old-fashioned value near downtown, yummy Sunday brunch buffet under 10 bucks, inexpensive Internet use. **Cons:** No bathtub, older floors and furnishings, so-so beach. ⊠ *Paseo Díaz Ordaz 901, Col. 5 de Diciembre* 🕾 *322/223–2000* ⊕ *www.hotelrosita.com* ⇨ *115 rooms* ⚿ *In-room: no a/c (some), no TV (some). In-hotel: restaurant, bar, pool, laundry service, public Wi-Fi.* ☰ *AE, MC, V* ¶○¶ *EP.*

$$$ 🏨 **Sheraton Buganvilias.** Juan Carlos Name, a disciple of modern-minimalist Mexican architect Luis Barragán, designed this looming high-rise near the Hotel Zone's south end and within walking distance of downtown. It's reliable, anonymous, and geared toward conventioneers and other groups. Rooms have a perky bright white-and–cherry red color scheme and very snug and comfortable beds with pillow-top mattresses and downy duvets. This is the closest of the major Zona Hotelera Norte hotels to downtown PV. **Pros:** Excellent Sunday brunch with mariachis, 24-hour Wi-Fi cheaper than those of many mega-hotels. **Con:** Slow elevators. ⊠ *Blvd. Francisco Medina Ascencio 999, Zona Hotelera Norte* 🕾 *322/226–0404, 800/325–3535 in U.S. and Canada* ⊕ *www.sheratonvallarta.com* ⇨ *480 rooms, 120 suites* ⚿ *In-room: safe, kitchen, refrigerator, Internet. In-hotel: 3 restaurants, room service, bar, tennis courts, pools, gym, spa, beachfront, concierge, children's programs (ages 4–12), laundry service, executive floor, public Internet, parking (no fee), no-smoking rooms* ☰ *AE, MC, V* ¶○¶ *EP, CP.*

MARINA VALLARTA

$$$$ 🏨 **CasaMagna Marriott.** The CasaMagna is hushed and stately in some
☾ places, lively and casual in others. Here's a classy property that nonethe-
★ less welcomes children. All of the restaurants—including a sleek Asian restaurant serving Thai, sushi, and teppanyaki and a large, pleasant sports bar—have kid's menus. The meandering grounds boast a large infinity pool as well as indigenous plant and chile gardens. Rooms have

an upbeat, classy decor; each has a balcony and most have an ocean view. The Marriott chain requires smoke detectors, sprinklers, thrice-filtered water, and other beyond-the-pale safety features. Access to the amazing spa is free with the purchase of a spa service. **Pros:** Lovely new spa, new gym equipment, good Japanese restaurant. **Con:** Unimpressive beach. ⊠*Paseo de la Marina 5, Marina Vallarta* ☎*322/226–0000, 888/236–2427 in U.S. and Canada* ⊕*www.casamagnapuertovallarta.com* ⇲*404 rooms, 29 suites* ⌂*In-room: safe, refrigerator, DVD, Wi-Fi. In-hotel: 4 restaurants, room service, bars, tennis courts, pools, gym, spa, beachfront, concierge, children's programs (ages 4–12), laundry service, public Internet, parking (no fee)* ⊟*AE, DC, MC, V* ⍥*EP.*

$$$$ ⍟ **Sol Meliá Puerto Vallarta.** The sprawling Meliá, on the beach and close to the golf course, is popular with families and hums with activity. An enormous birdcage with several parrots dominates the breezy lobby, which also houses an eclectic collection of Mexican art and memorabilia. The plazas beyond have still more artwork as well as garden areas, fountains, ponds, and such bits of whimsy as a supersize chessboard with plastic pieces as big as a toddler. There's a huge pool, an outdoor theater with nightly shows, and elaborate children's programs and amenities—including a climbing wall and a batting cage. Rooms are havens in subdued blues, creams, and sands. Considering it's an all-inclusive only, prices are extremely reasonable. **Pros:** Lots of activities for small children, giant pool. **Cons:** Small beach diminishes further at high tide, lots of children. ⊠*Paseo de la Marina Sur 7, Marina Vallarta* ☎*322/226–3000, 800/336–3542 in U.S.* ⊕*www.solmelia.com* ⇲*217 rooms, 4 suites* ⌂*In-room: safe, refrigerator, dial-up. In-hotel: 6 restaurants, bars, tennis courts, pool, gym, beachfront, concierge, children's programs (ages 4 mos.–13 yrs.), laundry service, public Internet, parking (no fee)* ⊟*AE, MC, V* ⍥*AI.*

$$$$ ⍟ **Velas Vallarta Suite Resort & Convention Center.** Silky sheets and cozy down comforters, multiple ceiling fans, and large flat-screen TVs are a few of the creature comforts that set Velas apart from the rest. Each large living area has two comfortably wide built-in couches in colorful prints and a round dining table. Huichol cross-stitch and modern Mexican art decorate the walls. Studios and one-, two-, and three-bedroom suites have the same amenities except that the studios don't have balconies or beach views. Tall palms, pink bougainvillea, and wild ginger with brilliant red plumes surround the three enormous pools. **Pros:** Large suites, 24-hour room service, pillow menu. **Con:**

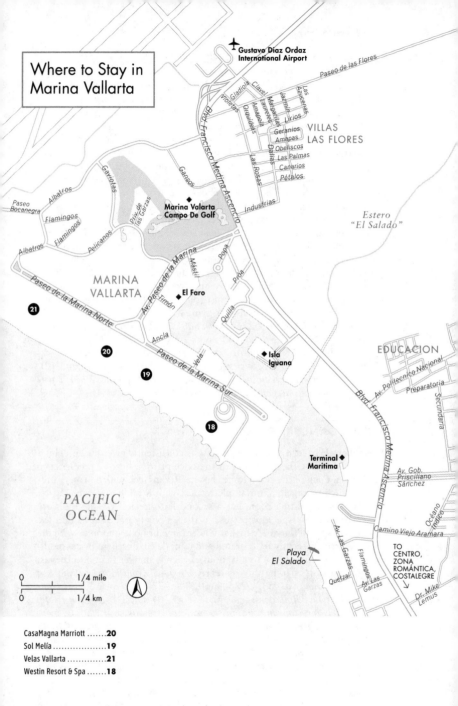

Where to Stay in Marina Vallarta

Gustavo Díaz Ordaz International Airport

Paseo de las Flores

VILLAS LAS FLORES

Gladiola
Clavel
Violetas
Orquídeas
Amapola
Amapas
Margaritas
Jazmín
Laureles
Lirios
Geranios
Amapas
Obeliscos
Dalias
Las Palmas
Canarios
Pétalos
Las Rosas
Las Azucenas

Blvd. Francisco Medina Ascencio

Industrias

Estero "El Salado"

Marina Valarta Campo De Golf

Albatros
Gaviotas
Garzas
Flamingos
Flamingos
Pelicanos
Albatros
Priv. de las Garzas

Paseo Bocanegra

MARINA VALLARTA

Av. Paseo de la Marina

Paseo de la Marina Norte

Ancla

Paseo de la Marina Sur

Timón

El Faro

Mástil

Popa

Proa

Quilla

Vela

Isla Iguana

EDUCACION

Av. Politécnico Nacional

Preparatoria

Secundaria

Blvd. Francisco Medina Ascencio

21

20

19

18

PACIFIC OCEAN

Terminal Marítima

Av. Gob. Priciliano Sánchez

Océano Índico

Camino Viejo Aramara

Playa El Salado

Av. Las Garzas

Quetzal

Flamingos

Av. Las Garzas

TO CENTRO, ZONA ROMÁNTICA, COSTALEGRE

Dr. Mike Lemus

| 0 | 1/4 mile |
| 0 | 1/4 km |

Small spa ⊠*Av. Costera s/n LH2, Marina Vallarta* ☏*322/221–0091 or 866/847–4609* ⊕*www.velasvallarta.com* ↪*339 suites* ⅃*In-room: safe, kitchen, refrigerato, dial-up. In-hotel: 2 restaurants, room service, bars, tennis courts, pools, gym, spa, beachfront, concierge, children's programs (ages 6–12), laundry service, public Internet, public Wi-Fi, parking (no fee), no-smoking rooms* ☰*AE, MC, V* ⓘ*AI.*

$$$$ ⚏**Westin Resort & Spa.** Hot pink! Electric yellow! Color aside, the Westin's buildings evoke ancient temples and are about as mammoth. There's not a bad sightline anywhere—whether you gaze out to the leafy courtyard or down an orange-tile, brightly painted corridor lined with Mexican art. The jarring echoes here are tempered by the rush of an enormous water feature. In the spacious, balconied rooms concrete-and-stone floors massage bare feet, and top-of-the-line mattresses with whisper-soft duvets make for heavenly siestas. Guest quarters above the sixth floor have ocean views; those below face the 600 palm trees surrounding the four beautiful pools. The Westin's Nikki Beach Club is still a classy restaurant/bar/lounge on the beach, although it's not as in vogue as it was for the first few years. **Pros:** Fabulous beds and pillows, impressive architecture and landscaping, attentive but not overzealous staff. **Cons:** small beach, fee for gym. ⊠*Paseo de la Marina Sur 205, Marina Vallarta* ☏*322/226–1100, 800/228–3000 in U.S. and Canada* ⊕*www.westinvallarta.com* ↪*266 rooms, 14 suites* ⅃*In-room: safe, Wi-Fi. In-hotel: 2 restaurants, room service, bars, tennis courts, pools, gym, spa, beachfront, concierge, children's programs (ages infant–12), laundry service, executive floor, public Internet, public Wi-Fi, parking (no fee), some pets allowed, no-smoking rooms* ☰*AE, DC, MC, V* ⓘ*BP.*

SOUTH ALONG BANDERAS BAY

$$$$ ⚏**Barceló La Jolla de Mismaloya.** Guests consistently give this hotel high
ⓒ   marks despite the reduction of the once-pristine beach by Hurricane Kenna. Each of the classy suites has an elegant feel, with a brown-and-taupe color scheme and ample terrace with a table and four chairs; the separate sitting room has a second flat-screen TV. The pools are surrounded by spacious patios, so there's plenty of room to find the perfect spot in the sun, whether you're on your honeymoon or with the kids. **Pros:** Recently redecorated and remodeled, excellent price for all-inclusive. **Cons:** No Wi-Fi in rooms; beach is smaller than it once was; construction ongoing through early 2009. ⊠*Zona Hotelera Sur, Km 11.5, Mismaloya* ☏*322/226–0660, 800/227–2356 in U.S. and Canada* ⊕*www.lajollademismaloya.com* ↪*304 suites* ⅃*In-room: safe. In-hotel: 3 restaurants, room service, bars, tennis court, pools, gym, spa, beachfront, diving, water sports, bicycles, concierge, children's programs (ages 4–9), laundry service, public Internet, public Wi-Fi, executive floor, parking (no fee), no-smoking rooms* ☰*MC, V* ⓘ*AI.*

$ ⚏**Casa Iguana All-Suites Hotel.** Palms and plants edge walkways that line the swimming pool and goldfish ponds. Balconies look down on this garden scene and on the palapa bar-restaurant. Standard suites have full kitchens, shower-only baths, chunky furniture with cast-iron hardware, and tiles with folkloric patterns. Electric orange and yellow

CLOSE UP

Don't Be (Time-Share) Shark Bait

In Puerto Vallarta, time-share sales-people are as unavoidable as death and taxes. And almost as dreaded. Although a slim minority of people actually enjoy going to one- to four-hour time-share presentations to get the freebies that range from Kahlua to rounds of golf, car rentals, meals, and shows, most folks find the experience incredibly annoying. For some it even casts a pall over their whole vacation.

The bottom line is, if the sharks smell interest, you're dead in the water. Time-share salespeople occupy tiny booths up and down main streets where tourists and cruise passengers walk. In general, while *vallartenses* are friendly, they don't accost you on the street to start a conversation. Those who do are selling something. Likewise, anyone calling you *amigo* is probably selling. The best solution is to walk by without responding, or say "No thanks" or "I'm not interested" as you continue walking. When they yell after you, don't feel compelled to explain yourself.

Some sly methods of avoidance that have worked for others are telling the tout that you're out of a job but dead interested in attending a presentation. They'll usually back off immediately. Or explaining confidentially that the person you're with is not your spouse. Time-share people are primarily inter-ested in married couples—married to each other, that is! But our advice is still to practice the art of total detach-ment with a polite rejection and then ignoring the salesperson altogether if he or she persists.

Even some very nice hotels (like the Westin) allow salespeople in their lobbies disguised as the Welcome Wagon or information gurus. Ask the concierge for the scoop on area activities, and avoid the so-called "information desk."

Time-share salespeople often pressure guests to attend time-share presenta-tions, guilt-tripping them ("My family relies on the commissions I get," for example) or offering discounts on the hotel room and services. The latter are sometimes difficult to redeem and cost more time than they're worth. And although it may be the salesper-son's livelihood, remember that this is your vacation, and you have every right to use the time as you wish.

plaids brighten spaces that can be dark at certain times of the day. The hotel is on a cobblestone street off the highway; if you don't want to hoof it into PV, take one of the local buses that pass every 15 minutes. The beach is a five-minute walk away; and the village of Mismaloya, with wandering chickens and even burros, is within braying distance. The all-inclusive plan isn't available during high season. **Pros:** Expe-rience village life not far from PV's bars and restaurants; onsite gro-cery store. **Cons:** Plaid fabrics abound, doesn't overlook water (but for this price, one can walk across the highway). ✉ *Av. 5 de Mayo 455, Mismaloya* ☎*322/228–0186, 877/893–7654 in U.S., 877/224–5057 in Canada* ⊕*www.casaiguanahotel.com* ⊃*49 2-bedroom suites, 3 3-bedroom suites* ⅊*In-room: kitchen, refrigerator. In-hotel: restaurant, room service, bar, pool, laundry facilities, public Wi-Fi, parking (no fee), no-smoking rooms* ⊟*AE, MC, V* ⦿ *EP.*

$$$$ ⚏**Dreams.** The dramatic view of the gorgeous, rock-edged beach is
☾   just one reason that this all-inclusive is special. Theme nights go a
Fodor'sChoice   bit beyond the usual Mexican fiestas: there are salsa dancing classes,
★   reggae and circus nights, and for sports night, ball games with hot
dogs and beer, and movies on the beach. Instead of buffet restaurants
there are five à la carte eateries featuring seafood, Mexican, Asian,
international, and an adults-only Italian eatery for dinner only. All of
the charming suites have fab views but only the newer ones have balconies, some with a hot tub. There are tons of activities for both kids
and adults, and no wristbands to clash with your resort-casual clothes.
Pros: Gorgeous private beach, easy drive or bus to downtown PV, no
ugly all-inclusive wristbands. **Cons:** No reservation restaurant system
means waiting to eat during busiest seasons. ⊠*Carretera a Barra de
Navidad (Carretera 200), at Playa Las Estacas Zona Hotelera Sur*
☎*322/226–5000, 866/237–3267 in U.S. and Canada* ⊕*www.dream-
sresorts.com* ➫*337 suites* ⧉*In-room: safe, refrigerator, DVD. In-
hotel: 5 restaurants, room service, bars, tennis courts, pools, gym, spa,
beachfront, water sports, bicycles, concierge, children's programs (ages
4–17), laundry service, parking (no fee), no-smoking rooms* ⊟*AE, D,
DC, MC, V* ⊺◯*AI.*

$$$$ ⚏**Majahuitas.** If travelers were animals, Majahuitas's guests would be
bears, not butterflies. Eating well and resting are the two top activities. After a 20-minute boat ride you (and, hopefully, your sweetie,
as this intimate place doesn't have a singles scene) arrive at a shell-
strewn beach where hermit crabs scuttle about seeking larger accommodations. Eight casitas crouch amid jungly plants (and biting bugs;
bring repellent) overlooking the tiny cove. Guest rooms are open to
the air and have low-wattage lights and tiny, solar-powered fans. It's
a romantic place that also happens to be good for families with tots.
Older kids, type-A adults, and anyone who doesn't read will be bored.
Pros: Plenty of opportunities for "me-and-you time," short boat ride
to other beaches like Yelapa and Las Animas. **Cons:** Zero possibility
for going out at night, party boats invade the smallish beach at mid-
day, no Internet or phone access. ⊠*Playa Majahuitas, Cabo Corrientes
Norte* ☎*322/293–4506, 800/728–9098 in U.S. and Canada* ⊕*www.
mexicoboutiquehotels.com/majahuitas* ➫*8 rooms* ⧉*In-room: no a/c,
no phone, no TV. In-hotel: restaurant, bar, beachfront, water sports*
⊟*AE, MC, V* ⊺◯*FAP* ☯*Closed Sept.*

$$ ⚏**Playa Conchas Chinas.** Studios here have functional kitchenettes, basic
cookware, and somewhat thin mattresses on wood-frame beds. Each
has a small tiled tub as well as a shower. The real pluses of this plain
Jane are the balconies with spectacular beach views and the location
above Conchas Chinas Beach, about a 20-minute walk to downtown
PV along the beach. The three-bedroom presidential suite has a sound
system and large-screen TV. **Pros:** Excellent view of rock-framed Con-
chas Chinas beach; a short drive or bus ride to downtown PV. **Cons:**
Some units smell funky. ⊠*Carretera a Barra de Navidad (Carretera
200) Km. 2.5, Conchas Chinas* ☎*322/221–5763 or 322/221–5230*
⊕*www.hotelconchaschinas.com* ➫*21 rooms, 2 suites* ⧉*In-room:
safe, kitchen, refrigerator. In-hotel: restaurant, bar, pool, beachfront,*

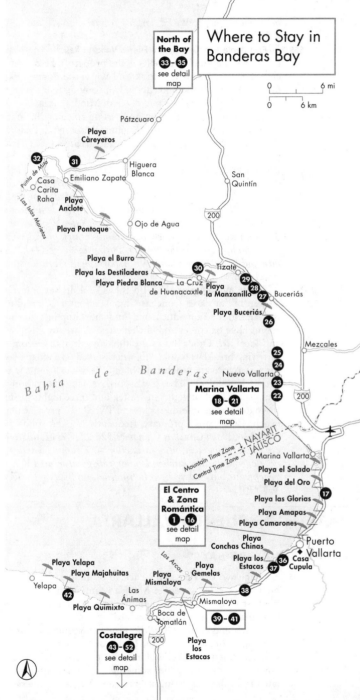

Where to Stay in Banderas Bay

0 ——————— 6 mi

0 ——————— 6 km

North of the Bay
33 - 35
see detail map

Pátzcuaro

Playa Càreyeros

Higuera Blanca

San Quintín

32 **31**

Punta de Mita

Casa Carita Raha

Emiliano Zapato

Las Islas Marietas

Playa Anclote

Playa Pontoque

Ojo de Agua

200

Playa el Burro

Playa las Destiladeras

Playa Piedra Blanca

La Cruz de Huanacaxtle

Tizate

30

Playa la Manzanillo

29 **28**

27 Bucerías

Playa Bucerías

26

Mezcales

25

24

Nuevo Vallarta

Marina Vallarta
18 - 21
see detail map

23

22

200

Bahía de Banderas

Mountain Time Zone

Central Time Zone

NAYARIT

JALISCO

Marina Vallarta

Playa el Salado

Playa del Oro

El Centro & Zona Romántica
1 - 16
see detail map

Playa las Glorias

17

Playa Amapas

Playa Camarones

Playa Conchas Chinas

Puerto Vallarta

Playa Yelapa

Playa Majahuitas

Los Arcos

Playa Mismaloya

Playa Gemelas

Playa los Estacas

36 Casa Cupula

37

Yelapa

42

Las Ánimas

Playa Quimixto

38

Boca de Tomatlán

Mismaloya

39 - 41

Costalegre
43 - 52
see detail map

200

Playa los Estacas

no elevator, public Wi-Fi, parking (no fee), no elevator =AE, MC, V
†○|EP.

$$$ 🏨**Presidente InterContinental Puerto Vallarta Resort.** The beautiful aqua-tone cove the hotel overlooks is the property's best asset. Rooms are classy, with a minimalist look and white-tile floors and citrus-color fabrics. You'll be asked to choose from among four experiences (Joy of Life, Renewal, Romance, and Peace of Mind) that involve changing the scents, music, stones, flowers, and certain amenities in your room to set the desired tone. This marketing gimmick doesn't dramatically enhance the hotel experience, though pillow menus are a nice touch. Ask about packages which may include golf, spa treatments, breakfast, and even free Wi-Fi and gym access. **Pros:** Lovely bay great for swimming; easy drive, bus, or taxi to downtown. **Cons:** Charge for room coffee, small gym and spa. ⊠*Carretera a Barra de Navidad, Km 8.6, Mismaloya* ☎*322/228–0191 or 888/424–6835 toll-free* ⊕*www.acquaesencia. com* ◚*97 rooms, 23 suites* ᗆ*In-room: safe, Wi-Fi (some). In-hotel: 3 restaurants, room service, bars, tennis court, pool, gym, spa, beachfront, diving, concierge, children's programs (ages 4–12), laundry service, public Internet, public Wi-Fi, parking (no fee), no-smoking rooms* =AE, D, MC, V †○|EP.

$$–$$$ 🏨**Quinta María Cortez.** This B&B has soul. Its seven levels ramble up
Fodor'sChoice   a steep hill at Playa Conchas Chinas, about a 20-minute walk along
★   the sand to the Romantic Zone (or a short hop in a bus or taxi). Most rooms have balconies and kitchenettes; all are furnished with antiques and local art. Other draws are the efficient and welcoming staff, the fortifying breakfast (cooked to order) served on a palapa-covered patio, the nearly private beach below, and the views from the rooftop sundeck. It's popular and has few rooms, so make reservations early. Minimum stays are five nights in winter, and three nights in summer. **Pros:** Intimate, personable digs; close to PV; above pretty Conchas Chinas beach. **Cons:** Small property, frequently booked solid. ⊠*Calle Sagitario 126, Playa Conchas Chinas* ☎*322/221–5317, 888/640–8100 reservations* ⊕*www.quinta-maria.com* ◚*7 rooms, 3 villas* ᗆ*In-room: no a/c (some), safe, kitchen (some), refrigerator, no TV. In-hotel: pool, beachfront, no elevator, public Internet, no kids under 17* =AE, MC, V †○|BP.

NORTH OF PUERTO VALLARTA

ALONG BANDERAS BAY

$ 🏨**Bungalows Los Picos.** This enclave of about a half-dozen groups of bungalows caters to large Mexican families much of the year, with the best value for the two- and three-bedroom bungalows. It attracts Canadian and American snowbirds in winter. On Playa del Beso, at the north end of Bucerías, the property requires a car or a taxi for straying from the pools or the beautiful beach for sightseeing or dining out. The restaurant is closed in low season. **Pro:** Great value for larger families. **Cons:** Young kids sometimes dominate swimming pools; isolated from shops, restaurants, and nightlife. ⊠*Carretera Tepic–Puerto*

Vallarta (Carretera 200), Km 140, Playa del Beso, Bucerías, Nayarit ☎*329/298–0470* ⊕*www.lospicos.com.mx* ⌑*56 bungalows for 4, 6, or 8 people* ⌂*In-room: , kitchen (some), refrigerator (some). In-hotel: restaurant, no elevator, public Internet* ⊟*MC, V.* ¶⊙*EP.*

$$$$ ⚏**Casa de Mita.** Architect-owner Marc Lindskog has created a nook
★ of nonchalant elegance, with updated country furnishings of wicker, leather, and wood; rock-floor showers without curtains or doors; and cheerful Pacific Coast architectural details. Mosquito netting lends romance to cozy, quilt-covered beds. Waves crashing onshore, their sound somehow magnified, create white noise that lulls you to sleep. In the morning, settle into a cushy chaise on your private patio to watch seabirds swim; at night watch the sun set behind Punta de Mita. These simple pleasures make this hideaway a winner. It doesn't hurt that the food is truly delicious, the bar is well-stocked with international labels, and it's all included in the room price. You can avoid the 10% surcharge for credit cards by using PayPal. **Pros:** Delicious food included in price, nearly private beach, free long-distance phone calls. **Cons:** Little nightlife in vicinity. ⊠*Playa Careyeros, Punta de Mita, Nayarit,* ☎*329/298–4114* ⊕*www.mexicoboutiquehotels.com/casalasbrisas* ⌑*8 rooms* ⌂*In-room: no phone, safe, refrigerator, no TV, Wi-Fi. In-hotel: restaurant, bar, pool, water sports, no elevator, concierge, public Wi-Fi, airport shuttle, no children under 16.* ¶⊙*AI.*

$$$$ ⚏**Four Seasons Resort.** The hotel and its fabulous spa perch above a
Fodor'sChoice lovely beach at the northern extreme of Bahía de Banderas, about 45
★ minutes from the PV airport and an hour north of downtown Puerto Vallarta. Spacious rooms occupy Mexican-style casitas of one, two, and three stories. Each room has elegant yet earthy furnishings and a private terrace or balcony—many with a sweeping sea view. The Jack Nicklaus–designed championship golf course has a challenging, optional 19th-island hole; the gym is first rate; and a good variety of sporting and beach equipment is on hand. Just offshore, the Marietas Islands are great for snorkeling, diving, whale-watching, and fishing. This is the place for indulging golf and spa fantasies, or just using the luxurious, top-notch facilities. It's a great spot for kids, too. **Pros:** Beautiful beach, yoga on the point, great gym equipment and game room for kids and adults, private yacht available for charter. **Cons:** Staff can seem overeager (you'll be saying "hola" a lot), very expensive spa treatments, stringent cancellation policy. ⊠*Bahía de Banderas, Punta de Mita, Nayarit* ☎*329/291–6019, 800/322–3442 in U.S., 800/268–6282 in Canada* ⊕*www.fshr.com/puntamita* ⌑*141 rooms, 27 suites* ⌂*In-room: safe, refrigerator, DVD, Wi-Fi. In-hotel: 3 restaurants, room service, bars, golf course, tennis courts, pool, gym, spa, beachfront, water sports, concierge, children's programs (ages 5–12), laundry service, public Internet, parking (no fee), no-smoking rooms* ⊟*AE, MC, V* ¶⊙*EP, BP.*

$$$$ ⚏**Grand Velas.** In scale and majesty, the public areas of this luxury brand compare to other Nuevo Vallarta all-inclusives like the Taj Majal to a roadside taco stand. Ceilings soar overhead, and the structure and furnishings are simultaneously minimalist and modern, yet earthy, incorporating stucco, rock, polished teak, and gleaming ecru

Continued on page 48

SPAAAHH

The trend of luxury spas in Mexico, and particularly in vacation hot spots like Puerto Vallarta, shows no signs of slowing. From elegant resort spas scented with essence of orange and bergamot to Aztec-inspired day spas, each has its own personality and signature treatments. Competition keeps creativity high, with an ever-changing menu of new treatments, many using native products like sage, chocolate, aloe vera, and even tequila.

Four Seasons Resort, Punta Mita

Spa Savvy

All of the spas listed here are open to nonguests, but reservations are essential. Guests of the hotel may get discounts. Spa customers can sometimes use other facilities at a resort, such as the restaurant, beach, pool, or gym. Ask when you book. Prices are generally on par with those of resort spas worldwide, but some deals are to be had, if you go with the less-expensive but still high-quality spas we lists. Or scout out hotel-spa packages and specials.

RESORT NAME	BODY TREATMENTS	SEASIDE TREATMENTS	TREATMENTS FOR TWO	FITNESS DAY PASS	HOT TUB	TEMAZCAL
CasaMagna Marriot	$75–$155	yes	yes	$50**	yes	no
Four Seasons	$85–$197	yes	yes	yes*	yes	yes
Gran Velas	$58–$178	yes	yes	$40	yes	no
Paradise Village	$40–$119	yes	yes	$20	yes	no
Terra Noble	$55–$65	no	yes	no	yes	yes

* A fitness day pass is free for Four Seasons guests; nonguests have access to all hotel facilities for half the room rate. **Fitness day passes at CasaMagna are $50 for nonguests, $15 for guests, and free with purchase of spa treatment.

TOP SPOTS

New and Worth Noting

OHTLI SPA, CASAMAGNA MARRIOTT
The modern yet organic-looking Ohtli spa and its attached, high-tech gym offer 22,000 square feet of elegant pampering. You can relax before or between treatments in the lounge, with a glass of water infused with love in the form of pink quartz crystals and messages of love in 13 languages. Come early to load up on this liquid love and to enjoy the cold pool, steam, sauna, and other elements of the separate men's and women's spa facilities.

Inspiration for this tasteful, soothing spa came from indigenous cultures. Treatment rooms are adorned with Huichol art and interior gardens to maintain a spiritual and nature-oriented mood. Many of the treatments—like the coconut exfoliation with deep-tissue massage—use local ingredients. The signature exfoliation treatment contains agave, cornmeal, and sea salt.

Body Treatments & Services: Exfoliation (8 kinds); wraps (7 kinds); massage (10 kinds).

Beauty Treatments: Facials (6 kinds); manicure; pedicure; waxing; children's treatments.

Prices: Body treatments $75–$155; facials $105–$150; hair $25–$90; manicure or pedicure $27–$90; waxing $25–$75.

Packages: Mother and daughter ice cream pedicure; other packages offered seasonally. *CasaMagna Marriott Puerto Vallarta, Paseo de la Marina 5, Marina Vallarta.* ☎ *322/226-0079* ⊕ *www.marriott.com* ▭ *AE, DC, MC, V.*

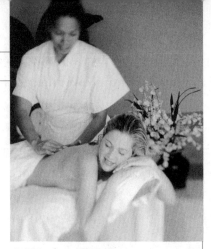

A Spa for All Seasons

FOUR SEASONS PUNTA MITA APUANE SPA
Professional service is the hallmark of this exclusive spa. An excellent kid's club allows you to enjoy spa treatments, knowing that your children are thoroughly engaged. The gym is first rate. An inspirational experience is a traditional temazcal ceremony, which takes place in a little building on a knoll near the sea.

Treatments are among the most expensive in the area, but everything is top drawer. Native products are used almost exclusively; the Punta Mita massage combines tequila and locally grown sage. And refreshing lime is mixed with tequila and salt for a margarita body scrub.

Body Treatments: Exfoliation; massage (9 types); Vichy hydrotherapy; wraps and scrubs (8 types); temazcal sweat lodge.

Beauty Treatments: Facials (7 types); manicure; pedicure; hair/scalp treatment.

Prices: Body treatments $85–$197; facials $98–$215; hair: $46–$100; manicure or pedicure $66–$92; waxing $27–$85.

Packages: Couples treatments such as Like Water for Chocolate—a chocolate scrub and facial; a hot-stone massage; and servings of fruit, chocolate fondue, and champagne. *Punta de Mita, Bahía de Banderas.* ☎ *329/291-6000* ⊕ *www.fourseasons.com/ puntamita.* ▭ *AE, DC, MC, V.*

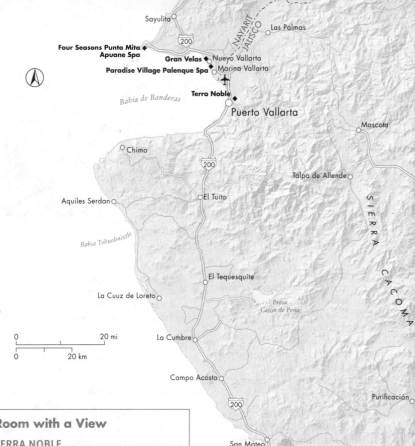

Sayulita

Las Palmas

NAYARIT
JALISCO

200

Four Seasons Punta Mita ◆
Apuane Spa

Nuevo Vallarta

Gran Velas ◆

Marina Vallarta

Paradise Village Palenque Spa ◆

Terra Noble ◆

Bahía de Banderas

Puerto Vallarta

Mascota

Chimo

200

Talpa de Allende

Aquiles Serdan

El Tuito

S
I
E
R
R
A

Bahía Tehualmixtle

El Tequesquite

*Presa
Cajón de Peña*

C
A
C
O
M
A

La Cuuz de Loreto

| 0 | | 20 mi |
| 0 | | 20 km |

La Cumbre

Campo Acosta

200

Purificación

San Mateo

Bahía Chamela

*Reserva de
la Biosfera*

La Huerta

Costa Careyes

80

El Tecuán

Bahía Tenacatita

El Tamarindo ◆

Cihuatlo

Barra de Navidad

Room with a View

TERRA NOBLE

Your cares begin to melt away as soon as you enter the rustic, garden-surrounded property of this day-spa aerie overlooking Banderas Bay. Familiar and unpretentious, Terra Noble is more accessible pricewise than some of the area's more elegant spas. After-treatment teas are served on an outdoor patio with a great sea view. Two-hour temazcal sweat lodge rituals cleanse on three levels: physically, mentally, and spiritually. Or recharge with clay and painting classes, and Tarot readings.

Body Treatments: Reflexology; massage; several wraps and scrubs; temazcal sweat lodge; yoga/meditation.

Beauty Treatments: Facials; manicure; pedicure.

Packages: A few economical packages such as the Stress Recovery (a sea-salt body scrub, a massage, and a facial), for $145.

Prices: Body treatments $50–$65; manicure/pedicure $25–$30.
Av. Tulipanes 595, at Fracc. Lomas de Terra Noble, Col. 5 de Diciembre. Tel. 322/223-3530 ⊕ *www.terranoble.com.* ▭ *MC, V.*

MORE TOP SPOTS

Something for Every Body

PARADISE VILLAGE PALENQUE SPA

On a peninsula between the beach and marina, this modern Maya temple of glass and marble is a cool, sweet-smelling oasis with separate wings for men and women; each is equipped with private hydrotherapy tubs, whirlpools, saunas, and steam rooms. The coed gym has state-of-the-art equipment and views of the ocean, plus aerobics classes in a separate studio and an indoor lap pool.

Drama Queen

Spa designer Diana Mestre, an old hand in these parts, brings together ancient healing arts and the latest technologies. The reasonably priced therapy selections are extensive, from an anti-cellulite seaweed wrap to milk baths with honey, amaranth, and orange oil or the raindrop aromatherapy massage, employing clove, sage, bergamot, and other essential oils.

Body Treatments: Aromatherapy; facials; electro-acuscope anti-pain & stress therapy; Reiki; exfoliation; hot-stone massage; hydrotherapy; wraps, scrubs, and body treatments (14 types); reflexology; shiatsu.

Beauty Treatments: Facials (10 types), manicure, pedicure.

Prices: Body treatments $40–$119; facials $40–$119; manicure/pedicure $23–$69; hair $35–$92; waxing $9–$63.

Packages: A wide variety of packages that allow switching treatments in an equivalent price bracket. The basic plan combines three 50-minute treatments: marine body scrub, holistic massage, and hydrating facial. *Paseo de los Cocoteros 1 Nuevo Vallarta. Tel. 322/226–6770 ⊕ www.paradisevillage.com. ▭ AE, MC, V.*

GRAN VELAS

The spa at Nuevo Vallarta's most elegant all-inclusive has dramatic architectural lines and plenty of marble, stone, teak, and tile. The 16,500-square-foot facility has 20 treatment rooms, and ample steam, sauna, and whirlpools. Lounge in the comfortable chaises in the "plunge lagoon" (with warm and cold pools) between or after treatments.

Reading the extensive menu of treatments can take hours—highlights are the chocolate, gold, or avocado wraps, Thai massage, European facial, cinnamon-sage foot scrub, and the challenging buttocks sculpt-lift. Adjoining the spa is an impressive fitness facility.

Body Treatments: Reflexology; massage (18 types); shiatsu; Vichy shower; exfoliation; wraps, scrubs, baths, and body treatments (32 types).

Beauty Treatments: Facials (12+); manicure/pedicure; hair care; waxing; makeup.

Prices: Body treatments: $58–$178; facials: $89—$148; manicure/pedicure: $20–$89; hair care: $29–$89; waxing: $29–$58; makeup: $78.

Packages: Happy Bride, Just for Men, and Detox Ritual packages, plus 10% discount for three or more treatments; otherwise, no packages. *Av. de los Cocoteros 98 Sur, Nuevo Vallarta. Tel. 322/226–8000 ⊕ www.grandvelas.com. ▭ AE, MC, V.*

GLOSSARY

acupuncture. Painless Chinese medicine during which needles are inserted into key spots on the body to restore the flow of *qi* and allow the body to heal itself.

aromatherapy. Massage and other treatments using plant-derived essential oils intended to relax the skin's connective tissues and stimulate the flow of lymph fluid.

ayurveda. An Indian philosophy that uses oils, massage, herbs, and diet and lifestyle modification to restore perfect balance to a body.

body brushing. Dry brushing of the skin to remove dead cells and stimulate circulation.

body polish. Use of scrubs, loofahs, and other exfoliants to remove dead skin cells.

hot-stone massage. Massage using smooth stones heated in water and applied to the skin with pressure or strokes or simply rested on the body.

hydrotherapy. Underwater massage, alternating hot and cold showers, and other water-oriented treatments.

reflexology. Massage on the pressure points of feet, hands, and ears.

reiki. A Japanese healing method involving universal life energy, the laying on of hands, and mental and spiritual balancing. It's intended to relieve acute emotional and physical conditions. Also called radiance technique.

salt glow. Rubbing the body with coarse salt to remove dead skin.

shiatsu. Japanese massage that uses pressure applied with fingers, hands, elbows, and feet.

shirodhara. Ayurvedic massage in which warm herbalized oil is trickled onto the center of the forehead, then gently rubbed into the hair and scalp.

sports massage. A deep-tissue massage to relieve muscle tension and residual pain from workouts.

Swedish massage. Stroking, kneading, and tapping to relax muscles. It was devised at the University of Stockholm in the 19th century by Per Henrik Ling.

Swiss shower. A multijet bath that alternates hot and cold water, often used after mud wraps and other body treatments.

Temazcal. Maya meditation in a sauna heated with volcanic rocks.

THE TEMAZCAL TRADITION

Increasingly popular at Mexico spas is the traditional sweat lodge, or *temazcalli*. Herb-scented water sizzles on heated lava rocks, filling the intimate space with purifying steam. Rituals blend indigenous and New Age practices, attempting to stimulate you emotionally, spiritually, and physically. For the sake of others, it's best to take a temazcal only if you're committed to the ceremony, or at least open-minded, and not claustrophobic.

Thai massage. Deep-tissue massage and passive stretching to ease stiff, tense, or short muscles.

thalassotherapy. Water-based treatments that incorporate seawater, seaweed, and algae.

Vichy shower. Treatment in which a person lies on a cushioned, waterproof mat and is showered by overhead water jets.

Watsu. A blend of shiatsu and deep-tissue massage with gentle stretches—all conducted in a warm pool.

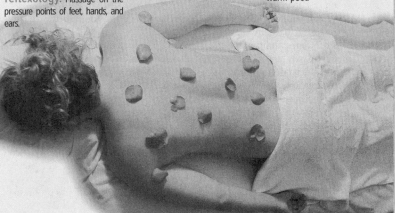

marble. The spa is excellent, and the views—with the garden-shrouded pool in the foreground and the beach beyond—are striking. Rooms are sleek, with elegant furnishings and appointments. In terms of food and drink, the high price entitles you to top-of-the-line spirits in minibars and restaurants, but the food, in our experience, is not exceptional, and for a rack rate of more than $1,000 per couple per night, all-inclusive, it should be. **Pros:** Exceptionally beautiful rooms and public spaces, lovely spa. **Cons:** Food could be better,

> **PILLOW TALK**
>
> If you're picky about your pillow, Grand Velas, Presidente Intercontinental, Four Seasons, or another top-drawer accommodation might prove to be the hotel of your dreams. Some of the swankiest hotels in the area have pillow menus with a half-dozen or more styles to choose from. Go with whisper-soft eiderdown or, if you're allergic to farm animals, 100% man-made materials.

Nuevo Vallarta location is far from PV (but 10 minutes by car from Bucerías). ✉ *Paseo de los Cocoteros 98 Sur, Nuevo Vallarta, Jalisco,* ☎ *322/226–8000, 877/398–2784 in U.S., 866/355–3359 in Canada* ⊕ *www.grandvelas.com* 🛏 *269 suites* ⅋ *In-room: safe, DVD, Wi-Fi. In-hotel: 4 restaurants, room service, bars, tennis court, pools, gym, spa, beachfront, children's programs (ages 4–12), laundry service, public Internet, airport shuttle, parking (no fee), some pets allowed (fee)* ▭ *AE, MC, V* ⦿ *AI.*

$ 🏨 **Marco's Place Suites & Villas.** Despite its name, this is a motel-like three-story property, and one of the few standard hotels in Bucerías, which is filled with apartment and condo rentals. Rooms are on the small side, with tiny baths, but are cheery and bright with comfortable beds. Sit on chaise lounges by the pool or at café tables outside the first-floor rooms. The property is a block from the beach. **Pros:** Bright, attractive rooms; several different outdoor spaces for reading or relaxing. **Con:** Street parking only. ✉ *Calle Juventino Espinoza 6–A, Bucerías, Nayarit* ☎ *329/298–0865* ⊕ *www.marcosplacevillas.com* 🛏 *15 rooms, 3 suites* ⅋ *In-room: kitchen, refrigerator. In-hotel: pool, no elevator* ▭ *No credit cards* ⦿ *EP.*

$$$$ 🏨 **Marival Resort and Suites.** Come here if you're looking for an all-inclusive bargain that includes a wealth of activities. Rooms have strong air-conditioning and amenities like hair dryers, irons and ironing boards, and small tubs, but also demonstrate an uninspired attempt at modern decor, not to mention cheap doors. There's an extra charge, inexplicably, for the use of in-room safes. Only a few units have ocean views, but there are plenty of individual palapas and lounge chairs at the beach. **Pros:** Value-priced; spotless rooms and immaculately kept grounds; premium booze brands. **Cons:** Rock-hard beds; musty smell in some rooms; cheap finishing touches like plastic chairs and fake plants. ✉ Paseo Cocoteros s/n at Blvd. Nuevo Vallarta, Nuevo Vallarta Jalisco ☎ 322/226–8200 ⊕ *www.gomarival.com* 🛏 373 rooms, 122 suites ⅋ In-room: kitchen (some). In-hotel: 6 restaurants, room service, bars, tennis courts, pools, gym, spa, beachfront, bicycles, children's programs (ages 4–17), public Internet, parking (no fee) ▭ MC, V ⦿ AI.

2

¢–$ ⊡**Palmeras.** A block from the beach, in an area with lots of good res-
taurants, Palmeras has small rooms with brightly painted interior walls
and modeled-stucco sunflowers serving as a kind of headboard behind
the bed. There's plenty of space to socialize around the large, clean,
rectangular pool. The more expensive rooms are larger, fresher, and
have a couch, satellite TV, and kitchenette; those on the second floor
have a partial ocean view. Smaller, older, street-facing rooms are half
the price of the newer units. **Pros:** Free Wi-Fi, inexpensive older rooms
for bargain hunters, one the best small hotels in Bucerías. **Con:** Some
rooms have odd layout. ⊠*Lázaro Cárdenas 35, Bucerías, Nayarit*
☎*329/298–1288, 647/722–4139 in the U.S.* ⊕*www.hotelpalmeras.*
com ⇋*21 rooms* ♿*In-room: no phone, kitchen (some), refrigerator,*
no TV (some), Wi-Fi. In-hotel: pool, no elevator, no-smoking rooms
⊟*MC, V* ⟨○⟩*EP.*

$$$ ⊡**Paradise Village.** This Nuevo Vallarta hotel and time-share property
♨   is perfect for families, with lots of activities geared to children. Many
people love it, although the property's dedication to time-share guests
makes some hotel guests feel short-shrifted. Most suites have balco-
nies with either marina or ocean views. Furnishings are attractive as
well as functional, with pretty cane sofa beds in a soothing palette and
well-equipped kitchens. Locals like to visit the clean, well-organized
spa, which smells divine, and is noted for its massages and facials.
The beach here is tranquil enough for swimming, although some small
waves are suitable for bodysurfing. **Pros:** Walk all the way to Bucerías
on the beach, full kitchen in all suites, efficient a/c units. **Cons:** Big
cats caged-in depressing zoo; no Internet room for guests. ⊠*Paseo de*
los Cocoteros 1, Nuevo Vallarta, Jalisco ☎*322/226–6770, 800/995–*
5714 Ext. 111 in U.S. and Canada ⊕*www.paradisevillage.com* ⇋*490*
suites ♿*In-room: safe, kitchen, refrigerator, Wi-Fi. In-hotel: 4 restau-*
rants, room service, bars, golf course, tennis courts, pools, gym, spa,
beachfront, children's programs (ages 4–11), concierge, public Wi-Fi,
parking (no fee) ⊟*AE, MC, V* ⟨○⟩*EP.*

$$ ⊡**Royal Decameron.** This high-volume hotel is at the south end of long
and lovely Bucerías Beach and has beautifully manicured grounds.
It also has quality entertainment, activities, and food, and strives to
maintain high sanitary standards. Rooms are plain and not particularly modern or appealing, with laminate bathroom counters and textured stucco interior walls that have been painted over many times.
Those in the older section have the best views since they were built
along the water. Reservations must be made through a brick-and-mor-
tar or online travel agency (e.g., Expedia.com, Travelocity.com, etc.).
Pros: Excellent deal for all-inclusive (room only and air packages, too);
long beach great for walking or jogging; Spanish and dance lessons
plus lots of other activities. **Cons:** So-so room decor, 35- to 45-minute
drive from downtown Vallarta ⊠*Calle Lázaro Cárdenas, Bucerías,*
Nayarit ☎*329/298–0226 or 800/279–3718 toll-free in the U.S., Can-*
ada ⊕*www.decameron.com* ⇋*620 rooms* ♿*In-room: safe (fee). In-*
hotel: 7 restaurants, bars, tennis courts, pools, bicycles, public Internet,
parking (no fee) ⊟*MC, V* ⟨○⟩*AI.*

$$–$$$ 🖵**Villa Bella.** Tropical plants give character to this privately owned property where tranquillity reigns. The hotel is on a hill above quiet La Cruz de Huanacaxtle, just north of Bucerías. Choose a garden-view room or ocean-facing suite in one of two villas that share common rooms—with TV, telephone, computer with Internet access, and DVD and CD players—as well as a swimming pool and gardens. Other pretty shared spaces include a dining area and kitchen in the guest villa, and second-story terraces off

> **GET YOUR ZZZ'S**
>
> Some accommodations in coastal Nayarit and Jalisco are along the main highway and experience heavy traffic. And resort hotels often have lobby bars in the middle of an open-air atrium leading directly to rooms, or rooftop discoteques, or outdoor theme nights with live music. When you book, request a room far from the noisiest part of the hotel.

some of the suites. Villa Bella is the perfect place to enjoy the simple charms of earthy La Cruz, a very Mexican village with a brand-new marina and a growing number of foreign residents and snowbirds. Payment is accepted only via PayPal. **Pros:** Free airport pickup, lap pool, free cocktail (or two) Monday through Saturday evening. **Cons:** Up a steep road, and best for those with a car; about an hour from Puerto Vallarta; little or no nightlife in immediate area. ⊠ *Calle del Monte Calvario 12, La Cruz de Huanacaxtle 63732, Nayarit* ☎ *329/295–5161, 329/295–5154, 877/273–6244 toll-free in U.S., 877/513–1662 toll-free in Canada* ⊕ *www.villabella-lacruz.com* 🛏 *2 rooms, 5 suites* ⌂ *In-room: no a/c (some), no phone, kitchen (some), no TV (some). In-hotel: restaurant, bar, pool, no elevator, airport shuttle, public Internet, no children under 12, no-smoking rooms* ⊟ *MC, V* ⍟ *CP.*

$$ 🖵**Villa Varadero.** Kids under 10 stay and eat for free with the all-inclu-
☾   sive plan at this small, friendly, four-story hotel in Nuevo Vallarta.
★   What's the bottom line, then? Families can stay for less than $90 per person per night, including tax. Other pluses are the wide beach with gentle surf and the chummy bar with its billiards salon, dart boards, dominoes, chess, and other games. The use of bikes, kayaks, and boogie boards is free for AI guests; there's a charge for use by EP guests. Only a few of the compact, well-maintained units have tubs, and decor is standard, although walls are painted in cheerful hues. **Pros:** Least-expensive all-inclusive in Nuevo Vallarta; small size makes for a less impersonal vacation. **Cons:** Ho-hum furnishings and room amenities; only one-bedroom suites have balconies. ⊠ *Retorno Nayarit, Lotes 83 and 84, Manzana XIII, Nuevo Vallarta, Jalisco* ☎ *322/297–0430, 800/238–9996 toll-free in the U.S., 877/742--6323 toll-free in Canada* ⊕ *www.villavaradero.com.mx* 🛏 *29 rooms, 29 suites* ⌂ *In-room: safe (some), kitchen (some), refrigerator. In-hotel: restaurant, bars, pool, beachfront, bicycles, laundry service, public Internet, parking (no fee)* ⊟ *AE, MC, V* ⍟ *AI, EP.*

CLOSE UP

An Over-the-Top Experience

You don't have to be a rock star to rent one of Vallarta's most beautiful homes, but a similar income or a never-ending trust fund might help.

Just beyond Destiladeras Beach at the north end of Banderas Bay, **Casa Canta Rana** (⊕ *www.casacantarana. com*) provides stunning views of the coast from inside a gated community. Indoor-outdoor living and dining spaces have bay and island views. Decorated with tasteful, seductively subdued furnishings, two of the three-bedroom suites share a tall palapa roof; the master suite has an indoor-outdoor shower and private patio. A maid, gardener, and pool boy are included. Additional staff, airport transfer, and other services are provided at additional cost. For the nanny, pilot, or bodyguard on your payroll, there's a separate apartment with bedroom, kitchen, and bath. High season (November 1–April 30) rate is $1,450 per night, with a four-night minimum.

What could be better than a former president's home, the site hand-picked for its almost incomprehensibly beautiful vistas of the sea? President Luis Echevarri's mansion, **Villa Vista Mágica,** is on a highly forested point between Sayulita and San Francisco, Nayarit. The circular, 10-bedroom

property comes with a cook who will prepare three meals a day (Mexican food from a Mexican cook). The Wave-Runners and two Suburbans are also at your disposal. This fabulous place costs a mere $42,000 a week (much more during holidays). To rent this—or a less-pricey property where you'll feel equally special and pampered—contact **Boutique Villas** (322/209–1992, or from the U.S 866/560–2281 ⊕ *www.boutiquevillas.com*).

Twenty years ago the private heaven of simple fisherfolk and their families, the spearhead-shape point at the northern point of Banderas Bay is today home to the gated, low-density community **Punta Mita** (☎888/647–0979 in U.S. and Canada ⊕ *www. puntamita.com.mx*). Here you find the Four Seasons (with the St. Regis resort to open in early 2008), as well as multiple golf courses, beach clubs, spas, and shops. Within the 1,500-acre retreat, the Four Seasons and other brands rent luxury villas whose high-season rates range from $4,000 to $10,000+ per night. Floor plans vary but there's consistency in the large outdoor living spaces; air-conditioned common areas and bedrooms with natural-hue, high-quality furnishings; and attentive staff members, including your own full-time chef.

NORTH OF BANDERAS BAY

$$ 🖵 **Costa Azul.** What makes this place attractive are the many activities ♻ offered: horseback riding, kayaking, hiking, surfing (with lessons), and excursions to the Marietas Islands or La Tobara mangroves near San Blas. The all-inclusive plan includes activities, but since the food is mainly mediocre and San Pancho has several excellent restaurants, the European Plan is recommended. Although the sandy beach faces the open ocean, it curves around to a spot that's safer for swimming. **Pros:** Great place to bond with kids of all ages, nice beach, outdoor activities are planned for you, free Wi-Fi in the bar/restaurant. **Cons:** Mediocre food, some guests have complained of disorganized and unhelpful staff members, and hotel maintenance has declined in recent years. ⌧*Carretera 200, Km 118, Fracc. Costa Azul, San Francisco, Nayarit* ☏*311/258–4210, 800/365–7613 toll-free in U.S.* ⊕*www.costaazul. com* ⇝*24 rooms, 3 villas* ⌂*In-room: no phone, kitchen (some), refrigerator (some), no TV. In-hotel: restaurant, bars, pool, beachfront, water sports, no elevator, laundry service, public Wi-Fi, airport shuttle, parking (no fee)* ▤*AE, D, DC, MC, V* †◯†*AI, EP, FAP.*

> **OM AWAY FROM HOME**
>
> **Via Yoga** (⊕ *www.viayoga.com*), based in Seattle, Washington, offers weeklong packages at Villa Amor that include twice-daily yoga classes with group activities, various disciplines of yoga, and, if you like, surfing classes and excursions.

$$–$$$ 🏨**Villa Amor.** What began as a hilltop home has slowly become an
★ amalgam of unusual, rustic-but-luxurious suites with indoor and outdoor living spaces. The higher up your room, the more beautiful the view of Sayulita's coast. The trade-off for such beauty? A long walk up a seemingly endless staircase and the dearth of room phones make contacting the front desk frustrating. Accommodations, managed by different owners, range from basic to honeymoon suites with terraces and plunge pools. Details like recessed color-glass light fixtures, talavera sinks in bathrooms, brick ceilings, wrought-iron table lamps, art in wall niches, and colorful cement floors add a lot of class. The property overlooks a rocky cove where you can fish from shore; a beautiful sandy beach is a few minutes' walk. The staff lends out bikes, kayaks, boogie boards, and snorkeling gear. **Pros:** Nice location across bay from Sayulita's main beach; staff arranges tours and tee times. **Cons:** Tons of stairs; no room phones; open-to-the-elements rooms can have creepy crawlies. ⌧*Playa Sayulita, Sayulita, Nayarit* ☏*329/291–3010* ⊕*www.villaamor.com* ⇝*32 villas* ⌂*In-room: no a/c (some), no phone, kitchen (some), refrigerator, no TV. In-hotel: restaurant, bar, water sports, bicycles, no elevator, laundry service, parking (no fee)* ▤*MC, V* †◯†*EP.*

$$ 🏨**Villas Buena Vida.** On beautiful Rincón de Guayabitos Beach, this property has three-story units, breeze-ruffled palms, and manicured walkways. Four guests are allowed in even the smallest rooms (which have two double beds and run-of-the-mill hotel furnishings), making this a deal for bargain hunters. Guayabitos is a Mexican resort town that's recently begun attracting snowbirds and travelers looking for less-touristy digs. The bay has calm surf that's good for swimming, a long flat beach embraced by twin headlands (great for walking), and boat trips to the quiet coves and solitary beaches along Jaltemba Bay. Be prepared for the staff to count every spoon and spatula when you check in and out. **Pros:** Beautiful bayside location, 5% cash discount. **Cons:** Uninspired furnishings, unreliable Internet access in rooms via Wi-Fi. ⌧*Retorno Laureles 2, Rincón de Guayabitos, Nayarit* ☏*327/274– 0231* ⊕*www.villasbuenavida.com* ⇝*36 rooms, 9 suites* ⌂*In-room: kitchen, refrigerator. In-hotel: restaurant, pools, no elevator, laundry facilities* ▤*MC, V* †◯†*EP.*

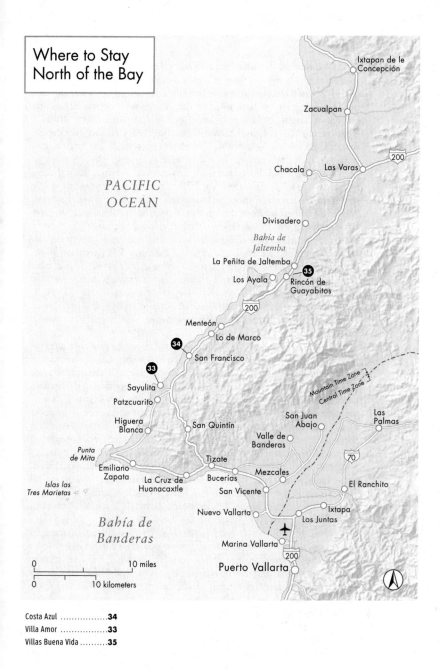

Where to Stay
North of the Bay

Ixtapan de le Concepción

Zacualpan

200

PACIFIC
OCEAN

Chacala   Las Varas

Divisadero

Bahía de Jaltemba

La Peñita de Jaltemba

35

Los Ayala   Rincón de Guayabitos

200

Menteón

Lo de Marco

34 San Francisco

33

Sayulita

Patzcuarito

Mountain Time Zone
Central Time Zone

Higuera Blanca

San Quintín

San Juan Abajo

Las Palmas

Valle de Banderas

Punta de Mita

Tizate

70

Emiliano Zapata

La Cruz de Huanacaxtle

Bucerías

Mezcales

El Ranchito

Islas las Tres Marietas

San Vicente

Nuevo Vallarta

Ixtapa
Los Juntas

Bahía de Banderas

Marina Vallarta

0   10 miles

0   10 kilometers

200

Puerto Vallarta

COSTALEGRE

$$$$ ⚙ **Las Alamandas.** Personal service and exclusivity lure movie stars and royalty to this low-key resort in a nature preserve about 1½ hours from both PV and Manzanillo. Suites are filled with folk art; their indoor-outdoor living rooms have modern furnishings with deliciously nubby fabrics in bright, bold colors and Guatemalan-cloth throw pillows. Request a TV, VCR, and movie from the library for an evening in; there's little else to do at night. There's lots more to do in the daytime, however, including picnics anywhere on the property (the thorn forest here is scrubby and dry rather than tropical and green) and boat rides on the Río San Nicolás. There's a 15% service charge and a two-night minimum; the average stay is seven nights. If you have to ask the price, you can't afford it. **Pros:** Stargazing from rooftop bar, stunning yet cozy architecture. **Cons:** Open-style bungalows not pleasant in rainy season, with mosquitoes and high humidity; not close to any restaurants or nightlife; riptides. ⊠ *Carretera 200, Km 85, Quemaro* ✛ *83 km (52 mi) south of PV, 133 km (83 mi) north of Barra de Navidad* ☎ *322/285–5500 or 888/882–9616* ⊕ *www.mexicoboutiquehotels. com/lasalamandas* ⟲ *14 suites* ⟳ *In-room: refrigerator, DVD, VCR. In-hotel: restaurant, room service, bars, tennis court, pool, gym, spa, beachfront, water sports, bicycles, concierge, laundry service, public Internet, parking (no fee)* ⊟ *MC, V* ⊙*EP, FAP.*

$$$$ ⚙ **El Careyes Beach Resort.** On a gorgeous bay framed by flowering vegeta-
★   tion, El Careyes is a boldly painted village of a resort. Guest rooms have large windows and private patios or balconies; suites have outdoor hot tubs. Colorful furnishings and artwork create a sophisticated Mexican palette. The full-service spa has fine European beauty and body treatments; a deli sells fine wines, prosciutto, and other necessities of the good life. A full range of water-sports equipment awaits you at the beach, and there are dune buggies and kayaks, too. There are more dining options in the area than at other Costalegre resorts, making a rental car a plus. It's a short walk to pretty Playa Rosa and a short drive to Bahía Tenacatita. **Pros:** Large spa menu, uniquely beautiful architecture, on a beautiful cove. **Cons:** Few computers makes it hard to check e-mail; only one restaurant; 5% service charge. ⊠ *Carretera a Barra de Navidad (Carretera 200), Km 53.5, Careyes, Jalisco,* ✛ *161 km (100 mi) south of PV, 55 km (34 mi) north of Barra de Navidad* ☎ *315/351–0000* ⊕ *www.elcareyes resort.com* ⟲ *22 rooms, 29 suites, 3 multi-bedroom casitas* ⟳ *In-room: safe, kitchen (some), refrigerator (some), DVD (some). In-hotel: restaurant, room service, bar, tennis courts, pool, gym, spa, beachfront, water sports, bicycles, laundry service, public Internet, public Wi-Fi, parking (no fee)* ⊟ *AE, MC, V* ⊙*EP.*

$$ ⚙ **Coconuts By the Sea.** A friendly couple of American expats (he's a
★   former Eastern Airlines pilot) own and run this charming cliff-top hide-away with a drop-dead gorgeous view of the ocean and Boca de Iguana Beach below. The furniture is stylish, and homey touches like lamps and fish-theme wall decorations make the snug apartments just right for holing up. The two apartments upstairs, with thatched roofs and kitchen and living room open to the elements, are not usually available in summer due to the rain; the rest of the year they're highly coveted.

One has an outdoor shower with a view. **Pros:** Homey apartments; great sea views. **Cons:** Its few rooms make last-minute reservations unlikely; long downhill walk to the beach ⊠*Playa Boca de Iguanas, 6 Dolphin Way, Bahía Tenacatita, Jalisco* ✛*195 km (121 mi) south of PV, 21 km (13 mi) north of Barra de Navidad* ☎ *314/338–6315* ⊕*www.coconutsbythesea.com* ⟿*4 rooms* ⟐*In-room: no phone, kitchen, refrigerator, Wi-Fi. In-hotel: pool, parking (no fee)* ⊟*No credit cards* ⵙ*EP.*

$$$$ ⬚**Grand Bay Isla Navidad.** On a 1,200-acre peninsula between the Pacific and the Navidad Lagoon, this no-holds-barred resort cascades down to a private, though not terribly scenic, brown-sand beach. An island unto itself, the lovely and rather snooty Grand Bay faces humble Barra de Navidad across the lagoon. Spanish arches, shady patios, cool fountains, and lush gardens contribute to the elegant architecture; tiered swimming pools are connected by slides and waterfalls. There's even a movie theater. If all this indulgence becomes too much, an inexpensive water taxi can take you over to the real world, two minutes away. There's a $15 per night service charge. **Pros:** AARP and AAA discounts, elegant property. **Cons:** Humble Barra de Navidad, the closest town, has no upscale restaurants; staff can be chilly; no ocean views. ⊠*Isla Navidad, Barra de Navidad, Jalisco* ☎*314/331–0500, 800/996–3426 in U.S.* ☎*315/355–6071* ⊕*www.wyndham.com* ⟿*158 rooms, 41 suites* ⟐*In-room: safe, refrigerator, kitchen (some), Ethernet, Wi-Fi. In-hotel: 3 restaurants, room service, bars, golf course, tennis courts, pools, gym, spa, concierge, laundry service, public Internet, public Wi-Fi, airport shuttle, parking (no fee), no-smoking rooms* ⊟*AE, MC, V* ⵙ*EP.*

$$$$ ⬚**Hotelito Desconocido.** Although every inch of the place is painted, tiled,
★ or otherwise decorated with bright Mexican colors and handicrafts, the effect is distinctive rather than fussy. Perhaps that's because rooms and suites incorporate local building styles and materials, including plank floors, reed mats, bamboo walls, and palm-frond roofs. They're cooled by battery-powered fans and lighted by lanterns, candles, and low-wattage lamps. Rustic but lovely bathrooms bring the outdoors in through large open windows. Signal for morning coffee by running up the red flag. On a long stretch of beach, this isolated hotel is an idyllic escape for its clientele: about 60% American, 25% European, and 100% laid-back. There's an obligatory meal plan of $184 for two people. **Pros:** Completely isolated, unique, and charming. **Cons:** Completely isolated, obligatory meal plan is rather pricey. ⊠*Playón de Mismaloya s/n, Cruz de Loreto, Jalisco* ✛*97 km (60 mi) south of PV, 119 km (74 mi) north of Barra de Navidad* ☎*322/281–4010, 800/851–1143 in U.S., 01800/013–1313 toll-free in Mexico* ⊕*www. hotelito.com* ⟿*16 rooms, 8 suites* ⟐*In-room: no a/c, no phone, no TV. In-hotel: 2 restaurants, bar, pool, spa, beachfront, water sports, bicycles, no elevator, concierge, public Internet, airport shuttle, parking (no fee)* ⊟*AE, MC, V* ⵙ*BP, FAP.*

$$ ⬚**La Paloma Oceanfront Retreat.** Room prices are reasonable considering the small studio apartments have almost everything home does, and four of them face the beach (where the waves are often good for

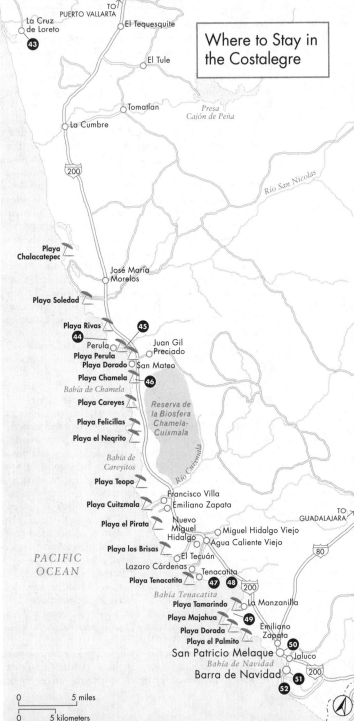

Where to Stay in the Costalegre

TO PUERTO VALLARTA

La Cruz de Loreto **43**

El Tequesquite

El Tule

Tomatlan

Presa Cajón de Peña

La Cumbre

200

Rio San Nicolas

Playa Chalacatepec

José María Morelos

Playa Soledad

Playa Rivas

44 **45**

Perula

Juan Gil Preciado

Playa Perula

Playa Dorado San Mateo

Playa Chamela **46**

Bahía de Chamela

Playa Careyes

Reserva de la Biosfera Chamela-Cuixmala

Playa Felicillas

Playa el Negrito

Río Cuixmala

Bahía de Careyitos

Playa Teopa

Francisco Villa

Playa Cuitzmala

Emiliano Zapata

Playa el Pirata

Nuevo Miguel Hidalgo

Miguel Hidalgo Viejo

TO GUADALAJARA

Agua Caliente Viejo

80

Playa los Brisas

El Tecuán

Lazaro Cárdenas

PACIFIC OCEAN

Tenacatita

Playa Tenacatita

47 **48** **200**

Bahía Tenacatita

La Manzanilla

Playa Tamarindo

Playa Majahua

49

Emiliano Zapata

Playa Dorada

50

Playa el Palmito

San Patricio Melaque

Jaluco

Bahía de Navidad

Barra de Navidad

51

200

52

0 5 miles

0 5 kilometers

boogie boarding, and always great for long walks along the bay). Each room is configured differently, but all are uniformly bright and cheerful, with private patios and paintings by the owner (she gives lessons in high season). There's a large pool and patio for outdoor barbecuing facing the ocean. There is a three-day minimum stay here; most visitors book by the week in high season. La Paloma now offers off-season discounts. **Pros:** Car onsite for rental by the day; alongside a beautiful bay; long beach perfect for walking and jogging. **Con:** Price hike in recent years, although still worth it! ⊠ *Av. Las Cabañas 13, San Patricio–Melaque,* ✛ *6 km (4 mi) north of Barra de Navidad* ☎ *315/355–5345* ⊕ *www.lapaloma-mexico.com* ⇴ *13 studio apartments* ⌂ *In-room: no a/c (some), no phone, kitchen, refrigerator, DVD (some). In-hotel: restaurant, pool, public Internet, public Wi-Fi, parking (no fee)* ⊟ *AE, MC, V (through PayPal only)* ⎮⊙⎮ *CP.*

> ### TURTLES 911
>
> Releasing tiny turtles into the sea, done in the evening when there are fewer predators, is a real thrill for kids, and for many adults as well. The Westin, Marriott Casa-Magna, Fiesta Americana, Velas Vallarta, and Dreams Resort in Puerto Vallarta; and Las Alamandas, Hotelito Desconocido, and El Tamarindo on the Costalegre have marine turtle conservation programs. They employ biologists to collect eggs from nests on nearby beaches, incubate them in protected sand pits, and help guests repatriate them into the wild blue sea.

$$$$ ⚎ **Punta Serena.** Guests come from New York and Italy to this adults-
★ only oasis of calm. Perched on a beautiful headland, "Point Serene" enjoys balmy breezes and life-changing views from the infinity hot tub; the beach far below and pool are clothing optional. Spa treatments are inventive: roses and red wine promote moisturizing; carotene and honey contribute to a glowing tan; and the "Mayan Wrap" connects you herbally to the glowing god within. Shamans lead healing steam ceremonies on weekends; mud-and-music therapies are on the beach; and activities like horseback riding, tennis (three courts), and nonmotorized water sports at the adjacent Blue Bay hotel are included in the price. Additionally, rooms have lovely furnishings and decor, and shared or private terraces, some with fab beach views. **Pros:** Gorgeous views; complimentary horseback ride and mangrove cruise; weekly temazcal, or ritual steam ceremony. **Cons:** Isolated; limited menu; cobblestone walkways and hills make walking difficult for some folks. ⊠ *Carretera Barra de Navidad–Puerto Vallarta (Carretera 200), Km 20, Tenacatita, Jalisco* ✛ *196 km (122 mi) south of PV, 20 km (12 mi) north of Barra de Navidad* ☎ *315/351–5427 or 315/351–5020* ⊕ *www.puntaserena. com* ⇴ *12 rooms, 12 suites* ⌂ *In-room: safe. In-hotel: restaurant, bar, pool, gym, spa, beachfront, laundry service, public Internet, parking (no fee), no kids under 18* ⊟ *AE, MC, V* ⎮⊙⎮ *AI.*

$$$$ ⚎ **El Tamarindo.** More than 2,000 acres of ecological reserve and jungle
Fodor's Choice surround this magical resort along 16 km (10 mi) of private coast. The
★ architecture utilizes simple design elements (with a Mediterranean flavor) and local building materials; world-renowned Ricardo Legorreta

was one of the architects. Many villas have outdoor living rooms. All have dark-wood floors, king-size beds, wet bars, ample bathrooms, and patios with plunge pools, hammocks, and chaise longues. Sofas are upholstered in rich textured fabrics, and all furnishings and details are spare and classy. At night the staff lights more than 1,500 candles around the villas to create a truly enchanting setting. The hotel receives our highest accolade, Fodor's Choice, for its stunning location, gorgeous rooms, and excellent golf course. **Pros:** Individual plunge pools, CD players with music in each room, daily yoga and pilates classes. **Cons:** 8% service fee on top of 17% sales and hotel taxes; isolated. ⊠ *Carretera Melaque–Puerto Vallarta (Carretera 200), Km 7.5, Cihuatlán, Jalisco* ✛*204 km (127 mi) south of PV, 12 km (7 mi) north of Barra de Navidad* ☎*315/351–5031, 01800/823—3037 toll-free in Mexico, 866/717–4316 from U.S. or Canada* ⊕*www.mexicoboutiquehotels.com/thetamarindo* ⮐*32 villas* ⧖*In-room: safe, no TV. In-hotel: restaurant, room service, bar, gym, spa, golf course, tennis court, pool, beachfront, diving, water sports, bicycles, concierge, laundry service, public Internet, airport shuttle, parking (no fee)* ⊟*AE, MC, V* ⊚*EP.*

$ ⊡ **Vagabundo.** This humble beach town on Chamela Bay is an excellent place off the gringo trail for swimming, fishing, or exploring the offshore islands. Simple hotel rooms surround a swimming pool in this motel-like, quiet, two-story hotel a block from the beach at Punta Perula. Bungalows have tiny but well-equipped kitchens; the restaurant serves breakfast and dinner. The hotel owner spent many years in the United States and speaks excellent English. **Pros:** Beautiful Chamela Bay within walking distance, bungalow with kitchenette doesn't cost much more than standard room. **Cons:** No Internet service yet; on the highway, not the beach. ⊠ *Calle Independencia 100, Punta Perula, Chamela Bay, Punta Perula, Jalisco* ✛*79 km (49 mi) south of PV, 137 km (85 mi) north of Barra de Navidad* ☎*315/333–9736* ⮐ *16 rooms, 5 bungalows* ⧖*In-room: kitchen (some), refrigerator (some). In-hotel: restaurant, pool, no elevator, laundry service* ⊟*No credit cards* ⊚*EP.*

¢–$$ ⊡ **Las Villas.** Aside from the luxurious and costly Grand Bay Isla Navidad and the behemoth Hotel Alondra, Barra de Navidad has only basic hotels with few rooms, and not a particularly good value compared to similar hotels elsewhere. This hotel with a domed brick ceiling, comfortable beds, and remote control air-conditioning is among the best choices. Ask for a free cot anytime for an additional guest. The two largest rooms have two twin beds as well as a king, plus DVD player and mini fridge. **Pros:** Well-situated with mom-and-pop groceries and restaurants in the area; right on the beach. **Cons:** Basic rooms, no credit cards currently accepted, no room phones, Wi-Fi not always working. ⊠ *Calle López de Legazpi 127, Barra de Navidad, Jalisco* ☎*315/355–5354, 01800/980–7060 toll-free in Mexico* ⊕*www.lasvillitas.com.mx* ⮐*9 rooms* ⧖*In-room: no phone, DVD (some), refrigerator (some). In-hotel: restaurant, bar, beachfront, public Wi-Fi* ⊟*No credit cards* ⊚*EP.*

COSTALEGRE HOTELS AT A GLANCE

HOTEL	Worth Noting	Cost	Rooms	Restaurants	On the Beach	Dive Shop	Pools	Spa	Golf Course	Tennis Courts	Health Club/Gym	Children's Program	Location
Las Alamandas	ultra-exclusive	$488–$599	14	1			1	yes		1	yes		Quemaro, Costalegre
El Careyes Beach Resort	impeccable decor	$315	55	1	yes		1	yes		2	yes		Careyes, Costalegre
Coconuts by the Sea	fab beach views	$150	4				1						Bahía Tenacatita
Grand Bay Isla Navidad	elegant but snooty	$340	199	3			3	yes	yes	3	yes		Barra de Navidad
Hotelito Desconocido	rustic-chic idyll	$410	24	2	yes		1	yes					Cruz de Loreto, Costalegre
La Paloma Retreat	well-equipped studios	$135	13	1	yes		1						San Patricio–Melaque
Punta Serena	adults-only oasis	$266	24	1	yes		1	yes					Bahía Tenacatita
El Tamarindo	stunning good taste	$625–$1,125	32	1	yes	yes	1	yes	yes	1	yes		Cihuatlán, Costalegre
Vagabundo	far from crowds	$42–$52	21	1			1				yes		Punta Perula
Las Vilitas	lovely bay	$78	10		yes		1						Bahía Tenacatita

Where to Eat

Food with a view.

WORD OF MOUTH

"If you go to Basilio Badillo (that's the street name, located about four blocks south of the river, also dubbed "restaurant row"), there are many moderate priced favorites such as Cafe de Olla, Fajita Republic, Joe Jacks Fish Shack, etc. It's easy to walk around this small area and pick out what you like. Most place have menus posted or available."

—suze

WHERE TO EAT PLANNER

Quick Take

Puerto Vallarta's restaurants are to die for, but what a misuse of earthly delights that would be. Variety, quality, and innovation are the norm whether you dine in a beachfront café or a swanky candlelighted restaurant. The best restaurants buy fresh fish and shellfish daily—and it's a great bargain. Vallarta's already superior restaurants really over-achieve during the 10-day Festival Gourmet International in mid-November.

Meals

PV restaurants cater to tourists with multicourse dinners, but traditionally, *comida* (late lunch) is the big meal of the day, usually consisting of soup and/or salad, bread or tortillas, a main dish, side dishes, and dessert. Traditional *cena* (dinner) is lighter; in fact, many people just have milk or hot chocolate and a sweet roll, or *tamales*.

Desayuno (breakfast) is served in cafés (coffee shops) and small restaurants. Choices might be hefty egg-and-chorizo or -ham dishes, enchiladas, or *chilaquiles* (fried tortilla strips covered in tomato sauce, shredded cheese, and meat or eggs). Tacos and quesadillas are delicious for breakfast; some of Vallarta's best taco stands set up shop by 9 am.

Foodie Hot Spots

PV's biggest concentration of restaurants is in the Zona Romántica, many in Colonia Emiliano Zapata. Once called Restaurant Row, Calle Basilio Badillo now has as many shops as restaurants, but on the surrounding streets eateries continue to crop up. Downtown has its fair share of choice places, too. All in all, gourmets will be happiest here in Old Vallarta, where an appetizer, sunset cocktail, or espresso and dessert isn't more than a $3 cab ride away.

Bucerías has good restaurants in the center of town. Marina Vallarta's worthwhile eateries are mainly in the resorts and surrounding the marina. Punta de Mita's restaurant scene is diversifying to bring more than ceviche and fish fillets to the palapas at El Anclote.

Beer & Spirits

Jalisco is far and away Mexico's most important tequila producing state. Mexican beers range from light beers like Corona and Sol to medium-bodied, golden beers like Pacífico and the more robust Bohemia, to dark beauties Negra Modelo and Indio.

Mealtimes

Mexican mealtimes are generally as follows. Upon rising: coffee, and perhaps pan dulce (sweet breads). Schedule permitting, Mexicans love to eat a hearty almuerzo, a full breakfast, at about 10. Comida, typically between 2 and 5 pm, is the main meal. Cena is between 8 pm and 9 pm.

Restaurants have long hours in PV, though seafood "shacks" on the beach often close by late afternoon or sunset. Outside the resorts of PV, southern Nayarit, and the Costalegre, restaurants may close by 7 or 8 pm, be sure to check so you don't go without supper. Unless otherwise noted, the restaurants listed in this guide are open daily for lunch and dinner.

Taco Primer

In this region, a taco is generally a diminutive corn tortilla heated on an oiled grill and filled with one of many meats, shrimp, or batter-fried fish.

If you're eating at an informal taco stand, your server may ask "Preparadito?"; he or she is asking if you want cilantro and onions. Then add your own condiments: salsa mexicana (chopped raw onions, tomatoes, and green chilies), guacamole, and pickled jalapeño peppers. Some restaurants go further with chopped nopal cactus and other items.

Reservations

Reservations are always a good idea. During low season, getting a table is usually a snap. But it's always wise to call ahead and make sure the place hasn't been reserved for a party.

What to Wear

We'd love to suggest resort casual or at least grunge chic, but not everyone likes to dress up.

The Mexicans are usually the best dressed, but even they forego jacket and tie for a nice button-down and slacks. The most elegant restaurants, like Café des Artistes, simply request that men wear T-shirts with sleeves.

If you enjoy looking like a million bucks, don't despair: looking good is always in style. The maitre d' will take notice.

Pricing

PV's extremely high number of excellent eateries—from corner taco stands to 5-star Diamond-Award winners—means competition is high, and that keeps prices reasonable. While some restaurants do charge as much as those in New York or L.A., there are tons of wonderful places ranging from moderate to downright cheap. To really experience Puerto Vallarta, try both ends of the spectrum, and everything in between.

Paying

Credit cards are widely accepted at pricier restaurants, especially MasterCard and Visa, and to a lesser extent American Express. More modest restaurants might accept cash only, and are leery of traveler's checks. Small eateries that do accept credit cards sometimes give a "discount" for cash (i.e., they charge a small fee for credit card use).

Tips on Tipping

Influenced by big tippers from the U.S., servers count on 10%–15%. In more humble establishments, where the bill is often shockingly low, tips are taken more casually than in the more prestigious restaurants. But in any case, we suggest tipping 15% for good service, a bit less for a flawed performance, and a bit more if the tab is ridiculously low.

DINING PRICE CATEGORIES

¢	$	$$	$$$	$$$$
Restaurants				
under $5	$5–$11	$12–$17	$18–$25	over $25

Restaurant prices are for a first course, excluding tax and service.

PUERTO VALLARTA

ZONA ROMÁNTICA

$ ✕**Andale.** Although many have been drinking, rather than eating, at
AMERICAN this local hangout for years, the restaurant serves great burgers, fries,
herb-garlic bread, black-bean soup, and jumbo shrimp, as well as daily
lunch and nightly drink specials at the chummy bar. The interior is
cool, dark, and informal; two rows of mini-tables line the sidewalk
outside. Service is generally attentive, although that doesn't mean the
food will arrive promptly. Plus-size patrons should beware the munch-
kin-size toilet stalls. ⊠*Av. Olas Altas 425, Col. E. Zapata* ☎*322/222–
1054* ☰*MC, V.*

$$ ✕**Archie's Wok.** This extremely popular South Side restaurant has a vari-
★ ety of Asian cuisines and dishes such as Thai garlic shrimp, *pancit* (Fili-
ASIAN pino stir-fry with pasta), and Singapore-style (lightly battered) fish, plus
lots of vegetarian dishes. Thursday through Saturday 7:30 to 10:30 PM
the soothing harp music of well-known local musican D'Rachel is the
perfect accompaniment to your meal. It opens for lunch only after 2 PM.
⊠*Calle Francisca Rodríguez 130, Col. E. Zapata* ☎*322/222–0411*
☰*MC, V* ☾*Closed Sun.*

$$$★ ✕**Le Bistro.** Start off with a soup of Mexican or Cuban origin and then
ECLECTIC move on to one of the international main dishes, like the cream of wild
spinach soup or mushroom-sherry soup, crepes, duck with blackberry
sauce, herbed Cornish hen, or sea scallops with jicama coleslaw. The
restaurant overlooks the Cuale River, and its eclectic decor draped in
ferns and tropical plants is a knockout, with carved-stone columns,
zebra chairs, wicker settees, and other sophisticated touches. During
breakfast, the tinkling of the piano keys is a lovely counterpoint to
the melody the river makes as it rushes over rocks below. ⊠*Isla Río
Cuale 16–A* ☎*322/222–0283* ⊕*www.lebistro.com.mx* ☰*AE, MC, V*
☾*Closed Sun. and mid-Aug.–mid-Oct.*

$$ ✕**Boca Bento.** This comely restaurant in the heart of the Romantic Zone
FUSION represents fusion of Latin American and Asian elements. The feeling is
simultaneously Eastern and modern, with contemporary music and art-
work. The small-plates concept has been abandoned in favor of a more
traditional menu of appetizers, soups, salads, and entrées with a side of
starch and vegetables: try the rib-eye steak, pork ribs with a honey-chili
glaze, or the cross-cultural mu shu carnitas with hoisin sauce. Open
daily for breakfast and dinner and always closed between 2 PM and
6 PM. ⊠*Calle Basilio Badillo 180, Col. E. Zapata* ☎*322/222–9108*
⊕*www.bocabento.com* ☰*AE. MC, V* ☾*Closed June–Oct.*

$$$ ✕**Brasil Steakhouse.** One of Vallarta's most popular venues for grilled
SEAFOOD meat is this all-you-can-eat place, where you're treated to never-end-
ing portions of beef ribs, turkey, several cuts of steak, pork tenderloin,
and grilled chicken. Waiters first bring chicken wings and direct you
to the salad bar before delivering skewers of meat of your choosing.
Lunch begins after 2 PM. ⊠*Venustiano Carranza 210, Col. E. Zapata*
☎*322/222–2909* ⊠*Calle Mastil s/n, Condominio Marina del Sol,
Local 1, Marina Vallarta* ☎*322/221–5026* ☰*AE, MC, V.*

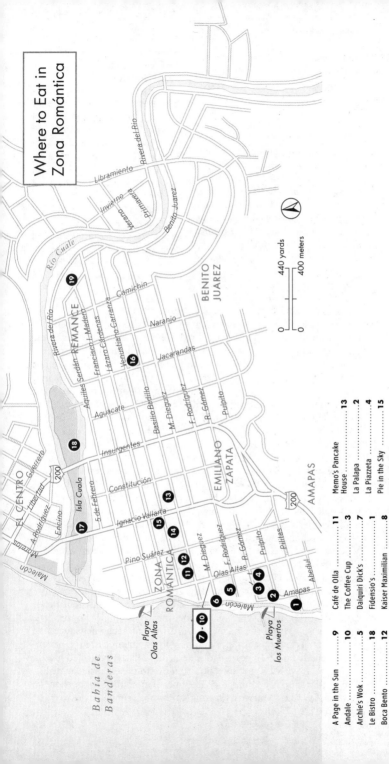

Where to Eat in Zona Romántica

3

0 440 yards
0 400 meters

EL CENTRO
BENITO JUAREZ
REMANCE
EMILIANO ZAPATA
AMAPAS
ZONA ROMÁNTICA

Bahía de Banderas

Río Cuale

Playa Olas Altas
Playa los Muertos

$$★
MEXICAN
✕**El Brujo.** The street corner on which the small restaurant is tucked means noise on either side. Service is reasonably attentive, although it sometimes seems grudging. Still, this is an expat (and gay) favorite, and no wonder: the food is seriously good and portions generous. The *molcajete*—a sizzling black pot of tender flank steak, grilled green onion, and soft white cheese in a delicious homemade sauce of dried red peppers—is served with a big plate of guacamole, refried beans, and made-at-the-moment corn or flour tortillas. ✉ *Venustiano Carranza 510, at Naranjo, Col. Remance* 🕾 *322/223–2036* ⊜ *Reservations not accepted* ⊟ *No credit cards* ⊘ *Closed Mon., 2 wks in late Sept.–early Oct.*

> **BREAKFASTS OF CHAMPIONS**
>
> In PV, **Memo's Pancake House** is a favorite; ritzier **La Palapa** and **Dacquiri Dick's** serve breakfast at the beach. **Langostino's** and **Playita de Lindo Mar** have more casual, oceanside morning fare. In Bucerías, head to **Famar** for an excellent Mexican breakfast or **Chayito's**, in San Francisco, for good coffee, fruit smoothies, and eggs. In the Costalegre, try **Casa de la Abuela** for excellent coffee and jazzy tunes and **El Dorado** for a full breakfast at the beach.

$
MEXICAN
✕**Café de Olla.** This earthy restaurant fills up as soon as it reopens for the season. Repeat visitors swear by the enchiladas and carne asadas; this is one of the few places in town to get a margarita made of raicilla (green-agave firewater as opposed to tequila). As reservations are not accepted, you may need to wait for a table, especially at breakfast and dinner. A large tree extends from the dining-room floor through the roof, local artwork adorns the walls, and salsa music often plays in the background. If you despair of waiting, the taco shop next door is reputedly very good. ✉ *Calle Basilio Badillo 168–A, Col. E. Zapata* 🕾 *322/223–1626* ⊜ *Reservations not accepted* ⊟ *No credit cards* ⊘ *Closed Tues. and Sept. 15–Oct. 15.*

¢
CAFE
✕**The Coffee Cup.** Coffee is sold in all its various presentations, including freshly ground by the kilo. You can munch on cookies, sandwiches, wraps, burritos, and breakfast breads, or get a fresh fruit smoothie. Use the single computer to access the Internet or send e-mails until a waiting customer's glare chase you off. They sell decaf coffee and there's a book exchange, too. It's no relation to the Coffee Cup in Marina Vallarta. ✉ *Calle Rodolfo Gómez 146–A, Col. E. Zapata* 🕾 *322/222–8584* ⊟ *No credit cards* ⊘ *No dinner Sun. Nov.–Apr.*

$$
Fodor'sChoice
★
ECLECTIC
✕**Daiquiri Dick's.** Locals come for the reasonably priced breakfasts (the homemade orange-almond granola is great); visitors come (often more than once during a vacation) for the good service and consistent Mexican and world cuisine. The lunch-dinner menu has fabulous appetizers, including superb lobster tacos with a drizzle of béchamel sauce and perfect, tangy jumbo-shrimp wontons. On the menu since the restaurant opened almost 30 years ago is Pescado Vallarta, or grilled fish on a stick. Start with a signature daiquiri; move to the extensive wine list. The tortilla soup is popular, too. The open patio dining room frames a view of Playa Los Muertos, creating a beautiful, simple scene to enjoy

MENU TRANSLATOR

Because eating is such an integral part of a Puerto Vallarta vacation, we've described here some of the dishes you're likely to find on area menus or in our reviews below. *Buen provecho!*

arrachera: skirt steak

carne asada: thin cut of flank or tenderloin (sometimes not *that* tender), grilled or broiled and usually served with beans, rice, and guacamole

carnitas: bites of steamed, fried pork served with tortillas and a variety of condiments

chilaquiles: pieces of corn tortillas fried and served with red or green sauce; good ones are crispy, not soggy, and topped with chopped onions and *queso cotija:* a crumbly white cheese

chile en nogada: a green poblano chili stuffed with a semi-sweet meat mixture and topped with walnut sauce and pomegranate seeds; the Mexican national dish, it's often served in September in honor of Independence Day

chile relleno: batter-fried green chili (mild to hot) stuffed with cheese, seafood, or a sweetish meat mixture; served in a mild red sauce

menudo: tripe stew

pozole: a rich pork- or chicken-based soup with hominy; a plate of accompanying condiments usually includes raw onions, radishes, cilantro, oregano, sliced cabbage, and tostadas

tostada: a crispy fried tortilla topped with beans and/or meat, cheese, and finely chopped lettuce or cabbage; or, the corn tortilla by itself, which is served with foods like ceviche and pozole

---

while you sip that mixed drink. ⊠*Av. Olas Altas 314, Col. E. Zapata* ☎*322/222–0566* ▤*MC, V* ⊘*Closed Sept. and Tues. May–Aug.*

$ ✕**Fidensio's.** Let the tide lick your toes and the sand caress shoeless
⟳ feet as simple yet tasty food is brought to your comfortable palapa-
ECLECTIC shaded cloth chair right at the ocean's edge. Made when you order them, the shrimp enchiladas—served with rice, a small handful of piping hot fries, and a miniature salad—are simply delicious. Many expats come for breakfast, or before 6 PM for burgers, nachos, club or tuna sandwiches, or a fresh fish fillet. Service is relaxed and friendly, not overbearing or phony; the only soundtrack is the sound of the waves. ⊠*Pilitas 90, Los Muerto Beach, Col. E. Zapata* ☎*322/222–5457* ▤*No credit cards* ⊘*No dinner.*

$$$ ✕**Kaiser Maximilian.** Viennese and Continental entrées dominate the
★ menu, which is modified each year when the restaurant participates in
CONTINENTAL PV's culinary festival. One favorite is herb-crusted rack of lamb served with horseradish and pureed vegetables au gratin; another is venison medallions in chestnut sauce served with braised white cabbage and steamed vegetables. The adjacent café (open 8 AM–midnight) has sandwiches, excellent desserts, and 20 specialty coffees—all of which are also available at the main restaurant. Because a stream of street peddlers is anathema to fine dining, eat in the charming, European-style

dining room, where handsome black-and-white-clad waiters look right at home amid dark-wood framed mirrors, brightly polished brass, and lace café curtains. ✉*Av. Olas Altas 380, Col. E. Zapata* ☎*322/223–0760* ▤*AE, MC, V* ⊘*Closed Sun.*

$$☾
SEAFOOD

✕**Langostino's.** Right on the beach just north of the pier at Playa Los Muertos, Langostino's is a great place to start the day with a heaping helping of Mexican rock, cranked up to a respectable volume. The house favorite at this professional and pleasant place is surf and turf, and the three seafood combos are a good value. The kids can play on the beach while you linger over coffee or suds. ✉*Los Muertos Beach at Calle Manuel M. Dieguez, Col. E. Zapata* ☎*322/222–0894* ▤*No credit cards.*

$
☾
AMERICAN

✕**Memo's Pancake House.** If your child can't find something he or she likes on the Pancake House menu, you might have an alien on your hands. There are 12 kinds of pancakes—including the Oh Henry, with chocolate bits and peanut butter—and eight kinds of waffles. Other breakfast items include machaca burritos, *chilaquiles,* and eggs Florentine, but these tend to be perfunctory: pancakes and waffles are your best bet. Waiters bustle around the large, fairly noisy dining room, which is bursting with local families on weekends and homesick travelers daily. The back patio—draped in pothos and serenaded by birds—experiences a greenhouse effect when the day heats up. Closes at 2 PM. ✉*Calle Basilio Badillo 289, Col. E. Zapata* ☎*322/222–6272* ⌨*Reservations not accepted* ▤*No credit cards* ⊘*No dinner.*

¢
CAFE

✕**A Page in the Sun.** This corner café in the middle of Olas Altas is always full of coffee drinkers reading newspapers and paperback books purchased here, or playing chess. The salads, sandwiches, and desserts on the menu are almost an afterthought. It's the location and the opportunity to hang out with one's friends that really count, plus the good coffee. ✉*Olas Altas 399, Col. E. Zapata* ☎*322/222–3608* ▤*No credit cards.*

$$$★
ECLECTIC

✕**La Palapa.** This large, welcoming, thatch-roof place is open to the breezes of Playa los Muertos and filled with wicker chandeliers, art-glass fixtures, and lazily rotating ceiling fans. The menu meanders among international dishes in modern presentation: roasted stuffed chicken breast, pork loin, or seared yellowfin tuna drizzled in cacao sauce. The seafood enchilada plate is divine. For a pricey but romantic evening, enjoy one of several set menus (265 pesos for two; reserve in advance) at a table right on the sand. This is a popular place for breakfast daily after 8 AM, for a lingering Sunday brunch, or solo guitar or Latin jazz combo nightly between 8 and 11. ✉*Calle Púlpito 103, Playa Los Muertos, Col. E. Zapata* ☎*322/222–5225* ▤*AE, D, MC, V.*

$
ITALIAN

✕**La Piazzeta.** Locals come for the delicious Naples-style pizza (the crust not too thick, not too thin, and cooked in a brick oven), but there's also great pasta and a good variety of entrées, like the cream-based salmon with caviar and lemon. For appetizers try the top-heavy (*con molto tomate*) bruschetta or steamed mussels with lemon, parsley, and butter. Most folks choose to sit on the open patio, but La Piazzeta also has an intimate dining room. The personal attention of the owner, Mimmo, guarantees repeat business. It's open 4 to midnight. ✉*Calle Rodolfo Gómez 143, Col. E. Zapata* ☎*322/222–0650* ▤*MC, V* ⊘*Closed Sun. No lunch.*

$$ **El Repollo Rojo.** Better known
ECLECTIC as the Red Cabbage (its English
name), this restaurant is by—but
doesn't overlook—the Cuale River.
It's hard to find the first time out,
but it's worth the effort for the
international comfort food. Home-
sick Canadians fill up on chicken
with mashed potatoes, gravy, and
cranberry sauce, while Italians

indulge in pasta with fresh tomatoes; there are even a few Russian
dishes. Frida's Dinner includes an aperitif of tequila followed by cream
of peanut soup, white or red wine, *chile en nogada* (a mild chili deco-
rated with colors of the Mexican flag), a main dish from the Yucatán or
Puebla, and flan for dessert. Romantic ballads fill the small space, and
the walls are crowded with movie posters and head shots of interna-
tional stars. Here's the quandary: some patrons rave about the service,
and others lambaste it. ⊠ *Calle Rivera del Río 204–A, El Remance*
☎ *322/223–0411* ▭ *No credit cards.* ⊘ *No lunch. Closed Sept. and
Sun. May–Oct.*

CENTRO & ENVIRONS

$ **Los Alcatraces.** For a breakfast of chilaquiles that are crisp, not soggy,
MEXICAN come to "The Calla Lilies." *Café de olla,* real Mexican coffee simmered
with cinnamon and *panela* (unrefined brown sugar), is served in a keep-
warm carafe; crumbly white cheese is brought from a ranch in the nearby
hills. All meals are economical, especially the combo plate: a quesa-
dilla, chiles rellenos, arrachera beef, rice, beans, and a taco. Weekdays,
a fixed-price lunch for under $5 consists of soup, main dish, beans, and
fruit drink. The only downside is traffic noise from the busy highway.
⊠ *Blvd. Federico M. Ascencio 1808, Col. Olímpica* ☎ *322/222–1182*
▭ *No credit cards* ⊘ *No lunch Sun.; no dinner Sat., Sun.*

$$ **El Andariego.** A few blocks past the north end of the malecón is this
MEXICAN lively Mexican restaurant. Lovely paintings of the city brighten the
walls, lighting is subdued, and the mood is romantic Mexico. The large
menu includes numerous salads, pasta dishes, lots of variety in chicken
and beef, and seafood and lobster prepared to your taste. You're
allowed to choose your poison (beef, cheese, or chicken fillings) for the
tacos and enchiladas on the combo plates. Enjoy live music (electric
guitar versions of "Proud Mary," or mariachi music) nightly between
5 and 11 PM. Breakfast is served, and there's free if not-always-reliable
wireless Internet in the restaurant and bar. ⊠ *Av. México 1358, at El
Salvador, Col. 5 de Diciembre* ☎ *322/222–0916* ⊕ *www.elandariego.
com.mx* ▭ *MC, V.*

$$ **El Arrayán.** The oilcloth table covers, enameled tin plates, exposed
Fodor's Choice rafters, and red roof tiles of this patio-restaurant conjure up nostalgia
★ for the quaint Mexican home of less frenetic times. Carmen Porras, the
MEXICAN hip, cute co-owner (with her parents), masquerades as your waitress,
dispensing interesting info about the origins of chiles en nogada (first

prepared for Emperor Agustín Iturbide—who knew?) and the other
Mexican comfort foods on her
menu. Here you'll find the things
abuelita (grandma) still loves to
cook, with a few subtle variations.
Highlights are chicken breasts
stuffed with zucchini blossoms and
chipotle-chili shrimp with a citrus sauce. For dessert try caramel
flan or a light pumpkin-caramel

ice. ⊠ *Calle Allende 344, at Calle Miramar, Centro* ☎ *322/222–7195*
☐ *MC, V* ☾ *Closed Tues. and Aug. No lunch.*

$$$ ✕ **Barcelona Tapas Bar.** One of the few places in town with both great
★   food and an excellent bay view, Barcelona has traditional Spanish tapas
SPANISH like *patatas alioli* (garlic potatoes), spicy garlic shrimp, and grilled
mushrooms. In addition to traditional paella, the restaurant serves a
seafood version. To start you off, attentive waiters bring a free appe-
tizer and delicious homemade bread. The six-course tasting menu lets
you try soup, salad, and dessert as well as tapas—choose your own or
follow the chef's suggestions. You can sit in a small, relatively quiet
room or the often crowded open-air patio. You'll have to pay for the
patio view by walking up a few dozen stairs. Cooking classes ($24) are
offered on Wednesdays in high season (November through April) and
include lunch. ⊠ *Matamoros at 31 de Octubre, Centro* ☎ *322/222–
0510* ⌔ *Reservations essential* ☐ *AE.*

$ ✕ **La Bodeguita del Medio.** Near the malecón's north end, this restaurant
CARIBBEAN with a fun-loving atmosphere has a bit of a sea view from its second-
floor dining room, and a Caribbean flavor. Specials vary by season; if
possible, try the roast pork, the Cuban-style paella, or the pork loin
in tamarind sauce; order rice, salad, or fried plantains separately. Like
its Havana namesake, La Bodeguita sells Cuban rum and cigars, and
the live music—like the cuisine—is pure *cubano*. During the day com-
rades hunch over their computers to take advantage of the free Wi-Fi;
sextet performs most nights until past midnight. Try the Havana spe-
cialty drink *mojito*: a blend of lime juice, sugar, mineral water, white
rum, and crushed fresh mint leaves. ⊠ *Paseo Díaz Ordáz 858, Centro*
☎ *322/223–1585* ☐ *AE, MC, V.*

$$$★   ✕ **Café des Artistes.** Several sleek dining spaces make up Café des Artistes,
ECLECTIC the liveliest of which is the courtyard garden with modern sculpture.
The main restaurant achieves a modern Casablanca feel with glass raindrops and tranquil music. Thierry Blouet's Cocina de Autor (closed
Sunday and September) is a limited-seating restaurant pairing four- to
six-course tasting menus with appropriate wines. Decor is restrained,
with a waterfall garden behind plate glass taking center stage. Many
diners end the night at the clubby cigar bar, but it's open to anyone,
as is Constantini Wine Bar, which offers some 50 vintages by the glass
as well as distilled spirits, appetizers, and live music most every night
of the week. ⊠ *Av. Guadalupe Sánchez 740, Centro* ☎ *322/222–3229*
☐ *AE, MC, V* ☾ *No lunch.*

$
MEXICAN
✗**El Campanario.** This little jewel is increasingly popular with budget travelers. Egg dishes and chilaquiles are served 9–11 AM, and an inexpensive daily lunch menu is served 2–5 PM. About $5 gets you soup, a main dish, drink, homemade tortillas, and dessert. Office workers come in for takeout, or drift in between 6 and 10 PM for tacos, *tortas* (Mexican-style sandwiches on crispy white rolls), or pozole. A recipe for the latter is given—along with a positive dining review—in a framed *Los Angeles Times* article from the 1980s. Fans swirl the air, doors are open to the street, and cheerful oilcloths cover wooden tables at this no-frills spot across from the cathedral. ⊠*Calle Hidalgo 339, Centro* ☎*322/223–1509* ⊟*No credit cards* ✆*Closed Sun., and often between 5 and 6 PM.*

> ### HANGOVER CURES
>
> For a hangover, menudo (tripe stew) and pozole are recommended, both with the addition of chopped fresh onions and cilantro, a generous squeeze of lime and as much chili as one can handle. Ceviche is another popular cure, with the same key ingredients: lime and chili.

$$$$★
MEXICAN
✗**Las Carmelitas.** Hawks soar on updrafts above lumpy, jungle-draped hills. The town and the big blue bay are spread out below in a breathtaking, 200-degree tableau. Under the palapa roof of this small, open restaurant romantic ballads play as waiters start you off with guacamole, fresh and cooked salsas, chopped cactus pad salad, and tostadas. Seared meats—served with grilled green onions and tortillas made on the spot—are the specialty, but you can also order seafood stew or soups. The restaurant opens at 1 PM. Don't despair about the $10 per person fee you pay to enter (apparently to discourage lookie-loos); it will be deducted from your tab. Or avoid the hassle altogether—the fee is waved for those who have made reservations. ⊠*Camino a la Aguacatera, Km 1.2, Fracc. Lomas de Terra Noble* ☎*322/303–2104* ⊟*No credit cards.*

$$
ECLECTIC
✗**Chez Elena.** Frequented in its heyday by Hollywood luminaries and the who's who of PV, this downtown restaurant still has a loyal following. The patio ambience is simple, but the wholesome food is satisfying, and portions are generous. House specialties include fajitas and Yucatan-style pork. Elena's is also known for its killer, handcrafted margaritas and its flaming coffee drinks. ⊠*Calle Matamoros 520, Centro* ☎*322/222–0161* ⊟*MC, V* ✆ *Closed June–Sept. No lunch.*

$$
★
SEAFOOD
✗**Cueto's.** Teams of engaging waiters, all family members, squeeze past the trio that croons romantic tunes throughout the day to refill beer glasses, remove empty plates, or bring more fresh tostadas and hot, crusty garlic bread. But don't fill up on nonessentials, as the recommended cream-based and mild-chili casseroles—with crab, clams, fish, shrimp, or mixed seafood—are so delicious you won't want to leave even one bite. The latest menu offering is a shrimpfest offering a couple dozen crustaceans prepared in seven different styles. You can have a complimentary margarita with dinner or a free digestif later on. Cueto's is a few blocks behind the Unidad Deportivo complex of soccer fields and baseball diamonds. ⊠*Calle Brasilia 469, Col. 5 de Diciembre (Zona Hotelera)* ☎*322/223–0363* ⊟*No credit cards.*

$

SEAFOOD

✕ **Marisco's La Tía.** Busy professionals stop in at "Auntie's" place to feed themselves and their families on super-sized burritos filled with octopus, shrimp, fish, or other local seafood standards. This simple, family-style venue at the north end of downtown is fine for a quick bite, pick up take out, or call for delivery. ✉ *Calle Honduras at Calle Perú,* ☎ *322/131-8536* ▭ *No credit cards.* ⊘ *Closed Sun.*

$$$

MEXICAN

✕ **Mestizo.** Vegetarians won't find much on this traditional Mexican-food menu, but can concoct a meal of spinach, beet, and jicama salad; squash blossom soup; and "antojitos," or grilled, corn-based snacks.

TACO PRIMER

In this region's informal eateries, a taco is generally a diminutive corn tortilla heated on an oiled grill filled with meat, shrimp, or batter-fried fish. If your server asks *"¿Preparadita?"*, he or she is asking if you want it with cilantro and onions. Add-your-own condiments are salsa mexicana (chopped raw onions, tomatoes, and green chilies), liquidy guacamole, and pickled jalapeño peppers. Some restaurants include chopped nopal cactus and other signature items.

Carnivores can feast on red snapper fillet with a mild poblano cream sauce; grilled goat with cactus; chicken with huitlacoche (corn fungus); or beef medallions. The garden setting, under a spreading arrayan tree, of this restored old home couldn't be prettier, or imbue a more traditional Mexican ambience. And the danzón music reminiscent of Old Mexico music salons only adds to the charm. ✉ *Calle Abasolo 233, Centro* ☎ *322/222-1333* ⊕ *www.mestizovallarta.com* ▭ *AE, MC, V* ⊘ *No lunch; closed Sun; closed May–mid-Oct.*

$

MEXICAN

✕ **Pepe's Tacos.** No longer the be-all and end-all of taco consumption in PV, Pepe's still can't be beat at 5 AM, when most sensible taco-makers are asleep. Although these diminutive tacos are a meat-lover's treat, there are quesadillas—and one taco with grilled onions and bell peppers, cheese, and canned mushrooms—for wayward vegetarians. Order tacos individually for about 70¢ each to try different types, or by the set. Or order one of several plates for two with a stack of tortillas. Expect plastic tablecloths and sports on several TVs at this open-door dive across from the Pemex station at the north end of Old Vallarta. ✉ *Honduras 173, between Avs. Peru and Mexico, Col. 5 de Diciembre* ☎ *322/223–1703* ▭ *No credit cards* ⊘ *Closed Mon. No lunch.*

$

☺

★

VEGETARIAN

✕ **Planeta Vegetariana.** Those who stumble upon this hog-less heaven can partake of the tasty meatless carne asada and a selection of main dishes that change daily. Choose from at least three delicious main dishes, plus beans, several types of rice, and a daily soup at this buffet-only place. Though the selection of overdressed salads is good, the greens tend to get wilted or soggy. A healthful fruit drink, coffee, or tea, and dessert is included in the reasonable price. Eggs are not used; items containing milk products are labeled as such. It's about a block north of the cathedral, downtown. ✉ *Iturbide 270, Centro* ☎ *322/222–3073* ▭ *No credit cards.*

$$$

ECLECTIC

✕ **River Cafe.** At night, candles flicker at white-skirted tables with comfortable cushioned chairs, and tiny white lights sparkle in palm trees surrounding the multilevel terrace. This riverside restaurant is recom-

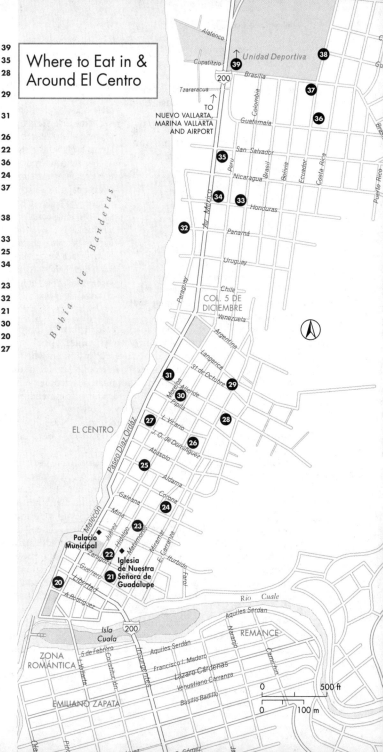

Where to Eat in & Around El Centro

mended for breakfast and for the evening ambience. Attentive waiters serve such international dishes as seafood fettuccini and vegetarian crepes; the wild mushroom soup and fried calamari with aioli sauce are especially recommended. If you're not into a romantic dinner, belly up to the intimate bar for a drink and—Thursday through Sunday evenings—listen to live jazz. Breakfast is served daily after 9 AM. ⊠*Isla Río Cuale, Local 4, Centro* ☎*322/223–0788* ⊟*AE, MC, V.*

■**TIP→** A waiter would never consider bringing you your check before you ask for it; that would be rude. However, it's also considered inappropriate to dally in bringing that check once you do ask for it.

> ### STREET-FOOD SMARTS
>
> Many think it's madness to eat "street food," but when you see professionals in pinstripes thronging to roadside stands, you've got to wonder why. Stands can be just as hygienic as restaurants, as they are actually tiny exhibition kitchens. Make sure the cook doesn't handle cash, or takes your money with a gloved hand. Plates sheathed in disposable plastic wrap solve the "washing-up-in-a-bucket" dilemma, and most stands have a place for customers to wash their hands. Ask locals for recommendations, or look for a stand bustling with trade.

$$$
ECLECTIC

✗ **Spiaggia.** Overhead lights impart a golden glow to this open, beachfront restaurant with cushy, linen-strewn tables. After dark, the harbor light up the big, simple deck covered by a giant white pavilion. A flautist adds to the romance Thursday through Sunday at dinner hour; during other times, a soundtrack dominated by robust female singers enhances the perky and modern mood. Our recommendations include the grilled veggies, the charcoal-grilled "cowboy" steak, and, for dessert, the extra creamy white chocolate parfait. Note that this place is also open for breakfast. ⊠ *Calle Uruguay 109, Col. 5 de Diciembre* ☎*322/223–3722* ⊟*AE, MC, V.*

$$$
Fodor'sChoice
★
ECLECTIC

✗**Trio.** Conviviality, hominess, and dedication on the parts of chefowners Bernhard Güth and Ulf Henriksson have made Trio one of Puerto Vallarta's best restaurants—hands-down. Fans, many of them members of PV's artsy crowd, marvel at the kitchen's ability to deliver perfect meal after perfect meal. Popular demand guarantees rack of lamb with fresh mint and for dessert, the warm chocolate cake. The kitchen often stays open until nearly midnight, and during high season the restaurant opens the back patio, second floor, and rooftop terrace. Waiters are professional yet unpretentious; either the sommelier or the maitre d' can help you with the wine. But the main reason to dine here is the consistently fabulous food at great value. ⊠*Calle Guerrero 264, Centro* ☎*322/222–2196* ⊟*AE, MC, V* ☯*No lunch.*

¢
MEXICAN

✗**Tutifruti.** If you find yourself near the main square at lunchtime, consider having a taco at this little stand. While we can't exactly call this *fast* food, the quesadillas and machaca (shredded beef) burritos are delicious; you can also get a sandwich or burger. Consider sharing, because the portions are large. For breakfast, order up a *licuado* (smoothie) made from fresh fruit and milk. If you're lucky, you might get one of the few stools at the tiled counter. ⊠*Calle Allende 200, between Av.*

Juaréz and Av. Guadalupe Sánchez, Centro ☎*322/222–1068* ▤*No credit cards* ⊘*Closed Sun. No dinner.*

$$$ ✕**Vitea.** When chefs Bernhard Güth and Ulf Henriksson, of Trio,
★ needed a challenge they cooked up this delightful seaside bistro. So
BISTRO what if your legs bump your partner's at the small tables? This will only make it easier to steal bites off her plate. The decor of the open, casual venue is as fresh as the food. Appetizers include the smoked salmon roll with crème fraiche and the spicy shrimp tempura; crab manicotti and other entrées are light and delicious. Half portions are available, or make a meal of the bistro's soups, sandwiches, and appetizers. ⊠*Libertad 2, near south end of Malecón, Centro* ☎*322/222–8703* ▤*MC, V* ⊘*Closed 1 wk. in late Sept.*

$$$ ✕ **Ztai.** Lounge music emanates from this cool, dark, modern restau-
ECLECTIC rant to the appealingly spare outdoor garden shaded by bamboo and fig trees. The food is quite good, and portions are large. Try the fresh and oh-so-lightly-fried calamari, the fruity shrimp ceviche, or the tender filet mignon. Asian flavors spice up the seafood recipes, while the meat dishes lean towards Continental cuisine—think herb-crusted lamb. After dinner you can recline with a chaser on one of the beds, sofas, or bar stools of Ztai's upstairs lounge. ⊠*Calle Morelos 737, Centro* ☎*322/222–0306* ▤*AE, MC, V.* ⊘*No lunch.*

MARINA VALLARTA

¢ ✕**The Coffee Cup.** Early-risers and those heading off on fishing char-
DELICATESSEN ters will appreciate the 5 AM opening time. There are fruit smoothies, and coffee in many manifestations, including frappés of Oreo cookie and German chocolate cake. Have a breakfast bagel (all day), wrap, deli sandwich, or homemade dessert. Located right on the marina, the café is filled with wonderful art for sale, and is open daily until 10 PM. ⊠*Condominios Puesto del Sol, Local 14–A, at marina, Marina Vallarta* ☎*322/221–2517* ▤*MC, V.*

$ ✕**Mariscos 8 Tostadas.** Extremely popular with locals, this large restau-
★ rant hums with activity and a varied, upbeat soundtrack with tunes
SEAFOOD by icons such as Bob Marley and Frank Sinatra. The menu is oddly translated—tuna sashimi appears as *atun fresco con salsa rasurada,* or "tuna cut thick with shaved sauce, alone if there was fishing" (the latter meaning that it's only available if the fish was caught that day)— indicating that this is a spot geared to locals, not tourists. The freshly caught, raw tuna, which is thicker than in U.S. sushi houses, but not too thick, is served in a shallow dish with soy sauce, micro-thin cucumber slices, sesame seeds, green onions, chili powder, and lime. Eat with tostadas until fit to burst. Avoid the shellfish, as the scallop tostadas, as the scallop tostadas, is virtually raw. The ceviche, however, couldn't be better—or fresher. There's a small storefront subsidiary in the parking lot at Plaza Marina; the charming original venue is behind Blockbuster Video in the Hotel Zone. ⊠*Calle Quilla at Calle Proa, Local 28–29, Marina Vallarta* ☎*322/221–3124* ▤*No credit cards* ⊘*No dinner* ⊠*Calle Río Guayaquil 413, at Calle Ecuador Col. Versalles (Zona Hotelera)* ⊹*Behind Blockbuster Video store* ☎*322/222–7691* ▤*No credit cards* ⊘*Closed*

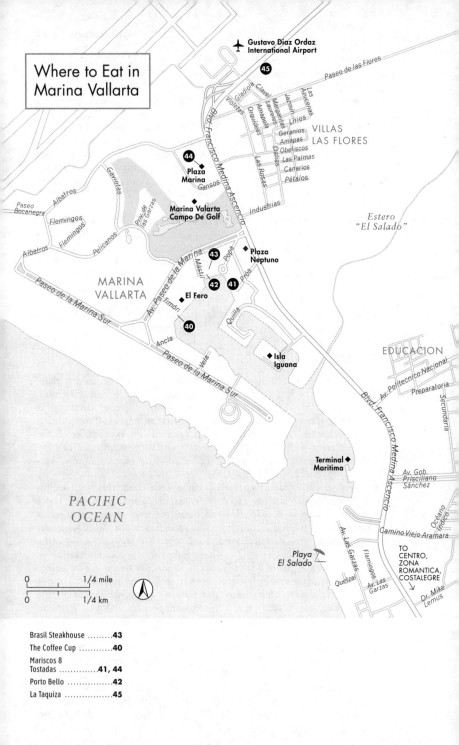

Where to Eat in Marina Vallarta

✈ Gustavo Diaz Ordaz
International Airport

45

Paseo de las Flores

VILLAS
LAS FLORES

Gladiola
Clavel
Violetas
Amapola
Orquideas
Jazmin
Margaritas
Laureles
Lirios
Geranios
Amapas
Dalias
Obeliscos
Las Palmas
Canarios
Pétalos
Las Azucenas

Las Rosas

Estero
"El Salado"

44
◆ Plaza
Marina

Gansos

◆ Marina Valarta
Campo De Golf

Industrias

Plaza
Neptuno

43

Popa

Mástil

Proa

42 **41**

◆ El Fero

Quilla

40

Ancla

Vela

Timón

MARINA
VALLARTA

Paseo de la Marina

Av. Paseo de la Marina

Paseo
Bocanegra

Albatros

Flemingos

Flemingos

Albatros

Gaviotas

Peñc de
las Garzas

Pelicanos

Paseo de la Marina Sur

Paseo de la Marina Sur

◆ Isla
Iguana

EDUCACION

Av. Politecnico Nacional

Preparatoria

Secundaria

Blvd. Francisco Medina Ascencio

Terminal ◆
Maritima

Av. Gob.
Priciliano
Sánchez

Océano
Indico

Camino Viejo Aramara

PACIFIC
OCEAN

Playa
El Salado

Av. Las Garzas

Flamingos

Quetzal

Av. Las
Garzas

TO
CENTRO,
ZONA
ROMANTICA,
COSTALEGRE

Dr. Mike
Lemus

0   1/4 mile
0   1/4 km

Sun. and two weeks in Sept. No dinner.

$$$
ITALIAN
✗**Porto Bello.** Yachties, locals, and other return visitors attest that everything on the menu here is good. And if you're not satisfied, the kitchen will give you something else without quibbling. Undoubtedly that's what makes Marina Vallarta's veteran restaurant its most popular as well. The dining room is diminutive and air-conditioned; the outdoor patio overlooking the marina is more elegant, with a white chiffon ceiling drape and

> ### NATURAL THIRST-BUSTER
>
> The guy on the malecón or in the main plaza with a giant gourd and a handful of plastic cups is selling *agua de tuba,* a refreshing, pleasant, yet innocuous drink made from the heart of the coconut palm. It's stored in a gourd container called a *huaje,* and served garnished with chopped walnuts and apples.

white ceiling fans. Since there are no lunch specials and the Italian menu is the same then as at dinner, most folks come in the evening. ✉*Marina del Sol, Local 7, Marina Vallarta* ☎*322/221–0003* ⊕*www.portobellovallarta.com* ⊟*MC, V.*

$
★
MEXICAN
✗**La Taquiza.** Here's a tip: Stop by this local's den on your way to the airport (it's just across the street), and get food to go. Dollar, Budget, and Thrifty rental car storefronts surround this bright and shiny hole-in-the-wall. You can order food, drop off your rental car, and then get a shuttle to the airport. Or eat in at the brightly polished green Formica tables (with matching chairs). The tasty lime drink, lunch specials, pinto bean soup, and the house specialty—tacos—are served in or on old-fashioned red pottery plates, bowls, and mugs. ✉*Blvd. Federico M. Ascencio 4594, Col. Villa Las Flores* ☎ *322/209–1131* ⊟*No credit cards* ⊘*Closed Sun. No dinner.*

SOUTH ALONG BANDERAS BAY

$$
☺
SEAFOOD
✗**El Edén.** The location, a jungly riverside place where the movie *Predator* was filmed, is as much of a draw as the mainly seafood fare. This is a place to spend time, splashing in the river or zinging through the air on a canopy tour. Not on the menu but worth asking about is the Festival de Camarones: shrimp is prepared breaded, butterflied, sautéed in garlic, and several other styles, and served with rice, tortillas, homemade chips, and various salsas. You might catch a ride at El Edén's downtown PV office, when they transport their canopy tour patrons; otherwise, plan to drive or take a cab. If it's not too busy, the restaurant will sometimes return patrons to the highway, where buses frequently pass. ✉*Carr. al Edén, Predio el Venado, 10 mins. east of Mismaloya* ☎*No phone* ⊟*No credit cards* ⊘*No dinner.*

$$$
ECLECTIC
✗**Le Kliff.** From a table on one of four tiers you can watch for whales in season or boats heading to the docks as the sun sets. Asian and Mediterranean flavors have been added to the recipes without great success. (The new chef, Everado Robles, may be able to set things right.) This open-air restaurant with an enormous palapa roof is a great bet for sunset hors d'oeuvres and cocktails. Some folks love the food, others feel it is not worth the inflated prices. Weddings are a big part of the

business, so call ahead to make sure it's not booked, and to reserve a table on the lowest deck, closest to the water. ⊠ *Carretera a Barra de Navidad, Km 17.5, just north of Boca de Tomatlán, Zona Hotelera Sur* ☎ *322/224–0975* ▭ *MC, V.*

$$
★
ECLECTIC

✕ **La Playita de Lindo Mar.** A favorite breakfast spot any day, or for the expansive, inexpensive Sunday brunch, this restaurant has a wonderful view of the waves crashing on or lapping at Conchas Chinas Beach. The breakfast menu wanders among savory crepes, fritattas, omelets, and the tasty *Huevos Felix:* eggs scrambled with fried corn tortillas, served with a grilled cactus pad, beans, and grilled serrano chilies. The multitude of lunch and dinner choices includes grilled burgers and chicken, shrimp fajitas, and lobster thermador. Open to the ocean air, the wood-and-palm front building looks right at home here. See the sign on Carretera a Mismaloya or follow your nose on the beach at Conchas Chinas. If you're driving, park in the hotel's lot and take the elevator down to the beach, or park in the small lot near the beach. Go before 11 AM for brunch, as they stop replenishing buffet dishes as the morning goes on. ⊠ *Carrertera a Barra de Navidad 2.5, Playa Conchas Chinas, at Hotel Lindo Mar* ☎ *322/221–5511* ▭ *MC, V.*

NORTH OF PUERTO VALLARTA

ALONG BANDERAS BAY

$
CAFE

✕ **The Bar Above.** This little place above Tapas del Mundo defies categorization. It's a martini bar without a bar (the owners, Buddy and Jorge, prefer that people come to converse with friends rather than hang out at a bar) that also serves dessert. Order from the day's offerings, maybe molten chocolate soufflé—the signature dish—or a charred pineapple bourbon shortcake. Lights are dim, the music is romantic, and there's an eagle's view of the ocean from the rooftop nest. ⊠ *Corner of Av. Mexico and Av. Hidalgo, 2 blocks north of central plaza, Bucerías* ☎ *329/298–1194* ▭ *No credit cards* ☉ *No lunch. Closed Sun., Aug., Sept., and Mon. in June, July, Oct.*

$$–$$$
STEAK

✕ **Brasil Nuevo Vallarta.** Although the food and presentation is the same as the steak house restaurant in downtown Vallarta *(⇨ above)*, this venue in Nuevo Vallarta's large, comprehensive mall has café seating on the corridor. Cuts of meat are easy to come by, but unimaginative use of herbs and spices (or lack thereof) makes the different cuts of meat taste surprisingly similar. Lunch is served only after 2 PM. ⊠ *Paradise Village Mall, 2nd fl., Nuevo Vallarta* ☎ *322/297–1164* ▭ *AE, MC, V.*

$
SEAFOOD

✕ **Columba.** Yearn for manta ray stew? Crave fresh tuna balls? Simply must have shark soup? The recipes here are geared to the local palate; if you're an adventurous eater with a hankering for fresh, strangely prepared (a lot of things are minced beyond recognition) seafood dishes, give Columba a try. It's on the road to the fishermen's beach in Cruz de Huanacaxtle. As a backup plan, have an appetizer here, then head for one of the other picks in Bucerías. This restaurant closes at 7 PM, and serves only beer and sodas as beverages. It has the least expensive

Continued on page 84

Mar Plata restaurant

MEXICO'S GOURMET TOWN

PV merges cooking styles and ingredients from all over the world

After huge cities like Guadalajara and Mexico City, Puerto Vallarta beats anywhere in the country for sheer number of excellent restaurants. Many talented chefs, drawn to this area by its natural beauty, have fallen in love with the place and opened restaurants, contributing to the varied world cuisine. Metaphorically duking it out, they create confits, reductions, tapanades, and tempuras. You, the visitor, are the clear winner, able to indulge in spring rolls or Filipino pancit, great pizza, melt-in-your-mouth beef carpaccio, and wonderful seafood dishes made with sea bass and tuna, shrimp, and shellfish plucked from local waters.

Competition creates excellence. "The high season is only five months long," says chef Bernhard Güth. "You have to be creative and good year-round to survive." PV doesn't have a signature cuisine—instead, it merges cooking styles and ingredients from all over the world. Traditional Mexican dishes are plentiful, but more often upscale restaurants use these as a springboard for their own specialties, infusing European techniques and classical recipes with new life. The most elegant restaurants present dishes so beautifully that you might dread the thought of disassembling these works of art.

TOP RESTAURANTS AND CHEFS

Stars among Puerto Vallarta's many fine chefs and restaurants, these trailblazers march to a different drummer.

Trio

Conviviality, hominess, and dedication on the parts of the chef-owners have made Trio one of Puerto Vallarta's best restaurants, hands-down. Fans, many of them members of PV's artsy crowd, marvel at the kitchen's ability to deliver perfect meal after perfect meal. Popular demand guarantees rack of lamb with fresh mint and for dessert, the warm chocolate cake.

Vitea

The chefs at Trio opened this oceanfront bistro in 2005— which all but guaranteed its success. In addition to the great oceanfront location and upbeat Caribbean soundtrack, Vitea charms with its wide range of Mediterranean-inspired, contemporary sandwiches, soups, small plates, and full entrées—all at accessible prices.

THE DUO AT TRIO AND VITEA When you ask patrons why they love Trio, they almost universally mention the personal attention of high-energy but low-key owner–chef **Bernhard Güth** and his colleague, **Ulf Henriksson**. Güth says "Our mission here is to hug all of our clients, mentally, to make them feel more than welcome."

TOP: Fish Dish from Trio
ABOVE: Bernhard Güth &
Ulf Henriksson

Daiquiri Dick's

Visitors come often more than once during a vacation for the excellent service and consistent and innovative Mexican and world cuisine. The menu has fabulous appetizers and fish. Start with a signature daiquiri; move to the lingering wine list. Twin patios face the sea—one covered, one not.

THE COLLABORATORS The fish on a stick has been around since Dick's was a palapa on the beach. But most of the stellar recipes originated with departed chef Rafael Nazario, and are now expertly executed by talented Mexican chef **Ignacio Uribe**. During high season, Seattle chef **Hnoi Latthitham** joins Uribe, adding sizzle and spice from her native Thailand.

Daiquiri Dick's fish on a stick

La Ola Rica

Presentation is artful, portions generous, and the decor—a cross between whimsical and chic—is as yummy as the food. Owners Gloria Honan and Triny Palomera Gil scour the coast each day for fresh ingredients, fish, and bread, and preside over the restaurant each night to make sure the food's as good as it can be.

SELF-MADE CHEF In 1996 **Gloria Honan** and her partner were selling espresso from a lopsided wooden table inviting potential clients to sign up for a meal. But when the pasta primavera proved wildly successful, they opened La Ola Rica in Triny's family home. Their expertise is self-taught. Gloria says, "Finding out what you are capable of and pushing yourself to hold high standards is a very rewarding experience."

Gloria Honan (chef-owner) and her partner, Triny Palomero Gil, co-owner

Mark's Bar & Grill

Standout dishes at this Bucerías restaurant include the homemade bread and pizza, great salads, and such entrées as macadamia-crusted fish fillets and lobster ravioli. The restaurant is cozy but chic, with glassware from Tonalá, special-order lamps from Guadalajara, and a red tile roof peaking through exposed beams. Vie for the back patio, open to the stars.

NATURAL TALENT Creative New Zealand transplant **Jan Benton** spent happy childhood hours digging potatoes, shaking walnuts from trees, and roaming for wild mushrooms. Her appreciation for wholesome, natural foods shows in her cuisine, of which Jan says: "Everything has its own reason to be on the plate. You'll not find a repeat flavor."

Still Life No. 1: Mussels

Café des Artistes

In Thierry Blouet's kitchen Mexican ingredients and European techniques produce such stellar dishes as cream of prawn and pumpkin soup, artichoke-and-potato terrine, and grilled tenderloin served with Camembert and smoky chipotle chile sauce.

THE MASTER Given the title of Master Chef of France in 2000, **Thierry Blouet** is well-spoken and confident, piling up the accolades and awards. Born in the Philippines to French parents, Chef Blouet describes his cooking as French cuisine with Mexican—and to a lesser extent, Asian—ingredients and spices. He is also president and co-founder of PV's Gourmet Festival, and in 2006 inaugurated Thierry's Prime Steakhouse.

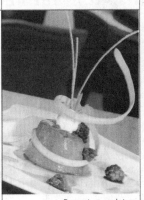

Dessert as sculpture

THE DISH ON THE DISHES

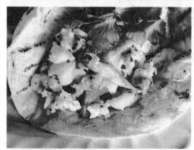

Lobster taco, Daiquiri Dick's

Puerto Vallarta has dozens of wonderful restaurants, and diligent research has produced the following list of some of the most exciting plates this gourmet town has to offer.

AMAZING APPETIZERS

Daiquiri Dick's **lobster tacos** are divine, and its shrimp wonton's wonderful melange of flavors dance a merengue in your mouth. At Trio, try the **anise-infused Portobello mushrooms** with vegetable vinaigrette. La Ola Rica has delightful **garlic mushrooms** and the sweetest **coconut shrimp** around.

SEAFOOD, MEXICAN-STYLE

The **mixed-seafood enchiladas** at La Palapa are wonderful, the best thing on the menu. Daiquiri Dick's **fish on a stick,** called Pescado Vallarta, has been pleasing crowds for nearly 30 years.

A-LIST ASIAN

Archie's Wok is the best place on the bay for multi-ethnic Asian cuisine, including Filipino, Thai, and Chinese. Favorite dishes are the **spicy Thai noodles** and **pancit** (Filipino noodle stir-fry). It's also great for vegetarians, with several wonderful stir-fried veggie dishes.

CHOCOLATE A-GO-GO

Indulge in a delicious **chocolate fondue** served with nutmeg ice cream at Café des Artistes. For special occasions, it's prepared on an creatively decorated tray with spun sugar and a liquid chocolate greeting. Trio's **warm chocolate cake** is legendary in PV. Make a pit stop at Pie in the Sky, in La Zona Romantica or Bucerías, for a bag of crunchy **chocolate chip cookies** for the road, or sit down for an addictive **chocolate brownie beso** (kiss), so rich it goes best with strong, black coffee.

IT'S ALL IN THE ATMOSPHERE

FOOD WITH A VIEW

Get a magnificent view of the city and bay, and a varied menu of excellent Spanish tapas at **Barcelona Tapas.**

DECADENT DECOR

Greco-Roman meets the tropics modern at **Le Bistro.** One of Vallarta's original gourmet restaurants, recently revitalized, has river-view dining among stone pillars and stands of towering bamboo. **Café des Artistes** has a magical, multilevel garden of ferns and figs, mangos and palms. Open to the ocean, **Vitea** is a casually hip

Boca Bento

bistro with clever and chic glass-and-metal furnishings. Two rows of tables outdoors facing the beach and boardwalk impart a European flavor. **Boca Bento** is serene, sensual, and open, with modern and elegant artwork, a soothing waterfall, and lots of candles. Grandiose yet romantic, **Mar Plata** is saved from looking industrial by innovative installations, fixtures, and antiques.

EPICUREAN EVENTS

Chocolate fondant with tomato and basil sorbet and white chocolate and raspberry sauce, Café des Artistes

INTERNATIONAL GOURMET FESTIVAL

Puerto Vallarta's dining scene owes its success in part to its annual gourmet festival, which has brought it international attention since 1994. During the eight-day food fling each November, chefs from Africa, Europe, South America, and the United States bring new twists on timeless classics. Starting with an elegant chef's cocktail reception, the festival continues with a full table of events. Each of the more than two dozen participating restaurants invites a guest chef to create special menus with wine pairings. Local and guest chefs teach cooking classes and seminars. The culmination is a gala dinner with live music, fireworks, and naturally, an over-the-top gourmet meal. ☎ *322/222–3229 Café des Artistes,* ⊕ *www.festivalgourmet.com.*

RESTAURANT WEEK

Most everyone in Vallarta works his or her tail off during the December to Easter high season. When *vallartenses* can finally take a breath—and then give a collective sigh of relief—they reward themselves with some reasonably priced nights out at the destination's best restaurants during this two-week (despite its name) event in Mayo. Each participating restaurant offers prix-fixe meals (with choices among appetizers, entrées, and desserts) for either 159 or 259 pesos. ☎ *322/221–0106.*

FOOD FOR A CAUSE

As if our clothes weren't already bursting at the seams, some of PV's most benevolent gastronomes began teaming up at fundraising events for local charities in 2005. Local chefs now produce Palomazo Gastronómico, or the "Culinary Jam Session," at least once a year. Along with four courses of haute cuisine, they serve up wine, song, and a warm and fuzzy feeling to boot. Cost is about $70 per person. ☎ 322/226–0017.

lobster around. ✉*Calle Marlin 14, at Calle Coral, Cruz de Huanacaxtle* ☎*329/295–5055* ▱*No credit cards* ⊘*Closed Mon. and wk after Easter.*

$$
SEAFOOD

✕**Dugarel Plays.** Do they mean "Dugarel's Place"? No matter, of Bucerías's many beachfront eateries, this one gets extra points for longevity, attentive service, good views north and south along the bay, and the best breezes. The menu is not extensive: there are several beef plates and Mexican dishes, and a larger assortment of fresh fish and seafood served with the usual rice and toasted bread, as well as veggies. ✉*Av. del Pacífico s/n, Bucerías* ☎*329/298–1757* ▱*No credit cards.*

TIME IS OF THE ESSENCE

The state of Nayarit (Nuevo Vallarta and points north) is in the Mountain Standard Time zone, while Jalisco (Marina Vallarta to Barra de Navidad) is on Central Standard Time. But because tourism in Bucerías and Nuevo Vallarta has always been linked to that of Puerto Vallarta, many Nayarit businesses run on Jalisco time. When making dinner reservations or checking restaurant hours, ask whether the place runs on *hora de Jalisco* (Jalisco time) or *hora de Nayarit*.

$
MEXICAN

✕**Famar.** This unassuming restaurant gets the vote of just about everyone we queried in Bucerías: expats and locals alike. Breakfast in the noisy front room includes chilaquiles, waffles, and omelettes. It's more peaceful on the back patio where the top picks are beef fajitas and shrimp Famar: the chef's secret recipe, containing shrimp, bacon, cheese, and salsa. Consistency and friendly, familial service is the name of the game. ✉*Héroes de Nacozari 105, Bucerías* ☎*329/298–0113* ▱*No credit cards* ⊘*Closed Sun.*

$$$
★
BISTRO

✕**Mark's Bar & Grill.** You can dine alone at the polished black-granite bar without feeling too lonely, or catch an important ball game. But seemingly a world away from the bar and TV is the charming restaurant known for its delightful decor and excellent cuisine. Both are best appreciated on the back patio, open to the stars. Standouts include the homemade bread and pizza, the salads, and the macadamia-crusted fresh fish fillets with mushroom ragout. The lamb is flown in from New Zealand; scallops, oysters and mussels, from Baja; and the black Angus beef, from Monterrey. Mixed organic lettuces, chives, and basil come from the lady down the street. The restaurant is elegant yet warm and inviting, with a golden glow over everything and roving musicians adding to the ambience. Order wine by the glass from the extensive list. ✉*Av. Lázaro Cárdenas 56, Bucerías* ☎*329/298–0303* ▱*MC, V* ⊘*No lunch.*

¢–$
★
CAFE

✕**Pie in the Sky.** Although the cars on the highway can be noisy, the lure of deliciously decadent mini-cheesecakes, pecan tarts, and crunchy chocolate cookies exerts a strong gravitational pull. The signature dessert here is the *beso,* a deep chocolate, soft-center brownie. Cakes, including gorgeous wedding cakes, are decorated by Zulem, a fine artist who excels with frosting as her medium. In addition to iced coffee and gourmet ice cream, Pie in the Sky has chicken potpie, spinach empanadas, and a spinach-and-cheese pizza. Sit a spell and take advan-

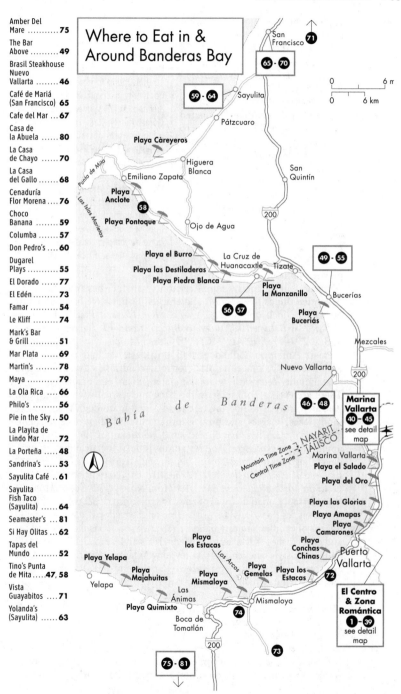

Where to Eat in & Around Banderas Bay

tage of the free Wi-Fi, at either location. ⊠*Héroes de Nacozari 202, Bucerías* ☎*329/298–0838* ⊠*Lázaro Cárdenas 247, at I. Vallarta, Col. E. Zapata* ☎*322/223–8183* ☰*AE, MC, V*

$$$
ARGENTINE

✕**La Porteña.** Restaurants are a hard sell in all-inclusive-dominated Nuevo Vallarta. This one seems to have broken the mold. Every cut of meat is grilled over mesquite, from the steaks to Angus prime rib (both imported from Texas). The adventurous yet tasty *chinculinas* (tender tripe appetizers) and chorizo turnovers certainly are authentic. Rice, veggies, and other sides must be ordered separately. The setting, an L-shape covered patio with kids' play equipment in the center, is Mexican, but the food is pure Argentine. Italian dishes and a few non-Argentine things like salmon and chicken dishes have been added. It opens for lunch only after 2 PM. ⊠*Blvd. Nayarit Pte. 250, Nuevo Vallarta* ✛*Between highway to Bucerías and El Tigre golf course* ☎*322/297–4950* ☰*AE, MC, V* ⊘*Closed Mon.*

> ## TACO NIGHTS
>
> Weekend nights in La Cruz de Huanacaxtle are Taco Nights (6 to 10 or 11); due to overwhelming popularity, it's now open Wednesday, too. At the home of the Diáz Gómez family (Calle Huachinango, 2 blocks north of traffic circle), locals and travelers socialize over delicious carne asada tacos, or quesadillas with freshly made flour or corn tortillas, excellent homemade salsas, and homemade flan for dessert. Bring your own beer or indulge in *horchata* or *agua de jamaica*, made, respectively, of rice and hibiscus plant.

$
ECLECTIC

✕**Philo's.** Ambitious Philo does it all: breakfast, lunch, dinner. It's a bar with live music, a meeting place for local fundraisers and events, and a community center (there are computers, yoga, and Spanish classes). There are even a pool table in the back and a small swimming pool. And if you were wondering, the food is good, although the menu of sandwiches, burgers, and pizza is less ambitious than it once was. Philo's special pizza has goat cheese, sundried tomatoes, onion, and pineapple—and they deliver! The restaurant is open for breakfast, as well, during high season (mid-November through April) ⊠*Calle Delfín 16, La Cruz de Huanacaxtle* ☎*329/295–5068* ☰*No credit cards.* ⊘*May–Oct.: no lunch and closed Sun. and Mon; Nov.–April: closed Mon.*

$$
☕
MEDITERRANEAN

✕**Sandrina's.** Canadian owner Sandy is as colorful as her wonderful art, which graces this locals' favorite. Dine on the back patio at night amid dozens of candles and tiny lights. The varied menu has plenty of salads and pasta dishes as well as such Mediterranean fare as chicken souvlaki and Greek-style chicken and pita bread with hummus or tzatziki. Order an espresso, delicious doctored coffee, or dessert from the bakery counter in the front, which opens at 9 AM. The main restaurant opens after 3 PM. ⊠*Av. Lázaro Cárdenas 33, Bucerías* ☎*329/298–0273* ⊕*www.sandrinas.com* ⌖*Reservations recommended.* ☰*MC, V* ⊘*No lunch. Closed Tues. and 2 wks in Sept.*

$
ECLECTIC

✕**Tapas del Mundo.** Here, worldly recipes of this and that are served in small plates perfect for sharing. Sit at one of three long bars around the open kitchen, soaking in the ambience created by the colorful American owners. Nosh on a hot pot of shrimp with guajillo chiles served with homemade tortillas, breaded olives, Anaheim chiles stuffed with goat cheese, or Oriental beef strips. Be apprised of the wonderful margaritas. The Bar Above, upstairs *(⇨above)*, sells desserts, coffee, and mixed drinks. ⊠ *Corner of Av. Mexico and Av. Hidalgo, 2 blocks north of central plaza, Bucerías* ☎*329/298–1194* ▭*No credit cards* ☉*Closed Sun. No lunch.*

$$ ✕**Tino's.** Vine-covered trees poke through the roof of the breeze-blessed,
★ covered outdoor eatery overlooking a placid lagoon. The Carvajal fam-
SEAFOOD ily has worked hard to make this a favorite Nuevo Vallarta restaurant, though the Punta de Mita branch is also nice, on a pretty beach and the original Pitillal location is popular for a trip back in time to Vallarta's roots. Tino's is full even midweek, mainly with groups of friends or businesspeople leisurely discussing deals. A multitude of solicitous, efficient waiters proffer green-lipped mussels meunière, crab enchiladas, oysters, and the regional specialty, fish *sarandeado* (rubbed with herbs and cooked over a wood fire). Concha de Tino is a dish with seafood, bacon, mushrooms, and spinach prettily presented in three seashells. ⊠*2a Entrada a Nuevo Vallarta, Km 1.2, Las Jarretaderas* ☎*322/297–0221* ▭*MC, V* ⊠*Av. El Anclote 64, El Anclote, Punta de Mita* ☎*329/291–6473* ⊠*Av 333 at Calle Revolución, Pitillal* ☎*322/225–2171 or 322/224–5584* ▭*MC, V*

NORTH OF BANDERAS BAY

$–$$ ✕**Cafe del Mar.** Chefs Eugene of Singapore and Amandine, a Belgian-
ECLECTIC Mexican, collaborate to create beautiful food focusing on seafood and chicken; the varied and excellent appetizers and desserts are especially recommended. The dishes blend Asian, Mediterranean, and haute Mexican cuisine in simple yet successful dishes. The setting itself is romantic and sophisticated. Tiny white lights and soft music accompany individual tables down the side of a hill to a vine-drenched trellis at the bottom. There's usually a guitarist serenading during Friday dinner; the restaurant is open for lunch as well. ⊠*Av. China 9, San Francisco* ☎*311/258–4251* ▭*MC, V* ☉*Closed Wed. and Aug. and Sept.*

¢ ✕ **Café de María.** Friendly owner María Ines oversees the produc-
CAFE tion—slow but steady—of your attractively presented fruit bowl with yogurt, spinach salad with sesame seeds and mandarin oranges, or just a mimosa or Bloody Mary, coffee, or a scoop of ice cream or carrot cake. The prices here are similar to those you'd find in the U.S., as are the lovely, clean bathrooms. Two rooms of this renovated former home overlook the street about a block from the town's main beach. ⊠*Av. Tercer Mundo 6 56, San Francisco* ☎*311/258–4439* ▭*No credit cards.* ☉*Closed Wed.; closed Sept. No dinner June–Aug.*

¢ ✕**La Casa de Chayo.** Here's a casual little place for breakfast a few
MEXICAN blocks from the beach in San Francisco, right next to La Ola Rica. Service inside or on the street-facing patio is easygoing but attentive. Between 8 and noon or 1 PM you can get the house favorites: huevos rancheros y chilaquiles as well as freshly squeezed orange juice, a banana strawberry smoothie, or an excellent fruit plate. ⊠*Av. Tercer*

Mundo 97, at Calle Mexico, San Francisco ☎329/258–4126 ☐*No credit cards* ⊘*Closed Tues. and July–Oct. No dinner.*

$–$$ ✕**La Casa del Gallo.** If a hole in the wall could be out of doors, this
ECLECTIC would be it. Frankly, it looks best by candlelight. But folks don't come
for the decor; they come for the fab filet mignon, great fish and shrimp,
and good pizza. Thursday at 7 PM there's a "save the sea turtles" presentation. The affable owner, Gallo, is also a musician who presents
tunes (often blues or acoustic guitar) whenever possible after 7:30 PM
(most often Thursday through Sunday in low season). Nightlife being
the exception rather than the rule in San Pancho, this is a great locals'
after-dark hangout. ⊠*Av. Tercer Mundo 7, San Francisco* ☎311/258–
4135 ☐*No credit cards* ⊘*Closed Tues. No lunch.*

¢–$ ✕**Choco Banana.** One of Sayulita's pioneer restaurants has really gotten
ᘓ spiffy, adding tile mosaic accents and generally beautifying its terrace
AMERICAN restaurant. The Wi-Fi doesn't hurt, either. BLTs and burgers, omelets
and bagels, and chicken with rice and chai tea are some of what you'll
find here. Service isn't fast, in keeping with laid-back Sayulita's surfer
attitude. This perennial favorite is almost always full of people eating
and loafing; there's a kid's menu for the truly young. It closes at 6 PM,
2 PM on Sunday. ⊠*Calle Revolución at Calle Delfín, on plaza, Sayulita*
☎329/291–3051 ☐*No credit cards.* ⊘*No dinner Sun.*

$$$ ✕**Don Pedro's.** Sayulita institution Don Pedro's has pizzas baked in
CONTINENTAL a wood-fire oven, prepared by European-trained chef and co-owner
Nicholas Parrillo. Also on the menu are consistently reliable seafood
dishes, tapanade, delicious ahi tuna, and mesquite-grilled filet mignon—
served with baby vegetables and mashed potatoes accompanied by pita
bread—which is just about the best around. The pretty second-floor
dining room, with the better view, is open when the bottom floor fills
up, usually during the high season (November to May). Call to find
out about live music during the week—sometimes salsa, sometimes
flamenco—during the dinner hour. This is a good spot for breakfast,
too, after 8 AM. ⊠*Calle Marlin 2, at beach, Sayulita* ☎329/291–3090
⊕www.donpedros.com ☐*MC, V* ⊘*Closed Sept.*

$$$–$$$$ ✕**Mar Plata.** Grandiose yet romantic, these impressive second-story
CONTINENTAL digs have a celestial seasoning of stars on the ceiling in the form of tin
lamps from Guadalajara. Dark-blue and deep terra-cotta walls juxta-
pose nicely; the huge space is saved from looking industrial by innova-
tive installations and fixtures. Co-owner and chef Amadine's recipes
wed traditional Argentine meats with updated Continental cuisine in
a happy transcontinental marriage. Portions are smallish, and entrées
exclude sides. There's live music Sunday and occasional flamenco
shows or tango classes. ⊠*Calle de Palmas 30, Col. Costa Azul, San
Francisco* ☎311/258–4424 ☐*MC, V* ⊘*Closed Mon. and Aug. and
Sept. No lunch.*

$$ ✕**La Ola Rica.** Oh. My. God. The food is good. *Really* good. Somehow
Fodor'sChoice chef and co-owner Gloria Honan (with Triny Palomera Gil) makes gar-
★ lic-sautéed mushrooms (a huge portion) into a minor miracle on toast.
ECLECTIC The cream of poblano-chili soup is simply to die for: not too spicy, but
wonderfully flavorful. And these are just the starters. The restaurant
is understandably popular, and reservations are encouraged. Locals

come for the coconut shrimp, lemon chicken, and medium-crust pizzas; everyone laps up the lovely margaritas. ⊠ *Av. Tercer Mundo s/n, San Francisco* ☎ *311/258–4123* ⊟ *MC, V* ⊘ *Closed Sun.; no lunch. Also closed Sun.–Wed. June, July, and Aug.–Oct. and closed Sat. June and July.*

DAILY SPECIALS

To save money, **look for the fixed-menu lunch** called either a *comida corrida* or a *menú del día*, served from about 1 to 4 in restaurants throughout Mexico, especially those geared to working-class folks.

$
MEXICAN
✗ **Sayulita Café.** The restaurant bills itself as "home of the perfect chile relleno," but it also serves other Mexican plates from Puebla and Oaxaca as well as Continental dishes like rib eye with baked potato. The restaurant and bar in this small, rather dark converted home look good by candlelight. From the sound system emerge jazz, classic, and Latin tunes; waiters with perfect English are the rule. ⊠ *Av. Revolución 37, Sayulita* ☎ *329/291–3511* ⊟ *No credit cards* ⊘ *Closed Sept. No lunch.*

$
SEAFOOD
✗ **Sayulita Fish Taco.** Although the namesake fish taco didn't really rock us on our last visit, Sayulita's limited number of eateries has gained it a place in the town's culinary roster. The attentive if leisurely service, central location and low prices make this a natural choice for banishing the munchies. The ability to select both the size and nature of the dish (choose, for example, fish, veggies, chicken, or shrimp prepared as a taco, burrito, or "bowl" or "shoe box" size) is another plus. ⊠ Jose Mariscal 13, *Sayulita* ☎ *329/291–3272* ⊟ *No credit cards* ⊘ *Closed Sun. and for vacation mid-Aug.–end of Sept.*

$
⊛
MEXICAN
✗ **Si Hay Olitas.** This simply decorated, open-front Mexican restaurant near tiny Sayulita's main plaza is the one most often recommended by locals for dependable Mexican and American fare. Order a giant burrito, vegetarian platter, burger or grilled chicken, or a seafood combo. There's a little of everything to choose from, and it's open for breakfast. The setting is casual and the menu has plenty of things that children will like. ⊠ *Av. Revolución 33, Sayulita* ☎ *329/291–3203* ⊟ *No credit cards.*

$$
MEXICAN
✗ **Vista Guayabitos.** Portions are large but the cooking is predictable at best. This restaurant's beauty lies in the setting, which couldn't be more dramatic. Enjoy lovely views of a solitary beach, an unattended island, and the beaches of Guayabitos. The hawk's-eye ocean view is especially wonderful around sunset. ⊠ *Carretera a Los Ayala, Km 1.5, Rincón de Guayabitos* ☎ *327/274–2589* ⊟ *MC, V.*

¢
FAST FOOD
✗ **Yolanda's.** Served up here is crackly, tasty chicken cooked while you watch in a cloud of steam over wood fire in half of a tin drum converted to a barbecue grill. Nothing fancy, just good old-fashioned food for the hungry. Take note that it's not cuisine, nor a fancy dining experience offered here; there are no tables or place to eat beyond a stand-up bar behind the grill. The memorable chicken is served take-out only with rice, corn tortillas, and a plastic bag of tasty salsa. Get the entire chicken for less than $8, half chicken for half that price. ⊠ *Calle José*

Mariscal s/n, next to Sayulita Fish Taco, Sayulita ☎*No Phone.* ▭*No credit cards.* ⊘*Closed Wed.*

COSTALEGRE

$ ✗**Ambar Del Mare.** A French woman from Provence brings a welcome
CONTINENTAL addition to Barra's circumspect culinary scene, along with good thin-crust pizzas, escargot, crepes, and other tasty French and Italian fare. Of the many pasta dishes, the lasagna, cannaloni, and ravioli use pasta made from scratch. The restaurant's compact size and good tunes, along with the small bar in the middle and the few tables looking out over the beach, give it a bistro feel. ⊠*Calle López de Legazpi 158, by Hotel Alondra, Barra de Navidad* ☎*315/355–8169* ▭*No credit cards* ⊘*No lunch. Closed Tues. and Wed. May–Nov.*

$ ✗**Casa de la Abuela.** The amiable and service-oriented owner, Miguel,
AMERICAN makes this one of the town's top choices for breakfast, snacks, or a light lunch. Listen to rock and jazz on the great sound system as you sip cappuccino and munch on the assortment of Mexican cookies that comes with it. Refills of the good American-style coffee are a given. Besides omelets, chilaquiles, fresh juices, and other breakfast food, Miguel and his family serve snacks like guacamole and chips, and burgers and fries for lunch. ⊠*Av. Miguel López de Legazpi 150, Barra de Navidad* ☎*No phone* ▭*No credit cards* ⊘*Closed Mon. No dinner.*

$ ✗**Cenaduría Flor Morena.** Some folks say these are the best enchiladas
★ they've ever eaten; others call it a "local institution." Locals and for-
MEXICAN eigners all pretty much agree that this hole in the wall on the main square is the best place around to get good, inexpensive Mexican favorites like pozole, tamales, and tacos. ⊠*Facing main plaza below the Catscan bar, San Patricio–Melaque* ☎*No phone* ▭*No credit cards* ⊘*Closed Mon. and Tues. No lunch.*

$ ✗**El Dorado.** This is the best place in town for seafood with an ocean view
SEAFOOD under a tall, peaked palapa roof. Besides seafood there are grilled chicken with baked potato, beef tips with rice and beans, soups, quesadillas, great guacamole, and fries. It's open all day (8 AM until 10 PM) and serves everyone from white-collar business types to families and friends meeting for lunch, to tourists cleaned up for an evening out. After your meal, kick your shoes off and take a walk on the beach. ⊠*Calle Gómez Farias 1, San Patricio–Melaque* ☎*315/355–5239* ▭*MC, V.*

$$ ✗**Martin's.** This second-floor,
MEXICAN palapa-roof restaurant is the most reliable in town for food and good cheer, and for hours of operation, too, as it's open year-round. There are Mexican- and American-style breakfasts, fajitas and shrimp for lunch and dinner, and sporadic serenades. This is as much a place for

> ### KNOW YOUR TORTILLAS
>
> In PV, tortillas are made of boiled and milled corn, griddle cooked, and served with just about every traditional dish. Butter to accompany tortillas is offered to *gringos* only. Foreigners also are given their choice of corn or flour tortillas, the latter native to northern Mexico and typically offered only with certain dishes, like *queso fundido* (cheese fondue).

socializing as for eating; at the bar you can quaff champagne, cognac, martinis, and wine. There's usually live music on Mondays in high season: jazz, flamenco, or Latin music, 8 PM to midnight. ✉*Calle Playa Blanco 70, La Manzanilla* ☎*315/351–5106* ⊟*No credit cards* ✆*Closed Tues. April–mid-Dec.; closed for vacation Sept. 19–Oct. 1.*

$$ ✕**Maya.** Two Canadian women have teamed up to bring sophistica-
★ tion to San Patricio–Melaque's dining scene. East meets West in con-
ECLECTIC temporary dishes such as tequila-lime prawns and corn, chorizo, and gouda-cheese fritters with a smoked jalapeno aioli. Favorite entrées include Szechuan prawns and prosciutto-wrapped chicken. Their hours of operation are complex and subject to change; it's best to check their Web site or confirm by phone. There's often live music including jazz or blues. ✉*Calle Alvaro Obregón 1, Villa Obregón, San Patricio–Melaque* ☎*315/102–0775 (cell phone)* ⊕*www.restaurantmaya.com* ⊟*No credit cards* ✆*Closed Sun., Mon. in Nov.; mid-May–Oct. No lunch.*

$$ ✕**Seamaster's.** Although most of the ocean-facing restaurants in Barra
SEAFOOD have a similar menu, this friendly family favorite is often recommended above the others. Have a shrimp or fish burger, the catch of the day bathed in garlic cream, or the house special: shrimp flambéed in brandy and Kahlua served in a nubby pineapple. The bar sometimes stays open late in high season, keeping clients around after the kitchen has shut down. ✉*Av. Miguel López de Legaspi 146, Barra de Navidad* ☎*315/355–5199* ⊟*No credit cards* ✆*Closed Tues.*

Beaches

Ixtapa

WORD OF MOUTH

"[For a low-key beach day], consider Bucerías, Yelapa, or even farther afield to a place like Melaque/Barra de Navidad (a three- to four-hour bus ride south), which has hordes of day-trippers each day. Bucerías, about 30 minutes north, is still fairly peaceful but growing."

— Stewbear

PUERTO VALLARTA SITS AT THE center of horseshoe-shape Bahía de Banderas (Banderas Bay), the second largest bay in North America (after the Hudson). Although Pacific Mexico's beaches are not the sugar-sand, crystal-water variety of the Caribbean, the beaches are lovely, the water unpolluted, and the coastline itself among the most majestic in Mexico.

Accounting for much of its beauty are the foothills that race down to meet the sea. Crowded with palms and cedars, the jungle's blue-green canopy forms a highly textured background to the deep blue ocean and creamy sand. Dozens of creeks and rivers follow the contours of these hills, creating estuaries, mangrove swamps, and other habitats for exploration. Exquisitely visible from cliff-side hotels and restaurants, the scalloped coast holds myriad coves and small bays perfect for shelling, sunning, swimming, and more strenuous activities.

At crowded Hotel Zone beaches and a few of the more popular stretches of sand north and south of town you can parasail, take boat rides, Jet Ski, kayak, boogie board, snorkel, and dive. If you want to explore the coast, some of the isolated beaches accessible by boat offer some of the above activities. Accessible by both land and sea are untouristy hideaways where there's little to distract you beyond the waves lapping at the shore. Almost any beach has at least one low-key seafood restaurant to provide simple fish lunches, cold beer, and warm pink sunsets.

GETTING ORIENTED

The mountainous backdrop of the beaches in Puerto Vallarta and to the north makes them beautiful—even though the water isn't translucent and the sand is grainy and brown, rather than powdery white. South of PV the mountains recede from the coast. The lovely yet lonely beaches and bays are fringed by dry tropical thorn forest with a wonderful variety of plant species. Several species of whales cruise down in winter and turtles spawn on the beaches. Throughout the region from southern Nayarit to the Costalegre, long, flat beaches invite walking and reefs and offshore breaks draw surfers; the omnipresent seafood shanties are perfect vantage points for sunsets on the sand.

BEACH REGIONS

PUERTO VALLARTA
Paralleling the Romantic Zone, Playa los Muertos is PV's most popular beach, with restaurants and bars with music; vendors selling barbecued fish on a stick; and people cruising the boardwalk. The beaches in the Hotel Zone and Marina Vallarta are a bit dull by comparison. At the south end of the bay are beautiful mountain-backed *playas* accessible only by boat.

NUEVO VALLARTA
One wide, flat, sandy beach stretches north of the Ameca River mouth for miles into the town of Bucerías. The generally calm water is good for swimming and, when conditions are right, bodysurfing or boogie

boarding. Activities are geared to all-inclusive hotel guests north of Paradise Village marina. Guys on the beach rent water-sports equipment, and most of the hotels rent equipment, too.

SOUTHERN NAYARIT

North of Nuevo Vallarta, rocky headlands sandwich scallops of sand from Bucerías to Chacala. These beaches attract boogie boarders, beachcombers, and those who make their own fun, as there are fewer services than in Vallarta. Surfing is big at Punta de Mita. Guayabitos, with its offshore island, is a vacation mecca for Mexican families and a refuge for snowbirds from Canada and the United States. Off the main highway, long, sandy roads lead to more isolated beaches such as Destiladeras.

THE COSTALEGRE

This is the domain of the independent traveler and the well-heeled recluse. High-end hotels on picturesque, rock-framed beaches arrange fishing and other pastimes. Other long, sandy beaches—many on large, semi-protected bays—are frequented by fishermen and local people relaxing at seafood shanties, and allow shelling, snorkeling, fishing, and trips to offshore islands. Having a car is helpful for exploring multiple beaches, although local bus service is available.

GO FOR:	IN PV:	NORTH OR SOUTH OF PV:
Wildlife	Los Arcos	Kayak adventures for La Manzanilla (Bahía Tenacatita); Islas Marietas (Punta de Mita)
Snorkeling	Los Arcos; Playa Conchas Chinas	Islas Marietas; Playa Mara
Walking or Jogging	Playa los Muertos	Nuevo Vallarta; Bucerís; Barra de Navidad and San Patricio Melaque (Bahía de Navidad)
Calm, Swimmable Waters	Hotel pool; Conchas Chinas	Los Ayala, Rincón de Guayabitos (Bahía de Jaltemba); Playa Las Minitas; Boca de Naranjo; Playa Chalacatepec
Surfing	N/A	El Anclote (Punta de Mita); Sayulita; Quimixto; Barra de Navidad
Eating/Drinking with Locals	Boca de Tomatlan	Chacala; Rincón de Guayabitos (Bahía de Jaltembo); Playa Tenacatita; Colimilla (Bahía de Navidad)

PUERTO VALLARTA

PV beaches are varied. Downtown Vallarta's main beach, Los Muertos, is a fun scene, with shoulder-to-shoulder establishments for drinking and eating under the shade. There's year-round action, although water-sports equipment rentals may be available on weekends only during the rainy season. The itinerant vendors are present year-round, however, and can be annoying. Immediately north of Los Muertos is contiguous Olas Altas Beach, with the same grainy brown sand but fewer vendors and services and sometimes waves big enough to surf or boogie. North of the malecón and Hotel Rosita, more stretches of sand front minor hotels. Hotel Zone beaches to the north offer opportunities to play in the sun during high season, although sand was dredged away by Hurricane Kenna in 2002. The beach at Marina Vallarta, between PV and Nuevo Vallarta, is swimmable but uninspired except for the beach toys and hotels that offer refreshments.

South of Vallarta proper are Conchas Chinas, a few smaller beaches, and Mismaloya. The wild beaches farther south (on the north side of Cabo Corriente, from Las Animas to Yelapa) didn't have electricity until the 1970s. They tend to fill up with day-trippers between December and April but are well worth a visit. At Los Muertos as well as beaches in the Hotel Zone and Marina Vallarta, you'll find Jet Skis, parasailing, and banana-boat rides in high season (December–April) and on weekends year-round.

GETTING THERE
The only public beach access (with on-street parking) at Marina Vallarta is between the airport and Condominios Grand Bay. There's little to stop you from walking through the major hotels, though, if you take a bus or cab to the area. The Hotel Zone and Centro beaches are easily accessed from the street. Take a bus or a cab, or drive your car; there's coveted curbside parking, or you can pay by the hour at the new Benito Juárez parking structure, just north of the Cuale River at the malecón and Calle Rodríguez.

DOWNTOWN PUERTO VALLARTA

Playa los Muertos is PV's original happenin' downtown beach. Facing Vallarta's South Side (south of the Río Cuale), this flat beach runs about 1½ km (1 mi) south to a rocky point called El Púlpito. Joggers cruise the cement boardwalk early morning and after sunset; vendors stalk the beach nonstop, hawking kites, jewelry, and sarapes as well as hair-braiding and alfresco massage. Their parade can range from entertaining (good bargainers can get excellent deals) to downright maddening. Restaurant-bars run the length of the beach; the bright blue umbrellas near the south end of the beach belong to the Blue Chairs resort, the hub of PV's effervescent gay scene.

The surf ranges from mild to choppy with an undertow; the small waves crunching the shore usually discourage mindless paddling. Strapping young men occasionally occupy the lifeguard tower, and local people fish from the small pier at the foot of Calle Francisca Rodríguez or cast nets from waist-deep water near the south end of the beach. Jet Skis zip around, but stay out beyond the small breakers, and are not too distracting to bathers and sunbathers. Guys on the beach offer banana-boat and parasailing rides. ■TIP→ **The steps (more than 100) at Calle Púlpito lead to a lookout with a great view of the beach and the bay.**

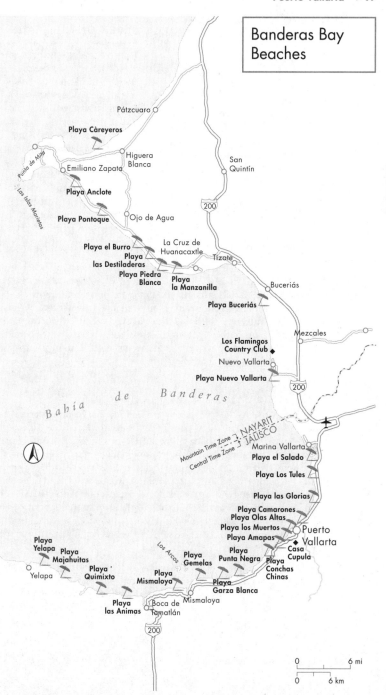

Banderas Bay Beaches

Pátzcuaro

Playa Cáreyeros

Higuera Blanca

San Quintín

Punta de Mita

Emiliano Zapata

Playa Anclote

Los Islas Marietas

Playa Pontoque

Ojo de Agua

200

Playa el Burro

La Cruz de Huanacaxtle

Playa las Destiladeras

Tizate

Playa Piedra Blanca

Playa la Manzanilla

Bucerías

Playa Bucerías

Mezcales

Los Flamingos Country Club

Nuevo Vallarta

Playa Nuevo Vallarta

200

Bahía   de   Banderas

Mountain Time Zone

Central Time Zone

NAYARIT

JALISCO

Marina Vallarta

Playa el Salado

Playa Los Tules

Playa las Glorias

Playa Camarones

Playa Olas Altas

Playa los Muertos

Puerto Vallarta

Playa Amapas

Casa Cupula

Playa Yelapa

Playa Majahuitas

Los Arcos

Playa Gemelas

Playa Punta Negra

Playa Conchas Chinas

Yelapa

Playa Quimixto

Playa Mismaloya

Playa Garza Blanca

Playa las Animas

Boca de Tomatlán

Mismaloya

200

0   6 mi

0   6 km

Playa Olas Altas means High Waves Beach, but the only waves suitable for body surfing or boogie boarding are near the Cuale River, at the north end of this small beach. Although Olas Altas more often refers to the neighborhood of bars and businesses near the ocean south of the Río Cuale, it is also the name of a few blocks of sand between Daiquiri Dick's restaurant and the Río Cuale. It attracts fewer families than Los Muertos, but is otherwise an extension of that beach. Facing Olas Altas Beach near Lázaro Cárdenas plaza are open-air stands selling beach accessories, small grocery stores, and easy access to beach-facing bars and restaurants.

> ### BEACH OF THE DEAD
>
> There are several versions of how Playa los Muertos got its name. One says that around the time it was founded, Indians attacked a mule train laden with silver and gold from the mountain towns, leaving the dead bodies of the muleteers on the beach. A version crediting pirates with the same deed seems more plausible. In 1935 anthropologist Dr. Isabel Kelly postulated that the place was an Indian cemetery.

The rock-strewn beach paralleling the malecón and the beach hotels like Rosita and El Pescador just north of it is **Playa Camarones**. Hurricane Kenna (2002) stole *mucho arena* (a lot of sand), however, and most people prefer to walk along the cement boardwalk rather than the beach here. Likewise, although the waves are gentle, the ocean floor is rocky and most bathers opt for the hotel pool. What you see here most often are small groups of men and boys surf casting, more for diversion than for hopes of great catches.

NORTH OF DOWNTOWN

The high-rise-backed **Zona Hotelera and Marina Vallarta beaches** have several names—**Playa Las Glorias** to the south, **Playa Los Tules** in the middle (around the Holiday Inn and Fiesta Americana), and **Playa El Salado** to the north. Most people, however, just refer to each beach by the hotel that it faces. These gray-beige, coarse-sand beaches are generally flat with a slope down to the water. Major winds and tides sometimes strew them with stones that make it less pleasant. (The Sheraton and its beachfront, at the south end of the strip, were hit hard by Hurricane Kenna in 2002, and in 2005 tons of sand were trucked in. The beach in front of it is therefore sandier than its neighbors, although still pocked with smooth, egg-size rocks.)

At Marina Vallarta, Playa **El Salado**—facing the Grand Velas, Meliá, Marriott, Mayan Palace, and the Westin—is pleasantly sandy. Colorful in high season with parasailers and with windsurfers rented or lent at area hotels, these beaches are actually more fun when crowded than when solitary. During fine weather and on weekends, and daily during high season, you can rent Jet Skis and pack onto colorful banana boats for bouncy tours of 10 minutes or longer. Some hotels rent small sailboats, sailboards, and sea kayaks to guests and to nonguests.

NAYARIT

At the northern end of Bahía de Banderas and farther into Nayarit state, to the north, are long, beautiful beaches fringed with tall trees or scrubby tropical forest. Only the most popular beaches like those of Nuevo Vallarta and Rincón de Guayabitos have much in the way of water-sports equipment rentals, but even the more secluded ones have stands or small restaurants serving cold coconut water, beer, and grilled fish with tortillas.

GETTING THERE

In Nuevo Vallarta, park on the street or in the parking lot of the tourism office, between Gran Velas and Maribal hotels. Buses arrive here as well, but the all-inclusive hotels that predominate cater to guests only, so bring your own supplies. It's a cinch to install yourself anywhere on Bucerías's long beach, with easy streetside parking. As most of the beaches north of here are off the main road, they are easiest to access by car (or taxi).

A new road (rather, the improvement of an old, narrow dirt-and-gravel road) connects Punta de Mita with Sayulita, San Francisco, and points to the north. However, if your destination is north of Punta de Mita, there's no need to follow the coast road to the point. Simply bear right instead of left after Bucerías, continuing on Carretera 200.

NUEVO VALLARTA TO PUNTA DE MITA

Several kilometers of pristine, if plain, beach face the hotels of **Playa Nuevo Vallarta.** The wide, flat, sandy beach is perfect for long walks: in fact, you could walk all the way to Bucerías, some 8 km (5 mi) to the north. Most of the hotels here are all-inclusives, so guests generally move between their hotel pool, bar, restaurant, and the beach in front. The same all-inclusive program means that nonguests are generally barred from the bars and restaurants.

Bucerías. Eight kilometers (5 mi) north of Nuevo Vallarta, the substantial town of Bucerías attracts a loyal flock of snowbirds, which has encouraged the establishment of apartments for rent and good restaurants. The beach here is endless: you could easily walk along its medium-coarse beige sands all the way south to Nuevo Vallarta. The surf is gentle enough for swimming, but also has body-surfable waves, and beginning surfers occasionally arrive with their longboards.

Just north of Bucerías, **La Cruz de Huanacaxtle,** better known as simply "La Cruz," has a fishing fleet but not much of a beach. A private marina is being developed as part of the Riviera Nayarit development plan. Like other Vallarta–Nayarit beaches, homey La Cruz is growing and becoming somewhat more sophisticated. On the north side of La Cruz, **Playa la Manzanilla** is a crescent of soft, gold sand where kids play in the shallow water while their parents sip cold drinks at one of several seafood shacks. It's somewhat protected by the Piedra Blanca headland to the north.

A few miles north of Piedra Blanca headland, **Destiladeras** is a 1½-km-long (1-mi-long) beach with white sand and good waves for bodysurfers and boogie-boarders. There's nothing much here except for a couple of seaside *enramadas* (thatch-roof shelters) serving fillets of fish and ceviche. **Punta el Burro,** at the north end of the beach, is a popular surf spot often accessed by boat from Punta de Mita.

⟳ **Punta de Mita,** about 40 km (25 mi) north of Puerto Vallarta, is home to the posh Four Seasons and the boutique resort Casa de Mita; other exclusive developments, condo complexes, a second golf course, and private villas are under construction. Just a few minutes past the entrance to the Four Seasons, the popular beach at **El Anclote** has a string of restaurants—once simple shacks but today of increasing sophistication—and price. This is a primo spot for viewing a sunset. Artificially calmed by several rock jetties and shallow for quite a ways out, it's also a good spot for children and average to not-strong swimmers to paddle and play, but there's a long slow wave for surfing, too. Most of the jewelry and sarape sellers and fishermen looking for customers have moved—or been moved—off the beach to more official digs in buildings along the same strip or facing the Four Seasons.

> **BEACH BLANKET BOTHER**
>
> Although it might feel rude, it's culturally permissible to simply ignore itinerant vendors, especially if you're in the middle of a conversation. However, being blatantly impolite (i.e., shouting at the vendor to take a hike) *is* rude—no matter where you're from. A wide grin and a firm *"No, gracias,"* with no further eye contact, is the best response—apart from "Yes, please, I'll take it," that is!

Accessible from El Anclote or the adjacent town of **Corral del Risco,** Punta de Mita has the most surf spots in the region, nearly a dozen, and the long swells here pump year-round. Divers favor the fairly clear waters and abundance of fish and coral on the bay side of the **Islas Marietas** about a half-hour offshore from El Anclote. In winter, especially January through March, these same islands are also a good place to spot orcas and humpback whales, which come to mate and give birth. Las Marietas is the destination for fishing, diving, and snorkeling; in addition, sealife viewing expeditions set out from El Anclote and Corral de Risco as well as from points up and down Banderas Bay.

NORTH OF BANDERAS BAY

As is happening up and down the Pacific Riviera, real estate north of the bay is booming. Mexicans are selling family holdings, jaded gringos are building private homes, and speculators from around the globe are grabbing what land they can, on and off the beach. For now, however, the Nayarit coast continues to enchant, with miles of lovely beaches bordered by arching headlands and Pacific hamlets drowsing in the tropical sun.

★ The increasingly popular town and beach of **Sayulita** is about 45 minutes north of PV on Carretera 200, just about 19 km (12 mi) north of Bucerías, and 35 km (22 mi) north of the airport. Until a few years ago, people liked to say it was like PV was 40 years ago. But today the sounds of construction ring through its narrow streets, which are now clogged with traffic in high season. Despite the growth, this small town is still laid-back and retains its surfer-friendly vibe. Fringed in lanky palms, Sayulita's heavenly beach curves along its small bay. A decent shore break here is good for beginning or novice surfers; the left point break is a bit more challenging. Skiffs on the beach have good rates for surfing or fishing safaris in area waters.

> ### WATER-TOY PRICES
>
> Prices for water toys in and around Vallarta are fairly consistent:
>
> WaveRunners: $45–$50 per half hour (one or two riders)
>
> parasailing: $35 for a 10-minute ride
>
> banana-boat rides: $15 for a 10-minute ride (usually four-person minimum)
>
> Hobie Cat or small sailboat: $40–$45 per hour

★ Ten minutes north of Sayulita, **San Francisco** is known to most people by its nickname: San Pancho. Just beginning to boom, it stretches between headlands to the north and south, and is accessed at the end of the town's main road: Avenida Tercer Mundo. You'll see men fishing from shore with nets as you walk the 1½-km-long (1-mi-long) beach of coarse beige sand. There's an undertow sometimes, but otherwise nothing to discourage reasonably strong swimmers. Its small waves occasionally support longboard surfing (especially in September), but this isn't a surf spot. In fact its small waves—too big for family splashing and too small for surfing—have probably maintained its innocence . . . until now. Popular with a hip crowd of European artists and intellectuals, San Pancho has just a few hotels but a growing number of good restaurants.

About 8 km (5 mi) north of San Pancho, **Lo de Marcos** is a humble town of quiet, wide streets that fill up on weekends and holidays with Mexican families renting the nondescript, bungalow-style motel rooms that predominate. After entering town on the main street, head left on the last road before the beach to reach **Playa las Minitas,** a small brown-sand beach on a pretty little cove framed by rocks. When not camped out at a half-dozen seafood shanties specializing in barbecued fish, local people bob in the super-tranquil surf. Continue another ½ km (¼ mi) along the road to **Playa los Venados,** which like Las Minitas, is a good spot for both swimming and snorkeling.

From south to north, the main beaches of **Bahía de Jaltemba** are: Los Ayala, Rincón de Guayabitos, and La Peñita.

A mini version of Guayabitos (⇨ *below*), **Playa los Ayala** has a level beach, mild surf, and an excellent view of **Isla del Coral,** to which glass-bottom boats ferry passengers for about $6 per person. On week-

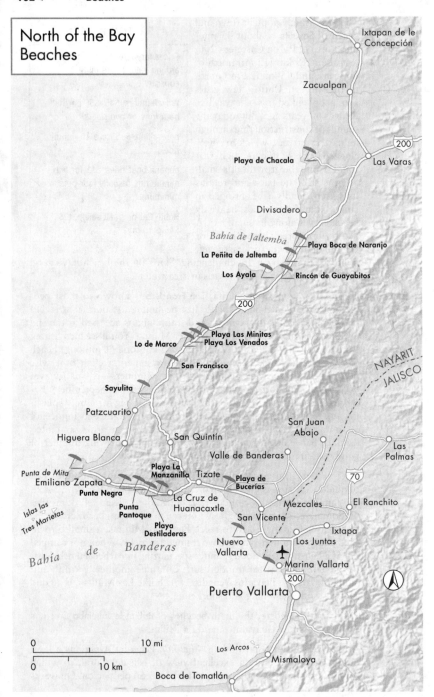

North of the Bay Beaches

Ixtapan de le Concepción

Zacualpan

Playa de Chacala

Las Varas

200

Divisadero

Bahía de Jaltemba

Playa Boca de Naranjo

La Peñita de Jaltemba

Los Ayala

Rincón de Guayabitos

200

Playa Las Minitas
Playa Los Venados

Lo de Marco

San Francisco

NAYARIT
JALISCO

Sayulita

Patzcuarito

Higuera Blanca

San Quintín

San Juan Abajo

Las Palmas

Playa La Manzanilla

Tizate

Valle de Banderas

Punta de Mita

Emiliano Zapata

Playa de Bucerías

70

Punta Negra

El Ranchito

Islas las Tres Marietas

Punta Pantoque

La Cruz de Huanacaxtle

Mezcales

Playa Destiladeras

San Vicente

Ixtapa

Bahía   *de*   *Banderas*

Nuevo Vallarta

Los Juntas

Marina Vallarta

200

Puerto Vallarta

0 ——————— 10 mi

0 ——————— 10 km

Los Arcos

Mismaloya

Boca de Tomatlán

ends, holidays, and in high season take a ride on a banana boat; most any time you can find a skiff owner to take you to **Playa Frideritas** or **Playa del Toro,** two pretty beaches for bathing that lie around the headland to the south, accessible only by boat. You can walk, however, over the hill at the south end of the beach to a seafood restaurant on a small scallop of beach called **Playa Frideras.**

☾ A couple of kilometers north of
★ Ayala along the highway, **Rincón de Guayabitos** bustles with legions of Mexican families on weekends and holidays; foreigners take up residence during the winter months. The main street, Avenida Nuevo Sol, has modest hotels, inexpensive restaurants, and scores of shops that all sell the same cheap bathing suits and plastic beach toys. One block closer to the sea are more hotels along with some vacation homes right on the sand. Colorfully painted stands on the beach sell fresh chilled fruit and coconuts; others serve up fresh seafood. This lovely beach bounded by headlands and the ocean is tranquil and perfectly suited for swimming.

Contiguous with Guayabitos, **La Peñita,** at the north end of the bay, has fewer hotels and the beach is often nearly abandoned except for a few fishermen. Its name means "little rock." The center for area business, La Peñita has banks, shoe stores, and ice-cream shops; a typical market held each Thursday offers knock-off CDs, polyester clothing, and fresh fruits and vegetables.

A few kilometers north of Peñita, a dusty road leads to **Boca de Naranjo,** a long, secluded sandy beach with excellent swimming. The rutted dirt road from the highway, although only about 4 km (2½ mi) long, takes almost a half hour to negotiate in most passenger cars. Enjoy great views of the coastline from one of nearly a dozen seafood shanties. Turtles nest here in August and September.

Some 30 km (19 mi) north north of Rincón de Guayabitos, **Chacala** is another 9 km (5 mi) from the highway through exuberant vegetation. Although most people are content to dine or drink at the handful of eateries right on the beach while imbibing the soft-scented sea air and the sight of the green-blue sea, you can bodysurf and boogie board here, too. Swimming is safest under the protective headland to the north of the cove; surfing is often very good, but you have to hire a boat to access the point break.

TURTLE RESCUE

In San Pancho, **Grupo Ecológico de la Costa Verde** (*Green Coast Ecological Group* ✉ *Av. Latino América 102, San Pancho* ☎ *311/258–4100* ⊕ *www.project-tortuga.org*) works to save the olive ridley, leatherback, and eastern Pacific green turtles that once swamped area beaches. Volunteers patrol beaches, collect eggs, maintain the nursery, tabulate data, and educate the public about their program. (Apply any time during the year, via the Web site, for an assignment June through November.) Slideshows to raise awareness and funds (buy a T-shirt to support the cause) are held each Thursday at 7 PM at La Casa de Gallo Restaurant.

4

SOUTH OF PUERTO VALLARTA

While coastal Nayarit is jumping on the development bandwagon, the isolated beaches of Cabo Corriente and those of southern Jalisco—some surrounded by ecological reserves—continue to languish for the time being in peaceful abandon. Things here are still less formal, and aside from the super-posh resorts like El Careyes, Hotelito Desconocido, and Las Alamandas, whose beaches are off-limits to nonguests, words like "laid-back" and "run-down" or "very basic" still apply, much to the delight of adventurous types.

GETTING THERE

Catch a green bus to Conchas Chinas, Mismaloya, or Boca de Tomatlán from the southwest corner of Calle Basilio Badillo and Constitución, Col. E. Zapata in Puerto Vallarta. Give the driver sufficient notice when you want to get off; pulling over along the narrow highway is challenging.

There are several ways to reach the beaches of southern Banderas Bay. Party boats (aka booze cruises) and privately chartered boats leave from Marina Vallarta's cruise-ship terminal (⇨ Chapter 7) and generally hit Las Animas, Quimixto, Majahuitas, and/or Yelapa. You can also hire a water taxi from Boca de Tomatlán ($6 one-way, usually on the hour 9 AM through noon, and again in early afternoon), from the pier at Los Muertos ($20 round-trip, 11 AM and in high season at 10:15 and 11 AM), or from the tiny pier next to Hotel Rosita ($20 round-trip, 11:30 AM). ■TIP➡ Note that weather and other variables can affect the water-taxi schedule. For maximum time at the beach of your choice and minimum frustration, head out early and relax over a soda or coffee at Boca de Tomatlán as you wait for the next available skiff to depart. You can catch the 4 PM taxi from Los Muertos to Yelapa if you're planning to spend the night; it will not return until the next day. Pangas (skiffs) for your party only can be hired at Boca, Mismaloya, or Los Muertos. The price depends on starting and ending points, but runs about $35 per hour for up to eight passengers.

It's best to have your own car for exploring the Costalegre, as many beaches are a few kilometers—down rutted dirt roads—from the highway. However, if you want to hang out in the small but tourist-oriented towns of San Patricio–Melaque and Barra de Navidad, you don't necessarily need wheels.

SOUTHERN BANDERAS BAY & CABO CORRIENTES

★ Frequented mainly by visitors staying in the area, **Playa Conchas Chinas** is a series of rocky coves with crystalline water. Millions of tiny white shells, broken and polished by the waves, form the sand; rocks that resemble petrified cow pies jut into the sea, separating one patch of beach from the next. These individual coves are perfect for reclusive sunbathing and, when the surf is mild, for snorkeling around the rocks; bring your own equipment. It's accessible from Calle Santa Barbara, the continuation of the cobblestone coast road originating at the south end of Los Muertos Beach, and also from Carretera 200 near El Set restaurant. Swimming is best at the cove just north of La Playita de Lindo Mar, below the Hotel Conchas Chinas (where the beach ends), as there are fewer rocks in the water. You can walk—be it on the sand, over the rocks, or on paths or steps built for this purpose—from Playa Los Muertos all the way to Conchas Chinas. The beach does not have services.

Though **Punta Negra,** about a mile south of Conchas Chinas, lost a lot of sand and allure during Hurricane Kenna, waves usually break gently on shore and the water is usually glassy and nice for swimming. It is accessible from Carretera a Mismaloya (Carretera 200) down a somewhat steep stone-and-cement path. Park off the highway at the north end of Condominios Jalisco Vacactional, near the blue Playa Punta Negra sign. The beach is mainly big round rocks, with little sand. There's shade under several tall trees sprouting from an old foundation, but there's sometimes trash from previous picnics. The beach has no facilities.

> ### SNORKELING SANCTUARY
>
> Protected area **Los Arcos** is an offshore group of giant rocks rising some 65 feet above the water, making the area great for snorkeling and diving. For reasonable fees, local men along the road to Mismaloya Beach run diving, snorkeling, fishing, and boat trips here and as far north as Punta de Mita and Las Marietas or the beach villages of Cabo Corrientes. Restaurants at Playa Mismaloya can also set you up.

Playa Garza Blanca, or "White Heron Beach," is a mirror image of Punta Negra Beach about half a mile away at the opposite end of the narrow cove. It's also signed, and accessible on foot by a dirt path. The beach does not have facilities.

Playa Mismaloya is the cove where *The Night of the Iguana* was made. Unfortunately, the big, tan Hotel La Jolla de Mismaloya looms large over the once-pristine bay, and Hurricane Kenna stole much of Mismaloya's white sand. Nonetheless, the place retains a certain cachet. It also has views of the famous cove from a couple full-service seafood restaurants on the south side of a wooden bridge over the mouth of the Río Mismaloya. Sun-seekers kick back in wooden beach chairs, waiters serve up food and drink, massage techs offer their (so-so) services alfresco, and Chico's Dive Shop sells dive packages and boat trips. The tiny village of Mismaloya is on the east side of Carretera 200, about 13 km (8 mi) south of PV.

Boca de Tomatlán is the name of both a small village and a rocky cove that lie at the mouth of the Río Horcones, about 5 km (3 mi) south of Mismaloya and 17 km (10½ mi) south of PV. Water taxis leave from Boca to the southern beaches; you can arrange snorkeling trips to Los Arcos. Five seaside cafés cluster at the water's edge.

☺ There's lots to do besides sunbathe at **Playa las Ánimas,** a largish beach 15 minutes south of Boca de Tomatlán by boat, so it tends to fill up with families on weekends and holidays. The usual seafood eateries line the sand, and you can also rent Jet Skis, ride a banana boat, or soar up into the sky behind a speedboat while dangling from a colorful parachute.

Between the sandy stretches of Las Animas and Majahuitas, and about 20 minutes by boat from Boca de Tomatlán, rocky **Quimixto** has calm, clear waters that attract boatloads of snorkelers. There's just a narrow beach here, with a few seafood eateries. Day-trippers routinely rent horses ($15 round-trip; ask at the restaurants) for the 25-minute ride—or only slightly longer walk—to a large, clear pool under a waterfall. You can bathe at the falls' base, and then have a cool drink at the casual restaurant. There's a fun, fast wave at the reef here, popular with surfers but because of its inaccessibility, rarely crowded.

Majahuitas—between the beaches of Quimixto and Yelapa and about 35 minutes by boat from Boca de Tomatlán—is the playground of people on day tours and guests of the exclusive Majahuitas Resort. The beach has no services for the average José; the lounge chairs and bathrooms are for hotel guests only. Palm trees shade the white beach of broken, sea-buffed shells. The blue-green water is clear, but tends to break right on shore.

★ The secluded village and ½-km-long (¼-mi-long) beach of **Yelapa** is about an hour southeast of downtown Puerto Vallarta, or a half hour from Boca de Tomatlán. Several seafood *enramadas* (thatch-roof huts) edge its fine, clean, grainy sand. During high season, parasailers float high above it all. From here you can hike 20 minutes into the jungle to see the small Cascada Cola del Caballo (Horse's Tail Waterfall), with a pool at its base for swimming. (The falls are often dry near the end of the dry season, especially April–early June.) A more ambitious expedition of several hours brings you to less-visited, very beautiful Cascada del Catedral (Cathedral Falls).

But, for the most part, Yelapa is *tranquilisimo:* a place to just kick back in a chair on the beach and sip something cold. Seemingly right when you really need it, Cheggy or Agustina, the pie ladies, will show up with their fantastic homemade pies.

Phones and electricity arrived in Yelapa around the turn of the 21st century. ■TIP→ **But bring all the money you'll need, as there is nothing as formal as a bank.**

Just south of the end of Banderas Bay are the lovely beaches of pristine, wonderful, fairly inaccessible **Cabo Corrientes.** These take an effort to visit, and preferably, a four-wheel-drive vehicle, although a sturdy, high-clearance vehicle will do. Public transportation goes there and back once a day from the small town of El Tuito (40 km [25 mi] south of Puerto Vallarta) along a rutted dirt road.

A somewhat difficult 40 km (25 mi) from the highway, the tiny town of **Aquiles Serdán** lies between the ocean and a river-fed lagoon. Boats hired here give access to miles of solitary, sandy beaches where primitive camping is permitted—providing you bring all of your own supplies and clean up after yourself. To get to Aquiles Serdán, bear right at the fork just past the village of Los Conejos.

Bearing left (and then right) just past Los Conejos brings you to bucolic **Tehualmixtle,** a sheltered cove that has, in addition to several restaurants, places to camp and basic rooms to rent. The pristine beach invites snorkeling and diving (bring your own equipment). Or you can explore the inland area with the help of an experienced guide at Candelarío's palapa. You'll find this little beachfront cabana at the end of the road that leads down through the village to the beach. If you're not sure which of the few small palapas it is, ask for Gaby, whose family runs the joint and who also coordinates tourism in the village.

THE COSTALEGRE

Most people come to the Costalegre—dubbed "The Happy Coast" by Jalisco's tourism authorities—to stay at luxury accommodations on lovely, clean beaches: Hotelito Desconocido, Las Alamandas, El Careyes, and El Tamarindo. Others head to southern Jalisco State without reservations to explore the coast at their leisure. Whether you kick back at an elegant resort or explore the wild side, the area between Cabo Corrientes and Barra de Navidad, the latter at the southern extreme of Jalisco state, will undoubtedly delight.

GETTING THERE

It's optimum to explore the beaches of southern Jalisco by car, SUV, or camper. Camping is permitted on most beaches, and these are often down a long dirt road from the highway. Fill up with gas at every opportunity, as gas stations are numbered. If you're in a rental car, reset the odometer and look for the kilometer signs at the side of the road. If you're driving a car marked in miles, not kilometers, the road signs are still useful, as many addresses are simply "Carretera 200" or "Carretera a Barra de Navidad" along with the marker number.

Buses leave from the **Central Camionero** (⊠ *Carretera Puerto Vallarta— Tepic [Carretera 200], Km 9, Col. Las Mojoneras* ☎ *322/290–1009*) in Puerto Vallarta.

COSTALEGRE

Some of the nicest beaches, with services, are now the private domain of gran turismo (government-rated five-star-plus) hotels. However, there are some delightful, pristine, and mainly isolated beaches along the Costalegre, most with few services aside from the ubiquitous seafood enramadas serving fish fillets and fresh ceviche.

A sylvan beach with no services, **Playa Chalacatepec** lies down a packed dirt road about 82 km (50 mi) south of El Tuito and 115 km (70 mi) south of Puerto Vallarta. The road to the beach is rutted and negotiable only by high-clearance passenger cars and smallish RVs. The reward for 8 km (5 mi) of bone-jarring travel is a beautiful rocky point, Punta Chalacatepec, with a sweep of protected white-sand beach to the north

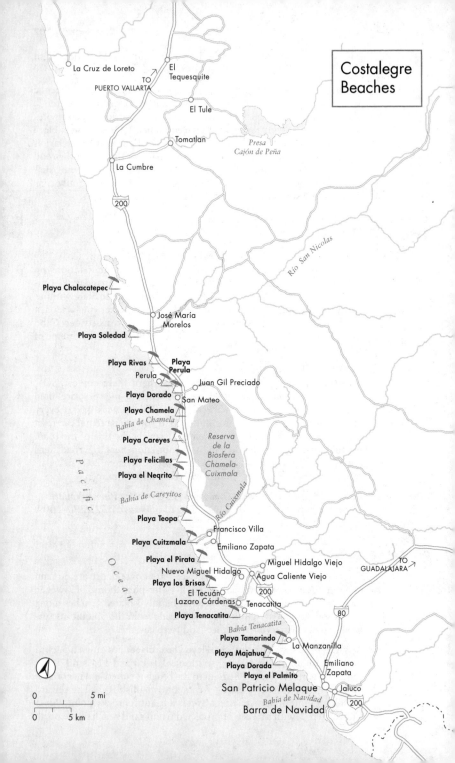

perfect for swimming, bodysurfing, and hunting for shells. Admire the tidepools at the point during low tide; take a walk of several kilometers along the open-ocean beach south of the point, where waves crash more dramatically, discouraging swimming. To get here, turn right into the town of José María Morelos (at Km 88). Just after 8 km (5 mi), leave the main road (which bears right) and head to the beach over a smaller track. From there it's less than a 1½ km (1 mi) to the beach.

The handful of islands just offshore of lovely **Bahía de Chamela,** about 131 km (81 mi) south of PV, protects the beaches from strong surf. The best place on the bay for swimming is **Playa Perula** (turnoff at Km 76, then 3 km [2 mi] on dirt road), in the protective embrace of a cove just below the Punta Perula headland. Fishermen there take visitors out to snorkel around the islands or to hunt for dorado, tuna, and mackerel; restaurants sitting on the coarse beige sand sell the same as fresh fillets and ceviche. The sand curves the length of the 8-km-long (5-mi-long) bay to **Playa Negrita,** with camping and RV accommodations and plenty of opportunities for shore fishing, swimming, and snorkeling. Almost every pretty beach in Mexico has its own humble restaurant; this one is no exception.

About 11 km (6½ mi) south of Bahía Chamela, **Playa Careyes** is a lovely soft-sand beach framed by headlands. When the water's not too rough, snorkeling is good around the rocks, where you can also fish.

You can walk south from Playa Careyes along the dunes to **Playa Teopa,** although guards protect sea turtle nests by barring visitors without written permission during the summer and fall nesting seasons. A road from the highway at Km 49.5 gains access to Playa Teopa by car; ask for written permission at Hotel El Careyes, a few kilometers to the north, or just roll up in your car and try your luck.

★ Named for the bay on which it lies, **Playa Tenacatita** is a lovely beach of soft sand about 34 km (20 mi) north of San Patricio Melaque and 172 km (106 mi) south of Puerto Vallarta. Dozens of identical seafood shacks line the shore; birds cruise the miles of beach, searching for their own fish. Waves crash against clumps of jagged rocks at the north end of the beach, which curves gracefully around to a headland. The water is sparkling blue. There are camping for RVs and tents at Punta Hermanos, where the water is calm, and local men offer fishing excursions. ■TIP→ **Of the string of restaurants on the beach, La Fiesta Mexicana is especially recommended.**

★ On the north end of Playa Tenacatita, **Playa Mora** has a coral reef close to the beach, making it an excellent place to snorkel.

A little more than 6 km (4 mi) south of Bahía de Tenacatita at Km 20, is the entrance to down-at-the-heels **Bahía de los Angeles Locos** all-inclusive hotel. It may be tacky and have a buffet that serves mediocre food, but it's got a great location and such amenities as tennis and banana boats. Sharing the property and some of the services is the buffed-out naturalistic resort at Punta Serena. Nearby Coconuts by the Sea

Lingering in Yelapa

If you can't tear yourself away at the end of the day (or you miss the last water taxi), consider renting one of the locally run rustic accommodations near the beach. Modest but charming in a bohemian way, Hotel La Lagunita (closed in the rainy season) has rooms right over the water. "Rustic chic" describes La Verana hotel, a five-star property represented by Mexico Boutique Hotels. It normally doesn't accept walk-ins, however, and a large deposit needs to be made in advance of your stay.

If you're lucky enough to be staying in Yelapa, there's plenty to do beyond the beach. Splash across the shallow lagoon or catch the water taxi to the main pier for a jungly walk past private homes and small shops; this is the Yelapa most folks never see.

Check out the candlelit Club Yates disco on the south side of the estu-ary (Wednesday and Saturday nights during high season [December through Easter week] and holidays). Or ask around for one of several yoga classes, schedule a therapeutic massage with Claudia (☎ 322/209–508 ✉ $50), or hire a local *pangero* (panga operator) for a trip to a secluded southern beach for swimming and a trek to a clandestine waterfall. For a simple meal in a tiny outdoor café, visit El Manguito ($$, ☎ 322/209–5061), just a few paces from the footbridge on the north side of the stream. Order shrimp, fish, lobster, beef, or just chips and salsa. It's open daily but closes between noon and 1 PM and again from 4 to 5 PM.

But the best part of staying in Yelapa is that after the booze cruises decamp and the water taxis put in for the night, you'll have the cool and groovy place to yourself.

guesthouse enjoys lovely breezes and excellent views from its breezy hilltop perch.

Farther south along Tenacatita Bay, **Playa Boca de Iguanas** is a wide, flat beach of fine gray-blond sand that stretches for several kilometers north of Playa Tenacatita. Gentle waves make it great for swimming, boogie boarding, and snorkeling, but beware the undertow. There are two RV parks here, and a couple of beach restaurants. The entrance is at Km 17.

☺ Two-kilometer-long (1-mi-long) **Playa la Manzanilla** is little more than a kilometer in from the highway, on the southern edge of Bahía de Tenacatita, 193 km (120 mi) south of Puerto Vallarta and 25 km (15½ mi) north of Barra de Navidad (at Km 14). Informal hotels and restaurants are interspersed with small businesses and modest houses along the main street of the town. Rocks dot the gray-gold sands and edge both ends of the wide beach. The bay is calm. At the beach road's north end, gigantic, rubbery-looking crocodiles lie heaped together just out of harm's way in a mangrove swamp. The fishing here is excellent; boat owners on the beach can take you fishing for snapper, sea bass, and others for $20–$25 an hour.

Twenty-one kilometers (13 mi) south of La Manzanilla, **Bahía de Navidad** represents the end of the Costalegre at the border with Colima

State. First up (from north to south) is **San Patricio–Melaque,** the most populous town on the Costalegre, with about 12,000 people. (The town is actually two towns that have now met in the middle.) While parts of town look dilapidated or abandoned, its long, coarse-white-sand beach is rather beautiful, with gentle waves. ■TIP➜ **The best swimming and boogie boarding is about half the length of town, in front of El Dorado restaurant.**

Fishermen congregate at the west end of San Patricio–Melaque, but it's most common to hire a panga for fishing at **Barra de Navidad** (usually called just "Barra"), a laid-back little town with sandy streets. At any time but at high tide you can walk between San Patricio and Barra, a distance of about 6 km (4 mi). It's about 4½ km (3 mi) on the highway from one town to the other.

4

Most of Barra is comprised of two streets on a long sandbar. Calle Veracruz faces the vast lagoon and **Isla Navidad,** now home to the posh Gran Bay resort. Water taxis take folks to the Gran Bay's golf course or marina, or to the seafood restaurants of **Colimilla,** on the lagoon's opposite shore. Avenida Miguel de Legazpi faces Barra's sloping brown-sand beach and the ocean. These and connecting streets have small shops, simple but charming restaurants, and—like everywhere along Mexico's Pacific coast—a host of friendly townspeople. ■TIP➜ **Surfers look for swells near the jetty, where the sea enters the lagoon.**

Shopping

Huichol bowls

WORD OF MOUTH

"Our favorite shopping area was the street of Basilio Badillo in the Zona Romántica: Unique crafts, jewelry, clothes, art, and shops."

–Janeyre

IT'S HARD TO DECIDE WHICH is more satisfying: shopping in Puerto Vallarta, or feasting at its glorious restaurants. There's enough of both to keep a bon vivant busy for weeks. But while gourmands return home with enlarged waistlines, gluttonous shoppers need an extra suitcase for the material booty they bring home.

Puerto Vallarta's highest concentration of shops and restaurants shares the same prime real estate: Old Vallarta. But as construction of hotels, time-shares, condos, and private mansions marches implacably north up the bay, new specialty stores and gourmet groceries follow the gravy train. To the south, the Costalegre is made up primarily of modest seaside towns and self-contained luxury resorts, and shopping opportunities are rare.

More than a half dozen malls line "the airport road," Boulevard Francisco M. Ascencio, which connects downtown with the hotel zone and Marina Vallarta. There you'll find folk art, resort clothing, and home furnishing stores amid supermarkets, and in some cases bars, movie theaters, and banks.

A 15% value added tax (locally called IVA, officially the impuesto al valor agregado) is levied on most purchases. (Note that it's often included in the price, and it's usually disregarded entirely by market vendors.) Foreign visitors can now reclaim this 15% by filling out paperwork at a kiosk in the Puerto Vallarta airport (and other major airports around the country). Purchases must be made using a major credit or debit card or cash at approved stores and businesses, and must total $115 or more. You must present a credit card at the time of purchase and obtain a receipt and an official refund form from the merchant. Tax paid on meals and lodgings won't be refunded.

SMART SOUVENIRS

ARTS & CRAFTS

Puerto Vallarta is an arts and crafts paradise, particularly if you're fond of ceramics, masks, fine art, and Huichol folk art (⇨ *"The Art of the Huichol," below).* Occasionally you'll find vivid handwoven and embroidered textiles from Oaxaca and Chiapas, and comfortable, family-size hammocks from Yucatán State. Handmade or silkscreened, blank greeting cards make inexpensive and lovely framed prints.

GLASS & PEWTER

Glassblowing and pewter were introduced by the Spanish. A wide range of decorative and utilitarian pewter items is produced in the area, as well as distinctive deep blue goblets, emerald-rimmed, chunky drinking glasses, and other glassware. All are excellent buys today.

JEWELRY

Many PV shop owners travel extensively during the summer months to procure silver jewelry from Taxco, north of Acapulco. For more information ⇨ *"One Man's Metal."*

POTTERY

After Guadalajara and its satellite towns Tlaquepaque and Tonalá—which produce ceramics made using patterns and colors hundreds of years old—Puerto Vallarta is the best place in the region to buy pottery, and at reasonable prices. PV shops also sell Talavera (majolica or maiolica) pottery from Puebla.

UNUSUAL GIFTS

For less-than-obvious souvenirs, go traditional and consider a *molinillo,* a carved wooden beater for frothing hot chocolate; you can find these at street vendors or traditional markets for about $1.50. A set of 10 or so *tiras de papel* (string of colored tissue-paper cuts) in a gift shop will only set you back about $2. Handmade huaraches (traditional sandals) are hard to break in (get them wet and let them dry on your feet), but last for years.

TIPS & TRICKS

Better deals are often given to cash customers—even though credit cards are nearly always accepted—because stores must pay a commission to the credit-card companies. U.S. dollars are almost universally accepted, although most shops pay a lower exchange rate than a bank (or ATM) or *casa de cambio* (money exchange). You may have to pay 5% to 10% more on credit-card purchases.

Bargaining is expected in markets and by beach vendors, who may ask as much as two or three times their bottom line. Occasionally an itinerant vendor will ask for the real value of the item, putting the energetic haggler into the awkward position of offering far too little. One vendor says he asks *norteamericanos* "for twice the asking price, since they always want to haggle." The trick is to **know an item's true worth** by comparison shopping. It's not common to bargain for already inexpensive trinkets like key chains or quartz-and-bead necklaces or bracelets.

Shop early. Though prices in shops are fixed, smaller shops may be willing to bargain if they're really keen to make a sale. Anyone even slightly superstitious considers the first sale of the day to be good luck, an auspicious start to the day. If your purchase would get the seller's day started on the right foot, you might just get a super deal.

HOURS OF OPERATION

Most stores are open daily 10–8 or even later in high season. A few close for siesta at 1 PM or 2 PM, then reopen at 4 PM. Perhaps half of PV's shops close on Sunday; those that do open usually close up by 2 or 3 in the afternoon. Many shops close altogether during the low season (August or September through mid-October). We've noted this whenever possible; however, some shops simply close up for several weeks if things get excruciatingly slow. In any case, low season hours are usually reduced, so call ahead during that time of year.

WATCH OUT   Watch that your credit card goes through the machine only once, so that no duplicates of your slip are made. If there's an error and a new slip needs to be drawn up, make sure the original is destroyed. Another scam is to ask you to wait while the clerk runs next door ostensibly to use another business's phone or to verify your number— but really to make extra copies. Don't let your card leave a store without you. While these scams are not common in Puerto Vallarta and we don't advocate excessive mistrust, taking certain precautions doesn't hurt.

> ### WALKING AND GAWKING
>
> On Wednesday evenings during high season (late October–April), the PV art community hosts Old Town artWalk (⇨ *Chapter 8*). Participating galleries welcome lookie loos as well as serious browsers between 6 PM and 10 PM; most provide at least a cocktail. Look for signs in the windows of participating galleries, or pick up a map at any of them ahead of time.

Don't buy items made from tortoiseshell or any sea turtle products: it's illegal, and Mexico's turtle species are endangered or threatened. These items are also not allowed into the U.S., Canada, or the U.K. Cowboy boots, hats, and sandals made from the leather of endangered species such as crocodiles may also be taken from you at customs, as will birds, or stuffed iguanas or parrots. Both the U.S. and Mexican governments also have strict laws and guidelines about the import–export of antiquities. Check with customs beforehand if you plan to buy anything unusual or particularly valuable.

Although Cuban cigars are readily available, American visitors aren't allowed to bring them into the U.S. and will have to enjoy them while in Mexico. However, Mexico produces some fine cigars from tobacco grown in Veracruz. Mexican cigars without the correct Mexican seals on the individual cigars and on the box may be confiscated.

PUERTO VALLARTA

ZONA ROMÁNTICA

ART

Fodor'sChoice   **Gallería Dante** (✉ *Calle Basilio Badillo 269, Col. E. Zapata* ☎ *322/222–*
★   *2477*) is a 6,000-square-foot gallery (PV's largest) and sculpture garden with classical, contemporary, and abstract works by more than 50 Mexican and international artists.

BOOKS & PERIODICALS

A Page in the Sun (✉ *Calle Olas Altas 399, Col. E. Zapata* ☎ *322/222–3608*). Folks read books they've bought or traded at this outdoor café. The tomes are organized according to genre and then alphabetized by author.

SHOPPING IN SPANISH

bakery: *panadería*	**market:** *mercado*
bookseller: *librería*	**notions store:** *mercería*
candy store: *dulcería* (often sells piñatas)	**stationery store:** *papelería*
	tobacconist: *tabaquería*
florist: *florería*	**toy store:** *juguetería*
furniture store: *mueblería*	**undergarment store:** *bonetería*
grocery store: *abarrotes*	
hardware store: *ferretería*	
health-food store: *tienda naturista*	
jewelry store: *joyería*	

CERAMICS, POTTERY & TILE

Mundo de Azulejos (⊠ *Av. Venustiano Carranza 374, Col. E. Zapata* ☎ *322/222–2675* ⊕ *www.talavera-tile.com*). Buy machine-made tiles from Monterrey, painted locally, for about 60¢ each at this shop. Slightly sturdier at about $1 each are the handmade tiles. You can get mosaic tile scenes (or order your own design), a place setting for eight, hand-painted sinks, or any number of soap dishes, cups, saucers, plates, or doodads. Around the corner and run by family members, Mundo de Cristal *(⇨ below)* has more plates and tableware in the same genre.

★ **Talavera Etc.** (⊠ *Av. Ignacio L. Vallarta 266, Col. E. Zapata* ☎ *322/222–4100* ⊗ *Closed Sun.*) is the exclusive representative of the Uriarte line, the oldest maker of Talavera in Mexico (est. 1805). They also sell reproductions of tiles from Puebla churches and small gift items. Look in the book to choose made-to-order pieces. In addition to being closed on Sunday, the shop is closed during lunch and for two weeks in September.

CLOTHING

★ **La Bohemia** (⊠ *Calle Constitución, at Calle Basilio Badillo, Col. E. Zapata* ☎ *322/222–3164* ⊠ *Plaza Neptuno, Av. Francisco M. Ascencio, Km 7.5 Marina Vallarta* ☎ *322/221–2160* ⊗ *Closed Sun.*) sells elegant clothing, some of it designed by the equally elegant owner, Toody. You'll find unique jewelry, accessories, and the San Miguel shoe—the elegant yet comfortable footware designed for walking on cobblestone streets like those of San Miguel and Puerto Vallarta.

D'Paola (⊠ *Calle Basilio Badillo 258, Col. E. Zapata* ☎ *322/223–2742* ⊗ *Closed Sun.*) has a large and somewhat unusual selection of pashmina, purses, and shawls and lots of muslin clothing. It's surrounded by other interesting shops.

Etnica Boutique (⊠ *Av. Olas Altas 388, Col. E. Zapata* ☎ *322/222–6763*) has a well-edited collection of cotton and linen dresses, shawls, purses, hats, sandals, and jewelry. A few items from Indonesia are mixed in with things from different regions of Mexico and Central America.

Manta Maya (⌧ *Basilio Badillo 300, at Av. Constitución, Col. E. Zapata* ☏*322/223–5915*) has mainly white- and cream-color women's and men's clothing, with the occasional brightly colored blouse or skirt tossed in for contrast. Like its sister stores in other resort cities, this small shop has smart clothes at reasonable prices.

Mar de Sueños (⌧ *Calle Basilio Badillo 277-B, Zona Romántica, Centro* ☏*322/222–7362* ☽*Closed Sun.*) carries classy Italian threads, including the stylish La Perla brand. The selection of linen blouses and exquisitely cut linen pants is perfect for PV's sultry climate. Or choose from Lycra™ tops, sexy silk lingerie, and several lines of bathing suits. Everything is top-notch and priced accordingly.

> ### TRUE MEXICAN TALAVERA
>
> Talavera, those blue-on-white ceramics, is named for the Spanish town where it originated. Authentic Mexican Talavera is produced in Puebla and parts of Tlaxcala and Guanajuato. The glazing process follows centuries-old "recipes." Look on the back or bottom of the piece for the factory name and state of origin. Manufacturers throughout Mexico produce Talavera-style pieces, which should sell for much less.

☙ **Myskova Beachwear Boutique** (⌧ *Calle Basilio Badillo 278, Col. E. Zapata* ☏*322/222–6091*) has its own line of bikinis, plus cover-ups, nylon slacks, and some items for children (sunglasses, bathing suits, flip-flops). There's a small line of jewelry, and Brazilian flip-flops for adults in a rainbow of colors.

Fodor'sChoice **Rebeca's** (⌧ *Olas Altas 403, Col. E. Zapata* ☏*322/222–2320*), open
★ daily, has a large selection of beachwear, including shorts, pseudo-Speedos, and bathing trunks for men; and sandals and fashionable flip-flops, attractive tankinis, lots of bikinis, and a few one-piece suits for women. Most of the goods are manufactured in Mexico.

Serafina (⌧ *Calle Basilio Badillo 260, Col. E. Zapata* ☏*322/223–4594*) is the place to go for over-the-top ethnic clothing, stamped leather purses from Guadalajara and belt buckles from San Miguel, as well as clunky necklaces and bracelets of quartz, amber, and turquoise. It also sells wonderful tchotchkes.

★ **Sirenas** (⌧ *Basilio Badillo 252B, Col. E. Zapata* ☏*322/223–1925* ☽*Closed Sun.*), a sister store to Serafina, is geared to women with eclectic tastes. Creative sisters from Tamaulipas State create chic and unusual, exuberant fantasy jewelry. Colorful clutches and makeup bags made from recycled packaging are an innovation from Mexico City. At this writing, the shop is filled with tight-fitting ribbed T-shirts edged in sequins and an assortment of ethnically inspired yet edgy and contemporary blouses and skirts from Indonesia and elsewhere.

FOLK ART & CRAFTS

★ **Lucy's CuCú Cabana** (⌧ *Calle Basilio Badillo 295, Col. E. Zapata* ☏*322/222–1220*). Here you can shop for inexpensive, one-of-a-kind folk art from Guerrero, Michoacán, Oaxaca, and elsewhere. Note that Lucy closes during lunch, on Sunday, and September through mid-October.

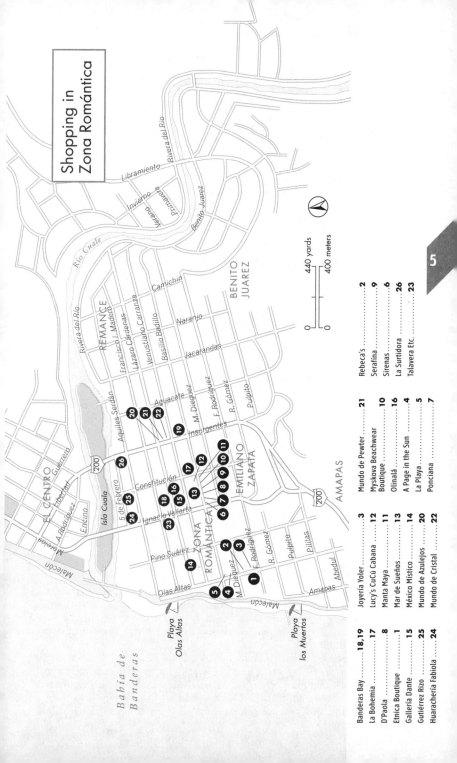

Shopping in Zona Romántica

México Místico (⊠ *Lazaro Cardenas 175, Col. E. Zapata* ☎ *322/223–1021*), across from Plaza Lázaro Cárdenas, sells custom or ready-made stained glass with traditional motifs such as hummingbirds, bearded irises, lighthouses, and angelfish; or less-traditional motifs, such as the Harley-Davidson logo.
Mundo de Cristal (⊠ *Av. Insurgentes 333, at Calle Basilio Badillo, Col. E. Zapata* ☎ *322/222–1426* ⊘ *Closed Sun. and Sat. afternoon*). Come for the glassware from

EXPAT HUMOR

The co-owner of Lucy's CuCú Cabana is Gil Gevens, who writes quirky epistles, often at his own expense, or the expense of other expats, about life in Puerto Vallarta. Gil writes regularly for the weekly English-language paper *Puerto Vallarta Tribune*, and you can buy his tongue-in-cheek books around town or at Lucy's.

Jalisco and Guanajuato states in sets or individually. Also available are Talavera place settings and individual platters, pitchers, and decorative pieces. Look in the back of the store for high-quality ceramics with realistic portrayals of fruits and flowers. You can have your purchase packed, but shipping is left to you.

Mundo de Pewter (⊠ *Av. Venustiano Carranza 358, Col. E. Zapata* ☎ *322/222–0503*). Relatives of the owners of Mundo de Cristal and Mundo de Azulejos *(➪ above)* own this shop, which is wedged in between the other two stores. Attractive, lead-free items in modern and traditional designs are sold here at reasonable prices. The practical, tarnish-free pieces can go from stovetop or oven to the dining table and be no worse for wear.

Olinalá (⊠ *Av. Lázaro Cárdenas 274, Col. E. Zapata* ☎ *322/222–4995 or 322/228–0659* ⊘ *Closed Sun. and Sept.and Oct.*) sells mainly painted ceremonial masks and a limited selection of other folk art from throughout Mexico.

GROCERY STORE

Gutiérrez Rizo (⊠ *Av. Constitución 136, between 5 de Febrero and Aquiles Serdan, Col. E. Zapata* ☎ *322/222–1367*). The most convenient market to the Romantic Zone has an ample liquor section, American-brand cereals, canned food, condiments, good produce, and ground-to-order coffee.

HOME FURNISHINGS

★ **Banderas Bay** (⊠ *Lázaro Cárdenas 263, Col. E. Zapata* ☎ *322/223–4352* ⊠ *Constitución 319A, Col. E. Zapata* ☎ *322/223–9871* ⊘ *Closed Sun.*). The American owners, who also own Daiquiri Dick's restaurant *(➪ Chapter 3)*, travel around the country for months in search of antiques, collectibles, handicrafts, and unique household items. About two-thirds of the merchandise is new. The shop, will pack and ship your purchases.

Ponciana (⊠ *Basilio Badillo 252–A, Col. E. Zapata* ☎ *322/222–2988*) has things you won't find at all the other stores, like porcelain replicas of antique dolls. The "antique" cupboards may have only original doors, but that's a common practice. Other antiques, perhaps an old reliquary, are transformed into wall art. You can also find tablecloths and placemats from Micho-acán, place settings, arty statuettes, matchboxes decorated with Frida Kahlo and Mexican movie themes, and other decorative items.

JEWELRY

Joyería Yoler (⊠*Calle Olas Altas
★ 391, Col. E. Zapata* ☎*322/222–
8713 or 322/222–9051*). Manager Ramon Cruz proudly shows off the store's collection of the Los Castillo family's silver jewelry made with lost-wax casting as well as hammering and burnishing techniques, small silver pitchers with lapis lazuli dragonfly handles, napkin rings, abalone pillboxes, and other lovely utilitarian pieces. The merchandise—which includes an extensive yet not overwhelming array of silver and semi-precious-stone jewelry—is nicely arranged in the ample shop.

> ## ALL THAT GLITTERS ISN'T SILVER
>
> There's a great selection of Mexican silver in PV, but watch out for "German silver" (aka *alpaca* or *chapa*): an alloy of iron, zinc, and nickel. Real silver is weightier, and is marked "925" (indicating a silver content of at least 92.5%) for sterling and "950" (at least 95% silver content) for finer pieces. When size permits, the manufacturer's name and the word "Mexico" should also appear.

LEATHER, SHOES & HANDBAGS

★ **Huarachería Fabiola** (⊠*Av. Ignacio L. Vallarta 145, Col. E. Zapata* ☎*322/222–9154*). Longtime visitors to Puerto Vallarta will remember this shop. Buy huaraches off the rack or order custom sandals for men or women. Most styles can be made in one to three days. Credit cards are not accepted.

EL CENTRO & ENVIRONS

ART

★ **Galería Arte Latinoamericana** (⊠*Calle Josefa O. de Domínguez 155, Centro* ☎*322/222–4406* ⊘*Closed Sun.*) sells contemporary art, primarily paintings. There are representative Indian portraits by Marta Gilbert and chunky village scenes—a cross between the Flintstones and Chagall—by Celeste Acevedo.

Galería Corona (⊠*Calle Corona 164, Centro* ☎*322/222–4210* ⊕*www. galeria-corona.com* ⊘*Closed Sun.*) is a small shop with some sculpture and art jewelry as well as etherial and painterly portraits and landscapes in various genres.

Galería 8 y Más (⊠*Calle Miramar 237, Centro* ☎*322/222–7971* ⊕*www.artismexico.com* ⊘*Closed Sun.*) started with eight Guadalajara artists and has expanded under new ownership to 45 artists from or residing in Jalisco. The large old building has glass, bronze, chalk, and oil paintings.

Galería Pacífico (⊠*Calle Aldama 174, Centro* ☎*322/222–1982* ⊕*www. galeriapacifico.com*), open since 1987, features the sculpture of Ramiz Barquet, who created the bronze *Nostalgia* piece on the malecón. Brewster Brockmann paints contemporary abstracts; Marco Alvarez, Alejandro Mondria, and Alfredo Langarica are other featured artists. The gallery is a resale specialist for the amazing representational work of the late Patrick Denoun, who died in a motorcycle accident in 2007.

Galería Uno (⊠ *Calle Morelos 561, Centro* ☎*322/222–0908*).You'll find wonderful, varied art in many mediums here. Owners Jan Lavender and Martina Goldberg love to showcase local talent, and during the season host individual shows that change up to three times a month. National and international artists represented include João Rodriguez, Esaú Andrade, and Daniel Palmer.

Galería Vallarta (⊠ *Av. Juárez 265, Centro* ☎*322/222–0290* ⊕*www. galeriavallarta.com*) is notable since, in addition to a large cadre of fine artists showing watercolors, oils, mixed media, and sculptures of bronze, wood, and ceramics, it has a comprehensive collection of lithographs and art prints, from the likes of Frida Kahlo and Diego Rivera to contemporaries such as Marta Gilbert. That it's open Sunday is a big plus.

Octavio Arte en Bronce (⊠ *Calle 21 de Marzo 1181, Col. Coapinole* ☎*322/229–1355* ⊕*www.octavioarteenbronce.com*). The artist who created the whale sculpture at the entrance to Marina Vallarta produces mainly monumental, ocean-theme statues. The lifelike bronze whales, dolphins, sea turtles, and sea lions range from table or desk size, on a wooden base, to larger, free-standing garden or patio models. The workshop is open weekdays 8 to 7 and Saturday 9 to 4, but it's still best to call ahead. The artist speaks excellent English and will sometimes show clients around the place.

Sergio Bustamante (⊠ *Av. Juárez 275, Centro* ☎*322/223–1405* ⊠*Paseo Díaz Ordáz 716, Centro* ☎*322/222–5480* ⊕*www.sergio bustamante.com.mx*) Internationally known Sergio Bustamante—the creator of life-size brass, copper, and ceramic animals, mermaids, suns, and moons—has a team of artisans to execute his never-ending pantheon of creative and quirky objets d'art, such as pots shaped like human torsos that sell for more than US$1,000. Paintings and jewelry are sold here as well.

BOOKS & PERIODICALS

Librería Guadalajara (⊠ *Plaza Genovesa, Av. Francisco M. Ascencio Local L4, Zona Hotelera* ☎*322/224–9084*) sells books in English and Spanish, and educational toys. Short hours on Sunday (10 to 2).

CERAMICS, POTTERY & TILE

Alfarería Tlaquepaque (⊠ *Av. México 1100, Col. 5 de diciembre* ☎*322/223–2121*) is a large store with a ton of red-clay items traditional to the area—in fact, their predecessors were crafted before the 1st century AD. Most of the merchandise, however, is tourist-quality at best.

Galería de Ollas (⊠ *Calle Corona 176, Centro* ☎*322/223–1045* ⊕*www.galeriadeollas.com*).The 300 or so potters from the village of Juan Mata Ortiz add their touches to the intensely—sometimes hypnotically—geometric designs of their ancestors from Paquimé. At this shop pieces range from about $60 to $10,000, with an average of about $400. Stop in during artWalk, or have a look at their great Web site.

■TIP→ Before you buy rustic ceramic plates, bowls, and cups, ask if there's lead in the glaze, unless you plan to use them for decoration only and not for food service.

★ **Majolica Antica** (⊠*Calle Corona 191, Centro* ☎*322/222–5118* ☉*Closed Sun.*) sells just that, which, according to knowledgeable shop owner Antonio Cordero, is also called Talavera or tin-glazed pottery. You get a certificate of origin with each piece of beautiful ornamental tile, utilitarian pitcher, plate, or place setting. It's open until 5 PM during the week and until 3 PM on Saturday.

CIGARS

La Casa del Habano (⊠*Aldama 170, Centro* ☎*322/223–2758* ☉*Closed Sun.*) sells only Cuban cigars, starting at $3.50 each and topping out at $44 for a Cohiba Millenium 2000. You can smoke your stogey downstairs in the casual lounge while sipping coffee or a shot of liquor.

■TIP→ If you're bringing any Mexican cigars back to the States, make sure they have the correct Mexican seals on both the individual cigars and on the box. Otherwise, they may be confiscated.

CLOTHING

Oahu (⊠*Calle Juárez 314, Centro* ☎*322/223–1058*) has men's surf and casual wear, including well-made flip-flops, high-quality T-shirts, as well as pint-size Hawaiian shirts for children. In fact, this is one of the best places to shop for children's casual wear and for water gear like board shorts and rash guards.

La Surtidora (⊠*Morelos 256, at Guerrero, Centro* ☎*322/222–1439*) (⊠*Av. 5 de Febrero at Insurgentes, Col. E. Zapata* ☎*322/222–0355*). This long-established shop has men's and women's clothing. The location near the bridge in Colonia E. Zapata has the larger selection. At first glance the items seem mainly matronly, but plowing through the racks will unearth fashionable cocktail dresses, trendy tops and T-shirts, plus men's guayaberas and slacks. Also at that location are shoes (high heels to flip-flops) and children's clothing.

DEPARTMENT STORE

LANS (⊠*Calle Juárez 867, at Pípila, Centro* ☎*322/226–9100* ⊠*Plaza Caracol, near Gigante supermarket, Blvd. Francisco M. Ascencio 2216, Zona Hotelera* ☎*322/226–0204*) is a multilevel department store with clothing for men, women, and children: look for Perry Ellis khakis, Levi's, Lee, and Dockers shirts and trousers, and jeans from Colombia. The store also sells housewares; purses and Swatch watches; Samsonite luggage; ladies' perfume and makeup (Chanel, Gucci, Estée Lauder); and men's undies.

FOLK ART & CRAFTS

Alas de Aguila (⊠*Av. Juárez 547, at Calle Corona, Centro* ☎*322/222–4039* ☉*Closed Sun.*). In addition to pewter there's a wide selection of Talavera-style objects—from soap holders and liquid soap dispensers to pitchers, platters, and picture frames—in a variety of patterns. Quality is middle-of-the-road; prices are excellent.

Galería Indígena (⊠*Av. Juárez 628, Centro* ☎*322/223–0800*) has an assortment of handicrafts: Huichol yarn paintings and beaded bowls

Shopping in and around El Centro

TO
NUEVO VALLARTA,
MARINA VALLARTA
AND AIRPORT

55 · 61

COL. 5 DE
DICIEMBRE

Paraguay

200

Chile

54

Venezuela

Argentina

Langarica

Bahía de
Banderas

Playa
Camarones

31 de Octubre

Malecón

200

53

52

51

Allende

Pipila

EL CENTRO

L. Vicario

49

50

J. O. de Domínguez

Paseo Díaz Ordaz

Morelos

47

Abasolo

46

48

42

43

44

45

Aldama

38

39

41

Corona

40

37

Galeana

Malecón

Mina

Juárez

Hidalgo

Matamoros

Miramar

E. Carranza

Palacio
Municipal

35

Iglesia de
Nuestra
Señora de
Guadalupe

36

Farol

E. Iturbide

33

31

34

Guerrero

Zaragoza

30

Morelos

Libertad

32

A. Rodríguez

29

28

Río Cuale

Isla Cuale

27

Río Cuale

ZONA
ROMÁNTICA

5 de Febrero

Constitución

Aquiles Serdán

Insurgentes

Francisco I. Madero

Jacarandas

I. Vallarta

Aguacate

200

0   440 yards

0   400 meters

EMILIANO ZAPATA

and statuettes, real Talavera ceramics from Puebla, decorative pieces in painted wood, and many other items.

El Instituto de la Artesanía Jalisciense (⊠*Calle Juárez 284, Centro* ☎*322/222–1301*) promotes Jalisco State's handicrafts, selling burnished clay bowls signed by the artist, blown glass, plates and bowls from Tonalá, and other items at fair prices. That said, Bustamante knockoffs and Huichol pieces in less-than-traditional themes (smiley faces not being one of the Huichols' typical motifs) are indications that quality is slipping. Still, there's a representative sampling of the state's ceramics, blue and red glassware, and *barro bruñido*: clay pieces finished by burnishing only. It's catercorner from La Plaza de Armas, and is open 9 to 9 daily.

Querubines (⊠*Av. Juárez 501–A, at Calle Galeana, Centro* ☎*322/223–1727*) has woven goods from Guatemala and southern Mexico, including tablecloths, napkins, placemats, and *rebozos* (stoles) made of rayon, silk, and cotton. The shop is in an old house that once belonged to Jesús Langarica, PV's first mayor. The structure's stone, cement, and brick floors make interesting backdrops for painted gourds from Michoacán, carved gourds from the Costa Chica (northern Oaxaca coast), and Talavera pottery.

GROCERY STORE

AgroGourmet (⊠*Blvd. Francisco M. Ascencio 2820, Zona Hotelera* ☎*322/221–2656* ⊠*Calle Róbalo 79, Col. Corral del Risco, Punta de Mita* ☎*329/291–6721*). If you crave country-style Texas sausage and other comfort foods from north of the border, try this store. You can find oils (sesame, grapeseed, nut, virgin olive), locally made pastas, homemade spaghetti sauce, lox, real maple syrup, and agave "nectar." A nice gift is the Mexican vanilla, in blown-glass containers.

JEWELRY

Alberto's (⊠*Av. Juárez 185, Centro* ☎*322/222–8317* ⊙*Closed Sun.*) The jewelers here, family to jewelers of the same surname in Zihuatanejo, are happy to explain, in English, which pieces carry authentic stones and which are composites or synthetics. Prices are reasonable.

Jades Maya (⊠*Leona Vicario 226–A, Centro* ☎*322/222–0371* ⊕*www.jadesmaya.com*). You can spend as little as $5 or as much as $5,000 on anything and everything jade here. The shop is open daily until 10 PM in high season. In addition to jewelry made from the 20 different colors of jade, there are replicas of ancient Mayan masks.

Joyería El Opalo (⊠*Local 13–A, Plaza Genovesa, Col. Las Glorias* ☎*322/224–6584*), a bright spot in a nearly abandoned mall, has managed to remain afloat through its cruise ship contacts. Silver jewelry ranges in price from $3 per gram for simpler pieces to $$30 a gram for the lighter, finer quality and more complex pieces. There's high-grade "950" silver jewelry in addition to the usual 0.925 sterling silver, and gold settings as well. Most of the semi-precious stones—amethyst, topaz, malachite, black onyx, and opal in 28 colors—are of Mexican origin. The diamond-cut necklaces are magnificent.

Joyas Finas Suneson (⊠*Calle Morelos 593, Centro* ☎*322/222–5715* ⊙*Closed Sun.*) specializes in silver jewelry and objets d'art by some

Continued on page 131

The intricately woven and beaded designs of the Huichols' art are as vibrant and fascinating as the traditions of its people, best known as the "Peyote People" for their traditional and ceremonial use of the hallucinogenic drug. Peyote-inspired visions are thought to be messages from God and are reflected in the art.

THE ART OF THE HUICHOL

Like the Lacandon Maya, the Huichol resisted assimilation by Spanish invaders, fleeing to inhospitable mountains and remote valleys. There they retained their pantheistic religion in which shamans lead the community in spiritual matters and the use of peyote facilitates communication directly with God.

Huichol is pronounced wee-CHOL; the people's name for themselves, however, is Wirarika (we-RAH-ri-ka), which means "healer."

Roads didn't reach larger Huichol communities until the mid-20th century, bringing electricity and other modern distractions. The collision with the outside world has had pros and cons, but art lovers have only benefited from their increased access to intricately patterned woven and beaded goods. Today the traditional souls that remain on the land—a significant population of perhaps 6,000 to 8,000—still create votive bowls, prayer arrows, jewelry, and bags, and sell them to finance elaborate religious ceremonies. The pieces go for as little as $5 or as much as $5,000, depending on the skill and fame of the artist and quality of materials.

Bead-covered
wooden statuette

UNDERSTANDING THE HUICHOL

When Spanish conquistadors arrived in the early 16th century, the Huichol, unwilling to work as slaves on the haciendas of the Spanish or to adopt their religion, fled to hard-to reach mountains and valleys of the Sierra Madre. They lived there, disconnected from society, for nearly 500 years. Beginning in the 1970s, roads and electricity made their way to tiny Huichol towns. The reintroduction to society has come at a high price: at least one ill-advised government project encouraged Huichol farmers to sell their land, and with it, their traditional lifestyle, in favor of a city existence. Today, about half of the population of perhaps 12,000 continues to live in ancestral villages and *rancheritas* (tiny individual farms).

THE POWER OF PRAYER

Spirituality and prayer infuse every aspect of Huichol life. They believe that without their prayers and offerings the sun wouldn't rise, the earth would cease spinning. It is hard, then, for them to reconcile their poverty with the relative easy living of "free-riders" (Huichol term for nonspiritual freeloaders) who enjoy fine cars and expensive houses thanks to the Huichols efforts to sustain the planet. But rather than hold our reckless materialism against us, the Huichol add us to their prayers.

Huichol yarn artist at work

THE PEYOTE PEOPLE

Visions inspired by the hallucinogenic peyote plant are considered by the Huichol to be messages from God, and to help in solving personal and communal problems. Indirectly, they provide inspiration for their almost psychedelic art. Just a generation or two ago, annual peyote-gathering pilgrimages were done on foot. Today the journey is still a man's chief obligation, but they now drive to the holy site at Wiricuta, in San Luis Potosi State. Peyote collected is used by the entire community—men, women, and children—throughout the year.

SHAMANISM

A Huichol man has a lifelong calling as a shaman. There are two shamanic paths: the path of the wolf, which is more aggressive, demanding, and powerful (wolf shamans profess the ability to morph into wolves); and the path of the deer, which is playful—even clownish—and less inclined to prove his power. A shaman chooses his own path.

Huichol craftsmen, Cabo San Lucas

SMART SHOPPING TIPS

Huichol art, sun face

of color. Beads should fit together tightly in straight lines, with no gaps.

YARN "PAINTINGS": Symmetry is not necessary, although there should be an overall sense of unity. Thinner thread results in finer, more costly work. Look for tightness, with no visible gaps or broken threads. Paintings should have a stamp of authenticity on the back, including artist's name and tribal affiliation.

BEADED ITEMS: The smaller the beads, the more delicate and expensive the piece. Beads with larger holes are fine for stringed work, but if used in bowls and statuettes cheapen the piece. Items made with iridescent beads from Japan are the priciest. Look for good-quality glass beads, definition, symmetry, and artful use

PRAYER ARROWS: Collectors and purists should look for the traditionally made arrows of brazilwood inserted into a bamboo shaft. The most interesting ones contain embroidery work, or tiny carved icons, or are painted with copal symbols indicative of their original, intended purpose, for example protecting a child or ensuring a successful corn crop.

WHERE TO SHOP

SUPPORTING HUICHOL TRADITIONS

Families that continue to work the land may dedicate a few hours a day to crafts, working to maintain their ceremonies, not to pay the cable bill. Buying directly from them can ensure a higher degree of artistry: the Huichol who make art to supplement farming work more slowly and with less pressure than their city-dwelling brethren. Shopping at stores like Peyote People and Hikuri supports artisans who live in their ancestral villages and practice the ancient traditions.

Peyote People treats the Huichol as a people, not a product. At their downtown Vallarta shop, the owners—a Mexican-Canadian couple—are happy to share with customers their wealth

of info about Huichol art and culture. They work with just a few farming families, providing all the materials and then paying for the finished product. ⊠ *Calle Juárez 222, Centro* ☎ *322/222–2303.*

Hikuri At the north end of Banderas Bay, is run by a British couple that pays asking prices to their Huichol suppliers and employs indigenous men in the adjoining carpentry and screen-printing shops. The men initially have little or no experience, and the jobs give them a leg up to move on to more profitable work. The excellent inventory includes fine yarn paintings. ⊠ *Calle Coral 66A, La Cruz de Huanacaxtle* ☎ *329/295–5071.*

The Huichol Collection Native artisans working on crafts and wearing their stunning and colorful clothing draw customers in. The shop has an excellent inventory, with some museum-quality pieces. Though the merchandise is genuine, the shop is also venue for timeshare sales— albeit with a soft sales pitch. ⊠ *Paseo Diaz Ordaz 732, Centro* ☎ *322/223–0661* ⊠ *Morelos 490, Centro* ☎ *322/223–2141.*

Galería Huichol sells yarn paintings, beaded bowls and statuettes, and some smaller items like beaded jewelry and Christmas ornaments. ⊠ *Paradise Plaza, 2nd fl., Nuevo Vallarta* ☎ *322/297–0342*

TRADITION TRANSFORMED

The art of the Huichol was, for centuries, made from undyed wool, shells, stones, and other natural materials. It was not until the 1970s that the Huichol began incorporating bright, zingy colors, without sacrificing the intricate patterns and symbols used for centuries. The result is strenuously colorful, yet dignified.

YARN PAINTINGS
Dramatic and vivid yarn paintings are highly symbolic, stylized visions of life.

VOTIVE BOWLS
Ceremonious votive bowls, made from gourds, are decorated with bright, stylized beadwork.

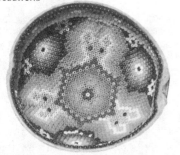

MASKS AND ANIMAL STATUETTES
Bead-covered wooden or ceramic masks and animal statuettes are other adaptations made for outsiders.

PRAYER ARROWS
Made for every ceremony, prayer arrows send petitions winging to God.

WOVEN SHOULDER BAGS
Carried by men, the bags are decorated with traditional Huichol icons.

For years, Huichol men as well as women wore **BEADED BRACELETS**; today earrings and necklaces are also made.

Diamond-shape **GOD'S EYES** of sticks and yarn protect children from harm.

HOW TO READ THE SYMBOLS

Spiders that come out at dawn are thought to welcome the rising sun.

The deer is the animal manifestation of the god Kahumari, who intercedes in heaven on earthlings' behalf.

Anything with horns or antlers symbolizes communion and oneness with God.

Yarn painting

■ The trilogy of corn, peyote, and deer represents three aspects of God. According to Huichol mythology, peyote sprang up in the footprints of the deer. Depicted like stylized flowers, peyote represents communication with God. Corn, the Huichol's

Corn symbol

staple food, symbolizes health and prosperity. An image drawn inside the root ball depicts the essence of God within it.

■ The double-headed eagle is the emblem of the omnipresent sky god.

Peyote

■ A nierika is a portal between the spirit world and our own. Often in the form of a yarn painting, a nierika can be round or square.

■ Salamanders and turtles are associated with rain; the former provoke the clouds. Turtles maintain underground springs and purify water.

■ A scorpion is the soldier of the sun.

Scorpion

■ The Huichol depict raindrops as tiny snakes; in yarn paintings they descend to enrich the fields.

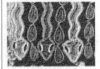

Snakes

Jose Beníctez Sánchez, (1938—) may be the elder statesman of yarn painters and has shown in Japan, Spain, the U.S., and at the Museum of Modern Art in Mexico City. His paintings sell for upward of $3,000 a piece.

of Mexico's finest designers. Most pieces have modern rather than traditional motifs, and designs are creative and unusual.

LEATHER, SHOES & HANDBAGS

★ **Rolling Stone** (⊠ *Paseo Diaz Ordáz 802, Centro* ☎ *322/223–1769*) is good for custom-made boots, sandals, and shoes (or off the rack) in a wide variety of leathers.

MALL

Plaza Caracol (⊠ *Blvd. Federico M. Ascencio, Km 2.5, Zona Hotelera across from Fiesta Americana hotel* ☎ *322/224–3239*), aka Gigante Plaza, is lively and full on weekends and evenings, even when others are dead. Its anchors are the Gigante supermarket and the adjacent LANS department store. Surrounding these are tiny stores dispensing electronics and ice cream, fresh flowers, manicures, and inexpensive haircuts. Adding to the commercial center's appeal is the sixplex movie theater.

MARKETS

Mercado de Artesanías (⊠ *Calle Agustín Rodríguez, between Calles Matamoros and Miramar, at base of bridge* ☎ *No phone*). Flowers, piñatas, produce, and plastics share space in indoor and outdoor stands with souvenirs and lesser-quality crafts. Upstairs, locals eat at long-established, family-run restaurants.

Mercado Isla Río Cuale (⊠ *Dividing El Centro from Colonia E. Zapata, access at Calle Morelos, Calle I. Vallarta, Calle Matamoros, Calle Constitución, Calle Libertad, Av. Insurgentes, and the malecón* ☎ *No phone*). Small shops and outdoor market stalls sell an interesting mix of wares at this informal and fun market. Harley-Davidson kerchiefs, Che paintings on velvet, and Madonna icons compete with the usual synthetic lace tablecloths, shell and quartz necklaces, and silver jewelry amid postcards and key chains. The market is partially shaded by enormous fig and rubber trees and serenaded by the rushing river; a half dozen cafés and restaurants provide sustenance.

WINE, BEER & SPIRITS

Anfitrión de México (⊠ *Calle Guerrero 278–A, Centro* ☎ *322/222–8130*) Here Argentine sommelier Cecilia Cabrera deals mainly with restaurants and hotels, but will also recommend and sell to the public wines imported from Chile, Argentina, France, Australia, and elsewhere.

La Playa (⊠ *Blvd. Francisco M. Ascencio, Km 1.5, Zona Hotelera ⊕ across from IMSS [Mexican Social Security Agency]* ☎ *322/224–7130* ⊠ *Calle Morelos at Calle Pípila, Centro* ☎ *322/223–1818* ⊠ *Olas Altas 246 at Basilio Badillo, Col. E. Zapata* ☎ *322/222–5304*) has tequila; wines from Chile, California (Gallo), and Spain; imported vodka and other spirits; and the cheapest beer around.

DO WEAR THEM OUT

Huaraches are woven leather sandals that seem to last several lifetimes. Traditionally worn by peasants, they're now sold by fewer shops, but in a slightly larger assortment of styles. Once broken in—and that takes a while—this classic, sturdy footwear will be a worthwhile addition to your closet.

5

MARINA VALLARTA

ART

Galería Em (✉ *Blvd. Francisco M. Ascencio 2758, entrance to Marina Vallarta* ☎ *322/221–1728 or 322/221–2856* ✉ *Las Palmas II, Local 17, Marina Vallarta* ☎ *322/221–2228*) sells art glass, stained glass, glass sculpture, and jewelry made of glass. You can commission a piece, or watch the artisans work at the shop on Blvd. Federico M. Ascencio.

BOOKS & PERIODICALS

Seven Deli (✉ *Plaza Marina, 2 doors down from McDonald's, Marina Vallarta* ☎ *322/221–0177*) has the New York Times and USA Today as well as *Cosmo, GQ, Vogue, People, Marie Claire,* and many other monthlies in English, along with many Spanish-language magazines.

CLOTHING

Boutique Osiris (✉ *Plaza Marina, Local F–6, Marina Vallarta* ☎ *322/221–0732*). The inventory may wax and wane a bit, but at its best has a nice selection of simple gauze, cotton, and linen clothing for day or evening wear, although it's more practical than formal or fancy.

Caprichoso (✉ *Plaza Neptuno, Av. Federico M. Ascencio, Km 7.5, Marina Vallarta* ☎ *322/221–3067*) sells sizes from XS to 2X. This is the only store in PV to stock the Oh My Gauze line of women's resort wear, and also sells Dunes, Juanita Banana, and unusual clothing by Chalí, with cut-out, painted flowers. Most of the inventory is cotton, including a smaller selection of clothing for men.

♻ **Gecko** (✉ *Condominios Puesto del Sol, Marina Vallarta* ☎ *322/221–2165*) is the place to go for beach togs for kids and teens. The selection of any one type of item isn't large, but there are bikinis, sunglasses, flip-flops, nice ball caps, and T-shirts. Board shorts and rash guards are stocked for surfers and wannabes.

★ **María de Guadalajara** (✉ *Puesta del Sol condominiums, Local 15–A, Marina, Marina Vallarta* ☎ *322/221–2566* ✉ *Calle Morelos 550, Centro* ☎ *322/222–2387* ⊕ *www.mariadeguadalajara.com*) has inspired jewelry and a fabulous line of women's cotton clothing. It's DIY chic here: you choose the colorful triangular sash of your liking, miraculously transforming pretty-but-baggy dresses into flattering and stylish frocks. The color palette is truly inspired. The selection for men is limited.

DEPARTMENT STORE

Liverpool (✉ *Av. Francisco M. Ascencio 2920, Plaza Galerías Marina Vallarta* ☎ *322/226–2200*). Vallartans are giddy about this department store anchoring 73,000 square feet of shopping on two floors at Plaza Galerías. The store sells everything from sporting goods to clothing, housewares, and more. There are two escalators, a restaurant, underground parking, a 12-plex cinema, and fast-food court with the ubiquitous McDonald's, Dominos Pizza, Chili's, and Starbucks.

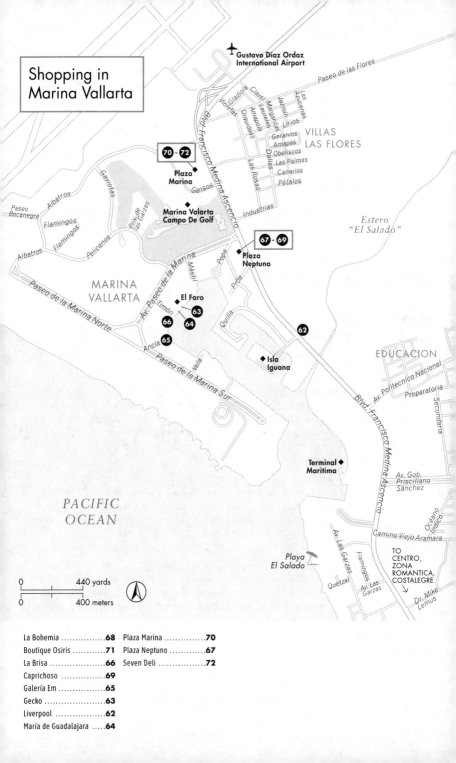

Shopping in Marina Vallarta

✈ **Gustavo Díaz Ordaz International Airport**

Paseo de las Flores

Gladiola
Clavel
Violetas
Amapola
Orquídeas
Margaritas
Laureles
Jazmín
Las Azucenas

Lirios
Geranios
Amapas
Obeliscos
Dalias
Las Palmas
Canarios
Pétalos

Las Rosas

VILLAS LAS FLORES

70 - 72

◆ **Plaza Marina**

Gansos

◆ **Marina Valarta Campo De Golf**

Industrias

Estero "El Salado"

Paseo Bocanegra

Albatros

Flamingos

Gaviotas

Prlv. de las Garzas

Flamingos

Albatros

Pelícanos

67 - 69

◆ **Plaza Neptuno**

Mástil

Popa

MARINA VALLARTA

Av. Paseo de la Marina

Proa

Timón

◆ **El Faro**

63

66

64

65

Ancla

Quilla

62

EDUCACION

Av. Politecnico Nacional

Preparatoria

Secundaria

Paseo de la Marina Norte

Vela

Paseo de la Marina Sur

◆ **Isla Iguana**

Blvd. Francisco Medina Ascencio

Blvd. Francisco Medina Ascencio

Av. Gob. Prisciliano Sánchez

◆ **Terminal Maritima**

PACIFIC OCEAN

Océano Índico

Camino Viejo Aramara

Av. Las Garzas

Flamingos

Quetzal

Av. Las Garzas

TO CENTRO, ZONA ROMANTICA, COSTALEGRE ↓

Dr. Mike Lemus

☂ *Playa El Salado*

```
0        440 yards
0        400 meters
```

JEWELRY

La Brisa (⊠ *Condominios Puesta del Sol, Local 11–B, Marina Vallarta* ☎ *322/221–2516*) is one of several silver stores owned by the same family. All have fair prices and no pressure; this one also has Talavera pottery for sale.

MALLS

Plaza Marina (⊠ *Carretera al Aeropuerto, Km 8, Marina Vallarta* ☎ *322/221–0490*), one long block north of Plaza Neptuno, has ATMs, dry cleaning, photo developing, a pharmacy, a café, Internet café, several bars, as well as numerous shops. The mall is anchored by the Comercial Mexicana supermarket. **Plaza Neptuno** (⊠ *Carretera al Aeropuerto, Km 7.5, Marina Vallarta* ☎ *No phone*) is a small mall in the heart of the marina district with a number of fine-home-furnishing shops, several classy clothing boutiques, and just behind it, a few good, casual restaurants.

NORTH OF PUERTO VALLARTA

NUEVO VALLARTA

CLOTHING

★ **D'Paola** (⊠ *Paradise Plaza, Local 11., Nuevo Vallarta* ☎ *322/297– 1030*) has dressier dresses and casual, unique resort wear in linen and cotton.

Ruly's Boutique (⊠ *Paradise Plaza, Local 10, Paseo de los Cocoteros 85 Sur, Nuevo Vallarta* ☎ *322/297–1724*) sells choice men's clothing. They have nice trousers, shirts, and shorts in a wide selection of handsome yet vibrant colors, as well as accessories, underwear, hats, and so on. The owner of Ruly's designs the clothing sold here and supervises its construction.

FOLK ART

La Aldaba (⊠ *Paradise Plaza, 2nd fl., Nuevo Vallarta* ☎ *322/297–0903*) has an interesting collection of gifts and small decorative items and housewares: Bustamante-inspired cat and moon candles, subtly painted sheet metal candleholders and wall art, and glass vases.

MALL

Paradise Plaza (⊠ *Paseo de los Cocoteros 85 Sur, Nuevo Vallarta* ☎ *322/226–6770*) is the most comprehensive plaza north of Marina Vallarta, with a food court, grocery store, several coffee and juice shops, Internet café, clothing and handicraft boutiques, and a bank, but no movie theater.

BUCERÍAS

BOOKS & PERIODICALS

Gringo's Books & Coffee (⊠ *Calle Morelos 7–A, Bucerías* ☎ *329/298–1767* ☉ *Closed Sun.*) sells novels a-go-go, including lots of beach reading.

FOLK ART
Jan Marie's Boutique (⊠ *Lázaro Cárdenas 56, Bucerías* ☎*329/298–0303*) has pottery, small housewares, tin frames sporting Botero-style fat ladies, and other gifts—the classy selection of Talavera pottery is both decorative and utilitarian. This is not the place for bargain hunters.

GROCERY STORES
Frutería Chabacano (⊠ *Calle Hidalgo 15, Bucerías* ☎*329/298–0692*) has the freshest fruits and vegetables in town. (Closed after 3 PM daily, and after 1 PM on Sunday.)
Super La Peque (⊠ *Morelos 7, Bucerías* ☎*329/298–0598*) has wine, liquor, cleaning supplies, junk food, and fresh fruit.

SAYULITA

BOOKS & PERIODICALS
Librería Sayulita (⊠ *Calle Manuel Navarrete 3, Sayulita* ☎*329/291–3382*) has new books in Spanish, used paperbacks in English, and magazines.

FOLK ART
★ **La Hamaca** (⊠ *Calle Revolución 110, Sayulita* ☎*329/291–3039*) has a wonderful inventory of folk art and utilitarian handicrafts; each piece is unique. Scoop up masks and pottery from Michoacán, textiles and shawls from Guatemala, hammocks from the Yucatán, and lacquered boxes from Olinalá. The store is open daily 9 to 9.

GROCERY STORE
Mi Tiendita (⊠ *Calle Marlin 44–A, Sayulita* ☎*329/291–3145*) sells deli sandwiches and groceries, as well as wine and beer.

SAN FRANCISCO

FOLK ART
Galería Corazón (⊠ *Av. América Latina 1, at Av. Tercer Mundo, San Pancho* ☎*311/258–4170*) specializes in high-end arts and crafts from Mexico. Hours are Tues.–Sat. noon–7 PM. Note, though, that it's closed mid-May through October.

GROCERY STORE
El Indio (⊠ *Av. América Latina 23 at Av. Mexico, San Pancho* ☎*311/258–4010*) is the most convenient place in San Pancho to get liquor, wine, milk, water, and other necessities.

HOME FURNISHINGS
Anthony Chetwynd Collection (⊠ *Calle Las Palmas 130, Col. Costa Azul, San Francisco* ☎ *311/258–4407*). The flamboyant, displaced Brit and owner travels to estates and villages all over Mexico to stock his antiques shop. About half the inventory is antique masks, chandeliers, reliquaries … whatever he can get his hands on. The rest are copies of the same, and some furnishings and housewares imported from Asia.

One Man's Metal

In less than a decade after William Spratling arrived in the mining town of Taxco—275 mi (170 km) north of Acapulco—he had transformed it into a flourishing silver center, the likes of which had not been seen since colonial times. In 1929 the writer-architect from New Orleans settled in the then-sleepy, dusty village because it was inexpensive and close to the pre-Hispanic Mexcala culture that he was studying in Guerrero Valley.

In Taxco—Mexico's premier "Silver City"—marvelously preserved white-stucco, red-tile-roof colonial buildings hug cobblestone streets that wind up and down the foothills of the Sierra Madre. Taxco (pronounced tahss-ko) is a living work of art. For centuries its silver mines drew foreign mining companies. In 1928 the government made it a national monument.

For hundreds of years Taxco's silver was made into bars and exported overseas. No one even considered developing a local jewelry industry. Journeying to a nearby town, Spratling hired a couple of goldsmiths and commissioned them to create jewelry, flatware, trays, and goblets from his own designs.

Ever the artist with a keen mind for drawing, design, and aesthetics, Spratling decided to experiment with silver using his designs. Shortly afterward, he set up his own workshop and began producing highly innovative pieces. By the 1940s Spratling's designs were gracing the necks of celebrities and being sold in high-end stores abroad.

Spratling also started a program to train local silversmiths; they were soon joined by foreigners interested in learning the craft. It wasn't long before there were thousands of silversmiths in the town, and Spratling was its wealthiest resident. He moved freely in Mexico's lively art scene, befriending muralists Diego Rivera (Rivera's wife, Frida Kahlo, wore Spratling necklaces) and David Alfaro Siqueiros as well as architect Miguel Covarrubios.

The U.S. ambassador to Mexico, Dwight Morrow, father of Anne Morrow, who married Charles Lindbergh, hired Spratling to help with the architectural details of his house in Cuernavaca. American movie stars were frequent guests at Spratling's home; once, he even designed furniture for Marilyn Monroe. Indeed, when his business failed in 1946, relief came in the form of an offer from the United States Department of the Interior: Spratling was asked to create a program of native crafts for Alaska. This work influenced his later designs.

Although he never regained the wealth he once had, he operated the workshop at his ranch and trained apprentices until he died in a car accident in 1969. A friend, Italian engineer Alberto Ulrich, took over the business and replicated Spratling's designs using his original molds. Ulrich died in 2002, and his children now operate the business.

Each summer PV shop owners travel to Taxco to procure silver jewelry.

After Dark

Mariachi

WORD OF MOUTH

"You get a very Mexican vibe in PV: beautiful location, charming cobbled streets, and a notorious nightlife. One of Mexico's best options as far as beach resorts go.

—Bain05

ORGANIC, OUTDOORSY VALLARTA SWITCHES GEARS after dark and rocks into the wee hours. After the beachgoers and sightseers have been showered and fed, Vallarta kicks up its heels and puts the baby to bed. Happy hour in martini lounges sets the stage for evening entertainment that might include a show, live music, or just hobnobbing under the heavens at a rooftop bar.

Many hotels have Mexican fiesta dinner shows, which can be lavish affairs with buffet dinners, folk dances, and even fireworks. Tour groups and individuals—mainly middle-age and older Americans and Canadians—make up the audience at the Saturday night buffet dinner show at Playa Los Arcos and other hotels. *Vaqueros* (cowboys) do rope tricks and dancers perform Mexican regional or pseudo-Aztec dances. The late-late crowd gets down after midnight at dance clubs, some of which stay open until 6 AM.

The scene mellows as you head north and south of Puerto Vallarta. In Punta de Mita, Bucerías, Sayulita, and San Francisco (aka San Pancho), local restaurants provide live music; the owners usually scare up someone good once or twice a week in high season. Along the Costalegre, tranquillity reigns. Most people head here for relaxation, and nightlife most often takes the form of stargazing, drink in hand. If you're visiting June through October (low season), attend live performances whenever offered, as they are few and far between.

Although there's definitely crossover, many Mexicans favor the upscale bars and clubs of the Hotel Zone and Marina Vallarta hotels, while foreigners tend to like the Mexican flavor of places downtown and the south side (the Zona Romántica), where dress is decidedly more casual.

⇨ *For more nightlife options, see "Gay Puerto Vallarta" (Chapter 10).*

BARS & PUBS

Like any resort destination worth its salt—the salt on the rim of the margarita glass, that is—PV has an enormous variety of watering holes. Bars on or overlooking the beach sell the view along with buckets of beer. Martini bars go to great lengths to impress with signature drinks, and sports bars serve up Canadian hockey and Monday-night football. Hotels have swim-up bars and lobby lounges, and these, as well as restaurant bars, are the main options in places like Nuevo Vallarta, Marina Vallarta, and most of the small towns to the north and south. ⇨ *For gay bars, see Chapter 10.*

ALL-PURPOSE BARS

Andale (⊠ *Av. Olas Altas 425, Col. E. Zapata* ☏ *322/222–1054*) fills up most nights. Crowds spill out onto the sidewalk as party-hearty men and women shimmy out of the narrow saloon, drinks in hand, to the strains of Chubby Checker and other vintage tunes. For a laugh, intoxicated or less inhibited patrons sometimes take a bumpy ride on the burro just outside Andale's door (a handler escorts the burro).

★ It's difficult to categorize **The Bar Above** (✉ *Av. México at Av. Hidalgo, 2 blocks north of central plaza, Bucerías* ☎ *329/298–1194*), a little place above Tapas del Mundo. It's a martini bar without a bar (the owner, Buddy, prefers that people come to converse with friends at tables rather than "hang out" at a bar) that also serves dessert. Molten

chocolate soufflé—the signature dish—or charred pineapple bourbon shortcake may be on the menu. Lights are dim, the music is romantic, and there's an eagle's view of the ocean from the rooftop crow's nest. It's closed every Sunday and in August and September. At other times, it's open 6 PM–11 PM.

Right on the sand across from Parque Lázaro Cárdenas, restaurant-bar **Burro's Bar** (✉ *Av. Olas Altas at Calle Lázaro Cárdenas, Col. E. Zapata* ☎ *No phone*) has bargain brewskis (three beers for three bucks) and equally inexpensive fruity margaritas by the pitcher. The seafood is less than inspired, but nachos and other munchies are good accompaniments to the drinks. Watch the waves and listen to Bob Marley and the Gypsy Kings among lots of gringo couples and a few middle-age Mexican vacationers. It opens daily at 10 AM.

Second-floor **La Cantina** (✉ *Morelos 709, at J.O. de Dominguez, Centro* ☎ *322/222–1734*), while not especially hip, has a good view of Banderas Bay and the boardwalk as well as canned (and sometimes live) Mexican tunes, especially *ranchera, norteño, grupera,* and *cumbia*.

The rooftop bar of **Chez Elena** (✉ *Hotel Los Cuatro Vientos, Matamoros 520, Centro* ☎ *322/222–0161*) is plain as can be, but the margaritas are first rate and the bay view expansive. It's disconcerting though, when you're the only one up there.

Geckos Pub (✉ *Calle Morelos, between Calles Madero and Av. Cárdenas Bucerías* ☎ *329/298–1861*) is an unassuming local watering hole with a billiards table. It's the kind of place a single woman can enter without feeling weird or being hassled as bartenders tend to keep an eye out for them in the small venue.

The tallest building around, **Hotel Alondra** (✉ *Calle Sinaloa 16, Barra de Navidad* ☎ *315/355–8372*), has a rooftop bar that's great for sunset cocktails.

Fodor's Choice **Memories** (✉ *Calle Mina 207, at Av. Juárez, Centro* ☎ *322/205–7906*)
★ is a wonderful little second-story nightspot. Right in downtown PV near the main plaza, it is frequented mainly by locals. The space is darkly romantic and a great place for a date, but still ideal for groups of friends, or for singles with a book. The extensive drink list includes "hair of the squirrel," with Frangelica, and lots of specialty alcoholic and nonalcoholic coffees. The classic-rock soundtrack pays homage to John Lennon, the Eagles, and Bob Marley; black-and-white

6

posters and photos honor other rock-and-rollers.

Called simply "Frog's" by the locals, **Señor Frog's** (⊠ *V. Carranza 218, at Ignacio I. Vallarta, Col. E. Zapata* ☎322/222–5171) is a good old-fashioned free-for-all for the young and the restless. There are black lights on the walls, sawdust on the floor, and a giant-screen TV above the tiny dance floor. Expect a foam party at least once a week, and other shenanigans.

Party Lounge (⊠ *Av. Mexico 993, across from Parque Hidalgo, Centro* ☎*No phone*) is open daily after 1 PM for stop-and-go drinks: mainly *litros*, that is, 32-ouncers of tequila sunrise, Long Island ice tea, piña colada, and the like. Because they have '70s, '80s, and lounge music rather than electronic music, the upstairs bar, open 8 PM to 4 AM, is popular with the middle-age and older set, foreign and domestic, as well as with the younger crowd.

The Shamrock (⊠ *Avenida México 22, Centro* ☎329/298–3073) is open daily after 11 AM. At this Irish-owned pub, the Wi-Fi flows freely throughout the chummy bar, and the chips, batter-fried cod, cottage pies, and burgers are great. When the amount of customers warrants it during busy season, the more sophisticated upstairs lounge opens to those seeking a quieter venue.

We Be Sausage Roadhouse Bar & Grill (⊠ *Av. de los Picos 102, Bucerías* ☎329/298–0954) is a pub owned by a Canadian sausage lover; have one of their excellent Italian-sausage sandwiches with your suds. Ball games are usually on the tube. It's closed Tuesday and Wednesday, and opens otherwise after 6 PM.

KARAOKE BAR

J.B. Golden Times (⊠ *Francisco I. Madero 176], Col. E. Zapata* ☎322/223–3609) started off as a salsa club but has since morphed into a karaoke bar. Cover varies from free to $10 per person, depending on the day of the week and the size of the crowd.

MARTINI BARS

★ **Apaches** (⊠ *Olas Altas 439, Col. E. Zapata* ☎322/222–5235) is gay friendly, lesbian friendly, *people* friendly. Heck, superwomen Mariann and her partner Endra would probably welcome you and your pet python with open arms, give you both a squeeze. PV's original martini bar, Apaches is the landing zone for expats reconnoitering after a long day, and a warm-up for late-night types. When the outside tables get jam packed in high season, the overflow heads into the narrow bar and the adjacent, equally narrow bistro. It opens after 5 PM; happy hour is 5 to 7. If you're alone, this is the place to make friends of all ages.

Garbo (✉*Pulpito 142, Olas Altas, Col. E. Zapata* ☎*322/223–5753*) is open nightly after 6. This is not the kind of place where you'll strike up a conversation; rather it's an upscale place to go with friends for a sophisticated, air-conditioned drink or two. Cigarette smoke perfumes the air, and a musician plays gentle electric guitar music nightly from 7 to 10 during high season (except Tuesday), less often the rest of the year.

The cozy **Kit Kat Club** (✉*Calle Púlpito 120, Col. E. Zapata* ☎*322/223–0093*) has great martinis and a retro feel. Both straights and gays are drawn to this elegant lounge, which has full meals as well as millions of $6 martinis. Most popular include the Peggy Lee (vodka, orange, and cranberry juices, and banana liqueur) and the Queen of Hearts (vodka, amaretto, cranberry juice, and 7UP).

LOUNGES

★ **Azul96** is one of Vallarta's trendiest new lounges. Downstairs, it's a fashionable restaurant and fashion statement with massive, boldly painted columns punctuating white-on-white minimalist decor. Up the elevator, enjoy an arresting cityscape along with sushi and appetizers. The minimalist feel of the restaurant is extended to the rooftop bar with high tables for four, sand at your feel and soft, innovative lighting. The speciality? Martinis. ✉*Morelos 696, Centro* ☎*322/222–1022* ⊕*www.azul96.com.*

Beyond its garden restaurant, multi-level **Ztai** (✉*Calle Morelos 737, Centro* ☎*322/222–0306* ✉ *No cover*) offers curtained poster-beds, super soft bar stools, and backless sofas in addition to more standard club seating. The mood of the bar is neon and minimalist, imbued with a peachy glow, and overlooking the ocean: C'est cool!

PIANO BARS

Bon vivants should head for **Constantini Wine Bar** (✉*Café des Artistes, Av. Guadalupe Sánchez 740, Centro* ☎*322/222–3229*), the latest innovation of hotshot restaurant Café des Artistes. Order one of 50 wines by the glass (more than 300 by the bottle, from 10 countries) and snack on caviar, bruschetta, and carpaccio—or go directly to dessert. Wine tastings are scheduled from time to time. There's live music most every night of the week.

At **El Faro** (✉*Royal Pacific Yacht Club, Marina Vallarta* ☎*322/221–0541*) you can admire the bay and marina from atop a 110-foot lighthouse. There's often live guitar or other romantic music Thursday through Saturday after 11 PM; on Sunday it starts at 9 PM. It's mainly a baby-boomer crowd, with lots of yachties.

RESTAURANT BARS

★ Soon after its 2004 inauguration, the sophisticated **Nikki Beach** (✉ *Westin hotel, Paseo de la Marina Sur 205, Marina Vallarta* ☎*322/226–1150*) hosted several events during the *Maxim* magazine model competi-

Continued on page 146

A cross-section of *la piña* (the heart) of the blue agave plant

¡TEQUILA!

If God were Mexican, tequila would surely be our heavenly reward, flowing in lieu of milk and honey. Local lore asserts that it was born when lightning hit a tall blue agave, cooking its heart.

Historians maintain that, following Spanish conquest and the introduction of the distillation process, tequila was developed from the ancient Aztec drink *pulque*. Whatever the true origin, Mexico's national drink long predated the Spanish, and is considered North America's oldest intoxicating spirit.

Conjuring up tequila, what might come to mind is late-night teary-eyed confessions or spaghetti-Western-style bar brawls. But tequila is more complex and worldly than many presume. By some accounts it's a digestive that reduces cholesterol and stress. Shots of the finest tequilas can cost upward of $100 each, and are meant to be savored as ardently as fine cognacs or single-malt scotches.

Just one of several agaves fermented and bottled in Mexico, tequila rose to fame during the Mexican Revolution when it became synonymous with national heritage and pride. Since the 1990s tequila has enjoyed a soaring popularity around the globe, and people the world over are starting to realize that tequila is more than a one-way ticket to a hangover.

The Blue Agave

Tequila is made from the blue agave plant (not from a cactus, as is commonly thought), a member of the lily family. Nearly 100,000 acres of blue agave are grown in Mexico today; the plant is native to the Sierra Madre region, still the center for agave fields and tequila production.

After the blue agave plant matures (which takes 8–12 years), its spiky leaves are removed and the heart cooked up to three days in a traditional pit oven (or convection oven) to concentrate the sugars. Seeping blood-red juice, the hearts are then ground and strained, then fermented and distilled at least two or three times.

Workers harvest *Agave tequilana Weber azul*

Mezcal

Liquor distilled from any maguey (agave) plant is called mezcal, so technically, tequila is a type of mezcal. But mezcal is usually used to describe a liquor made from any agave *except* the blue agave from which tequila is made. Originally hailing from Oaxaca, mezcal is as popular as tequila in Mexico, if not more so. Like tequila, quality varies widely from cheap firewater to smooth (and expensive) varieties with complex flavors. The type of maguey used influences the quality greatly.

At the fermentation stage, the agave is added to water.

Effortless Education

You can chat with your local bartender about the blue agave revolution, but the information you get may be flawed. Close to *casa*, you can learn a lot at **La Casa del Tequila** (✉ Calle Morelos 589, Centro ☎322/222–2000.) Ask the bartender to educate you as you taste a few of the 80 tequilas on hand.

TEQUILA TOURS

Near Boca de Tomatlán, **Agave Don Crispín** (✉ Las Juntas y Los Veranos, 10 mi south of PV ☎ 322/223–6002) is a small but proud producer of 100% agave tequila. Learn the basics of tequila production, and see the pit ovens and old-fashioned stills. If you're serious about tequila, you must go to tequila country. One of the most complete tours is with **Hacienda San José del Refugio** (✉ Amatitán, about 400 km [250 mi] east of PV, ☎ 33/3613–9585), producer of the Herradura brand. On the 9-hour **Tequila Express** (☎ 33/3880–9090 or through Ticketmaster at 33/3818–3800) train ride, blue agave fields zip by as you sip tequila and listen to roving mariachis. After a distillery tour, there's lunch, folk dancing, and *charro* (cowboy) demonstrations.

An assembly-line worker fills tequila bottles

José Cuervo is Mexico's largest tequila maker

CHOOSING A TEQUILA

Line 'em up!

Connoisseurs recommend imbibing nothing but 100% pure agave—with no added sugar or chemicals—even for mixed drinks. A tequila's quality is most directly related to the concentration of blue agave, and a higher agave content adds significantly to the price. This fact will be clearly marked on the label as TEQUILA 100% DE AGAVE or TEQUILA 100% PURO DE AGAVE. The cheapest varieties have 49% of their alcohol derived from sugars other than blue agave. (The max allowed by law.)

Aging tequila changes the flavor, but doesn't necessarily improve it. Whiskey and scotch inspired the aging process in oak barrels, which instills a smoky taste or imparts one of many other subtle bouquets. Some experts consider the unmitigated flavor of *blanco* (silver) superior to, or at least less influenced by Yankee and European tastes than that of *reposado* (aged) or *añejo* (mature).

Distinctions you should know (from— generally speaking—least to most expensive) are:

BLANCO (SILVER): Also known as white tequila (though "silver" is the official name), tequila blanco is clear as water. It is unaged—bottled immediately after distillation—and therefore has the purest agave taste of the tequila varieties.

ORO (GOLD): Also called *joven* (young) tequila, this is tequila blanco to which colorants or flavorings have been added, or that has been mixed with tequila aged in oak barrels, giving it a golden hue. Additives (all strictly regulated) such as caramel, oak tree extract, glycerin, and sugar syrup simulate the flavor of tequila aged in oak barrels.

REPOSADO (AGED): Aged in oak barrels 2 to 11 months, reposado is smoother and more flavorful than blanco, as it has acquired some of the oak flavor.

AÑEJO (EXTRA-AGED): Tequila aged more than one year in oak barrels; may also be called "mature tequila." This is the smoothest tequila variety, and the one that most resembles cognac or whiskey—ideal for sipping. Some feel that the agave taste is less noticeable.

CREAM OF THE CROP

In the tequila business, innovation and young energy aren't as successful as age and experience. Traditional *tequilera* families like those behind Don Julio, Sauza, and José Cuervo tend to get the most outstanding results, having pursued perfection for generations. All of our top picks are 100% blue agave.

Three faces of tequila.

El Tesoro de Don Felipe Platinum: Triple distilled, and produced the old-fashioned way, the agave hearts crushed with a stone grinder and baked in a brick oven

Don Eduardo: Youthful, crisp, and jubilant, with herby notes; triple distilled

Sauza's Tres Generaciones Blanco: Clean and balanced with hints of cinnamon

Chinaco Blanco: International World Spirits Competition judges proclaimed it "the epitome of tequila character, ... with a lively finish"

Amatitlán Reposado: A complex spirit with a suggestion of nutmeg and spice; awarded best in class at the 2005 International World Spirits Competition

Penacho Azteca Reposado: Another award winner by the same distillery as Amatitlán Reposado

Chinaco Reposado: Medium-dry rested tequila with an oak-spice bite and subtle fruit and flower aromas

Don Julio 1942: Exquisite, complex tequila with the aroma of toffee and vanilla

José Cuervo's Reserva de la Familia: Aged for three years in new oak barrels; rich flavor with touches of vanilla and herbs, and a long, graceful finish

Arette Gran Clase Añejo: Ultrasmooth, one of the suavest tequilas anywhere; aged for a full three years, it goes for $100 – $150 a bottle

A TEQUILA BY ANY OTHER NAME ISN'T TEQUILA

To be called "tequila" a drink must meet the following strict requirements, as put forth by Consejo Regulador de Tequila (Tequila Regulatory Council; CRT):

- made entirely in Mexico, and from blue agave grown in certain regions of Mexico (though it can be bottled elsewhere)

- distilled twice; some varieties are distilled three times

- contains at least 51% alcohol derived from Weber blue agave plant

- bears the official stamp of the CRT on the label

- if it is 100% blue agave, it must be bottled in Mexico at the plant at which it was made

tion, guaranteeing instant name recognition ... although much of its glamour has since worn off for the locals. Just about everything under the palapa roof is white, and hanging beds and furnishings encourage lounging. In the restaurant, hard-body waiters deliver dishes from Continental to Mediterranean to Asian, including sushi.

Vallartans decided that **Tribu Bar Lounge** (⊠ *Paseo de la Marina 220, Mayan Palace Marina, Marina Vallarta* ☎ *322/226–6000*) was a bit out of the way to become a serious hot spot, but Mexicans and foreigners in the Marina district still find it a dark and atmospheric space. DJ-spun music pulses house, lounge, techno or disco, and '80s music . . . whatever the crowd demands. Wednesday is usually salsa night, though the salsa is canned. There are also two billiard tables. It's open 5 PM to 1 AM (closed Monday), and there's no cover.

Victor's Place (Café Tacuba) (⊠ *Condominios Las Palmas, Local 9, Marina Vallarta* ☎ *322/221–2808*) is an excellent, inexpensive restaurant but doubles as a fun bar, well tended by the owner. Beer for a buck-fifty and inexpensive tequila-with-beer-chasers are practically a house rule. Nightly until 11 PM.

SPORTS BAR

With NASCAR on Sunday morning, NFL on Monday night, hockey, indispensable motocross, and welterweight fights, **Steve's Sports Bar** (⊠ *Basilio Badillo 286, Col. E. Zapata* ☎ *322/222–0256*) is a sports mecca. Five feeds and nine television sets guarantee broadcasts of many sporting events from various continents, simultaneously. There are piles of board games, too, and the burgers and fries couldn't be better.

LIVE MUSIC

Most of Puerto Vallarta's live music is performed in restaurants and bars, often on or overlooking the beach. ■TIP→ **Musical events happening anywhere in Vallarta are listed in** *Bay Vallarta*. This twice-monthly rag is an excellent source of detailed information for who's playing around Old Vallarta, the Zona Hotelera Norte, Marina Vallarta, and even as far north as Bucerías. More detail-oriented than most similar publications, *Bay Vallarta* lists showtimes, venues, genres, and cover charges. Live music is much less frequent in the smaller towns to the north and south of PV; to find out what's happening there, ask in tourist-oriented bars, restaurants, or hotels.

LATINO

FodorsChoice ★ **Blanco y Negro** (⊠ *Calle Lucerna at Calle Niza, behind Blockbuster Video store, Zona Hotelera* ☎ *322/293–2556*) is a wonderful place to have a drink with friends. The intimate café-bar is comfortable yet rustic, with *equipale* (leather-and-wood) love seats and traditional round cocktail tables. The music, which begins at 10:30, is *trova* (think Mexican Cat Stevens) by Latino legends Silvio Rodríguez and Pablo Milanés; some songs composed and sung by the owner are thrown in. There's never a cover. It's closed Sunday and Monday, otherwise open after 8 PM. **La Bodeguita del Medio** (✉ *Paseo Díaz Ordaz 858, Centro* ☎ *322/223–1585*) is a wonderful Cuban bar and restaurant with a friendly vibe. People of all ages come to dance salsa (and drink mojitos made with Cuban rum), so the small dance floor fills up as soon as the house sextet starts playing around 9 PM. There's no cover.

MUSIC ALFRESCO

The outdoor Los Arcos amphitheater frequently has some sort of live entertainment on weekends and evenings. It's as likely to be mimes or magicians as musicians, but always worth stopping for the camaraderie with local people.

Claudio's Meson Bay (✉ *Lázaro Cárdenas 17, by footbridge, Bucerías* ☎ *329/298–1634*) is a casual, open-sided, ocean-facing restaurant with live music (usually marimba). Marimba musicans or romantic duos show up daily to tap out these lighthearted melodies 6:30 to 10 PM (LESS OFTEN IN LOW SEASON)—which coincides with excellent all-you-can-eat buffets Monday, Wednesday, and Friday.

An institution for Mexican breakfast, **La Paloma** (✉ *Paseo Diaz Ordaz, at Aldama, Centro* ☎ *322/222–3675*) has otherwise average food but is recommended for sunset cocktails with live marimba and, later, mariachi music.

ROCK, JAZZ & BLUES

Philo's (✉ *Calle Delfin 15, La Cruz de Huanacaxtle* ☎ *329/295–5068*) is the unofficial cultural center and meeting place of La Cruz, with music, food, a large-screen TV, a diminutive swimming pool, and pool table. The namesake owner, a former record producer, also has a small recording studio here. The space is plain but there's excellent live music after 9 PM Thursday through Saturday year-round. Get down with rhythm and blues, country, and rock; or chow down on good pizza or on Thursday evenings, barbecue.

With the ambience (or lack thereof) of a small auditorium, **Roxy** (✉ *Av. Ignacio L. Vallarta 217, Col. E. Zapata* ☎ *No phone*) is a hit with locals and foreigners who like live blues, rock, reggae, and a little pop, mostly played by cover bands. The club doesn't begin to rock until around 10 PM, when the variable—but always small—cover charge begins. It's open daily until 4 AM in high season, otherwise closed Sunday.

DANCE CLUBS

You can dance salsa with the locals, groove to rock in English or *en español,* or even tango. Things slow down in the off-season, but during school vacations and the winter clubs stay open until 3, 5, or even 6 AM. Except those that double as restaurants, clubs don't open until 10 PM. ■ TIP→ **If you care about looking hip, don't show up at a club before** midnight—it will most likely be dead. Arriving around 10 PM, however, could save you a cover charge.

Have a late and leisurely dinner, take a walk on the beach and get some coffee, then stroll into the club cool as a cucumber at 12:30 AM or so.

Carlos O'Brien's (⊠ *Paseo Diaz Ordaz 796, Centro* ☎ *322/222–1444*) is the destination of choice for Vallarta's very young people—a mix of local teens and foreigners come after midnight to mingle and party, especially on weekends. Music is a bit of everything: rock, house, techno, banda, hip-hop, disco, you name it. The ground floor fills up from early afternoon, however, with cruise-shippers and other travelers seeking food and drinks in a relatively familiar atmosphere. There's an $8 cover on weekend nights and also during the week during high season. When the place is hopping it stays open until dawn.

★ **Christine** (⊠ *Krystal Vallarta, Av. de las Garzas s/n, Zona Hotelera* ☎ *322/224–6990 or 322/224–0202*) has spectacular light shows set to bass-thumping music that ranges from techno and house to disco, rock, and Mexican pop. Most people (young boomers and Gen-Xers) come for the duration (it doesn't close until 6 AM), as this is the top of the food chain for the PV dancing experience. The bar is open Wednesday through Sunday after 10 PM, and the cover is typically about $20. Exceptions include ladies' nights (no set night), when women get in free. On nights when it's open bar, the cover is $40 per person and drinks are unlimited.

Fodor'sChoice   In addition to pretty good Mediterranean dinners in the ground-floor
★ restaurant, **de Santos** (⊠ *Calle Morelos 771, at Leona Vicario, Centro* ☎ *322/223–3052*) starts the evening with chill out and lounge music that appeals to a mixed, though slightly older, crowd. Later, local and guest DJs spin the more danceable, beat-driven disco and house tunes that appeal to slightly younger folks. If the smoke and noise get to you, head upstairs to the rooftop bar, where you and your friends can fling yourselves on the giant futons for some stargazing. This is a see-and-be-seen place for locals, and the kitchen is generally open 'til 2 AM ; the whole place shuts down at 4 AM.

Popular with young, hip *vallartenses*, **Hilo** (⊠ *Paseo Díaz Ordaz 588, Centro* ☎ *322/223–5361*) attracts a mix of locals and visitors. It's mainly a young crowd, serving up house, techno, hip-hop, electronic, and Top 40. The ceiling is several stories high, and enormous bronze-colored statues give an epic feeling. It's open from 4 PM to 4 or 6 AM, but doesn't get rolling until midnight. The cover is $7–$10, or $30 with open bar.

★ **J.B.** (⊠ *Blvd. Francisco M. Ascencio 2043, Zona Hotelera* ☎ *322/224–4616*), pronounced "Hota Bay," is the best club in town for salsa. The age of the crowd varies, but tends toward thirty- and fortysomethings. J.B. is serious about dancing, so it feels young at heart. There's usually a band Thursday through Saturday nights, DJ music the rest of the week.

Those with *dos patas zurdas* (two left feet) can attend salsa lessons Thursday and Friday 8 to 10 PM; or take tango lessons on that schedule on Monday and Wednesday. Cost is $5 with no additional cover; otherwise, the cover is $9 (except Monday and Tuesday) after 10:30 PM.

Ready to party? Then head to **The Zoo** (⊠ *Paseo Díaz Ordaz 630, Centro* ☎ *322/222–4945*) for DJ-spun techno, Latin, reggae, and hip-hop. The adventurous can dance in the cage. It attracts a mixed crowd of mainly young locals and travelers, though after midnight the median age plunges. It's open until 6 AM when things are hopping. The restaurant is full in the early evening with cruise-ship passengers.

LET'S GET PHYSICAL

Tango aficionados since 1985, **Al and Barbara Garvey** (☎ *322/222–8895* or *415/513–4497 in the U.S.* ⊕ *www.tangobar-productions.com*) of San Francisco teach the Argentine dance for beginner through advanced levels. They also give private lessons and meet up with fellow dancers for practice at Vallarta's Latin dance club, J.B. The Garveys are usually around only during the winter season; call or check their Web site for schedules.

FILM

Movie tickets here are less than half what they are in the U.S. and Canada. Many theaters have discounted prices on Wednesday. See theater Web sites or ⊕ www.vallartaonline.com/cinema. **Cinépolis** (⊠ *Plaza Soriana, Av. Francisco Villa 1642–A, Pitillal* ☎ *322/225–1251* ⊕ *www.cinepolis.com.mx*) was, until Cinemark showed up, PV's newest theater. Next to Soriana department stores at the south entrance to El Pitillal, it has 15 screens and shows in English and Spanish. Tickets are about $4.

Easy to access in the heart of the Hotel Zone, **Cinemark** (⊠ *Ave. de los Tules 178, Plaza Caracol, Zona Hotelera* ☎ *322/224–8927*) is on the second floor at the south end of Plaza Caracol. The latest films are shown on its 10 screens. Tickets are about $3.50.

Versalles (⊠ *Av. Francisco Villa 799, Col. Versalles* ☎ *322/225–8766*) has six screens. Tickets: $4.

MORE AFTER-DARK OPTIONS

Enjoy a show, cruise, or see silver-studded mariachis. Most hotels have lounge music. Drag shows (⇨ *Chapter 10*) are crowd pleasers—whether the crowd is straight or gay.

COFFEEHOUSES

⇨ *For more coffeehouses, see "Where to Eat" in Chapter 3.* **Pie in the Sky Vallarta** (⊠ *Lázaro Cárdenas 247, Col. E. Zapata* ☎ *322/223–8183*) serves excellent coffee as well as *the* most scrumptious pies, cookies, and

Mexican Rhythms & Roots

Salsa, merengue, *cumbia* . . . do they leave you spinning, even off the dance floor? This primer is designed to help you wrap your mind around Latin beats popular in Pacific Mexico. Unfortunately, it can't cure two left feet.

These and other popular Latin dance rhythms were born of African drumming brought to the Caribbean by slaves. Dancing was vital to West African religious ceremonies; these rhythms spread with importation of slaves to the New World. Evolving regional tastes and additional instruments have produced the Latin music enjoyed today from Tierra del Fuego to Toronto, and beyond.

While the steps in most dances can be reduced to some basics, these flat-footed styles of dancing are completely foreign to most non-Latins. Dance classes can definitely help your self-esteem as well as your performance. In Puerto Vallarta, the dance club J.B. is the place to go for lessons.

From Colombia, wildly popular **cumbia** combines vocals, wind, and percussion instruments. With a marked rhythm (usually 4/4 time), the sensual music is relatively easy to dance to. Hip-hop and reggae influences have produced urban cumbia, with up-tempo, accordion-driven melodies. Listen to Kumbia Kings, La Onda, Control, and Big Circo to get into the cumbia groove.

Fast-paced and with short, precise rhythms, **merengue** originated in the Dominican Republic. Although the music sounds almost frantic, the feet aren't meant to keep pace with the melody. Check out Elvis Crespo's 2004 album *Saboréalo*.

Born in Cuba of Spanish and African antecedents, **son** is played on accordion, guitar, and drums. The folkloric music was translated to various dialects in different parts of Mexico. "La Bamba" is a good example of *son jarrocho* (from Veracruz).

American Prohibition sent high-rollers sailing down Cuba way, and they came back swinging to son, mambo, and rumba played by full orchestras—think Dezi Arnaz and his famous song "Babalou." In New York these styles morphed into **salsa**, popularized by such luminaries as Tito Puente and Celia Cruz and carried on today by superstars like Marc Anthony. Wind instruments (trumpet, trombone), piano, guitar, and plenty of percussion make up this highly spiced music.

Mexicans love these African-inspired beats, but are especially proud of homegrown genres, like **música norteña**, which has its roots in rural, northern Mexico (in Texas, it's called *conjunto*). The traditional instruments are the *bajo sexto* (a 12-string guitar), bass, and accordion; modern groups add the trap drums for a distinctive rhythmic pulse. It's danced like a very lively polka, which is one of its main influences. Norteña is the music of choice for working-class Mexicans and Mexican-Americans in the United States.

A subset of música norteña is the **corrido**, popularized during the Mexican Revolution. Like the ballads sung by wandering European minstrels, corridos informed isolated Mexican communities of the adventures of Emiliano Zapata, Pancho Villa, and their compatriots. Today's "narco-corridos" portray dubious characters: the drug lords who run Mexico's infamous cartels. Popular norteño artists include Michael Salgado and the pioneering Los Tigres del Norte, whose album

Americas Sin Fronteras was terrifically popular way back in 1987.

But the quintessential Mexican music is **mariachi**, a marriage of European instruments and native sensibilities born right here in Jalisco, Mexico. Guitars, violins, and trumpets are accompanied by the *vihuela* (a small, round-backed guitar) and the larger, deep-throated *guitarrón*. Professional mariachis perform at birthdays and funerals, engagements, anniversaries, and life's other milestones. You won't find mariachi music at nightclubs, however; the huapango, jarocho, and other dances the music accompanies are folk dances. F *For more about mariachi, see* "Mariachi: Born in Jalisco" *in Chapter 9.*

For concerts, clubbing, and dancing, Mexicans look to the contemporary music scene. Latin jazz was born when legendary Cuban musician Chano Pozo teamed up with the great bebop trumpeter Dizzy Gillespie. Current Latin jazz acts worth applauding are Puerto Ricans Eddie Palmieri and David Sanchez; representing pop, Obie Bermúdez also hails from that Caribbean mecca of music. Check out Latin pop by Cuba's Bebo Valdez, and rock en español by Colombian-born Juanes as well as Mexico's own los Jaguares, El Tri, Ely Guerra, Molotov, and the veteran band Maná.

cakes. There's free Wi-Fi for those with their trusty laptops.

Dark and romantic, albeit open to the winds, **Café San Angel** (⌀*Av. Olas Altas 449, at Calle Francisca Rodriguez, Col. E. Zapata* ☎*322/223–1273*) is a favorite with the gay crowd. It has tables along the sidewalk and comfortable couches and chairs within. The menu holds soups, sandwiches, salads, and a great frappuccino.

DINNER CRUISES

⇨*See "Cruises" in Chapter 7.*

DRINKS ON THE BEACH

Playa Los Muertos is the destination of choice for a sunset cocktail and dinner on the beach. Strolling mariachi bands serenade diners overlooking the sand; at some tables the waves kiss your toes under the table. Candles and torches light the scene, along with the moon. After dinner you can take a stroll or sit on the beach, or head to another restaurant bar for a coffee or after-dinner *digestif* to the tunes of marimba, folk music, or jazz.

SHOWS

In addition to those listed here, many hotels have buffet dinners with mariachis, folkloric dancers and charros (elegantly dressed horsemen, who, in this case, perform mostly roping tricks, as horses are a bit too messy for the stage and most of their feats on horseback involve running at top speed in a specially designed arena called a lienzo charro). All-inclusive hotels generally include nightly entertainment in the room price. ⇨*For more dinner shows, see "Theater" in Chapter 8.*

Enjoy Vallarta's original dinner show Thursday or Sunday at **La Iguana** (⌀*Calle Lázaro Cárdenas 311, Col. E. Zapata* ☎*322/222–0105*). Large troops of professional mariachis entertain, beautiful women dance in colorful costumes, couples dance, kids whack piñatas, and fireworks light up the sky. The simulated cockfight is supposed to be painless for the roosters, and nearly so for alarmed foreign visitors. There's an open bar, and the buffet has 40 selections. Most folks deem this party worth the price of $65 per person.

El Mariachi Loco (⌀*Lázaro Cárdenas 254, at Calle I. Vallarta Centro* ☎*322/223–2205*) is the place to see mariachi musicians. The mariachis begin at 9 PM Monday through Wednesday; the rest of the week an organ player and drummer warm up the crowd before the mariachis come onstage at 11:30 PM. On weekends a comedian and ranchera group are added to the mix at around 1 AM. Cover is $5.

Playa Los Arcos (⌀*Av. Olas Altas 380, Col. E. Zapata* ☎*322/222–1583*) has a theme dinner show Monday, Wednesday, and Saturday 6–10:30 PM. The show, which costs $18, includes a buffet and one cocktail. The most popular theme night is Saturday's Mexico Night, with mariachis, rope tricks, and folkloric dance.

Adventure

Snorkeling

WORD OF MOUTH

"Vallarta Adventures has two different excursions to Las Caletas that are each very nice. One is a whale-watching trip (with free booze) during the day. When you get to Las Caletas you get a very good meal, then have a couple of hours to just hang around, swim, snorkel, or hike. The other is Rhythms of the Night. You leave in the evening, have a nice dinner and then a fun show in an outdoor amphitheater. Las Caletas has no electricity so everything is lighted by torches."

—DouginABQ

PUERTO VALLARTA IS THE BEST adventure-vacation destination on Mexico's Pacific Coast, at least for the sheer variety of activities. The water's warm and swimmable year-round, although downright bath-like July through September. The big blue bay attracts sea turtles, humpback whales, several species of dolphins, and a growing number of snorkelers and divers. The fishing is excellent—from deep-sea angling for gigantic marlin and sailfish to trolling near shore for roosters and red snapper. Banderas Bay and the beaches to the north and south have waves for surfing as well as plenty of calm bays and inlets for swimming.

Among the lush subtropical mountains—so close to the coast and laced with streams and rivers rushing to the ocean—are challenging mountain biking trails for the fit, and, for those who prefer gas-driven excitement, dune and ATV safaris into the hills. Many family-owned ranches have horse-riding tours at reasonable prices—lasting from an hour or two to overnight forays into the Sierra.

Most tour operators provide transportation from strategic pickup points, usually in downtown Puerto Vallarta, Marina Vallarta, and Nuevo Vallarta and sometimes in Conchas Chinas, but you'll save traveling from one end of the bay to the other by choosing an outfitter near your neck of the woods. Party boats and private yachts are great for accessing gorgeous and hard-to-reach beaches, primarily south of Vallarta along Cabo Corrientes.

Most of the tour operators are in Puerto Vallarta, but whenever possible we've listed some of the companies springing up to meet the needs of visitors staying north and south of town.

OUTDOOR ACTIVITIES & SPORTS

ATV & DUNE BUGGY TOURS

There's an increasing number of ATV, dune buggy, and jeep tours heading to the hills around Puerto Vallarta. Sharing a vehicle with a partner means a significant savings. Also take into consideration location; some head south of PV proper, others to the north. Most rides are to small communities, ranches, and rivers north, south, and east of Puerto Vallarta.

LOGISTICS

A valid driver's license and a major credit card are required. Wear lightweight long pants, sturdy shoes, bandanna (some operators provide one as a keepsake) and/or tight-fitting hat, sunglasses, and both sunscreen and mosquito repellent. In rainy season (July–October) it's hotter and wetter—ideal for splashing through puddles and streams; the rest of the year is cooler but dusty. In either season, prepare to get dirty. Four-hour tours go for $75–$120; full-day trips to San Sebastián cost about $165 for one or $175 for two riders.

MULTI-ADVENTURE OUTFITTERS

Don't see what you want here? Try one of these outfitters, whose multitude of tours includes bird-watching, ATV tours, whale-watching, biking, hot-air ballooning, sailing, and much, much more.

Ecotours (☎ *322/223–3130 or 322/222–6606* ⊕ *www.ecotoursvallarta.com*). **Immersion Adventures** (⊠ *La Manzanilla* ☎ *315/351–5341* ⊕ *www.immersionadventures.com*).

Tours Soltero (⊠ *San Patricio Melaque* ☎ *315/355–6777* ✑ *rays-toursmelaque@yahoo.com*). **Vallarta Adventures** (☎ *322/297–1212 Nuevo Vallarta, 322/221–0657 Marina Vallarta, 888/303–2653 from U.S. and Canada* ⊕ *www. vallarta-adventures.com*). **Wild Vallarta** (☎ *322/222–8928 or 877/314–9453 from the U.S. or Canada* ⊕ *www.wildvallarta.com*).

OUTFITTERS

Adventure ATV Jungle Treks (⊠ *Basilio Badillo 400, Col. E. Zapata* ☎ *322/223–0392*) leads daily three-hour dune buggy tours ($120 for one or two riders) and ATV tours ($75 for one rider or $95 for two) that head into the hills behind Vallarta. Convenient to Marina Vallarta and Nuevo Vallarta, **Best Tours** (⊠ *Orquidia 117, Col. Villa Las Flores* ☎ *322/221–3066*) runs custom tours in addition to twice-daily, three-hour ATV ($75 one rider, $95 two riders) and dune buggy ($120) tours; kids under 11 ride free with a parent.

★ **Wild Vallarta** (☎ *322/222–8928 or 877/314–9453 from the U.S. or Canada* ⊕ *www.wildvallarta.com*) has full-day and half-day tours in Honda four-wheel ATVs and open-frame, five-speed buggies with VW engines. The long and rugged ATV tour to San Sebastián, high in the Sierra, requires some experience, but four-hour trips are fine for beginners. (Consider riding two per ATV for the tequila tasting, solving the drinking-and-driving conundrum if you plan to gulp rather than sip.)

CANOPY TOURS

Puerto Vallarta's newest thrill is canopy tours, which are better described as high-octane thrill rides. On a canopy tour you'll "fly" from treetop to treetop, securely fastened to a zip line. Despite the inherent danger of dangling from a cable hundreds of feet off the ground, the operators we list have excellent safety records. It's permissible to take photos while zipping along so if you're brave, bring your camera along, with a neck strap to leave hands free.

LOGISTICS

■TIP→ **Don't take a tour when rain threatens.** A thunderstorm isn't the time to hang out near trees attached to metal cables, and rain makes the activity scary to say the least. Even during the rainy season, however, mornings and *early* afternoons are generally sunny. Check with each operator regarding maximum weight (usually 250 pounds) and minimum ages for kids.

OUTFITTERS

★ **Canopy El Edén** (✉ *Office: Plaza Romy, Calle Vallarta 228, Interior 1, Col. E. Zapata* ☎*322/222–2516* ⊕*www.canopyeleden.com*) has daily trips to the spirited Mismaloya River and adjacent restaurant. During the 3½-hour adventure ($81), which departs from the downtown office, you zip along 10 lines through the trees and above the river. To take full advantage of the lovely setting and good restaurant, take the first tour (they depart Monday through Friday at 9, 10, 11, 12, and 1:30 and weekends at 9, 11, and 1—sometimes less frequently in low season) and bring your swimsuit. The schedule includes about an hour to spend at the river or restaurant. If there's room, you can return with a later group. If you wish to stay longer and there's room, you can return to Vallarta with a later group; otherwise take a taxi or ask the restaurant staff for a lift to the highway, where buses frequently pass.

Fodor'sChoice Vallarta's top canopy tour is **Canopy Tour de Los Veranos** (✉ *Office: Calle*
★ *Francisca Rodríguez 336, Centro* ☎*322/223–0504 or 877/563–4113 from the U.S.* ⊕*www.canopytours-vallarta.com*). Slightly more expensive than some competitors ($79), Los Veranos also has the most zip lines (14), the longest zip line (600 feet), the highest zip line (500 feet off the ground), and the most impressive scenery: crossing the Rio Los Horcones half a dozen times on several miles of cables. Departures are from the office, across from the Pemex station at the south side of Puerto Vallarta, on the hour between 9 and 2, with reduced hours in low season (June through November). It's the only PV tour company that doesn't require helmets. After your canopy tour, there's time to scale the climbing wall, play in the Los Horcones River, eat at the restaurant, or hang out at the bar overlooking the river, but check to make sure that a ride back to town is available.

Luis Verdin of **Rancho Mi Chaparrita** (✉ *Manuel Rodriguez Sanchez 14, Sayulita* ☎*329/291–3112* ⊕*www.michaparrita.com*) runs a 10-zip-line tour on his family ranch. Access the ranch on his lively, healthy horses via the beach and backcountry for a complete adventure. Canopy tours are $75; a canopy tour plus the horseback ride is $95.

The most convenient canopy tour if you're staying in Nuevo Vallarta is **Vallarta Adventures** (✉ *Paseo de las Palmas 39–A, Nuevo Vallarta* ☎*322/297–1212, 888/303–2653 in U.S. and Canada* ✉*Edifício Marina Golf, Local 13–C, Calle Mástil, Marina Vallarta* ☎*322/221–0657* ⊕*www.vallarta-adventures.com*), although it's not the best show in town. Participants use gloved hands rather than a braking device to slow down or stop, and must return to town right after their zip line canopy adventure with no time for other activities. It's $79 per person.

FISHING

Sportfishing is excellent off Puerto Vallarta, and fisherfolk have landed monster marlin well over 500 pounds. Surf casting from shore nets snook, roosters, and jack crevalles. Hire a *panga* (skiff) to hunt for Spanish mackerel, sea bass, amberjack, snapper, bonito, and roosterfish on full- or half-day trips within the bay. Yachts are best for big-game fishing: yellowfin tuna; blue, striped, and black marlin; and dorado. Hire them for four to 10 hours, or overnight. Catch-and-release of billfish is encouraged. If you don't want to charter a boat, you can also join a "party" boat.

SEASONAL CATCHES

Sailfish and dorado are abundant practically year-round. (Though dorado drop out a bit in early summer and sailfish dip slightly in spring.)

Winter: bonito, dorado, jack crevalle, sailfish, striped marlin, wahoo

Spring: amberjack, jack crevalle, grouper, mackerel, red snapper

Summer: grouper, roosterfish, yellowfin tuna

Fall: black marlin, blue marlin, sailfish, striped marlin, yellowfin tuna, wahoo

Most sportfishing yachts are based at Marina Vallarta; only a few call "home" the marina at Paradise Village, in Nuevo Vallarta. Pangas can be hired in the traditional fishing villages of Mismaloya and Boca de Tomatlán, just south of town; in the Costalegre towns of La Manzanilla and Barra de Navidad; and in the north, La Cruz de Huanacaxtle, as well as at El Anclote and Nuevo Corral del Risco, Punta de Mita. The resort hotels of the Costalegre and Punta de Mita arrange fishing excursions for their guests. Bass fishing at Cajón de Peña, about 1½ hours south of Vallarta, nets 10-pounders on a good day.

LOGISTICS

Most captains and crews are thoroughly bilingual, at least when it comes to boating and fishing.

LICENSES Licenses are necessary, but don't worry about procuring yours on your own. If the captain hasn't arranged it ahead of time, he will make sure that a SEMARNAP official is on hand to sell you one before the boat departs. Cost is about $13 per day; there are no weekly rates.

PRICES Prices generally range $300–$400 for four hours on a yacht to $600–$1,050 for a day-long cruise for four to eight anglers. A longer trip is recommended for chasing the big guys, as it takes you to prime fishing grounds like Los Bancos and Cobeteña.

Party boats range from $125 to $140 per person for an eight-hour day. Drinking water is generally included in the price; box lunches and beer or soda may be sold separately or included, or sometimes it's BYOB. Pangas and superpangas, the latter with shade and a head of some sort, charge $185 to $400 for four to eight hours and generally accommodate one to three or four anglers. For a boat and round-trip transportation to Cajón de Peña, an all-day affair, expect to pay $150 to $600 per person.

OUTFITTERS

CharterDreams(⊠*Marina Las Palmas II, Locales 11 and 12, Marina Vallarta* ☎*322/221–0690* ⊕*www.charterdreams.com*) has a variety of excursions, from trips with one to three people in *pangas* (skiffs) for bass fishing to cruises with up to eight people aboard luxury yachts. Although most fisherfolk choose to leave around the smack of dawn, you set your own itinerary. The same rates apply for whale-watching or private sightseeing or snorkeling tours: $400 for four hours, $450 to $650 for six hours, and $500 to $800 for eight hours, depending on the boat.

In Barra de Navidad, at the southern end of the Costalegre, contact **Gerardo Kosonoy** (☎*315/355–5739 or 315/354–2251 (mobile)* ⊘*hakunakosonoy@yahoo.com*) for fishing excursions. Alternately, you can easily round up another fisherman with a panga from one of the two large fishing co-ops on the lagoon side of town. There's usually at least one representative hoping for clients at the water taxi dock. Gerardo and his compadres charge 400 pesos ($37) per hour or 2,500 pesos ($238) for seven hours, for one to four passengers. There's a four-hour minimum.

★ **Master Baiter** (⊠*Puesto del Sol Condominiums, near lighthouse, Marina Vallarta* ☎*322/209–0498 or 322/209–0499* ⊕*www.mbsportfishing. com* ⊠*Calle 31 de Octubre 107, across from McDonald's, Centro* ☎*322/222–4043*) is a comprehensive fishing outfitter with a proven track record. Its superpanga fleet consists of 26-foot skiffs with shade and bathroom; some have GPS. The 8-, 10-, and 12-hour yacht charters allow enough time to fish El Morro, Corbeteña, and beyond. An overnight trip ($2,650) allows further exploration, and includes meals and drinks. Both storefronts (downtown Vallarta and Marina Vallarta) sell fishing tackle, although there's a better selection at the Marina store.

Do you remember the seductive-looking divers in *Night of the Iguana?* Well, their progeny might be among the local guys of **Mismaloya Divers** (⊠*Road to Mismaloya Beach, Mismaloya* ☎*322/228–0020*). Panga trips here are comparatively inexpensive, usually around $40 per person (minimum four people) within the bay or $100 per person to the Marietas (five lines, one to four passengers), including a light breakfast or lunch and water. Local fishermen at Punta de Mita have formed the **Sociedad Cooperativa de Servicios Turísticos** (*Tourist Services Cooperative* ⊠*Av. El Anclote 1, Manz. 17, Corral del Risco, Punta de Mita* ☎*329/291–6298* ⊕*www.prodigyweb.net.mx/cooperativapuntamita*). The families who run this co-op were forcibly relocated from their original town of Corral del Risco due to the development of luxurious digs like the Four Seasons. The guides may not speak English as fluently as the more polished PV operators, but they know the local waters, and the fees go directly to them and their families. Sportfishing costs about $60 to $70 per hour, with a four-hour minimum, for up to four people. Two hours of whale-watching or snorkeling around the Marietas Islands, for up to eight people, costs $114 per person. Anyone older than six but younger than 60 also pays $2 for a wristband allowing entrance to the Marietas, a national aquatic park.

ANNUAL EVENTS

MARCH

The entire month is dedicated to racing and boating activities, beginning with the **Banderas Bay Regatta** (☎ *322/297–2222* ⊕ *www. banderasbayregatta.com*), which starts in San Diego, California, and ends here with a great awards banquet. Throughout the month there are cocktail parties, charity events, receptions, seminars, additional races, and boat parades. A 1,000-mile race between San Diego and Puerto Vallarta, co-hosted by the two cities' yacht clubs, begins around the third week of February and ends during March festivities. Check ⊕ *www.vallartayachtclub.com* for details.

MAY

Begun in the early '90s, the five-day **Annual Sports Classic** (*contact Veronica Alarcon at the Sheraton Buganvilias:* ☎ *322/226–0404 Ext. 6038* ⊕ *www.puertovallarta. net/news/sports-classic-2008.php*) invites amateurs, pros, and semipros to compete in basketball, soccer, bowling, tennis, beach volleyball, a 5k race, and an aerobics marathon. Most events take place at the Agustin Flores Contreras Stadium, Los Arcos Amphitheater, and the beach in front of the Holiday Inn.

NOVEMBER

The **Puerto Vallarta International Half Marathon** (⊕ *www.maratonvallarta.com*), held in early November, gets bigger each year. There's a 5K run, too, and a big pasta dinner on the beach the day before the race.

The **International Puerto Vallarta Sailfish and Marlin Tournament** (☎ *322/225–5467* ⊕ *www. fishvallarta.com*) celebrated its 50th anniversary in 2005. The entry fee is more than $1,300 per line, but the prizes and prestige of winning are great. Categories are dorado, tuna, marlin, and sailfish.

Captain Peter Vines of **Vallarta Tour and Travel** (⊠ *Marina Los Palmas Local 4, in front of Dock B, Marina Vallarta* ☎ *322/294–6240 or 866/682–1971 from the U.S. and Canada*) can accommodate eight fisherfolk with top-of-the-line equipment, including the latest electronics, sonar, radar, and two radios. Rates are very reasonable (four hours $400, six hours $500, eight hours $600, 12 hours $800), especially since they include lunch, beer, soda, and fish-cleaning service at the end of the day. Transportation from your hotel is included in the full-day bass-fishing expedition to Cajón de Peña, which is essentially a charter service.

GOLF

"Not a bad mango in the bunch" is how one golf aficionada described Puerto Vallarta's courses. From the Four Seasons Punta Mita to the Gran Bay at Barra de Navidad, the region is a close second to Los Cabos in variety of play at a range of prices. Well-known designers are represented, including Jack Nicklaus and Tim Weiskopf.

LOGISTICS

Most of these courses offer first-class services including driving ranges and putting greens, lessons, clinics, pro shops, and clubhouses.

COURSES

★ Joe Finger designed the 18-hole course at **Marina Vallarta** (✉ *Paseo de la Marina s/n, Marina Vallarta* ☎ *322/221–0545 or 322/221–0073*); the $128 greens fee includes practice balls and a shared cart. It's the area's second-oldest course and is closest and most convenient for golfers staying in the Hotel Zone, Old Puerto Vallarta, and Marina Vallarta. Very flat, it's way more challenging than it looks, with lots of water hazards. Speaking of hazards, the alligators have a way of blending into the scenery. They might surprise you, but they supposedly don't bite. Some of the best views in the area belong to the aptly named **Vista Vallarta** (✉ *Circuito Universidad 653, Col. San Nicolás* ☎ *322/290–0030 or 322/290–0040*). There are 18 holes designed by Jack Nicklaus and another 18 by Tom Weiskopf. The greens fee for the course, which is a few miles northwest of the Marina Vallarta area, is $174. A shared cart and tax are included.

★ At the Paradise Village hotel and condo complex, **El Tigre** (✉ *Paseo de los Cocoteros 18, Nuevo Vallarta* ☎ *322/297–0773, 866/843–5951 in U.S., 800/214–7758 in Canada* ⊕ *www.eltigregolf.com*) is an 18-hole course with 12 water features. The greens fee of $167 includes a shared cart, water, practice balls, and tax. Don't be surprised if you see a guy driving around with tiger cubs in his truck: the course's namesake and mascot is the passion of the club's director. El Tigre has a fun island par 3. **Four Seasons Punta Mita** (✉ *Punta de Mita* ☎ *329/291–6000* ⊕ *www.fourseasons.com*) was designed by Jack Nicklaus. Nonguests are permitted to play the 195-acre, par-72 course; however, they must pay the hotel's day use fee of 50 percent of the room rate (approximately $300 plus 28 percent taxes and service charge), which covers use of a guest room and hotel facilities until dark. Reservations are essential. The greens fee is $195 plus 25 percent tax and service and includes the golf cart. The club's claim to fame is that it has perhaps the only natural island green in golf. Drive your cart to it at low tide; otherwise hop aboard a special amphibious vessel (weather permitting) to cross the water. There are seven other oceanfront links, as well as an optional par 3, the resort's signature hole.

Designed by Percy Clifford in 1978, PV's original course, **Los Flamingos Country Club** (✉ *Carretera a Bucerías, Km 145, 12 km (8 mi) north of airport, Nuevo Vallarta* ☎ *329/296–5006* ⊕ *www.flamingosgolf.com.mx*), has been totally renovated. The 18-hole course at the northern extremity of Nuevo Vallarta has new irrigation and sprinkler systems to maintain the rejuvenated greens. The high-season greens fee is $139, including a shared cart and a bucket of balls. Nine of the 18 holes at **Mayan Palace** (✉ *Paseo de las Moras s/n, Fracc. Nautico Turistico, Nuevo Vallarta* ☎ *322/226-4000 Ext. 4600*) are being completely redesigned by Jack Nicklaus and will reopen in early 2009. Until then players repeat the remaining nine holes for $124. The fee includes cart, use of practice range, and return transportation to hotel. Twilight fees (after 1 PM) are almost half that price, at $75.

Fodor'sChoice ★ About two hours south of Vallarta on the Costalegre is the area's best course. At least six of the holes at **El Tamarindo** (⊠ *Carretera Melaque–Puerto Vallarta, Careterra 200, Km 7.5, Cihuatlán* ☎ *315/351–5032 Ext. 4*) play along the ocean; some

are cliffside holes with fabulous views, others go right down to the beach. On a slow day, golfers are encouraged at tee time to have a swim or a picnic on the beach during their round, or to play a hole a second time if they wish. Designed by David Fleming, the breathtaking course is the playground of birds, deer, and other wildlife. It's an awesome feeling to nail the course's most challenging hole, the 9th: a par-3 with a small green surrounded by bunkers. The greens fee is $210, including cart and tax. Resort guests get priority for tee times; call up to a week ahead to check availability. **Isla Navidad** (⊠ *Isla Navidad, Barra de Navidad* ☎ *314/337–9006* ⊕ *www.islanavidad.com*) must have the best variety of play in the area, with three 9-hole courses of different flavors: mountain, lagoon, and ocean. Designed by Robert VanHagge, the course is beautifully sculpted, with lovely contours. Greens fees are $184 for 9 holes or $207 for 18, including driving range practice, cart, and tax.

7

HORSEBACK RIDING

Most of the horse riding outfits are based on family ranches in the foothill towns of the Sierra like Las Palmas. Horses are permitted on the beach in smaller towns like Sayulita and San Francisco, but not in Vallarta proper, so expect to ride into the hills for sunset-viewing there.

LOGISTICS

Outfitters pick you up either from the hotel or strategic locations north and south of town and return you to your hotel or to the pickup point. Short rides depart morning and afternoon, while longer rides are generally in the morning only, at least during winter hours of early sunset.

Ask at the beachfront restaurants of tiny towns like Yelapa, Quimixto, and Las Animas, south of PV, to hook up with horses for treks into the jungle. Horses are generally well cared for, and some are exceptionally fit and frolicky.

OUTFITTERS

Hacienda de Doña Engracia (⊠ *Carretera a las Palmas, Km 10, La Desembocada* ☎ *322/224–0410* ⊕ *www.haciendadonaengracia.com*) has, among other activities, a three-hour horseback excursion ($56 per person). After the river has receded at the end of the wet season (this dry period usually lasts from late November through June), you ride one hour to a series of three hot springs, where you spend an hour before heading back, crossing a river mid-trip. In rainy season, the tour through jungly hills is impressive but, because you often can't cross the swollen streams, it doesn't go to the hot springs. Some of the large stable of horses are of Arabian stock. At the hacienda, you can fish in the small artificial lake, do a tequila tasting, go mountain biking, or lunch at the restaurant. Most people arrive as part of a cruise-ship excursion or dune buggy tour with Wild Vallarta *(⇨ ATV Tours, above)* or other adventure companies, but you can drive on your own as well.

★ **Rancho Charro** (☎322/224–0114 ⊕*www.ranchoelcharro.com*) provides transportation to and from your hotel for rides to rivers and waterfalls. Choices include three-hour ($56), five-hour ($68), and all-day rides ($100), and several multiday camping-riding combos.

★ The friendly folks at family-owned **Rancho Manolo** (⊠*Highway 200, Km 12, at Mismaloya bridge, Mismaloya* ☎322/228–0018 *day, 322/222–3694 evening*) take you into the mountains they know so well. The usual tour is to El Edén, the restaurant-and-river property where the movie *Predator* was filmed. The three-hour trip (45 minutes each way, with 1½ hours for a meal or for splashing in the river) costs just $33.

The horses of **Rancho Ojo de Agua** (⊠*Cerrada de Cardenal 227, Fracc. Aralias, Puerto Vallarta* ☎322/224–0607 ⊕*www.ranchojodeagua. com*) are part Mexican quarter horse and part Thoroughbred; according to proud owner Mari González, the stock comes from the Mexican cavalry. The family-owned business conducts sunset and half-day horseback rides (three to five hours, $63 and $70), the latter including lunch and time for a swim in a mountain stream. Also available at some times of year is a full-day excursion (seven hours, most of which on the horse) into the Sierra Madre ($95) or an overnight ($250), which includes four meals and either tent or cabin camping.

Rancho Mi Chaparrita (⊠*Manuel Rodriguez Sanchez 14, Sayulita* ☎329/291–3112 ⊕*www.michaparrita.com*) has very nice, healthy horses willing to run (or walk, if you ask them nicely). Ride on the beach, in the tropical forest, or a combination of the two for $25 an hour.

Though the trail rides at **Club de Polo Costa Careyes** (⊠*Km 53.5, Carretera 200, Carretera a Barra de Navidad, El Careyes* ☎315/351–0320 ⊕*www.mexicopolo.com*) are expensive at $100 for 45 minutes to an hour, you know you're getting an exceptional mount. Trips leave in early morning or around sunset. Tours are mid-November through mid-April only.

KAYAKING

Except on very calm, glassy days, the open ocean is really too rough for enjoyable kayaking, and the few kayaking outfitters there mainly offer this activity in combination with snorkeling, dolphin-watching, or boating excursions to area beaches. The best places for kayaking-and-birding combos are the mangroves, estuaries, large bays, and islands of the Costalegre, south of Puerto Vallarta.

LOGISTICS

Many of the larger beachfront hotels—especially the all-inclusives—rent or loan sea kayaks to their guests. Double kayaks are easier on the arms than single kayaks. Since the wind usually picks up in the afternoon, morning is generally the best time to paddle. Stick to coves if you want to avoid energy-draining chop and big waves. Kayaks range from $8 to $12 an hour or $23 to $35 per day. All-inclusives like Dreams, just south of Puerto Vallarta, usually don't charge their guests for kayaks.

○ Rent kayaks or take a half-day, full-day, or two-day paddling and birding tour with **Immersion Adventures** (⊠ *Entrada Camino a La Manzanilla, La Manzanilla* ☎ *315/351–5341* ⊕ *www.immersionadventures.com*). Although the company has an office on the entrance road to La Manzanilla, it's best to book your excursions at least a week ahead of your arrival. Opportunities include trips to offshore islands Cocinas and Iglesias, the riparian environment of Ríos Purificación or Cuixmala, or five- to six-hour coastal forays with time for snorkeling.

In addition to its other curricula, **Ecotours** (⊠ *Ignacio L. Vallarta 243, Col. E. Zapata* ☎ *322/223–3130 or 322/222–6606* ⊕ *www.ecotours vallarta.com*), in downtown Vallarta, has kayaking tours from Boca de Tomatlán ($70). After paddling around a rocky point you end at tiny Playa Colomitos, where there's time for snorkeling and then a snack. You'll spend 1½ to 2 hours kayaking and though it's fun being on the water, the scenery is not exactly breathtaking.

Vallarta Adventures (⊠ *Paseo de las Palmas 39–A, Nuevo Vallarta* ☎ *322/ 297–1212, 888/303–2653 in U.S. and Canada* ⊠ *Edifício Marina Golf, Local 13–C, Calle Mástil, Marina Vallarta* ☎ *322/221–0657* ⊕ *www.vallarta-adventures.com*) includes kayaking in its boat trip to Las Caletas, the company's private beach; the coastline here is fun to explore. The only other option is on dolphin-watching trips, where there are about five kayaks per boatload of up to 100 passengers, most of whom choose to snorkel.

> **PICKUP POLO**
>
> Rent a pony and join a game of polo at the **Club de Polo Costa Careyes** (⊠ *Km 53.5 Carretera 200, Carretera a Barra de Navidad, El Careyes* ☎ *315/351–0320* ⊕ *www.careyes.com*). The cost is $400–$600 per game for four to five chuckers; includes horse rental, polo pro, and greens fee. Spectators are welcome, too, at no charge, to watch the various tournaments (mid-April–November). Ask about packages including accommodations, clinics (mid-February through mid-March only), and lessons.

7

MOUNTAIN BIKING

Although the tropical climate makes it hot for biking, the Puerto Vallarta area is lovely and has challenging and varied terrain. Based in Puerto Vallarta, the major biking operators lead rides up river valleys, to Yelapa, and from the old mining town of San Sebastian (reached via plane; included in price), high in the Sierra, back to Vallarta. It's about 45 kilometers of twisty downhill.

In the rainy season, showers are mainly in the late afternoon and evening, so bike tours can take place year-round. In summer and fall rivers and waterfalls are voluptuous and breathtaking. A popular ending point for rides into the foothills, they offer a place to rest, rinse off (there's lots of mud), and have a snack or meal. During the dry season, it's relatively cooler and less humid. The very best months for biking are January and February: the weather is coolest and the vegetation, rivers, and waterfalls still reasonably lush after the end of the rainy season in October.

LOGISTICS

PRICES Four- to five-hour rides average $60 to $70; Yelapa costs $115–$160. The ride down from San Sebastián, including one-way plane trip, goes for around $240. Rides of more than a half day include lunch, and all include helmet, gloves, and bikes.

OUTFITTERS

Oscar del Díos of **Bike Mex** (✉ *Calle Guerrero 361, Centro* ☎*322/223–1834 or 322/223–1680*) can tailor rides to your level of fitness and ability. He has a technical, single-track ride for the very advanced and local rides for all levels. The all-day downhill from San Sebastian (take the plane up and ride back for $240) is less popular now that the road has been paved and has more vehicular traffic. More popular is the daily "killer donkey" experience; cost is $68 for the round-trip. Excursions include guide, gear (24-speed mountain bikes), and a light breakfast and snacks. Multiday excursions can be arranged. A few streets behind Vallarta's cathedral, **Eco Ride** (✉ *Calle Miramar 382, Centro* ☎*322/222–7912* ⊕*www.ecoridemex.com*) caters to intermediate and expert cyclists. Rides start at the shop and go up the Río Cuale, passing some hamlets along single tracks and dirt roads. A few rides include time at local swimming holes; the Yelapa ride ($114)—with two 10-km (6-mi) uphills and a 20-km (12-mi) downhill—returns by boat.

Family-operated **Vallarta Bikes** (✉ *Fransico Villa 1442, Col. Los Sauces* ☎*322/293–1142* ⊕*www.vallartabikes.com*) has custom tours of up to 10 days. More common, however, are set itineraries for beginner to advanced cyclists. A three- to four-hour beginner's ride to La Pileta ($43) is popular, as the departure point is near the town center and the destination a year-round swimming hole. This easy downhill includes lunch, as do all Vallarta Bikes' tours. The six-hour, 35-km (22-mi) tour to Yelapa ($143) is more physical, but the reward is lunch overlooking Yelapa's beautiful beach and returning by water taxi. Owner-guide Alejandro González leads groups whenever possible. He will certainly push you, but don't expect him to hold your hand.

MULTISPORT TOURS

Natura Expeditions (✉ *Carretera Aeropuerto, Km 5.5, Zona Hotelera* ☎ *322/224–0410* ⊕ *www.mexon line.com/viva.htm*) has nature-oriented excursions, including bass and deep-sea fishing, scuba diving, hiking, horseback riding, and biking.

Canadian expat Ray Calhoun and his wife Eva run **Tours Soltero** (✉ *Privada Las Cabañas 26, San Patricio Melaque* ☎ *315/355–6777* ✐ *raystoursmelaque@yahoo. com*). They rent mountain bikes, snorkeling equipment, and boogie boards ($10 per day), and lead active tours from their base in San Patricio Melaque to neighboring beaches and towns. Typical tours are snorkeling in Tenacatita with boogie boarding at Boca de Iguana, from 10 to 5 ($31), and a day trip to the state capital, Colima, which includes lunch and a stop at a typical hacienda cum museum ($62). Tours run any day, all year with a minimum of four customers.

> ### A CUT ABOVE
>
> With some 15 years' experience, dozens of tours, and a staff of some 350, the well-respected **Vallarta Adventures** (✉ *Paseo de las Palmas 39–A, Nuevo Vallarta* ☎ *322/297–1212, 888/303–2653 in U.S. and Canada* ✉ *Edifício Marina Golf, Local 13–C, Calle Mástil, Marina Vallarta* ☎ *322/221–0657* ⊕ *www. vallarta-adventures.com*) is the obvious choice for high-end hotel concierges and cruise-ship activity directors.

SAILING

Although large Bahía de Banderas and towns to the north and south have lots of beautiful beaches to explore and wildlife to see, there are few sailing adventures for the public. Most boating companies don't want to rely on the wind to get to area beaches for the day's activities. The companies below are recommended for their true sailing skills and reliable vessels.

LOGISTICS

For insurance reasons, companies or individuals here don't rent bareboat (uncrewed) yachts even to seasoned sailors. Those who want to crew the ship themselves can do semi-bareboat charters, where the captain comes along but allows the clients to sail the boat.

OUTFITTERS

Recommended by Pat Henry (now retired) of the Coming About School of Sailing is **Dos Amantes** (✉ *Marina Vallarta* ☎ *044322/140–3171* ✐ *dos_amantes_lacey@hotmail.com*). The easy-going owners, Joe and Lori Lacey, will tailor a day or overnight of sailing to their clients' wishes: giving sailing tips or sailing the boat themselves, providing gourmet food, snorkeling and sunset-viewing opportunities, and most anything else.

Puerto Vallarta Tours (☎ *322/222–4935 or 866/217–9704 from the U.S. or Canada* ⊕ *www.puertovallartatours.net*) offers a variety of sailing adventures, from all-day sails to Yelapa or more remote Pizota, to half-day treks to Los Arcos, or private sailing charters. Prices for shared cruises range from $45 per person for a four-hour tour to Los Arcos to $76 for a full-day jaunt to Pizota.

Vallarta Adventures (✉ *Paseo de las Palmas 39–A, Nuevo Vallarta* ☎ *322/297–1212, 888/303–2653 in U.S. and Canada* ✉ *Edifício Marina Golf, Local 13–C, Calle Mástil, Marina Vallarta* ☎ *322/221–0657* ⊕ *www.vallarta-adventures.com*) has day and sunset sails during high season for about $85 and $75 per person, respectively. They'll do individual charters as well. Another option for chartering your own private sailboat is to contact captain Andre Schwartz of **Casa Naval** (✉ *El Faro de la Marina, Marina Vallarta* ☎ *322/100–4154 or 322/148-2203* ✉ *zenigma1947@yahoo.com*). Based in Marina Vallarta the captain-owner has a comfortable Beneteau Oceanis 390 called the *Dèjá-Vu Again,* a 39-foot vessel that accommodates eight for trips of four hours to several days. He charges $100 per hour for up to 10 passengers, with a discount of 10 percent for trip of four hours or more.

SCUBA DIVING & SNORKELING

The ocean isn't nearly as clear as the Caribbean, but the warm, nutrient-rich water attracts a varied community of sea creatures. Many of the resort hotels rent or loan snorkeling equipment and have introductory dive courses at their pools. The underwater preserve surrounding Los Arcos, a rock formation off Playa Mismaloya, is a popular spot for diving and snorkeling. The rocky bay at Quimixto, about 32 km (20 mi) south of PV and accessible only by boat, is a good snorkeling spot. *Pangeros* based in Boca, Mismaloya, Yelapa and elsewhere can be hired to take you to spots off the tourist trail.

On the north side of things, Punta de Mita, about 80 km (50 mi) north of PV, has the Marietas Islands, with lava tubes and caves and at least 10 good places to snorkel and dive, including spots for advanced divers. El Morro Islands, with their big fish lurking in the underwater pinnacles and caves, are also suitable for experienced divers.

LOGISTICS
June through September is the very best time for snorkeling and diving, although it's fine all year long. In summer, however, the water is not only its warmest and calmest but visibility is best—80 to 120 feet on a good day—and you can spot gigantic manta rays, several species of eel, sea turtles, large and many species of colorful fish. In winter, although conditions are less favorable, some luck will yield orca and humpback whale sightings, an awesome experience.

OUTFITTERS
For PADI- or NAUI-certification, equipment rentals, and one- or two-tank dives, contact **Chico's Dive Shop** (✉ *Paseo Díaz Ordáz 772, Centro* ☎ *322/222–1895* ✉ *Mismaloya Beach, in front of Barceló La Jolla de Mismaloya, Mismaloya* ☎ *322/228–0248* ⊕ *www.chicos-diveshop.com*). Trips to Los Arcos accommodate snorkelers ($25 per person) as well as those who want a one- or two-tank dive ($65 and $95, respectively). Book several days ahead for a night dive ($73 for one

tank). From the Mismaloya shop, you can rent kayaks and mountain bikes ($10 per hour for either one). In Nayarit, **Vallarta Undersea** (⊠*Héroes de Nacozarí 152, Bucerías* ☎*329/298–2364* ⊕*www.vallartaundersea.com*) teaches PADI dive courses; runs dive trips; and sells, rents, and repairs dive equipment. The Vallarta branch, which goes by the name **Pacific Scuba** (⊠*Federico M. Ascencio, Zona Hotelera* ☎*322/209–0334* ⊕*www.vallartaundersea.com*), is across the street from Peninsula Mall.

WHEN TO CATCH A WAVE

Locals have lots of folk wisdom about when to catch the best waves. Some say it's best right before a good rain, others believe it's when the tide is moving toward an extreme high or low.

★ **Ecotours,** an authorized equipment dealer, has English-speaking PADI dive masters. Two-tank dives run $85 to $100; longer trips to Corbeteña cost $120. All two-tank trips include lunch, refreshments, and gear. The PADI dive masters at **Pacific Scuba** (⊠*Blvd. Francisco Medina Ascencio 2486, Zona Hotelera* ☎*322/209–0364* ⊕*www.pacificscuba.com.mx*) teach courses, rent equipment, and arrange trips. A two-tank package to one of at least six sites (including Los Arcos, Marietas Islands, or Corbeteña) costs $82 to $150 and includes lunch and all gear. Three-day packages are available, too.

★ Tours with **Sociedad Cooperativa de Servicios Turísticos** (⊠*Av. El Anclote 1, Manz. 17, Corral del Risco* ☎*329/291–6298* ⊕*www.prodigyweb.net.mx/cooperativapuntamita*) are a great deal if you have a group: two hours of snorkeling around the Marietas Islands, for up to eight people, costs just $120. **Vallarta Adventures** (⊠*Paseo de las Palmas 39–A, Nuevo Vallarta* ☎*322/297–1212, 888/303–2653 in U.S. and Canada* ⊠*Edifício Marina Golf, Local 13–C, Calle Mástil, Marina Vallarta* ☎*322/221–0657* ⊕*www.vallarta-adventures.com*) has daylong, two-tank tours of El Morro Islands ($115), El Corbeteña ($125), and less-visited sites like Los Anegados ($90) and El Sequial ($125). Most are offered just once a week. Their expert PADI guides accommodate snorkelers as well as divers. They also have introductory dive classes for children and adults ($35), and open-water certification.

SURFING

The main surfing areas are in the north, in Nayarit State, including (from south to north) Destiladeras, Sayulita, and nearly a dozen breaks off Punta de Mita, where offshore breaks for intermediate and advanced surfers are best accessed by boat. The best spots for beginners are shore breaks like those at El Anclote and Sayulita; in the south, Barra de Navidad is also appropriate for beginners.

LOGISTICS

SEASONS Waves are largest and most consistent between June and December; the water is also warmest during the rainy season (late June–October), averaging nearly 80° July through September.

PRICES   Surfboard rentals start at $10 an hour or $25 a day. Surfing trips run around $40 per hour, usually with a three- or four-hour minimum. Shops sell rash guards (not usually the need for a full wet suit here), boogie boards, wax, and other necessities. For good info and links check out ⊕*www.surf-mexico.com.*

OUTFITTERS

On the beach at Sayulita is **Captain Pablo** (✉*Calle Las Gaviotas at beach, Sayulita* ☎*329/291–2070 early morning and evenings only* ✍*pandpsouthworth@hotmail.com*), where you can rent equipment or take surfing lessons with Patricia: $25 should get you to your feet (board included). Surf tours, gear included, cost $180 for four hours (up to four surfers).

On the beach at Sayulita, **Sininen** (✉*Calle Delfín 4–S, Sayulita* ☎*329/291–3186*) rents ($20 per day, $30 for 24 hours) and sells surfboards and surf paraphernalia. In Barra look for **South Swell Surf Shop** (✉*Hotel La Alondra, Suite 2, Calle Sinaloa 16, Barra de Navidad* ☎*315/100–4332 cell*) for all your ripping requirements. If you're not ripping yet, they offer lessons for about $40 per person for two hours, including equipment.

WILDLIFE-WATCHING

Banderas Bay and the contiguous coast and inland areas are blessed with abundant species of birds and beasties. Diverse habitats from riparian forests to offshore islands are home to a wide range of native and migratory birds, including about two dozen endemic species. Beyond birds, most of the wildlife spotting is marine: whales (late November through end of March), dolphins, marine turtles, and giant manta rays, among many other species.

BIRD-WATCHING

Although there aren't a lot of dedicated birding operators here, this region is perfect for the pastime, as Vallarta has more than 350 species in a wide variety of habitats, including shoreline, rivers, marshes, lagoons, mangroves, and tropical and evergreen forests. In the mangroves, standouts are the great blue heron, mangrove cuckoo, and vireo. Ocean and shore birds include brown and blue-footed boobies and red-billed tropic birds. Military macaws patrol the thorn forests, and songbirds of all stripes serenade the pine-oak forests.

LOGISTICS   Most people come on trips through birding clubs or organizations like those below, or hire a private birding guide. Outfitters charge $45–$60 for half-day tours and $100–$125 for full-day tours.

OUTFITTERS   **Ecotours** (✉*Ignacio L. Vallarta 243, Col. E. Zapata* ☎*322/223–3130 or 322/222–6606* ⊕*www.ecotoursvallarta.com*) runs four different six-hour tours ($73 per person each) to different ecosystems. Bring plenty of insect repellent, especially in the rainy months. Clients of **Immersion Adventures** (✉*Entrada Camino a La Manzanilla, La Manzanilla* ☎*315/351–5341* ⊕*www.immersionadventures.com*) sneak up on their idols via kayak, accessing mangrove swamps and riparian environments as well as hiking along jungle trails. **Victor Emanuel Nature Tours** (*512/328–5221, 800/328–8368 in U.S. and Canada www.ventbird.com*) has several yearly small-group birding tours of the Puerto Vallarta from Rancho Primavera, just south of PV proper.

Mark Stackhouse, of **Westwings Birding Tours** (*866/552–0221 from the U.S. www.westwings.com*), leads tours of Nayarit, Jalisco and Colima. According to Mark, a 30-year birder, it's possible to see about 25 percent of the birds found throughout Mexico on day trips from a San Blas Hotel. Contact Mark with plenty of lead time to arrange private birding tours; group trips are described on the Web site. **Wings** (*520/320–9868, 888/293–6443 in U.S. and Canada www.wings-birds.com*) based in Tucson, Arizona, leads several weeklong tours each year to the mangroves and tropical forest around San Blas, Jalisco, and Colima.

DOLPHIN ENCOUNTERS

Many folks find the idea of captive dolphins disturbing; others cherish the opportunity to interact with these intelligent creatures that communicate through body language as well as an audible code we humans have yet to decipher. Decide whether you support the idea of captive-dolphin encounters, and act accordingly. Listed below are operators with captive dolphin programs as well as one that has an open-ocean encounter. As these gregarious mammals are fond of bow-surfing, most bay-tripping boats will encounter dolphins as they motor along the bay, providing more opportunities to see dolphins as well as leaping manta rays and other sea life.

LOGISTICS Dolphins are abundant in the bay year-round, though not 24/7. Dolphin encounters limit the number of humans per encounter, and usually allow just two visits a day, so call early in your stay to book.

OUTFITTERS For both the Dolphin Encounter ($69) and the Dolphin Swim ($99)
★ with **Dolphin Discovery** (*Sea Life Park, Carretera a Tepic, Km 155, Nuevo Vallarta 322/297–0724, 866/393–5158 toll-free in the U.S., 866/793–1905 toll-free in Canada www.sealifeparkvallarta.com*) you spend about 30 of the 45-minute experience in the water interacting with dolphins. In the Royal Dolphin Swim ($149), you still get only 30 minutes in the pool, but at a higher ratio of cetaceans to humans, you get more face time. Mexican-owned **Wildlife Connection** (*Calle Francia 140, Dpto. 7, Col. Versalles, Puerto Vallarta 322/225–3621 www.wildlifeconnection.com*) uses two-motor skiffs equipped with listening equipment to find pods of dolphins in the wild blue sea. You can then jump in the water to swim with these beautiful creatures in their own environment. The most common destination is around the Marietas Islands. The cost is $65 per person for a three- to four-hour tour, including travel time, and tours are conducted April through December only. There's no guarantee, however, that the dolphins will stick around for the fun. There's also a combined tour searching for whales and dolphins, $80 a pop, December through March only.

HIKING

The coastal fringe and the hills behind Vallarta—with streams and rivers heading down from the mountains—are beautiful areas for exploring, but few tour operators have hiking and walking trips. If you plan an impromptu exploration, it's best to take along a local familiar with the area.

CAUTION

Several organizations, including Greenpeace, the Humane Society (U.S.), and the Whale and Dolphin Conservation Society have spoken out against captive dolphin encounters, asserting that some water parks get dolphins from restricted areas, and that the confined conditions at some parks put the dolphins' health at risk. Consider putting the $100-plus fee toward a snorkeling, whale-watching, or noncaptive dolphin encounter, where you can see marine life in its natural state.

LOGISTICS Some of the biking tour operators (⇨*Biking, above*) will lead hiking outings as well, if you ask.

OUTFITTERS **Ecotours** (✉*Ignacio L. Vallarta 243, Col. E. Zapata* ☎*322/223–3130 or 322/222–6606* ⊕*www.ecotoursvallarta.com*) leads a very short hike (about one hour total hiking) or a three-hour hike around El Nogalito River with a pit stop at a rocky, waterfall-fed pool for a dip. En route to either you'll see a small number of birds, butterflies, and tropical plants.

Vallarta Adventures (✉*Paseo de las Palmas 39–A, Nuevo Vallarta* ☎*322/297–1212, 888/303–2653 in U.S. and Canada* ✉*Edifício Marina Golf, Local 13–C, Calle Mástil, Marina Vallarta* ☎*322/221–0657* ⊕*www.vallarta-adventures.com*) has an outdoor adventure tour ($95) combining a speedboat ride and mule trek with rappelling, hiking, and a partial canopy tour. Although hikes are generally led by knowledgeable naturalists, the emphasis is on physical activity rather than flora and fauna sightings. Participants must be 12 or over and 220 pounds or under.

TURTLE-WATCHING & REPATRIATION

Mexico has seven of the eight sea turtle species in the world. Three of those species live in and around Banderas Bay. The most prevalent is the olive ridley, or *golfina*. The fastest growing and earliest to mature of the Pacific Coast turtles, they are much more numerous than the Careyes and leatherbacks; the latter are the least frequently sighted. Researchers estimate there are one to 10 leatherbacks for every 1,000 olive ridleys in the Puerto Vallarta area. The tour companies listed offer educational programs combined with hands-on activities.

After the female turtle creates a nest in the sand, the eggs incubate for approximately 60 days. The babies must bust out of eggs and earth on their own, and with luck they will head for the ocean under cover of night. Birds, crabs, and other wild animals are relentless predators. For every 1,000 baby turtles born, only one survives to adulthood. Fortunately the average nest holds several hundred eggs.

LOGISTICS Tours run from summer through late fall. Wear shoes or sandals that are comfortable for walking in the sand, bring a sweatshirt or light jacket, and plan to stay out late in the evening for most turtle repatriation programs, as that is when predators are less active. Most tours cost $46–$50 per person and last three to four hours.

OUTFITTERS Learn about and interact with nature through **Ecotours** (⊠*Ignacio L. Vallarta 243, Col. E. Zapata* ☎*322/223–3130 or 322/222–6606* ⊕*www. ecotoursvallarta.com*), which offers three-hour turtle tours ($46) August through early December. Depending on the time of year, you may walk the beach searching for females depositing their eggs in the sand and help remove these eggs for safekeeping. Whether or not you find egg-laying females, there are always little turtles for releasing to the wild at the end of the evening. Tours are Monday through Saturday. Trained biologists from **Wildlife Connection** (⊠*Calle Francia 140, Col. Versalles, Puerto Vallarta* ☎*322/225–3621* ⊕*www.wildlifeconnection.com*) lead turtle repatriation programs. During the four-hour tours you'll drive ATVs to the beach to find and collect recently deposited eggs, if possible, and then blast over to Boca de Tomates Beach to liberate tiny turtles under the relative protection of darkness.

WHALE-WATCHING

Most of the boats on the bay, whether fishing boats or tour boats, also run whale-watching tours (December–mid-March). Some boats are equipped with hydrophones for listening to the whales' songs and carry trained marine biologists; others use the usual crew and simply look for signs of cetaceans. The species you're most likely to see are humpback and killer whales (a gray whale occasionally), false killer whales, and bottlenose, spinner, and pantropic spotted dolphins (yup, dolphins are whales, too!).

LOGISTICS Whale-watching is only available December through March. Prime breeding grounds are around the Marietas Islands. The larger boats leave from Marina Vallarta, but fishermen in villages like Corral del Risco, Mismaloya, Boca de Tomatlán, and even Yelapa and Las Animas can be hired for less formal, more intimate trips to look for whales. The larger boats are more likely to have radio equipment useful for communicating with others about the location of whale pods. Some outfitters offer a discount if you sign up online.

OUTFITTERS **Ecotours** (⊠*Ignacio L. Vallarta 243, Col. E. Zapata* ☎*322/223–3130 or 322/222–6606* ⊕*www.ecotoursvallarta.com*) operates excursions aboard boats with hydrophones. After a brief lecture about cetacean ecosystems, board a boat at Punta de Mita for a three-hour tour. Tours are daily in season (mid-December–mid-March) and cost $85. **Sociedad Cooperativa de Servicios Turísticos** (⊠*Av. El Anclote 1, Manz. 17, Nuevo Corral del Risco* ☎*329/291–6298* ⊕*www.prodigyweb.net. mx/cooperativapuntamita*) has whale-watching around the Marietas Islands ($1,200 for one to eight people). You search until whales are spotted, and then have a half-hour of viewing time before returning to dry land.

Vallarta Adventures (⊠*Paseo de las Palmas 39–A, Nuevo Vallarta* ☎*322/297–1212, 888/303–2653 in U.S. and Canada* ⊠*Edifício Marina Golf, Local 13–C, Calle Mástil, Marina Vallarta* ☎*322/221–*

0657 ⊕www.vallarta-adventures. com) has professional guides who assist you in spotting dolphins and whales as you snorkel, dive, or kayak at various sites on and around Banderas Bay. Sailing trips for seeking cetaceans are also available ($85). Professional biologists at **Wildlife Connection** (⊠*Calle Francia 140, Col. Versalles, Puerto Vallarta* ☎*322/225–3621* ⊕*www. wildlifeconnection.com*) are dedicated to educating the public about area wildlife; the outfit gives tours in season ($74).

WORD OF MOUTH
"There is no electricity [on the Rhythms of the Night tour], so dinner and the trails are all lit by candles. Very cool and romantic. I would highly recommend this."
–MichelleY

OTHER ADVENTURES

CRUISES

Daytime bay cruises generally begin with a quick jaunt to Los Arcos Underwater Preserve, off Mismaloya Beach. There's about a half hour for snorkeling or swimming—sometimes with legions of little jellyfish in addition to the turtles that feed on them. Cruises then proceed to Yelapa, Quimixto, or Playa las Ánimas, or to Islas Marietas for whale-watching (in winter), snorkeling, swimming, and lunch. Horseback riding might be available at an additional cost (about $15).

There are plenty of similar tours available; the following are among the most popular and professional.

LOGISTICS
Buy your ticket from licensed vendors at Parque Lázaro Cárdenas, just north of the Cuale River, along the boardwalk at Los Muertos Beach, and at sportfishing operators such as Master Baiters.

Prices are somewhat fluid; like car salespeople, the ticket sellers give discounts or jack up the price as they see fit. Full-day booze cruises cost about $45–$70 per person, including open bar, Continental breakfast, lunch, snorkeling, and/or kayaks. Dinner cruises cost $75–$80. Expect to pay a small port fee (about $2) at the maritime pier in addition to the cost of the ticket.

OUTFITTERS
Cruceros Princesa (⊠*Terminal Marítima, Marina Vallarta* ☎*322/224–4777*) has full-day and half-day trips to the beaches of southern Bahía de Banderas with snorkeling, beach time, and lunch. Half-day cruises generally go to Los Arcos or Las Animas; full-day cruises access several different spots, such as Yelapa and Majahuitas or Los Arcos, or Quimixto and Playa las Ánimas, as well as jaunts to Islas Marietas for half-day whale-watching (in winter), snorkeling, swimming, and lunch. The boat "Zarape" heads to Los Arcos for 40 minutes of snorkeling,

and then continues to Las Animas and Quimixto. After beach time there's lunch aboard the boat on the return trip ($38).

Cruceros Santamaría (⊠ *Paseo de la Marina Sur 161, Interior 14, Las Palmas I Condominiums, Marina Vallarta* ☎ *322/221–2511* ⊕ *www.santamariacruises.com*) has two different full-day tours to Los Arcos and Las Ánimas with visits to either Quimixto or Yelapa. It also rents boats for large private parties. You can buy tickets from their office or booth vendors.

☾ A really-and-truly sailing vessel that has circumnavigated the world more than once, the *Marigalante* (⊠ *Paseo Díaz Ordáz 770, Centro* ☎ *322/223–0309 or 322/223–1662* ⊕ *www.marigalante.com.mx*) has a pirate crew that keeps things hopping for preteens and even older kids with fun and games. The dinner cruise, with open bar and pre-Hispanic show, is geared for adults and has some bawdy pirate humor. Women who don't want to be "kidnapped" may prefer the day cruise or another operator.

★ **Vallarta Adventures** (⊠ *Paseo de las Palmas 39–A, Nuevo Vallarta* ☎ *322/297–1212, 888/303–2653 in U.S. and Canada* ⊠ *Edifício Marina Golf, Local 13-C, Calle Mástil, Marina Vallarta* ☎ *322/221–0657* ⊕ *www.vallarta-adventures.com*) has day or evening cruises to Caletas Beach, its exclusive domain. Although the day cruise can accommodate 150 passengers, there's plenty of room to spread out: boulder-bordered coves, sandy beaches, hammocks in the shade, and jungle trails ensure that you won't feel like a cow about to be branded "tourist." The Caletas by Day cruise includes snorkeling, kayaking, hiking, and lunch (scuba or spa treatments available for additional fees). The Rhythms of the Night evening cruise includes dinner on the beach and a show at the amphitheater. Most folks love the show—men and women dressed as voluptuous natives do a modern dance to dramatic lighting and music. Kids under 10 are not allowed. Both tours cost $85.

WATER PARK

☾ Traditionally more popular with Mexican families than foreigners, **Sea Life Park** *(formerly Splash)* has added dolphin encounters *(⇨ above)* to attract a wider audience. Kids love the place just as it was: They can still plummet down enormous waterslides, swim, and play on playground equipment and carnival rides. There are restaurants and bars; to take advantage of the three shows (birds, sea lions, and dolphins), arrive by noon, as they're presented once only between then and 1:10 PM. ⊠ *Carretera a Tepic, Km 155, Nuevo Vallarta* ☎ *322/297-0724* ⊠ *$12* ⊙ *Daily 10–6.*

Culture

Huichol artisan

WORD OF MOUTH

"We only touched on the flea market and malecón/Old Town area, and I wish we had taken more time to stroll and take it all in. I would recommend not rushing through Old Town. I think it's one thing that sets PV apart from so many tropical/beach destinations—so many of them are limited to beaches and resort experiences."

—Stephie

8

In the 1950s, Puerto Vallarta was like an extended family: everyone knew everyone else. Most of the inhabitants were from related families who had come down from the mountain mining towns after the turn of the century. People sat in front of their houses in the evening, chatting; the action was in the street. Until the explosion of outside interest, most of PV's intellectual and artistic life has centered

> ### GET THE SCOOP
>
> One of the best sources of information for upcoming events is *Bay Vallarta*, published twice a month. The free bilingual publication gets scooped up fast from hotels, restaurants, car rental agencies, and other places frequented by visitors.

around traditional Mexican culture, which is synonymous with the Catholic religion. Today there are plenty of bars and nightclubs, but less live theater and music than locals would like. The fine arts scene, however, is thriving. Local and foreign artists are established and respected painters and sculptors represented by PV's finest galleries. High season is the time to see these artists at their best, especially on Wednesday evenings, when everyone in town turns out for artWalk.

ARCHITECTURE

La Iglesia de Nuestra Señora de Guadalupe *(Church of Our Lady of Guadalupe)* is dedicated to the patron saint of Mexico and of Puerto Vallarta. The holy mother's image, by Ignacio Ramírez, is the centerpiece of the cathedral's slender marble altarpiece. The brick bell tower is topped by a lacy-looking crown that replicates the one worn by Carlota, short-lived empress of Mexico. The wrought-iron crown toppled during an earthquake that shook this area of the Pacific Coast in October 1995, but was soon replaced with a fiberglass version, supported, as was the original, by a squadron of stone angels. ⊠ *Calle Hidalgo, Centro* ☎ *No phone* ⊘ *7:30* AM–8 PM.

THE ARTS

DANCE

Under the direction of Professor Carlos Enrique Barrios Limón at the Centro Cultural Cuale, **Grupo Folklórico Municipal Xiutla** (⊠ *Centro Cultural Cuale, East end of Isla Río Cuale, Centro* ☎ *322/223–0095*) is a talented troupe of folkloric dancers. During the group's career of more than a decade, the 250 young people have performed at various venues around PV as well as elsewhere in Mexico, Canada, the United States, and Europe. Performances are often held outdoors at Los Arcos amphitheater or Parque Lázaro Cárdenas as well as at more formal venues around the city, and announced through the usual channels (*Bay Vallarta*, flyers, etc.).

FILM

Biblioteca Los Mangos (⊠*Av. Francisco Villa 1001, Col. Los Mangos* ☎*322/224–9966*) shows art films, musicals, and blockbusters. The current schedule is Friday at 7 PM and Saturday at 4 PM, but call to check showtimes; tickets are $1.50.

PV's original extravaganza for movie buffs and movie stars alike is the **Festival Internacional de Cine de Puerto Vallarta** (⊕*cinefest.pv.udg. mx*). Held during four days each March (sometimes April), the festival honors the best full-length feature film with a "golden iguana" award. Full-length, documentary, and short-subject films are shown around town at Cinépolis (about $4 each) or under the stars at Los Arcos Amphitheater; flyers all over town advertise the movies, or contact the movie houses directly *(⇨ Chapter 6)*. The public is invited to attend lectures and listen to discourses on local radio programs.

> ### PUBLIC HOLIDAYS
>
> Post offices, government and private offices, and banks are closed on public holidays (ATMs are plentiful, however). On Labor Day even tourist-related businesses like restaurants may be closed, as they prefer to give all employees the day off with pay. Public holidays include:
>
> **January 1:** Año Nuevo (New Year's Day)
> **February 5:** Día de la Constitución (Constitution Day)
> **March 25:** Aniversário de Benito Juárez (Juárez's Birthday)
> **May 1:** Día del Trabajador (Labor Day)
> **September 15:** Día de la Independencia (Independence Day)
> **November 20:** Día de la Revolución Mexicana (Mexican Revolution Day)

Beginning in late November or early December, the public is invited to see movies of many genres, at reasonable prices, during the five-day **Vallarta Film Festival** (☎*322/297–1947 or 322/297–1605* ⊕*www.vallarta filmfestival.com*). Films and seminars are held at the Cinemark Plaza Caracol (Plaza Caracol, Zona Hotelera ☎*322/224–8927*). Film industry types come to hobnob and honor each other with awards for best director, picture, cinematographer, and actor.

FINE ART

See Chapter 5 for art gallery descriptions and locations. An artist of worldwide renown, **Evelyn Boren** (⊠*Casa Bugambilla, Calle Bouganvillea s/n, Sayulita* ☎*329/291–3095*) lives and works in Sayulita each winter. Represented by Galeria Café des Artistes and other Puerto Vallarta shops, Boren shares her colorful landscapes with the public each Wednesday afternoon between 1 and 4 (Nayarit time) January through March. Her house is on the beach just south of the plaza.

The late Manuel Lepe's 1981 mural depicting Puerto Vallarta as a fanciful seaside fishing and farming village is painted above the stairs on the second floor of the **Palácio Municipal** (⊠*Av. Juárez, on Plaza de Armas, Centro* ☎*322/222–4565*), PV's city hall. Lepe is known for his blissful, primitive-style scenes of the city, filled with smiling angels. This one is rather tired, and the naïf work has been surpassed by his devotees. Still, Lepe is considered the father of PV naïf, and the mural is worth a quick look. The interior hallways surrounding the government building's central plaza sometimes host photography or fine art exhibitions. The tourism office is on the first floor. The Palacio is open weekdays 9 to 5.

An annual event since 1996, **Old Town artWalk** (☎322/222–1982) showcases artwork at 15 galleries. The galleries stay open late, usually offering an appetizer or snack as well as wine, beer, or soft drinks.

FOLKLORIC DANCE

Zapateado, the dancing characterized by rhythmical foot-stomping, is accompanied by *sones,* narrative, and up-tempo mariachi songs written specifically for the dances. Anywhere between 200 and 300 sones are known to exist, but the best-known is the *Jarabe Tapatío* (Mexican Hat Dance), whose dance includes the emblematic move of the male dancer putting his sombrero on the ground as a sign of respect to his female companion.

Browse paintings, jewelry, ceramics, glass, and folk art while hobnobbing with some of PV's most respected artists. If you don't have a map, pick one up from one of the perennially participating galleries, which include Galería Arte Latinoamericano, Galería Corona, Galería 8 y Más, Galería Pacífico, Galería Uno, Galería Vallarta, and Galería de Ollas (⇨*Chapter 5*). This walk is held from 6 PM to 10 PM, from the last week of October until late April.

MUSIC

Auditorio CECATI (*Centro de Capacitación Turística e Industrial* ✉*Calle Hidalgo 300, Centro* ☎*322/222–4910*) is the venue for musical or theatrical performances. It's right in the middle of the Old Town, and tickets generally inexpensive—about $10 for adults, half that for kids.

Vallarta's *banda municipal* (☎*322/223–2500*) serenades its citizens Thursday and Sunday evenings between 6 and 7, sometimes a bit later. Couples dance around the main plaza to *cumbias* (a distinctive style of popular Latin dance music that originated in Colombia), emanating from the central kiosk. Everyone's welcome to join in, and most of the dancers are just regular folks, both visitors and *vallartenses,* having some fun. Some days, however, the band plays *danzón,* a complicated, stylized box-step that originated in Cuba and is best left to those who know the steps.

THEATER

The small **Santa Barbara Theater** (✉*Olas Altas 351, Col. E. Zapata* ☎*322/223–2048* ⊕*www.santabarbaratheater.com*) is the place to see English-language shows, mainly musicals, November through April. It's community theater, not high art, but the productions are fun. A four-course dinner and a show are usually $35; tickets for the show alone run about $22.

FLIGHT OF THE VOLADORES

A relatively new phenomenon on the malecón are performances by *los voladores de Papantla,* the Papantla "flyers" near Los Arcos. Dressed in exquisite costumes of red velveteen pants decorated with sequins, mirrors, embroidery, and fringe, five men climb a 30-meter (98-foot) pole. Four of them dive from the top of the platform as the leader "speaks" to them from the pinnacle with fife and drum. Held by a rope tied to one foot, the men wing around the pole exactly 13 times before landing on the ground. The total number of revolutions adds up to the ritualistically significant number of 52. Native to Veracruz State, this traditional performance is held Thursday and Sunday evenings at 6 PM and 8 PM in low season, and every hour on the hour from 6 PM to 9 PM in high season (December through April).

Inexpensive (or even free) musical and theatrical events are often presented at **Centro Universitario de la Costa** (*CUC* ⊠ *Carretera a Ixtapa, Km 2.5, Ixtapa* ✛ *Outskirts of Ixtapa* ☎ *322/226–2263*). Performances include experimental and classical theater. Productions are in Spanish, but because they are very visual, they're enjoyable even if you don't speak the language. Check the principal newspapers *El Tribunal de la Bahía* and *Vallarta Opina* for upcoming events. Tickets are usually $5 to $10.

CLASSES & WORKSHOPS

A good source of information for current classes is the bimonthly, free *Bay Vallarta,* which always lists a Web page or phone number for further information.

You can matriculate mid-session at the informal **Centro Cultural Cuale** (⊠ *East end of Isla Río Cuale, Centro* ☎ *322/223–0095*) for classes like painting, drawing, and acting for children and for adults. Most of the instructors speak some English, others are fluent.

English-speaking artist Alicia Buena gives ceramics and painting classes for individuals or groups at **Terra Noble** (⊠ *Av. Tulipanes 595, Fracc. Lomas de Terra Noble, Col. 5 de Diciembre* ☎ *322/223–3530* ⊕ *www. terranoble.com*). The cost is a rather pricey $55 per person for the 1½-hour class. To schedule, call Terra Noble two days before you'd like to attend a class.

MUSEUMS

Not terribly exciting but free and smack in the middle of downtown, the small **Museo de la Marina** (⊠ *Calle Zaragoza between Av. Juárez and the malecón, at the southwest corner of the main plaza, Centro* ☎ *322/223–5357* ☒ *Free* ☉ *10–7:30 Tues.–Sun.*) has maritime exhib-

LIZ + RICHARD

The affair between Richard Burton and Elizabeth Taylor practically ignited tourism to PV, which was an idyllic beach town when the couple first visited in 1963. Taylor tagged along when Burton starred in *The Night of the Iguana*, shot in and around Mismaloya beach. The fiery Welsh actor purchased Casa Kimberley (on Calle Zaragoza, a few blocks behind the cathedral) for Liz's 32nd birthday and connected it to his home across the street with a pink-and-white "love bridge." Taylor's relationship with PV lasted longer than that with her fellow actor and two-time husband; she owned the house for 26 years and left most of her possessions behind when she sold it. Casa Kimberely later became a B&B; in 2007 litigation regarding ownership shut it—and tours of it—down.

its labeled in Spanish. There are a few interesting artifacts as well as maps, miniatures, and scale models of ships.

Pre-Columbian figures and Indian artifacts are on display at the **Museo Arqueológico** *(Archeological Museum)*. There's a general explanation of Western Pacific cultures and shaft tombs, and abbreviated but attractive exhibits of Aztatlán and Purépecha cultures and the Spanish conquest. ⊠ *Western tip of Isla Río Cuale, Centro* ☎*No phone* ✉*By donation* ⊗*Mon.–Sat. 10–7.*

CULTURAL CENTERS

The **Centro Cultural Cuale** (⊠*East end of Isla Río Cuale, Aquiles Serdán 437, Int. 38, Centro* ☎*322/223–0095*) sells the work of local artists, has art and dance classes *(⇨ Classes, above)*, and hosts cultural events. Cost of classes is nominal and cultural events are free. The free bimonthly *Bay Vallarta*, available at tourist-oriented shops, hotels, and restaurants, is the best source of information on current classes.

Biblioteca Los Mangos (⊠*Av. Francisco Villa 1001, Col. Los Mangos* ☎*322/224–9966*) has lots of reasonably priced art classes *(⇨ Classes and Workshops, above)*, and free or inexpensive monthly events, such as dance performances. Themed performances are scheduled around Day of the Dead, Christmas, Easter, and other holidays.

Philo's (⊠*Calle Delfin 15, La Cruz de Huanacaxtle* ☎*329/295–5068*) is the unofficial cultural center of La Cruz, north of Bucerías. Spanish classes are Thursday and Saturday at 11 AM for beginners and at 10 AM for intermediate speakers. Classes are free, but donations are greatly appreciated.

FESTIVALS & EVENTS

WINTER

JANUARY

Held for the first time in 2005, the **Perrotón** (*Dog Show* ☎322/223–2500) has become an annual event. In addition to lectures, there are contests including ugliest dog, dog and owner who most resemble each other, most beautiful dog, and exhibitions of agility and obedience.

FEBRUARY

The four-day **Festival de Música San Pancho** (*San Pancho Music Festival* ☎311/258–4135) is an amalgam of the area's best regional musicians; snowbirds also participate. The free jamboree, usually held in mid- to late February, gets bigger and more organized each year. The 2008 event featured bluegrass, blues, jazz, funk and standards in addition to cumbia and Mexican classics. Look for flyers around town that describe events and their venues. San Pancho is about 50 minutes north of downtown Puerto Vallarta.

> **CULTURAL TOURS**
>
> **Puerto Vallarta Tours** (☎866/217-9704 ⊕www.puertovallartatours.net) runs all-day guided bus tours to Tepic, Nayarit, for sightseeing, shopping, and learning about the Huichol Indians. **Vallarta Adventures** (✉Paseo de las Palmas 39–A, Nuevo Vallarta ☎322/297–1212, 888/303-2653 in U.S. and Canada ✉Edifício Marina Golf, Local 13-C, Calle Mástil, Marina Vallarta ☎322/221-0657 ⊕www.vallarta-adventures.com), has its own Huichol Indian tour, once a week, which includes round-trip air transportation into the highlands of the Sierra.

Tours, hotel rooms, works of art, and dinner at participating restaurants are auctioned during the **Benefício Annual Para la Biblioteca Los Mangos,** a benefit to support the city's only public library. Contact Ricardo Murrieta (☎322/224–9966) for more information. *Charros* (cowboys) from all over Mexico compete in the four-day **Campeonato Charro Nacional** (*National Charro Championship* ☎322/224–0001) at Mojoneras. In addition to men's rope and riding tricks and the female competitors, there are mariachis, a parade, and exhibitions of charro-related art. Admission is $7–$12.

SPRING

APRIL

★ The **International Film Festival of Puerto Vallarta** (⇨*Film, above*) is a huge event that draws filmgoers from around the globe. Most of the events and ceremonies are for filmmakers, but the public can enjoy the art and blockbuster films shown during the weeklong event.

MAY

★ **Las Fiestas de Mayo** (*May Festivals* ☎322/223–2500) is a traditional three-week fair with fireworks and regional crafts and foods that is more popular with locals than visitors. Here in Jalisco, no such festival would be complete without *charreadas* (rodeos) and cockfights. Restaurants lower their prices for two weeks at the beginning of low season during **Restaurant Week** (⇨ *"Mexico's Gourmet Town," in Chapter 3*), also known as the May Food Festival.

SUMMER

JUNE
June 1 is **Día de la Marina** (☎*322/ 224–2352*). Like other Mexican ports, PV celebrates Navy Day with free boat rides (inquire at the Terminal Marítima or the XII Zona Naval Militar, just to the south). Watch colorfully decorated boats depart from here to make offerings on the water to sailors lost at sea.

> ## THREE KINGS DAY
>
> El Día de los Santos Reyes (January 6) was the traditional day of gift-giving in Latin America until Santa Claus invaded from the North (or North Pole, depending on your beliefs). Although many families now give gifts on Christmas or Christmas Eve, Three Kings Day is still an important family celebration. The children receive token "gifts of the Magi." Atole (a drink of finely ground rice or corn) or hot chocolate is served along with the *rosca de reyes*, a ring-shape cake. The person whose portion contains a tiny baby Jesus figurine must host a follow-up party on Candlemass, February 2.

JULY AND AUGUST
During school vacations, **children's events** (☎*322/223–2500*), like the release of baby marine turtles, are scheduled to educate, entertain, and heighten awareness of ecological issues.

Barra de Navidad celebrates its patron saint, **San Antonio de Padua,** the week preceding July 13 with religious parades, mass, street parties, and fireworks. **Cristo de los Brazos Caídos** is honored August 30–September 1 in much the same way as Saint Anthony.

FALL

SEPTEMBER
The **Celebration of Independence** is held on September 15 and 16, beginning on the evening of September 15 with the traditional *Grito de Dolores*. It translates as "Cry of Pain," but also references the town of Dolores Hidalgo, where the famous cry for freedom was uttered by priest Miguel Hidalgo. Late in the evening on September 15 there are mariachis, speeches, and other demonstrations of national pride. On September 16, witness parades and charros on horseback along the length of the boardwalk.

NOVEMBER
Fodor'sChoice The **Festival Gourmet International** is one of PV's biggest events
★   (⇨ *"Mexico's Gourmet Town," in Chapter 3*). The **Vallarta Film Festival** (⇨ *Film, above*) is an opportunity to see great indie films.

On the Boardwalk

Puerto Vallarta's **malecón** is the Champs Élysées of PV—only shorter, warmer, and less expensive. Along the mile-long cement walkway bordering the sea, small groups of young studs check out their feminine counterparts, all in meticulously pulled-together casual clothes; cruise-ship passengers stretch their legs; and landlocked tourists take a walk before dinner. Even those who have lived here all their lives come out to watch the red sun sink into the gray-blue water beyond the bay.

Every night and weekend is a parade. Vendors sell *agua de tuba,* a refreshing coconut-palm-heart drink. Empanada, corn-on-the-cob, and fried banana stands congregate near the Friendship Fountain and its trio of leaping bronze dolphins. Peddlers sell helium balloons and cotton candy. Clowns, magicians, and musicians entertain in the Los Arcos amphitheater.

Some of PV's most endearing art pieces are not in galleries, but here *en pleine aire.* Stretching along the seawalk is a series of bronze sculptures that are constantly touched, photographed, and climbed on. These nonstop caresses give a bright bronze luster to strategic body parts of Neptune and the Nereid, a mermaid and her man. Higher up on its pedestal, Puerto Vallarta's well-known seahorse icon retains a more traditional (and dignified) patina.

Rotunda on the Sea, a wacky grouping of chair-people by Alejandro Colunga, is a good spot to sit and watch the sea and the swirl of people enjoying life, although around sunset, others waiting their turn make it hard to linger.

The three mysterious figures that compose In Search of Reason, by world-famous artist Sergio Bustamante, are just as otherworldly as the jewelry, painting, and statuettes sold in his three Vallarta shops. Look for the pillow-headed figures climbing a ladder to the sky. Across from Carlos O'Brien's restaurant, Ramiz Barquet's Nostalgia is an ode to the artist's reunion with the love of his life at this very spot. You can find more of Barquet's work at Galería Pacífico.

Gary Thompson, owner of Galería Pacífico, leads public sculpture walking tours mid-November through mid-April. The free two-hour tours, which do not require reservations, leave Tuesday mornings at 9:30 from the Millennium sculpture, next to the Hotel Rosita, after a briefing by its creator, artist Mathis Lidice. Tours end at the gallery, where sculptor Ramiz Barquet answers questions and presents a brief demonstration of modeling in clay.

✉ *Extending south from Calle 31 de Octubre to Los Arcos outdoor amphitheater and the town square.*

8

NOVEMBER 28–DECEMBER 12

★ Puerto Vallarta's most important celebration of faith—and also one of the most elaborate spectacles of the year—is **Fiestas de la Virgin of Guadalupe** (☎ *322/223–2500*), designed to honor the Virgin of Guadalupe, the city's patron saint and the patroness of all Mexico. Exuberance fills the air as the end of November approaches and each participating business organizes its own procession. The most elaborate ones include allegorical floats and giant papier-mâché *matachines,* or dolls (for lack of a better word), and culminate in their own private mass. Throughout the afternoon and evening, groups snake down Calle Juárez from the north or the south, ending at the Cathedral in Old Vallarta.

THE NATURAL WORLD

Open since late 2005, the **Zoológico de Vallarta** (⊠ *Camino al Edén 700, Mismaloya* ☎ *322/228–0501* ⊕ *www.zoologicodevallarta.com* ✉ *$10* ⊙ *Daily 10–6)* is home to some 450 animals representing the different continents. The zoo's captive breeding program means you'll see baby emus, kitten-like Bengal tigers, and tiny little capuchin monkeys, among other species. Plants are also being cultivated for reintroduction in areas that have been damaged by mining or other industries. Five of the 64 hectares have been developed. Currently there's a restaurant on site and parking at no additional charge. The $80 VIP tour, available through advance reservation for up to 10 people (English or Spanish), includes face time with interesting animal species, a T-shirt, and a meal.

> ## THE RICOS Y FAMOSOS
>
> Mid-November through the end of April, three-hour **villa tours** (☎ *322/222–5466)* by the International Friendship Club get you inside the garden walls of some inspiring PV homes. English-speaking guides lead groups on air-conditioned buses: Tuesday to the north shore ($50 per person), Wednesday and Thursday to the south shore (US$35) per person tour to the south shore. Tours depart promptly at 11 AM (arrive by 10:30) from the Hotel Posada Río Cuale (Calle Aquiles Serdán 242). Lunch is included. The fee benefits local charities.

Located on 20 acres of land 12 miles south of Puerto Vallarta, the **Puerto Vallarta Botanical Gardens** (⊠ *Carretera a Barra de Navidad Km. 24, Las Juntas y Los Veranos* ☎ *322/223–6182* ⊕ *www.vallartabotanical gardensac.org* ⊙ Closed Mon. ✉ *$3)* features more than 3,000 species of plants. Set within the tropical dry forest at 1,300 feet above sea level, its trails lead to palm, agave and rose gardens as well as a tree fern grotto, orchid house, and displays of Mexican wildflowers and carnivorous plants. There's free parking and a lovely, open-sided restaurant serving a wide array of salads as well as pizza and Mexican dishes. Beverages include wine and a full bar. Go to their Web site to arrange a four-hour birding or hiking tour, with lunch, for $85 per person.

Overnight Excursions

Guadalajara

WORD OF MOUTH

"Last year we went to Mexico City and drove to Guadalajara, Tequila, and then on to PV—loved it and are planning to drive again this year. We only drive during the day and use main highways, as much as we can."

—Safa 1

EXCURSIONS FROM PUERTO VALLARTA

TOP REASONS TO GO

★ **Alchemic atmosphere:** San Blas's basic but charismatic attractions—beaches, markets, churches, and boat trips—combine like magic for a destination that's greater than the sum of its parts.

★ **Highland rambles:** Drop-dead-gorgeous hills and river valleys from Talpa to San Sebastián get you out into nature and away from coastal humidity.

★ **Amazing photography:** In the mountain towns, even amateur photographers can capture excellent small-town and nature shots.

★ **Palatable history:** Soak up Mexican history and culture in Guadalajara's churches, museums, and political murals.

★ **Getting the goods:** From megamalls to entire pre-Hispanic townships, Guadalajara has excellent housewares and handcrafts at great prices.

1 San Blas. Change happens slowly in San Blas, which has yet to experience a tourism boom. Cruise wide dirt streets on one-speed bikes, read books in the shade, dig your toes in the sand, and just enjoy life—one lazy day at a time. Blue mountains and green hills provide a beautiful backdrop.

Lake Chapala, Jalisco

Sand sculpture on the Beach

2 The Mountain Towns.
Former mining and supply towns Talpa, Mascota, and tiny San Sebastián were isolated for centuries by narrow roads and dangerous drop-offs and remain postcards of the past. Soak up the small-town atmosphere and alpine air.

3 Greater Guadalajara.
Home to cherished archetypes like mariachi, charrería (elegant "rodeos"), and tequila, Guadalajara is often called "the Mexican's Mexico." The metropolitan area includes former farming community Zapopan, and two districts known for crafts: Tlaquepaque and neighboring Tonalá. Outside the city are unique archaeological digs at Teuchitlán, lakeside retreat Chapala, artists' and expats' enclave Ajijic, and Tequila, famous for . . . do we even need to say it?

GETTING ORIENTED

About 156 km (95 mi) north of PV, mountain-backed San Blas has beaches and birding. Inland 340 km (211 mi) or so from PV, Jalisco capital Guadalajara (pop. 4 million) sits in the Atemajac Valley, circled by Sierra Madre peaks. Sleepy mountain towns Talpa, Mascota, and San Sebastián lie about halfway between PV and Guadalajara; each offers a glimpse of rural life from centuries long gone.

9

Tonalá Ceramics

OVERNIGHT EXCURSIONS PLANNER

Coming and Going

If you plan to visit both Puerto Vallarta and Guadalajara, consider flying into one and out of the other. It costs little more than a round-trip ticket to either city. To do the trip one-way, go by bus ($32–$37), as drop-off charges for rental cars are steep. (Leave extra time if you're flying the same day.) The bus from PV is an alternative, as drivers are experts at navigating mountain roads, which are occasionally in disrepair. Access to Mascota and Talpa from Guadalajara is more direct, and fully paved. The road from PV is sometimes impassable in rainy season. Buses take you directly from PV to San Blas, or you can get off at nearby beaches, but a car is handier for exploring the coast. The mostly two-lane PV–San Blas road is curvy but otherwise fine.

■TIP→Most small towns that don't have official stations sell gas from a home or store. Ask around before heading out on the highway low on gas.

Driving Times from Puerto Vallarta

San Blas	3–3.5 hours
San Sebastián	1.5–2 hours
Mascota	2.5–3 hours
Talpa de Allende	3–3.5 hours
Guadalajara	4.5–5 hours

Day Trips versus Extended Stays

The San Blas area is best as an overnight unless you go with an organized tour (F Tour Companies), though you could easily drive to Platanitos, south of San Blas, for a day at the beach.

If busing or driving to the mountain towns, plan to overnight unless you take the day tour with Vallarta Adventures. Alternately, you can fly on your own with Aerotaxis de la Bahía (P 322/221–1990) for a quick day trip or an overnight stay.

Guadalajara is too far to go for the day from Vallarta or San Blas, and at least two days is recommended.

How Much Can You Do?

What you can (physically) do and what you should do are very different things. To get the most out of your excursion from Puerto Vallarta, don't overdo it. It's a vacation—it's supposed to be fun, and possibly even relaxing! If you'll be in the Sayulita, San Francisco, and Chacala areas in Nayarit, it's easy to do an overnight jaunt up to San Blas, enjoying the myriad beaches and small towns as you travel up and back. Or make San Blas your base and explore from there.

You could also feasibly spend one night in San Blas and two in Guadalajara, about four hours driving and five hours by bus. For lovers of the road less traveled, two to three nights in the mountain towns gives you ample time to explore San Sebastián, Mascota, and Talpa as well as the surrounding countryside. Or you could spend one night in the mountains and continue to Guadalajara the next day. To fully appreciate Guadalajara, plan to spend at least two nights.

Tour Companies

Eco San Blas Safari (☎ 322/222–1922) leads all-day tours ($115 per person) Tuesday through Thursday from PV to San Blas with a boat trip to La Tovara. It's a full day, but at least you're not driving. **TB Tours** (✉ Calle Cisne 129, Fracc Los Sauces ☎ 322-224-7733 or 322-225-0479 ⊕ www.tvtourspv.com) leads tours to San Blas, with a visit to the old fort and the town, and to La Tovara mangroves and the crocodile farm. It's a full-day tour including breakfast in San Francisco en route, the boat tour, guide, lunch and hotel pick-up and return. Cost is about $100 per person. There are tours year-round, but only on Thursday.

Contact the **Cámera de Comercio** (Chamber of Commerce ✉ Av. Vallarta 4095, Zona Minerva, Guadalajara ☎ 33/3121–0378 or 33/3122–7701) for information about the all-day tour aboard the **Tequila Expres Train.** The cost is about $83, including lunch, mariachi serenades, and tequila.

Highly recommended **Vallarta Adventures** (✉ Edifício Marina Golf, Local 13–C, Calle Mástil, Marina Vallarta, Puerto Vallarta ☎ 322/297–1212 or 322/221–0657, 888/303–2653 in U.S. and Canada ⊕ www.vallarta-adventures.com) has daily, seven-hour jeep tours to San Sebastín ($75). It also runs air trips to San Sebastián on Tuesday, Thursday and Saturday ($155) with occasional jaunts to Mascota and Talpa. On Monday is a flight to and day tour of San Blas ($255), followed by land trips to several other Nayarit villages, including the island Mexitlán, possible homeland of the Aztec empire.

The bilingual guides of Ajijic's **Charter Club Tours** (✉ Carretera Chapala-Jocotepec, Plaza Montana mall, Ajijic ☎ 376/766–1777 ⊕ www.charterclubtours.com.mx) lead tours of Guadalajara, shopping and factory trips in Tlaquepaque and Tonala, and treks to Jalisco's lesser-known towns.

When to Go

With its springlike climate, Guadalajara can be visited any time of year, though in winter pollution can cause raw throats, sore eyes, and sinus irritation. Book well in advance to visit during the October Festival or other holidays. Roads can be dangerous during summer rains; June through October aren't the best time to visit the mountain towns by land.

San Blas and the coast begin to heat up in May; during the late June through October rainy season both the ambient and ocean temps are highest.

Festivals & Special Events

Guadalajara's major events include a May cultural festival; suburb Tlaquepaque celebrates the June ceramics festival.

The International Mariachi and Tequila Festival, in September, teams mariachi bands with the philharmonic orchestra. Also in Guadalajara, the entire month of October is given up to mariachis, *charreadas* (rodeos), soccer matches, and theater; the blessed Virgin of Zapopan is feted the week preceding October 12.

In the Sierra Madre, Talpa's equally admired icon brings the faithful en masse four times a year for street dances and mariachi serenades.

At the San Blas Festival (February 3), a statue of the town's patron saint gets a boat ride around the bay.

9

SAN BLAS & ENVIRONS

The cool thing about San Blas and the surrounding beaches—if you like this sort of thing—is that they're untouristy and authentic. Sure, there's an expat community, but it's minuscule compared to that of Puerto Vallarta. Parts of San Blas itself are deliciously disheveled, or should we say, ungentrified. The lively square is a nice place to polish off an ice-cream cone and watch the world. If you're looking for organized activities and perfect English speakers, this isn't the place for you.

Most people come to the San Blas area for basic R&R, to enjoy the long beaches and seafood shanties. The town's sights can be seen in a day, but stay for a few days at least to catch up on your reading, visit the beaches, and savor the town as it deserves. La Tovara jungle cruise through the mangroves should not be missed.

SAN BLAS

Most travelers come here looking for Old Mexico, or the "real Mexico," or the Mexico they remember from the 1960s. (Those who come on day tours from PV sometimes appear bewildered, glancing about for the small-town charm they've been promised.) New Spain's first official Pacific port has experienced a long, slow slide into obscurity since losing out to better-equipped ports in the late 19th century. But there's something to be said for being a bit player rather than a superstar. Industrious but not overworked, residents of this drowsy seaside city hit the beaches on weekends and celebrate their good fortune during numerous saints' days and civic festivals. You can, too.

GETTING HERE & AROUND

If you want to head directly to San Blas from outside Mexico, fly to Tepic (via Mexico City or direct from Tijuana), 69 km (43 mi) from San Blas. But the majority of visitors going to PV start there, and road-trip up to San Blas. To get to San Blas from Tepic, Nayarit, head north on Highway 15D, then west on Highway 11. Mexicana de Aviación and Aeromexico do the Mexico City–Tepic route, while AeroCalifornia serves Tepic from Ciudad Juárez (across the border from El Paso, Texas) and Tijuana and Avolar fly direct from Tijuana.

The Puerto Vallarta bus station is less than 5 kilometers (a couple of miles) north of the PV airport; there are usually four daily departures for San Blas ($12; 3.5 hours). These buses generally don't stop, and most don't have bathrooms. Departure times vary throughout the year, but at this writing, there are no departures after 4:30 PM. To get to Platanitos Beach, about an hour south of San Blas, take the Puerto Vallarta bus. ■TIP→ **Always check the return schedule with the driver when taking an out-of-town bus.** A taxi from Puerto Vallarta or from the airport costs about $100.

San Blas

TO
LA TOVARA ↗

◆ Embarcadero
La Tovara

◆ 54
◆ Tickets to
La Tovara

Cementerio Cerro de ◆
San Basilio

El Templo de ◆
Virgen del Rosario

◆ Contaduría

54

Zacatecas

Aviación

Bravo

Gómez ◆ *Farías*

Zapata

Echeverría

Xucatán

Canalizo *Sonora*

Sinaloa

Juárez

Michoacán

Templo de San Blas ◆ ◆ Tourism Office

◆ Plaza Principal

Mercado ◆
José María

Restaurant Casa
◆ de Canibal

Querétaro

Oaxaca

Restaurant La Isla ◆

Batallón de San Blas

Paredes

9

Hotel Hacienda
◆ Flamingos

Matanchen

Del Puerto

Aduana ◆

Arista

Comonfort

◆ Hotel Casa Roxanna

◆ Hotel Garza Canela

Campeche

Virgilio Uribe

⊗

0 — 1 mi
0 — 1 km

Playa Borrego

A car is handy for more extensive explorations of the coast between Puerto Vallarta and around San Blas. Within San Blas, the streets are wide, traffic is almost nonexistent, and with the exception of the streets immediately surrounding the main plaza, parking is easy. From Puerto Vallarta, abandon Highway 200 just past Las Varas in favor of the coast road (follow the sign toward Zacualpan, where you must go around the main plaza to continue on the unsigned road.

> ### BIRDER'S PARADISE
>
> More than 500 species of birds settle in the San Blas area; 23 are endemic. Organize a birding tour through Hotel Garza Canela (⇨ below). In January, you can attend the **International Festival of Migratory Birds** for bird-watching tours and conferences with experts and fellow enthusiasts.

Ask locals "¿San Blas?," and they'll point you in the right direction). The distance of about 160 km (100 mi) takes three to four hours.

From Guadalajara, you can take 15D (the toll road, about $40) to the Miramar turnoff to San Blas. It's actually much faster and less congested, however, to take Highway 15 at Tequepexpan and head west through Compostela on Highway 68 (toll about US$5); merge with Highway 200 until Las Varas, then head north on the coastal route (Highway 66) to San Blas.

To really go native, rent a bike from Wala Restaurant, a half block up from the plaza on Calle Juárez, and cruise to your heart's content. To get to the beaches south of town, to Matanchén Bay, and to the village of Santa Cruz, take a bus (they usually leave on the hour) from the bus station across the street from the church on the main plaza. To come back, just stand by the side of the road and flag down a passing bus.

ESSENTIALS

Bank Banamex (⊠ *Calle Juárez 36, 1 block east of plaza, San Blas* ☎ *323/285–0031* ⊕ *www.banamex.com.mx*).

Bus Contact Transportes Norte de Sonora (☎ *323/285–0043 in San Blas, 322/290–0110 in Puerto Vallarta*).

Medical Assistance Centro de Salud San Blas (⊠ *Calle H. Batallón at Calle Yucatán, San Blas* ☎ *323/285–0232*). **Emergency Hotline** (☎ *066*). **Farmacia Económica** (⊠ *Calle H. Batallón at Calle Mercado, San Blas* ☎ *323/285–0111*) closes between 2 and 4:30 PM and for the night at 9 PM.

Tourist Board Oficina de Turismo de San Blas (⊠ *Calles Canalizo and Sinaloa in Municipal Palace, 2nd floor, on main plaza San Blas* ☎ *323/285–0221 or 323/285–0005*).

WHAT TO SEE

San Blas has a few fun places to visit, but don't expect to be bowled over.

Check out the outside of the chaste little **Templo de San Blas,** called *La Iglesia Vieja* (the Old Church) by residents, on the town's busy plaza. It's rarely open these days, nevertheless you can admire its diminutive beauty and look for the words to Henry Wadsworth Longfellow's poem "The Bells of San Blas," inscribed on a brass plaque. (The long-gone bells were actually at the church dedicated to the Virgin of the Rosary, on Cerro de San Basilio.)

> **BEHIND THE MUSIC**
>
> If you're a fan of the rock group Maná, it's interesting to note that the song "Muelle de San Blas" ("San Blas's Wharf") refers to a tiny dock and a few wooden posts hosting friendly looking pelicans, just south of the Aduana.

Browse for fruits or good photo-ops at the market, **Mercado José María** (⌂ *Calle H. Battalón de San Blas, between Calles Sonora and Sinaloa*), where you can take a load off at Chito's for a milk shake or fresh fruit juice.

The old **Aduana** (*Customs House* ⌂ *Calle Juárez, near Calle del Puerto*) has been partially restored and is now a cultural center with sporadic art or photography shows and theatrical productions.

For a bird's-eye view of town and the coast, hike or drive up Calle Juárez, the main drag, to Cerro de San Basilio. Cannons protect the ruined **Contaduría** (*Counting House* ⌂ *Cerro de San Basilio*), built during colonial times when San Blas was New Spain's first official port.

Continuing down the road from the Contaduría brings you to **El Templo de la Virgen del Rosario**. Note the new floor in the otherwise ruined structure; the governor's daughter didn't want to soil the hem of her gown when she married here in 2005. A bit farther on, San Blas's little cemetery is backed by the sea and the mountains.

WHERE TO EAT

$ ✕ **Casa del Canibal.** How does grilled chicken served with mashed potatoes and big hunks of steamed broccoli sound? Or a big Caesar salad with garlic toast? There are also beef stroganoff, penne primavera, and a few other international dishes. The small bar, more popular with gringos than with locals, closes down by 9 or 10 PM. Sunday brunch, from 9 to noon, features freshly brewed Nayarit coffee, Bloody Marys, eggs Benedict, pastries, and fresh fruit. ⌂ *Calle Juárez 53* ☎ *323/285–1412* ⊕ *www.casadelcanibal.com* ▭ *No credit cards* ⊙ *No lunch. Closed Mon. and Tues., and July–mid-Oct.*

$ ✕ **La Isla.** Shell lamps; pictures made entirely of scallops, bivalves, and starfish; shell-drenched chandeliers … every inch of wall space is decorated in different denizens of the sea. Service isn't particularly brisk (pretty much par for the course in laid-back San Blas), but the seafood, filet mignon, and fajitas are all quite good. Afterward stroll over to the main plaza a few blocks away. ⌂ *Calle Mercado at Calle Paredes* ☎ *323/285–0407* ▭ *No credit cards* ⊙ *Closed Mon.*

WHERE TO STAY

$ ⬚ **Casa Roxanna.** This is an attractive little enclave of cozy, very clean (and painted yearly) cottages with screened windows. Full kitchens with lots of pots and pans invite cooking, but the real draws are the lovingly tended gardens surrounding the lodgings, the covered patio, and the sparkling, three-lane lap pool. If you love it, settle in a while; monthly rates are usually available. Pros: Personable staff, great lap pool. Cons: So-so a/c units, lackluster interior decor. ⊠ *Callejón El Rey 1, San Blas,* ☎ *323/285–0573* ⊕ *www.casaroxanna.com* ☞ *6 cottages* ♤ *In-room: no phone, kitchen (some), refrigerator (some). In-hotel: pool, laundry facilities, parking (no fee), public Wi-Fi* ⊟ No credit cards ⊙|EP.

$$ 🏨 **Hacienda Flamingos.** Built in 1882, this restored mansion-turned-hotel was once part of a large hacienda. The restoration is stunning: surrounding a pretty, plant-filled courtyard is a covered veranda of lovely floor tiles, with lazily rotating ceiling fans, antique furniture, and groupings of chairs for a casual conversation. Opening off the veranda, elegant suites have also been restored to their original glory. It's right across from the cultural center and near the market and town plaza. Pros: Lovely decor, close to town center. Cons: Sometimes eerily devoid of other guests, staff can be chilly. ⊠ *Calle Juárez 105, San Blas* ☎ *323/285–0485* ⊕ *www.sanblas.com.mx* ☞ *20 rooms* ♤ *In-room: no phone, DVD. In-hotel: pool, gym, no elevator, laundry facilities, public Wi-Fi, parking (no fee)* ⊟ MC, V ⊙|EP.

$$ 🏨 **Hotel Garza Canela.** Opened decades ago by a family of dedicated
★ bird-watchers, this meandering, three-story hotel with expansive grounds is the home base of choice for birding groups. Rooms have small balconies and polished limestone floors; junior suites have large whirlpool tubs. Betty Vasquez, who runs the French restaurant here, studied at Le Cordón Bleu in France; she prepares elegant and very tasty meals. Pros: Very good French restaurant, suites have jacuzzi tub. Cons: Estuary location means there are some biting bugs, one shared computer for checking Internet in lobby, no Wi-Fi after 8 PM. ⊠ *Calle Paredes 106 Sur, San Blas* ☎ *323/285–0112 or 323/285–0480; 01800/713–2313 toll-free in Mexico* ⊕ *www.garzacanela.com* ☞ *44 rooms, 6 suites* ♤ *In-room: no phone. In-hotel: restaurant, pool, no elevator, public Internet, parking (no fee)* ⊟ AE, MC, V ⊙|EP.

OUTDOOR ACTIVITIES & SPORTS

BOAT TOUR A series of narrow waterways wends through the mangroves to **La**
★ **Tobara**, San Blas's most famous attraction. Turtles on logs, crocs that
☾ *look* like logs, birds, iguanas, and exotic orchids make this maze of mud-brown canals a magical place. Begin the tranquil ride ($9 per person; four-person minimum or $34 [360 pesos] total for fewer than four) at the El Conchal Bridge, at the entrance-exit to San Blas, or the village of Matanchén. Boats depart when there are enough customers, which isn't usually a problem. Either way you'll end up, after a 45-minute boat ride, at the freshwater pool fed by a natural spring. Rest at the snack shop overlooking the water or jump in using the rope swing, keeping an eye out for the allegedly benign resident croc. There's an optional trip to a crocodile farm for a few dollars more, making it a three-hour instead of a two-hour tour.

ECOTOUR **Singayta** (⊠ *8 km [5 mi] from San Blas on road to Tepic* ⊕ *www.singayta. com*) is a typical Nayarit village that is attempting to support itself through simple and un-gimmicky ecotours. The basic tour includes a look around the town, where original adobe structures compete with more practical but less picturesque structures with corrugated tin roofs. Take a short guided hike through the surrounding jungle, and a boat ride around the estuary ($5 for up to four people). Or rent mountain bikes ($3 per hour) to check out

> **BEST BEACH BITE**
>
> For a marvelous albeit simple barbecue fish feast, visit **Enramada Ruiz,** a sinfully simple yet sublime seafood shanty on Playa Platanitos.

a broader area. This is primo birding territory. The townspeople are most geared up for tours on weekends and during school holidays and vacations: Christmas, Easter, and July, and August. The easiest way to book a tour is to look for English-speaking Juan Bananas, who sells banana bread from a shop called Tumba de Yako (look for the sign on the unmarked road Av. H. Batallón between Calles Comonfort and Canalizo, en route to Playa Borrego). He can set up a visit and/or guide you there. Groups of five or more can call ahead to make a reservation with Juan (☎323/285–0462, ✉ ecomanglar@yahoo.com) or with Camilo Paz (☎311/109–8123); call at least a day ahead if you want to have a meal.

THE BEACHES NEAR SAN BLAS

Like San Blas itself, the surrounding beaches attract mostly local people and travelers fleeing glitzier resort scenes. Beaches here are almost uniformly long, flat, and walkable, with light brown sand, moderate waves, and seriously bothersome no-see-ums, especially around sunrise and sunset (and during the waxing and waning moons). Almost as ubiquitous as these biting bugs are simple *ramadas* (open-sided, palm-thatch-roof eateries) on the beach whose owners don't mind if you hang out all day, jumping in the ocean and then back in your shaded hammock to continue devouring John Grisham or leafing through magazines. Order a cold lemonade or a beer, or have a meal of fillet of fish, ceviche, or chips and guacamole. Don't expect a full menu, rather what's fresh and available. All these beaches are accessible by bus from San Blas's centrally located bus station.

Fodor'sChoice ★ ℭ You can walk or ride a bike to long, lovely **Playa Borrego,** just 1 km (½ mi) south of town. Rent a surfboard at Stoners' or Mar y Sol restaurant to attack the year-round (but sporadic) shore or jetty breaks there, or stroll down to the southern end to admire the lovely, palm-fringed estuary.

About 6 km (4 mi) south of Playa Borrego, at the northern edge of Bahía de Matanchén, **Playa Las Islitas** used to be legendary among surfers for its long wave, but this has diminished in recent years; the beach is now suitable for swimming, body surfing, and boogie boarding.

★ At the south end of the Matanchén Bay, **Playa Los Cocos and Playa Miramar** are both great for long walks and for hanging out at ramadas.

Adjacent to Miramar Beach is the well-kept fishing village of **Santa Cruz**. Take a walk on the beach or around the town; buy a soft drink, find the bakery and pick up some banana bread. Outdoor dances are occasionally held on the diminutive central plaza.

★ Beyond Matanchén Bay the road heads inland and reemerges about 8 km (5 mi) later at **Playa Platanitos**, a lovely little beach in a sheltered cove. Fishermen park their skiffs here, and simple shacks cook up the catch of the day.

WHERE TO STAY

¢–$ ⬚**Casa Mañana.** Some of the pleasant rooms overlook the beach from
☾ a balcony or terrace, but most people stay here for easy access to the good burgers, guacamole, and seafood platter for two ($14) at the adjoining El Alebrije restaurant. The bar, with its cool, brick-floor interior open to the beach, is also popular. Other perks: the long beach, large pool, and hiking and other outdoor activities. Pros: Good burgers; nice beachfront location. Con: Must take a bus or taxi to and from San Blas. ✉*South end of Playa Los Cocos, 13 km (8 mi) south of San Blas* ☎*323/254–9090* ⊕*www.casa-manana.com* ⤶*26 rooms* ⚷*In-hotel: restaurant, bar, pool, beachfront, parking (no fee)* ▭*MC, V* ⦿*EP.*

THE MOUNTAIN TOWNS

A trip into the Sierra Madre is an excellent way to escape the coastal heat and the hordes of vacationers. The Spanish arrived to extract ore from these mountains at the end of the 16th century; after the Mexican Revolution the mines were largely abandoned in favor of richer veins. The isolation of these tiny towns has kept them old-fashioned.

The air is crisp and clean and scented of pine, the valley and mountain views are spectacular, and the highland towns earthy, unassuming, and charming. Whitewashed adobe homes radiate from town plazas where old gents remember youthful exploits. Saturday night boys and girls court each other alfresco while oompah bands entertain their parents from the bandstand. Although most of the hotels in the region have only basic amenities (construction on a massively improved road from PV is encouraging entrepreneurs, however), the chill mountain air and kilos of blankets can produce a delicious night's sleep.

GETTING HERE & AROUND

For an effortless excursion, go on a tour throuogh Vallarta Adventures day tour. They have excellent day tours to San Sebastián by jeep ($75) or by small plane ($155). The small-plane ride provides a wonderful photo op and aerial introduction to the Sierra Madre.

For more flexibility or to spend the night in a cozy, no-frills hotel or a refurbished hacienda, charter a twin-engine Cessna through Aerotaxis de la Bahía in PV. For one to seven passengers the rate is about US$600 split among them to San Sebastián, US$600 to Mascota, and $650 to Talpa de Allende. Add to these fares 15% sales tax and US$20 per per-

GREAT ITINERARIES

If you're not joining an organized day tour, there are many possible itineraries, depending on whether you leave from PV or from Guadalajara, your tolerance for driving mountain roads, and your desire to explore (i.e., either to see lots or just relax and enjoy the tranquillity, mountain-and-valley views, and quaint lifestyle).

From Puerto Vallarta, consider a two-day trip to the area beginning in San Sebastián and returning to PV (or Guadalajara) from Talpa de Allende. There are many ways to go; keys are not driving at night and enjoying the slow pace. Drive to San Sebastian, enjoying the mountain scenery en route. After a look around the quaint old mining village and an early lunch, continue to Mascota, the area's largest town and a good base. Spend the night in Mascota. The Sierra Lodge on Lake Juanacatlán, which serves excellent food, can be added as an overnight trip, but they don't take day-trippers. If you prefer, take a day trip from Mascota to Talpa de Allende, whose raison d'être is the tiny, beloved Virgin statue in the town's ornate basilica.

Each of the three towns has hills to be climbed for excellent vistas and photos. Otherwise, activities include wandering the streets, visiting small museums and Catholic churches, tasting regional food, and drinking in the mountain air and old-fashioned ambience. Make sure you get where you're going before dark, as mountain roads are unlighted, narrow, and in many cases have sheer drop-offs.

son air travelers' tax. ■TIP➔ **The return flight is free if you fly back with the pilot within three hours of arrival.**

ATM (Autotransportes Talpa–Mascota) buses depart from their bus station in PV (Calle Lucerna 128, Col. Versalles) three times a day at around 9 AM, 2:30, and 6 PM, stopping at La Estancia (11 km [7 mi] from San Sebastián; 1½ hours), then Mascota (2 to 2½ hours) and Talpa (3½ hours).

Buses also depart several times a day from Guadalajara's new bus station (Entronque carretera libre a Zapotlanejo, Modules 3 and 4). Note that the bus does not enter San Sebastián; you can usually find a cab (or someone heading to town) for about $12, sharing the cab with others to split the cost. You'll be dropped at a small rest area at the side of the road, where local men in trucks or taxis usually are available to transport you to town.

From Puerto Vallarta it's about 80 km (50 mi; 2 hours) to San Sebastián, 2.5 to 3 to Mascota, and an additional 30 minutes to Talpa. The road is paved and finished as far as the turnoff to San Sebastian at La Estancia. A suspension bridge was inaugurated in early 2007 to cover the last 8 km (5 mi) of the road leading to San Sebastián and Mascota, which used to get washed out regularly in the rainy season. (Note: this road may become dangerous or at least frightening during the rainy season, when landslides can occur.) Lago Juanacatlán is an hour from Mascota on a rough one-lane road of dirt and rock.

Taxis are easily found near the main square in Talpa, Mascota, and San Sebastián.

ESSENTIALS

Air Contact **Aerotaxis de la Bahia** (☎ *322/221–1990*).

Banks **Bancomer** (✉ *Calle Constitución at Calle Hidalgo, Mascota* ☎ *388/386–0387*). **Banco HSBC** (✉ *Calle Independencia, across from la presidencia [town hall], Talpa* ☎ *388/385–0197*).

Bus Contact **Autotransportes Talpa–Mascota** (*ATM* ☎ *322/222–4816 in Puerto Vallarta, 388/386–0093 in Mascota, 388/385–0015 in Talpa, 33/3600–0588, 33/3619–7549 in Guadalajara*).

Medical Assitance **Centro de Salud de Mascota** (✉ *Calle Dávalos 70, Mascota* ☎ *388/386–0174*).**Farmacia Estrella** (✉ *Calle 5 de Mayo, at Calle Ayuntamiento, Mascota* ☎ *388/386–0285*). **Farmacia del Oeste** (✉ *Calle Cuauhtemoc at Calle López Mateos, across from plaza, San Sebastián* ☎ *322/297–2833*). **Farmacia San Miguel** (✉ *Calle Independencia, at Calle Anahuac, across from square, Talpa* ☎ *388/385–0085*).

Tour & Visitor Information **Oficina de Turismo de Mascota** (✉ *La Presidencia [Town Hall], Calle Ayuntamiento, at Calle Constitución, facing plaza, Mascota* ☎ *388/386–1179*). **Oficina de Turismo de San Sebastián** (✉ *Calle López Mateos, around corner from la presidencia (town hall), San Sebastián* ☎ *322/297–2938*). **Oficina de Turismo de Talpa** (✉ *La Presidencia (Town Hall), Calle Independencia s/n, 2 blocks north of plaza, Talpa de Allende* ☎ *388/385–0009 or 388/385–0287*). **Vallarta Adventures** (☎ *322/297–1212* ⊕ *www.vallarta-adventures.com*)

SAN SEBASTIÁN

If, physically, there are only about 80 km (50 mi) between Puerto Vallarta and San Sebastián, metaphorically they're as far apart as the Earth and the moon. Sleepy San Sebastián is the Mayberry of Mexico, but a little less lively. It's the kind of place where you feel weird walking past people without saying hello, even though you don't know them from Adam. The miners that built the town have long gone, and more recently, younger folks are drifting away in search of opportunity. Most of the 800 or so people who have stayed seem perfectly content with life as it is, although rat-race dropouts and entrepreneurs are making their way here along improved roads.

WHAT TO SEE

The most interesting thing to see in San Sebastián is the town itself. Walk the cobblestone streets and handsome brick sidewalks, admiring the white-faced adobe structures surrounding the plaza. Take any side street and wander at will. Enjoy the enormous walnut trees lining the road into town, and diminutive peach trees peaking over garden walls. The reason to go to this cozy, lazy, beautiful town at 5,250 feet above sea level is to look inward, reflecting on life, or outward, greeting or chatting as best you can with those you meet. Look anywhere, in fact, except a laptop or if possible, a television screen. That's just missing the point.

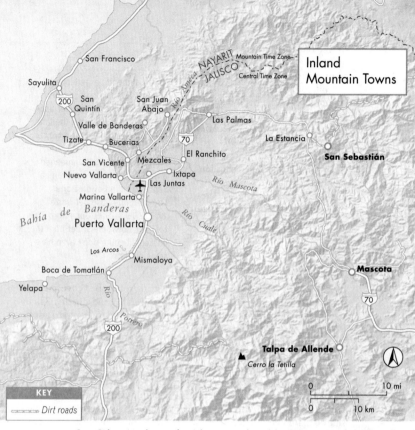

San Sebastián has a few things to do, although none of them is the reason to visit.

Stop in the *abarrotes* (general store) on the north side of the square for a beverage or a spool of thread; then head directly behind it to **Iglesia de San Sebastián** a typically restored 1800s-era church that comes to life in the days preceding its saint's day, January 20.

You're welcome any time at the **Casa Museo de Doña Conchita** (⊠*Calle Juárez 2* ☎*322/297–2860* ☏*$1*). The aged but affable lady loves to show visitors photos of her venerable family—which she traces back six generations. See bank notes from the mining days, bloomers, shirts made by hand by the lady for her many children, and other old memorabilia. If you speak Spanish, ask Doña Conchita to tell you about the ghosts that haunt her house, which is right on the square between the basketball court and *la presidencia,* or town hall. Hours are somewhat flexible, but stated hours are Monday through Saturday 10 AM to 3 PM and 5 PM to 7 PM; Sunday 11:30 to 3.

WHERE TO STAY & EAT

$ ✕**Fonda de Doña Lupita.** Typical food of the countryside—enchiladas, tamales, pozole, beefsteak with beans and tortillas, and so on—is served in an equally typical family home. The house has been enlarged to welcome guests, and the friendly owner does her part. Straw-bottom chairs are comfortable enough, and the oilcloths shiny and new. The small bar is at the back behind the large, open kitchen. It's open for breakfast, too. ⊠ *Calle Cuauhtemoc 89* ☎ *322/297–2803* ▭ *No credit cards.*

$$ ▥ **La Galerita de San Sebastián.** A pair of displaced *tapatíos* (Guadalajarans) has created a cluster of pretty cabins on their property about four blocks from the plaza. Comfortable futons in each room provide a place to sleep, nap, or to view satellite TV on the small computer screen. The double-sided fire-

> ### WARM CUPPA CORN?
>
> For an authentic experience, pop into any *fonda* or *lonchería* (simple eateries, the former usually in someone's home, the latter open for lunch only) for a typical *atole con piloncillo* (hot corn drink sweetened with unrefined brown sugar) and a simple meal. Some, like the **Fonda Doña Leo** (⊠ *Calle Paso del Norte* ☎ *322/297–2909, open from 7 AM to 3 PM*), down the street from the basketball court, don't even have signs out front.

place heats the bedroom and adjoining sitting room. Bed coverings and matching drapes of earthy, muted colors are all good quality. This is the most modern place to stay in San Sebastián, and is geared to adults. Pros: Stylish; has in-room fireplaces. Cons: Pricey compared to other area digs; credit cards not accepted. ⊠ *Camino a Las Galeritas 62, Barrio La Otra Banda, San Sebastián* ☎ *322/297–3040* ⊕ *www.lagalerita. com.mx* ⇱*3 bungalows* ⚬ *In-room: no a/c, no phone, refrigerator. In-hotel: restaurant, parking (no fee)* ▭ *No credit cards* ⏍ *BP.*

$ ▥ **Real de San Sebastián.** Small rooms are dominated by snug king beds in curtained alcoves in this interesting B&B. It has a (somewhat cramped) shared main living space with a cushy plush couch facing a large-screen satellite TV, and more formal round tables where afternoon coffee or hot chocolate is served. In the morning take complimentary coffee and rolls in bed, served through a small service window. The manager, Margarito Salcedo, is friendly and solicitous. Pros: Friendly, helpful hosts; good value. Cons: Living room is dated; guest rooms are dominated by the bed and don't have phones; credit cards aren't accepted. ⊠ *Calle Zaragoza 41, San Sebastián* ☎ *322/297–3224* ⊕ *www.sansebastian deloeste.com* ⇱*6 rooms* ⚬ *In-room: no a/c, no phone, no TV. In-hotel: restaurant, no elevator* ▭ *No credit cards* ⏍ *CP.*

OUTDOOR ACTIVITIES & SPORTS

Local men can be hired for a truck ride up to **La Bufa**, a half-dome visible from the town square. One such man is Obed Dueña (☎ *322/297–2864*), who charges about $30 for the trip, whether for two or 16 people. It's the same price if you ride with him or hike back. The truck will wait while you climb—about 15 minutes to the top—and enjoy the wonderful view of the town, surrounding valleys, and, on a clear day, Puerto Vallarta. San Sebastián was founded as a silver-and-gold mining town; ask the driver to stop for a quick visit to a mine en route. The excursion takes about 3 hours all told. Or you can hike both ways; it takes most folks 2 to 2½ hours to reach the top, and half to two-thirds that time to return. Another great destination for a walk is **Hacienda Jalisco** (⇨*above*), a 20-minute walk from San Sebastián's plaza; for about $2 you can have a look around the beautiful property and the common areas on the first floor of the traditionally decorated country inn.

MASCOTA

Mascota's cool but sunny climate is perfect for growing citrus, avocados, nuts, wheat, corn, and other crops. Fed by the Mascota and Ameca rivers and many springs and year-round streams, the blue-green hills and valleys surrounding town are lusciously forested; beyond them rise indigo mountains to form a painterly tableau. This former mining town and municipal seat is home to some 13,000 people. Its banks, shops, and a hospital serve surrounding villages. On its coat of arms are a pine tree, deer, and rattlesnake. The town's name derives from the Nahuatl words for deer and snake.

WHAT TO SEE

★ Mascota's pride is **La Iglesia de la Preciosa Sangre** (*Church of the Precious Blood*), started in 1909 but unfinished due to the revolution and the ensuing Cristero Revolt. Weddings, concerts, and plays are sometimes held here under the ruins of Gothic arches. Note the 3-D blood squirting from Jesus's wound in the chapel—you could hardly miss it.

Walk around the **plaza,** where old gents share stories and kids chase balloons. Couples dance the stately *danzón* on Thursday and Saturday evenings as the band plays in the wrought-iron bandstand. The town produces ceramics, saddles, and *raicilla,* a relative of tequila made from the green agave plant (tequila comes from the blue one).

On one corner of the plaza is the town's white-spire **Iglesia de la Virgen de los Dolores.** The Virgin of Sorrow is feted on September 15, which segues into Mexican Independence Day on the 16th.

A block beyond the other end of the plaza, the **Museo de Mascota** (✉*Calle Morelos, near Calle Allende*) is worth a look. Open Monday through Saturday 10–2 and 4–8, the museum closes between 3 and 5.

Around the corner from the Mascota Museum, the **Casa de la Cultura** (✉*Calle Allende 115*) has rotating exhibits of photography and art. It's open 10–2 and 4–7 Monday through Saturday.

WHERE TO EAT

$ ✕**La Casa de Mi Abuela.** Everyone and his mother likes "Grandma's House," which is conveniently open all day (and evening), every day, starting at around 8 AM with breakfast. In addition to beans, rice, *carne asada,* and other recognizable Mexican food, there are

> ### MASCOTA'S MARTYR
>
> In 1927, during the anticlerical Cristero movement, Mascota's young priest refused to abandon his post. Soldiers peeled the skin from his hands and feet before forcing him to walk to a large oak tree, where he was hanged. Mascota's hero, José María Robles was canonized in 2000 by Pope John Paul II.

9

backcountry recipes that are much less familiar to the average traveler. ⊠ *Calle Corona, at Calle Zaragoza, Mascota* ☎ *No phone.*

$ ✕ **Café Napolés.** Primarily a coffee-and-dessert stop and fashionable hangout for Mascotans, this snug little eatery serves big breakfasts, too. Sit on the small, street-facing patio, in the diminutive dining room, or facing the glass case featuring fantastic-looking cakes, pies, and tarts. Closes between 2:30 and 4:30 PM Monday through Saturday, and between 2:30 and 7 PM on Sunday. ⊠ *Calle Hidalgo 105, Centro-Mascota* ☎ *388/386–0051* ▭ *No credit cards.*

¢ ✕ **Navidad.** It is named for the small town 14 km from Mascota, not the Christmas holiday, which is the only day this restaurant closes. The cavernous space, lined in red brick, makes the restaurant look rather generic, but it's actually family-owned and -run and oh-so-personable. Best yet, it's open 7 AM to nearly midnight. Try the regional dishes like goat stew and enchiladas, as well as pizza, or a daily special such as beef tongue, jocoque, or perhaps another mystery dish. ⊠ *Calle Juan Díaz de Sandi 28, CentroMascota* ☎ *388/386–0469* ▭ *No credit cards.*

WHERE TO STAY

$ ⊡ **Mesón de Santa Elena.** Beautiful rooms in this converted 19th-cen-
★ tury house have lovely old tile floors, beige cotton drapes covering huge windows, rag-rolled walls, and wonderful tile floors and sinks. The dining room has old-fashioned cupboards and there are dining tables inside and out on two patios festooned with flowers and large potted plants. Second-floor rooms have views of fields and mountains to the west. Pros: Two blocks from the town square, feels like you're a guest in someone's home, Internet cafe about a block away. Cons: Internet intermittent in some rooms, feels like you're a guest in someone's home. ⊠ *Hidalgo 155, Mascota* ☎ *388/386–0313* ⊕ *www.meson desantaelena.com* ⤴ *10 rooms, 2 suites* ⌂ *In-room: no a/c, no phone, no TV. In-hotel: restaurant (breakfast only), no elevator, public Wi-Fi* ▭ *No credit cards* ⍾ *AI, BP, EP.*

$$ ⊡ **Rancho La Esmeralda.** Catering to small groups and father-and-son outings, this ranch-style lodging near the entrance to town also accepts individual travelers. All interiors are pine-wood simple, with ceiling beams and tile roofs, and plain furnishings. The villas have kitchens, and most have a porch and fireplace; many sport a king-size bed. This working ranch offers horseback riding and also rents bicycles and ATVs. Because most guests are Guadalajarans on weekends, mid-week prices are discounted 30%. Pros: Newer construction, fireplaces and king-size beds, substantial mid-week discount. Cons: 10-minute drive from town center, bumpy cobblestone entry road. ⊠ *Calle Salvador Chavez 47,* ☎ *388/386–0953* ⊕ *www.rancholaesmeralda.com.mx* ⤴ *8 rooms, 6 cabins* ⌂ *In room: kitchen (some), refrigerator (some), Wi-Fi. In hotel: Restaurant (weekends and holidays only), public Wi-Fi, parking (no fee).* ▭ *MC, V.*

$$$ ⊡ **Sierra Lago.** An hour north of Mascota, this lodge of knotty pine is a tranquil lakeside retreat. Sail or kayak or just read a book in the steamy hot tub. If you choose the all-inclusive plan, drinks are included, as are activities like fishing, horseback riding, kayaking, and mountain biking. The clean mountain air is sure to give your appetite a boost; if he

has time, the chef will cook up your freshly caught fish. Pros: Beautiful scenery and mountain air, activities included in all-inclusive's room rate. Cons: No phone in room, no Internet access. ✉*Domicilio Conocido, Lago Juanacatlán* ☎*877/845–5247 (reservations only)* ⊕*www. sierralago.com* ⬛*23 cabins* ⚲*In-room: no phone. In-hotel: restaurant, bar, tennis court, pool, bicycles, parking (no fee)* ▤*MC, V* ⎍*AI.*

OUTDOOR ACTIVITIES & SPORTS

★ The beautiful countryside just outside town is ideal for hikes and drives. From Mascota's plaza you can walk up Calle Morelos out of town to **Cerro de la Cruz.** The hike to the summit takes about a half hour and rewards with great valley views. The newish **Presa Corinches,** a dam about 5 km (3 mi) south of town, has bass fishing, picnic spots (for cars and RVs), and a restaurant where locals go for fish feasts on holidays and weekend afternoons. To get to the dam, head east on Calle Juárez (a block south of the plaza) and follow the signs to the reservoir. Take a walk along the shore or set up a tent near the fringe of pine-oak forest coming down to meet the cool blue water, which is fine for swimming when the weather is warm. **Lago Juanacatlán** is a lovely lake in a volcanic crater at 7,000 feet above sea level. Nestled in the El Galope River valley, the pristine lake is surrounded by alpine woods, and the trip from Mascota past fields of flowers and self-sufficient *ranchos* is bucolic.

SHOPPING

Stores in town sell homemade preserves, locally grown coffee, raicilla (an alcoholic drink of undistilled green agave), and sweets. A good place to shop for local products and produce is the **Mercado municipal** (✉*Calle P. Sánchez, at Hidalgo, 1 block west of plaza*).

TALPA DE ALLENDE

Another tranquil town surrounded by pine-oak forests, Talpa, as it's called, has just over 7,000 inhabitants but welcomes 4 million visitors a year. They come to pay homage or ask favors of the diminutive Virgen del Rosario de Talpa, Jalisco's most revered Virgin. Some people walk three days from Puerto Vallarta as penance or a sign of devotion; others come by car or truck but return annually to show their faith.

WHAT TO SEE

★ On the large town plaza, the **Basílica de Talpa** is the main show in town. The twin-spire limestone temple is Gothic with neoclassic elements. After visiting the diminutive, royally clad Virgin in her side chapel, stroll around the surrounding square. Shops and stalls sell sweets, miniature icons of the Virgin in every possible presentation, T-shirts, and other souvenirs. *Chicle* (gum) is harvested in the area, and you'll find small keepsakes in the shapes of shoes, flowers, and animals made of the (nonsticky) raw material.

WHERE TO EAT

$ ✗**Casa Grande.** This excellent steak house also serves grilled chicken and seafood. Under a roof but open on all sides and with an incredible view, it's highly recommended by visitors and locals. Lunch is served after 2 PM, and the kitchen stays open until 10:30. ✉ *Calle Juárez 53, Talpa de Allende* ☎ *388/385–0709* ▤ *MC, V* ⊘ *Closed Tues.*

$ ✕**El Herradero.** "The Blacksmith" will win no awards for cuisine, or, for that matter, decoration. But it's often filled with families of pilgrims, and the locals recommend it, too. The menu offers mainly meat dishes, including burgers with fries, plus antojitos: gorditas and sopes (cornmeal based, fried concoctions topped with beans and salsa),

> **HOLY CITY**
>
> During several major annual fiestas, the town swells with visitors. The Fiesta de la Candelaria culminates in Candlemass, February 2. The town's patron saint, St. Joseph, is honored March 19. May 12, September 10, September 19, and October 7 mark rituals devoted to the Virgin del Rosario de Talpa.

pozole (hominy soup), and quesadillas. The tortillas are made fresh out back. Half orders are available, and there's a bar serving national booze and beer. ✉ *Calle 23 de Junio #8, Centro Talpa de Allende* ☎ *388/385–0376* ▤ *No credit cards.*

WHERE TO STAY

$ ▥**Hacienda Jacarandas.** The charming, two-story building has high ceilings, wide corridors, and comfortable guest rooms with fine and folk art. Bougainvillea in shades of purple and pink climb up the cream-color exterior walls, and the rooftop terrace—with a terrific view—is a nice place to laze away a morning or afternoon, in the sun or under the covered portion. The 62-acre property has a small lake. Pros: You get to stay in a restored hacienda, savvy hoteliers who know how to treat foreign guests. Cons: Has been for sale for some years, no elevator, credit cards not accepted. ✉ *Rancho Portrellos, just over bridge at southeast end of town, Talpa de Allende* ☎ *333/447–7366* ⊕ *www. haciendajacarandas.com* 🛏 *6 rooms* ⚐ *In-hotel: restaurant, bar, pool, no elevator* ▤ *No credit cards* ⊘ *Closed Easter–June* ﴾◎﴿*BP.*

¢ ▥**Renovación.** Basic yet comfortable rooms in this three-story hotel (opened in 2007) have king-size beds with dark blue, hunting-theme spreads and desks of shiny lacquered wood. The remote-controlled TV is bolted to the wall near the ceiling. It's located on the main road into town, just a few short blocks from the plaza and town hall. The price goes up on weekends, although only January through May. Pros: Brand-new construction, a couple of blocks from the main plaza. Cons: No elevator, no credit cards accepted. ✉ *Calle Independencia 45, Centro* ☎ *388/385–1412* 🛏 *18 rooms* ⚐ *In-hotel: no elevator.* ▤ *No credit cards.*

THE GUADALAJARA REGION

Guadalajara rests on a mile-high plain of the Sierra Madre Occidental, surrounded on three sides by rugged hills and on the fourth by the spectacular Oblatos Canyon. Mexico's second largest city has a population of 4 million and is the capital of Jalisco State. This cosmopolitan if traditional and quintessentially Mexican city offers a range of activities. Shop for handicrafts, housewares, and especially fine ceramics in smart shops or family-owned factories. Dress up for drinks, dinner, and dancing in smart Zona Minerva, in downtown Guadalajara, or put on your comfy walking shoes to visit satellite neighborhoods of indigenous origin. For shoppers and metropolis lovers, this is a great complement to a Puerto Vallarta vacation.

An hour's drive in just about any direction from Guadalajara will bring you out of the fray and into the countryside. Due south is Lake Chapala, Mexico's largest natural lake. Bordering it are several villages with large expat communities, including Chapala and Ajijic, a village of bougainvillea and cobblestone roads. Tequila, where the famous firewater is brewed, is northwest of Guadalajara. Teuchitlán, south of Tequila, has the Guachimontones ruins. The placid lakeside area makes for a weeklong (expats would say lifelong) getaway, while Tequila and Teuchitlán are great for day-trippers.

2–3 DAYS IN THE GUADALAJARA REGION

The four primary municipalities of metropolitan Guadalajara are Guadalajara, Zapopan, Tlaquepaque, and Tonalá. With the exception of Zapopan, the areas of interest to visitors can each be navigated on foot in a few hours, though each deserves at least half a day. Zapopan requires more time since it's a sprawling suburb with lots of shopping. Due west of Guadalajara's Centro Histórico, Zona Minerva is the place to go for great restaurants and after-dark action. Plan on a third day if you want to visit outlying areas like Lake Chapala and Teuchitlán.

On the morning of Day 1, visit historic Guadalajara, checking out the cathedral and other landmarks on the interconnecting plazas. Enormous Mercado Libertad (aka Mercado San Juan de Dios) is several long blocks east of Plaza Fundadores, or take the subway two blocks south of the cathedral on Avenida Juárez. If it's Sunday, see a charreada; otherwise head to Zapopan to see the basilica, the Huichol Museum, and the Art Museum of Zapopan, and spend 15 minutes at *la presidencia municipal* (city hall) to admire the leftist-theme mural inside. If you have more time, check out the market, two blocks west at Calles Eva Briseño and Hidalgo, and a couple of surrounding churches before grabbing a drink or a bite on Paseo Teopinztle, two blocks south. Freshen up at your hotel, then dine in downtown Guadalajara or the Zona Minerva.

Spend the second day shopping and visiting churches and museums in the old towns of Tonalá and in more compact, walkable Tlaquepaque. If you're here on Thursday or Sunday, don't miss the Tonalá crafts market, with its super deals. El Parián in Tlaquepaque is a great place to enjoy a mariachi serenade with a cool refreshment. Have Mexican food for lunch or dinner in one of Tlaquepaque's charming restaurants. If you don't want to shop, consider spending the day hiking in Barranca de Oblatos or visiting the playground, park, and gardens at Parque Azul. Arrive in the morning to avoid crowds; leave before dark.

If you've got three days in Guadalajara, you'll have time to visit Tequila or Lake Chapala. It's a refreshing change to get out of the city and admire the relatively dry hills and valleys, noting the fields of blue agave that are Tequila's reason for being. Tequila is en route to San Blas and Puerto Vallarta. Lake Chapala and the towns on the shore work well as a day excursion if you have a car.

LOGISTICS & TIPS Allot a minimum of three hours for the Centro Histórico, longer if you really want to enjoy the sculptures and street scene. Mornings are generally the least crowded time of day, although the light is particularly beautiful in the afternoons when jugglers, street musicians, and other informal entertainers tend to emerge.

Beware of heavy traffic and *topes* (speed bumps). Traffic circles are common at busy intersections.

Tonalá's crafts market and Mercado Libertad are the region's top two marketplaces. Allot yourself plenty of time and energy to explore both. El Trocadero is a weekly antiques market at the north end of Avenida Chapultepec. Feel free to drive a hard bargain at all three.

GUADALAJARA

Metropolitan Guadalajara's sights are divided into four major areas: Guadalajara, Zapopan, Tlaquepaque, and Tonalá. Within Guadalajara are many districts and neighborhoods. Of most interest to visitors is the Centro Histórico (Historic District), a rather small section of town that's part of the larger downtown area (El Centro). Outside the Centro Histórico, Guadalajara resembles any large, sometimes polluted city with gnarly traffic. On the west side are Zona Minerva, the most modern section of the city and the place to go for dining, dancing, shopping in large malls, and high-rise hotels. The Centro Histórico, Tlaquepaque, and Tonalá can each be navigated on foot in a few hours, though they deserve at least half a day. Zapopan's high-end hotels, bars, shops, and cafés are spread out, but historic Zapopan is reasonably compact. Likewise, Tonalá is a lot more spread out than more tourist-oriented, walkable Tlaquepaque.

GETTING HERE & AROUND

BY AIR Many major airlines fly nonstop from the U.S. to Guadalajara. Aeropuerto Internacional Libertador Miguel Hidalgo is 16½ km (10 mi) south of the city, en route to Chapala. Autotransportaciones Aeropuerto operates a 24-hour taxi stand with service to any place in the Guadalajara area; buy tickets at the counters at the national and international exits. Some hotels also offer airport pickup shuttles; these need to be arranged in advance.

BY BUS & SUBWAY Although flying from your hometown to Guadalajara, then back home from PV can be a good deal, flying round-trip to Guadalajara from PV is not. The bus is much cheaper, scenic, and efficient. Luxury buses between Puerto Vallarta and Guadalajara take 4½ hours and cost $33–$37. With one wide seat on one side of the aisle and only two on the other, ETN is the most upscale line, and has about nine trips a day to and from Puerto Vallarta, except Sunday, with only one. Within Mexico, they accept advance reservations with a credit card.

Estrella Blanca is an umbrella of different bus lines; many head straight for Guadalajara. TAP (Transportes al Pacifico) is a first-class line that serves major Pacific coast destinations between Ixtapa/Zihuatanejo and the U.S. border, including service to Guadalajara, Puerto Vallarta, and Tepic. ■TIP→ **Many bus lines do not accept credit cards.** Guadalajara's Nueva Central Camionera (New Central Bus Station) is 10 km (6 mi) southeast of downtown.

Most city buses (45¢) run from every few minutes to every half hour between 6 AM and 9 PM; some run until 11 PM. ⚠ **The city's public transit buses are infamously fatal; drivers killed more than 100 pedestrians annually in the late 1990s before the government intervened. These poorly designed, noisy, noxious buses are still driven ruthlessly and cause at least a dozen deaths per year.**

Large mint-green Tur and red Cardinal buses are the safest, quickest, and least crowded and go to Zapopan, Tlaquepaque, and Tonalá for around 80¢. Wait for these along Avenida 16 de Septiembre.

Autotransportes Guadalajara–Chapala serves the lakeside towns from Guadalajara's new bus station (Central Camionera Nueva) and from the old bus station (Antigua Central Camionera); cost is around $4. It's 45 minutes to Chapala and another 15 minutes to Ajijic; there are departures every half hour from 6 AM to 9:30 PM. Make sure you ask for the *directo* (direct) as opposed to *clase segunda* (second-class) bus, which stops at every little pueblo en route.

Guadalajara's underground *tren ligero* (light train) system is clean, safe, and efficient. Trains run every 10 minutes from 5 AM to midnight; a token for one trip costs about 40¢.

BY CAR   Metropolitan Guadalajara's traffic gets intense, especially at rush hour; parking can be scarce. Streets shoot off at diagonals from roundabouts (called *glorietas*), and on main arteries, turns (including U-turns and left turns) are usually made from right-side lateral roads (called *laterales*)—which can be confusing for drivers unfamiliar with big city traffic. ■TIP→ **Ubiquitous and inexpensive, taxis are the best way to go in Guadalajara.**

BY TAXI   Taxis are easily hailed on the street in the Centro Histórico, Zapopan, Tlaquepaque, and most other areas of Guadalajara. All cabs are supposed to use meters (in Spanish, *taximetro*)—you can insist the driver use it or else agree on a fixed price at the outset. Many hotels have rate sheets showing the fare to major destinations and parts of town.

Taxi is the best way to get to Tonalá or Tlaquepaque (about $7). To continue from Tlaquepaque to Tonalá, take a taxi from Avenida Río Nilo southeast directly into town and the intersection of Avenida de los Tonaltecas ($4–$6; 5–10 minutes depending on traffic).

ESSENTIALS

Air Contacts Aeroméxico (☎01800/021-4000 or 01800/021–4010 ⊕www. aeromexico.com). **American Airlines** (☎33/3616–4090, 33/3688–5518 (airport) or 01800/904–6000 ⊕www.aa.com). **Continental** (☎33/3647–4251 33/3688–5141

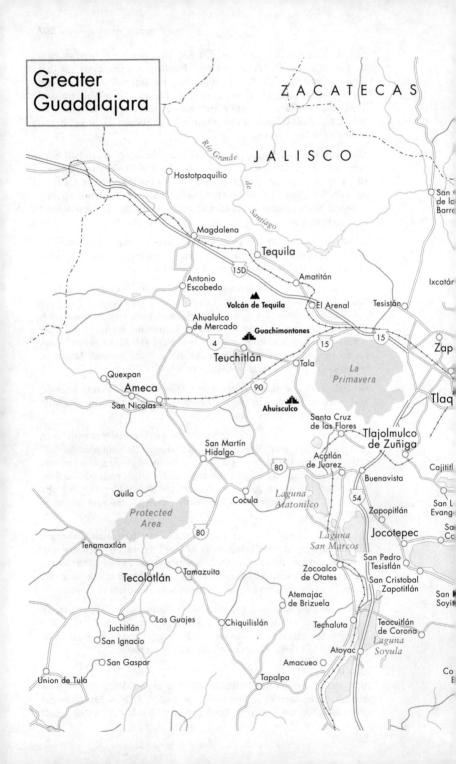

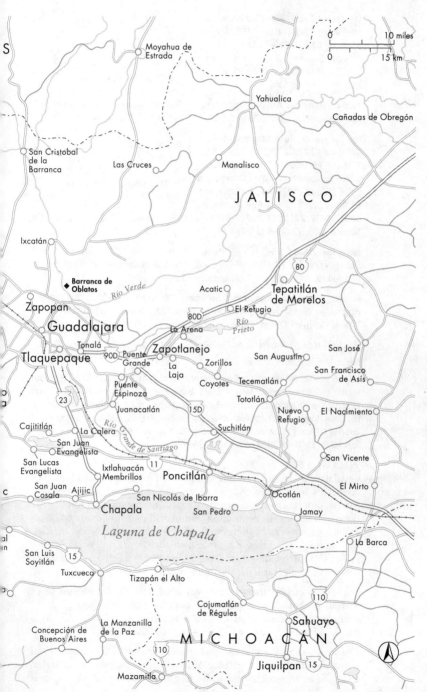

S

Moyahua de Estrada

Yahualica

Cañadas de Obregón

San Cristobal de la Barranca

Las Cruces

Manalisco

J A L I S C O

Ixcatán

♦ Barranca de Oblatos

Río Verde

Acatic

80

Tepatitlán de Morelos

Zapopan

Guadalajara

80D

El Refugio

Río Prieto

La Arena

Tonalá

Zapotlanejo

San José

Tlaquepaque

90D

Puente Grande

La Laja

Zorillos

San Augustín

San Francisco de Asís

Puente Espinoza

Coyotes

Tecematlán

Juanacatlán

15D

Tototlán

Cajititlán

La Calera

Río Grande de Santiago

Suchitlán

Nuevo Refugio

El Nacimiento

San Juan Evangelista

San Lucas Evangelista

Ixtlahuacán Membrillos

11

Poncitlán

San Vicente

San Juan Cosala

Ajijic

San Nicolás de Ibarra

Ocotlán

El Mirto

Chapala

San Pedro

Jamay

Laguna de Chapala

La Barca

San Luis Soyitlán

15

Tuxcueca

Tizapán el Alto

110

Cojumatlán de Régules

Sahuayo

Concepción de Buenos Aires

La Manzanilla de la Paz

110

M I C H O A C Á N

Mazamitla

Jiquilpan

15

9

0 ──── 10 miles
0 ──── 15 km

(airport), or *01800/900–5000* ⊕ *www.con tinental.com).* **Delta Air Lines** (☎ *33/3630– 3530* or *01800/902–2100 toll-free in Mexico* ⊕ *www.delta.com).* **Mexicana** (☎ *33/3615–3227* or *01800/502–2000* ⊕ *www.mexicana.com).*

Airport Transfers Autotransportacio- nes Aeropuerto (☎ *33/3688–5293).*

Bus Contacts Autotransportes Gua- dalajara Chapala (☎ *33/3619–5675).* **ETN** (☎ *33/3600–0477* or *01800/360– 4200* ⊕ *www.etn.com.mx).* **Greyhound** (☎ *33/3647–5070 in Guadalajara, 01800/710–8819 toll-free in Mexico,*

> ### HORSING AROUND
>
> *Calandrias* (horse-drawn carriages) take in the sights of the Centro Histórico; it's $20 for a long tour and $15 for a short one. Tapatío Tour, an open-top, double-decker bus, loops Zona Rosa ($11; daily 10 AM–8 PM every 30 minutes). Get on and off as much as you like to explore the sights. The bus departs from the Rotunda, a plaza on the Cathedral's north side.

800/231–2222 in U.S., 800/661–8747 in Canada ⊕ *www.greyhound.com).* **Estrella Blanca** (☎ *33/3679–0404).* **TAP** (☎ *33/3668–5920).*

Taxis Taxi Plaza del Sol (< > ⊠ *Glorieta Minerva, Minerva,* ☎ *33/3631–5262).* **Taxi Sitio Miverva no. 22** (☎ *33/3630–0050).* **Taxi Tlaquepaque** (⊠ *Calles Progreso and Juárez, Tlaquepaque, Tlaquepaque* ☎ *33/3633–0662).*

Medical Assistance Emergency Hotlines (☎ *066, 065 for Red Cross ambulance).* **Farmacias Guadalajara** (⊠ *Av. Javier Mina 221, between Calle Cabañas and Vicente Guerrero, Centro Histórico, Guadalajara* ☎ *33/3617–8555).*

Hospital México-Americano (⊠ *Calle Colomos 2110, Centro Histórico, Guada- lajara* ☎ *33/3641–3141).*

Tour & Visitor Information Guadalajara Municipal Tourist Office (⊠ *Monu- mento Los Arcos, Pedro Morelos 1596, 1 block east of Minerva Fountain, Zona Minerva, Guadalajara* ☎ *33/3668–1600).* **Tlaquepaque Municipal Tourist Office** (⊠ *Calle Morelos 288, Tlaquepaque* ☎ *33/3562–7050 Ext. 2318).* **Tonalá Municipal Tourist Office** (⊠ *Av. de los Tonaltecas Sur 140, in La Casa de los Artesanos, Tonalá* ☎ *33/3284–3092* or *33/3284–3093).*

WHAT TO SEE

EL CENTRO & THE CENTRO HISTÓRICO Guadalajara's historical center is a blend of modern and old buildings connected by a series of large plazas radiating from the Cathedral. Many colonial-era structures were razed; others stand crumbling, as there's no money for restoration. But overall there are many colonial- and Republican-era buildings with impressive carved limestone facades, tiled steeples and domes, magnificent wooden doors, and wrought-iron grills. The surrounding parks, plazas, and fountains have Corinthian columns and a great sense of community.

For a taste of how the wealthy once lived, visit the **Casa-Museo López Portillo,** a mansion with a stunning collection of 17th- through 20th- century furniture and accessories. ⊠ *Calle Liceo 177, Centro Histórico* ☎ *33/3613–2411* ☐ *Free* ☉ *Tues.–Sat. 10–6, Sun. 10–5.*

★ Construction was begun in 1561 on the **Catedral,** a downtown focal point and an intriguing mélange of Baroque, Gothic, and other styles. Exquisite altarpieces line the walls. In a loft above the main entrance is

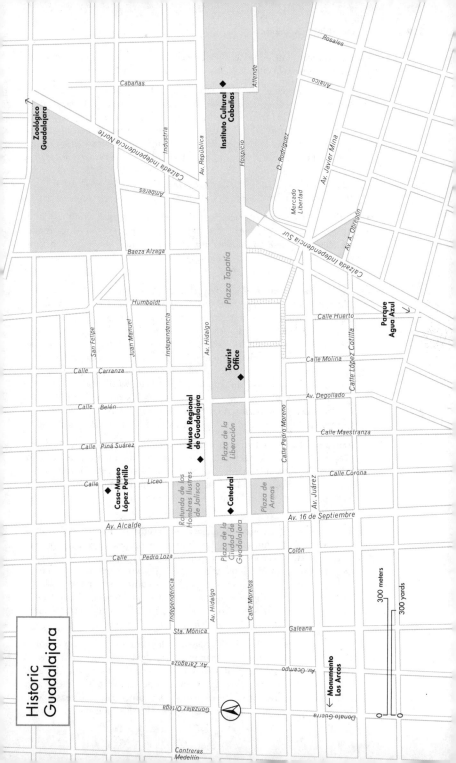

a magnificent late-19th-century French organ. ⊠*Av. Alcalde, between Av. Hidalgo and Calle Morelos, Centro Histórico* ⊙*Daily 8–8.*

Fodor's Choice
★
☼

Originally a shelter for the elderly and orphans, the neoclassical-style **Instituto Cultural Cabañas** has 106 rooms and 23 flower-filled patios that now house art exhibitions. Kids love the murals by Orozco, as well as his smaller paintings and cartoons and the labyrinthine compound in general. Large-scale theater, dance, and musical performances occasionally take place on a patio here. The Tolsá Chapel hosts more-intimate events. ⊠*Calle Cabañas 8, Centro Histórico* ☎*33/3668–1647* ⊠*$7 (foreigners), $3.50 (nationals); free Sun.* ⊙*Tues.–Sat. 10–6, Sun. 10–3; occasionally closed for maintenance.*

★ Artifacts from prehistoric times through the Spanish conquest and an impressive collection of European and Mexican paintings make the **Museo Regional de Guadalajara,** a grand former seminary, worth a visit. Admission is $4 per person. ⊠*Calle Liceo 60, Centro Histórico* ☎*33/3614–5257* ⊠*$3; free Sun.* ⊙*Tues.–Sat. 9–5:30, Sun. 9–4:30.*

☼ Popular **Parque Agua Azul** has playgrounds, caged birds, an orchid house, and acres of trees and grass crisscrossed by walking paths. There aren't many butterflies in the huge, geodesic butterfly sanctuary, but the semi-tropical garden inside still merits a visit. The Museo de la Paleontología (⊠*Av. Dr. R. Michel 520, Centro Histórico* ☎*33/3619–7043*), on the park's east side, has plant and animal fossils as well as exhibits on the origin of the planet. Admission is 90¢, and the museum is open Tuesday through Saturday 10–6 and Sunday 11–4. (There's no museum entrance inside Agua Azul; you must walk to the park's north side.) ⊠*Calz. Independencia Sur, between González Gallo and Las Palmas, south of Centro Histórico, El Centro* ☎*33/3619–0333* ⊠*40¢* ⊙*Daily 10–6.*

North of El Centro, **Barranca de Oblatos** is a multipronged, 2,000-foot-deep ravine with hiking trails and the narrow Cascada Cola de Caballo (Horsetail Waterfall), named for its horsetail shape. A portion of the canyon complex, called Barranca de Huetitán (Huetitán Canyon), has a steep, winding, 5-km (3-mi) trail to the river below. The trails are less strenuous at the Barranca de Oblatos entrance.

☼ The city's zoo, **Zoológico Guadalajara,** on the edge of the jagged Barranca de Huetitán, has more than 1,500 animals representing 360 species. There are two aviaries, a kids' zoo, and a herpetarium with 130 species of reptiles, amphibians, and fish. For 50¢ you can take a train tour of the grounds. Admission to the adjacent amusement park is $1.30. ⊠*Paseo del Zoológico 600, off Calz. Independencia, Zona Huentitán* ⊹*North of town near Barranca de Oblatos* ☎*33/3674–4488* ⊠*$4.50* ⊙*Wed.–Sun. 10–6 (daily during school vacations).*

TLAQUEPAQUE Another ancient pueblo that's gone upscale is crafts-crazy Tlaquepaque. Fabulous shopping for fine ceramics coupled with the attractive town's compact size make it appealing to Guadalajarans and visitors. Along its cobblestone streets are a wealth of old homes converted to shops and restaurants. B&Bs with jungly gardens, warming fires, and reasonable prices easily convince many travelers to make this their base.

LIVE PERFORMANCE

The State Band of Jalisco and the Municipal Band sometimes play at the bandstand on Tuesday around 6:30 PM. Small, triangular Plaza de los Mariachis, south of the Mercado Libertad, was once the ideal place to tip up a beer and experience mariachi, the most Mexican of music, at about $15 a pop. Now boxed in by a busy street, a market, and a run-down neighborhood, it's safest to visit in the day or early evening. For about the same amount of money but a more tourist-friendly atmosphere, mariachis at El Parián, in Tlaquepaque, will treat you to a song or two as you sip margaritas at this enormous, partly covered conglomeration of 17 cantinas diagonal from the town's main plaza. Once a marketplace dating from 1883, it has traditional *cazuela* drinks, which are made of fruit and tequila and served in ceramic pots.

The internationally acclaimed **Ballet Folclórico of the University of Guadalajara** (⊕ *www.ballet.udg. mx*) performs traditional Mexican folkloric dances and music in the Teatro Diana (☎ *33/3614–7072)* most Sundays at 10 AM; tickets are $3–$25. The state-funded **Orquesta Filarmónica de Jalisco** (*Philharmonic Orchestra of Jalisco* ⊕ *www. ofj.com.mx*) performs pieces by Mexican composers mixed with standard orchestral fare. When in season (it varies), the OFJ performs Sunday at 12:30 PM and Friday at 8:30 PM; tickets are $5–$15.

Ask your concierge or the tourism office about other performances around town, or check the newspaper.

Fodor'sChoice ★ On display at the **Museo del Premio Nacional de la Cerámica Pantaleon Panduro** are prize-winning pieces from the museum's annual June ceramics competition. You can request an English-speaking guide at possibly the best collection of modern Mexican pottery anywhere. ⊠ *Calle Priciliano Sánchez at Calle Flórida, Tlaquepaque* ☎ *33/3562–7036* 🆓 *Free* ☉ *Mon.–Sat. 10–6, Sun. 10–3.*

In a colonial mansion, the **Museo Regional de la Cerámica** has displays (in Spanish) explaining common processes used by local ceramics artisans; presentation isn't always strong. ⊠ *Calle Independencia 37, Tlaquepaque* ☎ *33/3635–5404* 🆓 *Free* ☉ *Tues.–Sat. 10–6.*

ZAPOPAN Expanding over the years, Guadalajara's population of about 4 million now encompasses pre-Hispanic towns like Zapopan. The country's former corn-producing capital, Zapopan is now a wealthy enclave of modern hotels and malls. Beyond, some farming communities remain, but the central district is now home to two remarkable museums and one of Mexico's most revered religious icons.

★ The vast **Basílica de la Virgen de Zapopan,** with an ornate plateresque facade and *mudéjar* (Moorish) tile dome is home to Our Lady of Zapopan: a 10-inch-high, corn-paste statue venerated for miraculous healings and answered prayers. Every October 12, more than a million people pack the streets around the basilica for an all-night fiesta capped by an early-morning procession. Don't miss the adjoining Huichol Museum (⇨below), which has Huichol art for sale.

★ Better known by its initials, MAZ, the **Museo de Arte de Zapopan** is Guadalajara's top contemporary art gallery. It regularly holds expositions of distinguished Latin American painters, photographers, and sculptors. ⊠*Andador 20 de Noviembre 166, Zapopan* ☎*33/3818–2200* ☎*$2.30; free Tues.* ☉*Tues.Sun. 10–6.*

★ The Huichol Indians are famed for their fierce independence, their use of peyote in religious ceremonies, and their exquisite beadwork and yarn "paintings" (⇨ *"The Art of the Huichol," in Chapter 5)*. At the **Museo Huichol Wixarica de Zapopan,** bilingual placards explain the fascinating Huichol religion and worldview while somewhat hokey maniquins display intricately embroidered clothing. The gift shop sells a small inventory of beaded items, prayer arrows, and god's eyes. ⊠*Av. Hidalgo, 152, Zona Zapopan Norte* ☎*33/3636–4430* ☎*50¢* ☉*Mon.–Sat. 9:30–1:30 and 3:30–6, Sun. 10–2.*

WHERE TO EAT

Tapatíos love foreign food, but homegrown dishes won't ever lose their flavor. The trademark local dish is *torta ahogada,* literally a "drowned [pork] sandwich" soaked in tomato sauce and topped with onions and hot sauce. Other favorites are *carne en su jugo* (beef stew with bacon bits and beans), *birria* (hearty goat or lamb stew), and *pozole* (hominy and pork in tomato broth). Seafood is popular and is available in trendy restaurants as well as at stands. The best Mexican food is near the main attractions downtown. The most popular non-Mexican restaurants are scattered about western Guadalajara, in Zona Minerva.

CENTRO HISTÓRICO

$
★
MEXICAN
✕**La Fonda de San Miguel.** Located in a former convent, La Fonda is perhaps the Centro's most exceptional eatery. Innovative Mexican eats are presented in a soaring courtyard centered around a stone fountain and hung with a spectacular array of shining tin stars and folk art from Tlaquepaque and Tonalá. Relish the freshly made tortillas and the shrimp in tasty mole sauce. Live performances include a duo that plays midweek 3 to 5 PM, and a folkloric show Thursday through Saturday at 9 PM. (See the current schedule on the restaurant's Web site.) ⊠*Donato Guerra 25, Centro Histórico* ☎*33/3613–0809* ⊕ *www.lafondadesan miguel.com* ⊟*AE, MC, V* ☉*No dinner in June.*

$
MEXICAN
✕**Tacos Providencia del Centro.** This is the place for traditional Guadalajara street-stand fare. Tacos *al pastor* top the clean restaurant's menu, and they come with every possible filling, including *trompa* (pig snout). Quesadillas and *gringas* (tortillas filled with cheese and meat) are also available. ⊠*Calle Morelos 84-A, at Plaza Tapatía, Centro Histórico* ☎*33/3613–9914* ⊟*No credit cards.*

TLAQUEPAQUE

$$
★
MEXICAN
✕**Casa Fuerte.** Relax with tasty Mexican dishes at the tables along the sidewalk or under the palms and by the fountain in the patio. You'll be tempted by the sidewalk tables facing the pedestrian street, but duck

Continued on page 220

MARIACHI: BORN IN JALISCO

by Sean Mattson

's 4 AM and you're sound asleep somewhere in Mexico. Suddenly you're jolted awake by trumpets blasting in rapid succession. Before you can mutter a groggy protest, ten men with booming voices break into song. Nearby, a woman stirs from her slumber. The man who brought her the serenade peeks toward her window from behind the lead singer's sombrero, hoping his sign of devotion is appreciated—and doesn't launch his girlfriend's father into a shoe-throwing fury.

At the heart of Mexican popular culture, mariachi is the music of love and heartache, of the daily travails of life, and nationalistic pride. This soundtrack of Mexican tradition was born in the same region as tequila, the Mexican hat dance, and *charrería* (Mexican rodeo), whose culture largely defines Mexican chivalry and machismo.

Today, mariachi bands are the life of the party. They perform at weddings, birthdays, public festivals, restaurants, and city plazas. The most famous bands perform across the globe. Guadalajara's annual mariachi festival draws mariachis from around the world.

The origin of the word *mariachi* is a source of some controversy. The legend is that it evolved from the French word *mariage* (marriage), stemming from the French occupation in the mid-1800s. But leading mariachi historians now debunk that myth, citing evidence that the word has its origins in the Nahuatl language of the Coca Indians.

THE RISE OF MARIACHI

Historians trace the roots of mariachi to Cocula, a small agricultural town south of Guadalajara. There, in the 17th century, Franciscan monks trained the local indigenous populations in the use of stringed instruments, teaching them the religious songs to help win their conversion.

The aristocracy, who preferred the more refined contemporary European music, held early mariachi groups in disdain. But by the late 19th century, mariachi had become enormously popular among peasants and indigenous people in Cocula, eventually spreading throughout southern Jalisco and into neighboring states.

MODERN MARIACHI INSTRUMENTS

Traditional mariachi groups consisted of two violins (the melody), and a vihuela and guitarrón (the harmony). Some long-gone groups used a *tambor* or drum, not used in modern mariachi. All members of the group shared singing responsibilities.

TRUMPETS
Added to the traditional mariachi lineup in the 1930s when mariachis hit the big screen, at the insistence of a pioneer in Mexican radio and television

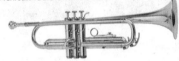

VIOLINS
Essential to any mariachi group

THE FOLK HARP
Longstanding mariachi instrument, used today by large ensembles and by some traditional troupes

THE GUITARRÓN
A large-bellied bass guitar

GUITARS
The round-backed vihuela is smaller and higher-pitched than the standard guitar

5-string Vihuela   6-string guitar

In 1905, Mexican dictator Porfirio Díaz visited Cocula and was received with a performance of a mariachi group. Impressed with the performance, Diaz invited the group to Mexico City where, after a few years and a revolution, mariachi flourished. Over the next two decades, more groups followed to Mexico City. Mariachi groups gained wide popularity by the 1930s, when movie stars as Jorge Negrete and Pedro Infante began portraying mariachi musicians in their films.

MARIACHI STYLE

■ The mariachi *traje* (suit) consists of matching vest, *chaleco* (short jacket), and form-fitting pants, and a complementary *moño* (large bow tie). Simple *trajes* have soutache trim or embroidery; finer versions have suede patterns on the jacket with metal buttons down the pants legs. Trajes come in all colors, but formal costumes are black.

■ Sombreros made from pressed rabbit fur are the highest quality.

■ The modern mariachi's dress is an adaptation of *charro*, or Mexican cowboy, attire, first worn by the members of an early mariachi group led by Cirilo Marmolejo and adopted for Mexican movies of the 1930s–50s. A complete formal outfit can cost as much as US$3,000.

■ *Botonaduras* (decorative buttons on the pants legs) can be simple, or ornate, made of silver or gold. A brooch on the front of the jacket often matches the botonadura.

■ Black leather *botines* (half-boots) are standard mariachi footwear.

WHERE AND HOW TO HEAR MARIACHI

HIRE A MARIACHI GROUP

There may be no better way to thoroughly surprise (or embarrass) your significant other, or a more memorable way to pop the question, than with a mariachi serenade. Hiring a band is easy. Just go to Plaza de los Mariachis, beside Mercado Libertad in downtown Guadalajara. Pablo Garcia, whose Mariachi Atotonilco has been working the plaza for almost 40 years, says a serenade runs about 2,000 pesos, or just under US$200. Normal procedure is to negotiate price and either leave a deposit (ask for a business card and a receipt) and have the band meet you at a determined location, or, as Mexicans usually do, accompany the band to the unexpecting lady.

HIT THE INTERNATIONAL MARIACHI FESTIVAL

The last weekend of every August, some 700 mariachi groups from around the world descend upon Guadalajara for the annual International Mariachi Festival. Mexico's most famous mariachi groups—Mariachi Vargas de Tecalitlán, Mariachi los Camperos, and Mariachi de América—play huge concerts in Guadalajara's Degollado Theater, accompanied by the Jalisco Philharmonic Orchestra. The weeklong annual charro championship is held simultaneously, bringing together the nation's top cowboys and mariachis.

THE WORLD'S BEST MARIACHI BAND

At least, the world's most *famous* mariachi band, Mariachi Vargas de Tecalitlán was founded in 1897, when the norm was four-man groups with simple stringed instruments. Started by Gaspar Vargas in Tecalitlán, Jalisco, the mariachi troupe shot to fame in the 1930s after winning a regional mariachi contest, which earned them the favor of Mexican president Lázaro Cárdenas. The group quickly became an icon of Mexican cinema, performing in and recording music for films. Now in its fifth generation, Mariachi Vargas performs the world over and has recorded more than 50 albums, and music for more than 200 films.

The *gabán* (poncho) was worn traditionally for warmth.

CATCH YEAR-ROUND PERFORMANCES

If you miss Guadalajara's mariachi festival you can still get your fill of high- quality mariachi performances on street corners, in city plazas, and at many restaurants. An estimated 150 mariachi groups are currently active in the City of Roses.

Restaurants, most notably Guadalajara's Casa Bariachi chain, hire mariachi groups, whose performance is generally included with your table (though tips won't be refused). On occasion, mariachis perform free nighttime concerts in Guadalajara's Plaza de Armas. Another venue, the Plaza de Mariachi, beside Guadalajara's landmark Mercado Libertad, is a longstanding attraction, albeit during the day—at night it's better known for crime than mariachi.

Tlaquepaque's El Parían, a former market turned series of bars around a tree-filled central patio, is a fantastic intimate setting for mariachi music. Between free performances in the central kiosk, you can request serenades at about $20 per song or negotiate deals for longer performances for your table.

ALL ABOARD THE TEQUILA TRAIN!

To experience the Jalisco quartet of traditions—mariachi, charreria, folkloric dance, and tequila—in one adventure, take the Tequila Express. It includes a train ride from Guadalajara through fields of blue agave to a tequila-making hacienda, live mariachi music, all the food and drink you can handle, and a charro and folkloric dance performance.

WORKING HARD FOR THE MONEY

It is becoming harder for mariachi groups to make a living at the trade. The increasing cost of living has made nighttime serenades, once a staple of a mariachi's diet of work, expensive ($200 and up) and out of the reach of many locals. Performers generally work day jobs to make ends meet.

THE COWBOY CONNECTION

Mariachi and Mexican rodeo, or *charreada* (Mexico's official sport), go together like hot dogs and baseball. Both charreada and mariachi music evolved in the western Mexican countryside, where daily ranching chores like branding bulls eventually took on a competitive edge. The first of Mexico's 800 charro associations was founded in Guadalajara in 1920, and to this day holds a two-hour rodeo every Sunday. Throughout the competition, mariachi music is heard from the stands, but the key mariachi performance is at the end of a competition when female riders called *escaramuzas* perform synchronized moves, riding side-saddle in traditional ribboned and brightly colored western Mexican dresses.

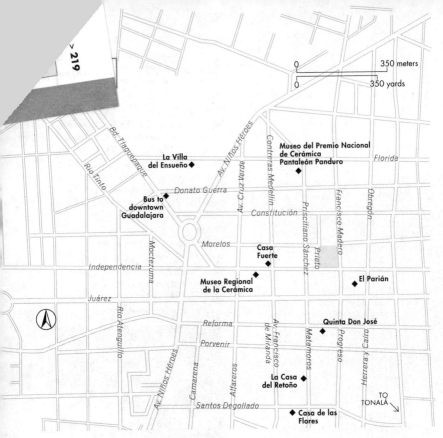

inside before you decide: the oversize garden patio surrounding a huge old tree is magnificent. Try the house specialties: chicken stuffed with *huitlacoche* (a corn fungus that's Mexico's answer to the truffle) and shrimp in tamarind sauce. Live, romantic music accompanies lunch every day except Monday. Closes at 8 PM. ⊠ *Calle Independencia 224, Tlaquepaque* ☎ *33/3639–6481* ▭ *AE, MC, V.*

TONALÁ

$ ✕ **El Rincón del Sol.** A covered patio invites you to sip margaritas while
MEXICAN listening to live guitar music (Tuesday to Sunday afternoons). Try one of the steak or chicken dishes or the classic *chiles en nogada* (in walnut sauce) in the colors of the Mexican flag. The waitstaff is helpful, as is the owner, who is right on-site to supervise. ⊠ *Av. 16 de Septiembre 61, Tonalá* ☎ *33/3683–1989 or 33/3683–1940* ▭ *MC, V.*

ZONA MINERVA

$ ✕ **Karne Garibaldi.** Lightning service is made possible by the menu's sin-
MEXICAN gle item: *carne en su jugo,* a combination of finely diced beef and bacon simmered in rich beef broth and served with grilled onions, tortillas, and refried beans mixed with corn. The original location on Calle Garibalde is in a less desirable neighborhood than the Plaza del Sol branch. ⊠ *Calle Garibaldi 1306, Zona Minerva* ☎ *33/3121–1663* ▭ *AE, MC, V.* ⊠ *Mariano Otero 3019, Zona Plaza del Sol* ☎ *33/3121–1663.*

$$ ✕**Pierrot.** Nose through this hushed French dining room's extensive
★ wine list for a drink to accompany the mouthwatering trout amandine
MEXICAN or pâté-stuffed chicken breast in tarragon sauce. Wall-mounted lamps
and fresh flowers on each table are among the intimate, homey restau-
rant's gracious touches. In business since the early 1980s, it is still very
popular with the locals, and plenty busy with business types in suits
throughout the week. It opens for lunch after 1 PM, and offers two daily
lunch specials. ⊠*Calle Justo Sierra 2355, Zona Minerva* ☎*33/3630–
2087* ⊟*AE, MC, V* ☽*Closed Sun.*

$$ ✕**Sacromonte.** Come here for creative Mexican food, superior service,
★ and warm ambience. You're surrounded by *artesanías* in the dining
MEXICAN area, and there's live music every afternoon from about 2 to 5, and
Friday through Sunday evenings after 9, light jazz. Try a juicy steak
or *La Corona de Reina Isabel*—a crown of intertwined shrimp in lobster sauce. ⊠*Pedro Moreno 1398, Zona Minerva* ☎*33/3825–5447*
⊟*MC, V* ⌟*Reservations essential* ☽*No dinner Sun.*

$ ✕**La Trattoria.** Guadalajara's top Italian restaurant is a bustling fam-
★ ily place. The menu's highlights include spaghetti *frutti di mare* (with
ITALIAN seafood), *scaloppine alla Marsala* (beef medallions with Marsala and
mushrooms), and fresh garlic bread. All meals include a trip to the
salad bar. Make a reservation if you're eating after 8 PM. ⊠*Av. Niños
Héroes 3051, Zona Minerva* ☎*33/3122–1817* ⊟*AE, MC, V.*

WHERE TO STAY

Choosing a place to stay is a matter of location and price; tourists are
often drawn to the Centro Histórico, where colonial-style hotels are
convenient to historical and other sights, or to Tlaquepaque's genial
B&Bs. Businesspeople head for the Zona Minerva, specifically around
Avenida López Mateos Sur, a 16-km (10-mi) strip extending from the
Minerva Fountain to the Plaza del Sol shopping center, where they can
take advantage of modern office facilities and four-star comforts.

CENTRO HISTÓRICO

$$$ ▥**Holiday Inn Centro Histórico.** Here's a spiffy, reliable international
chain in the heart of historic Guadalajara. In 2007 they brought in
new mattresses, bedding, pillows—the works, all done up in a gold-
and-white color scheme. Rooms have a work station and plasma TV;
in the bath is a glassed-in shower but no tub. The inexpensive breakfast
buffet is offered daily, and the restaurant serves national and inter-
national dishes. Pros: 24-hour business center and 24-hour gym, free
Wi-Fi in rooms, free airport shuttle. Cons: No heat, small gym, no
pool. ⊠*Av. Juárez 211, Centro* ☎*33/3560–1200, 800/HOLIDAY in
U.S. and Europe* ⊕*www.holidaycentrogdl.com* ⇥*90 rooms and suites*
⌂*In room: safe, Wi-Fi. In hotel: restaurant, room service, bar, laundry
facilities, laundry service, public Internet, public Wi-Fi, parking (no
fee), airport shuttle.* ⊟*AE, MC, V.*

$$ ▥**Hotel de Mendoza.** This refined hotel with postcolonial architecture
★ and hand-carved furniture is on a relatively calm side street a block
from Teatro Degollado. Suites are worth the extra cost: standard rooms
are comfortable but small. Balconies overlook the courtyard pool
from some rooms. Pros: Free Wi-Fi and use of hotel computers; suites

have balconies and queen-size tubs; package for about $100 gets you a room, breakfast, and parking. Cons: Standard rooms have shower only; only a portion of the rooms have balconies, and those can't be reserved ahead. ⊠*Calle Venustiano Carranza 16, Centro Histórico,* 🕾*33/3942–5151, 01800/361–2600 in Mexico* ⊕*www.demendoza. com.mx* 📞*110 rooms, 17 suites* ♿*In room: Wi-Fi. In-hotel: restaurant, pool, gym, parking (fee), public Wi-Fi.* ⊟*AE, MC, V* ⦿*EP.*

$$ ★   🏨 **Hotel Morales.** Renovated in 2005 after being abandoned for 30 years, this downtown hotel—originally a 19th-century rooming house—is elegant and quiet. Demure guest rooms have crown molding, blond wood floors, and satiny gold-and-beige furnishings. Café tables on the roof provide an escape from the more formal lobby with its international restaurant. Among the distinguished guests who have stayed here are the bullfighter El Cordobéz; cinema star Cantinflas; and the Brazilian soccer hero Pelé. Pros: Downtown elegance on the cheap, free in-room coffee, double-paned windows. Cons: No Wi-Fi in rooms. ⊠*Ave. Ramón Corona 243, Centro* 🕾*33/3658–5232* ⊕*www.hotelmorales. com.mx* 📞*59 rooms, 7 suites.* ♿*In-room: safe. In-hotel: restaurant, public Wi-Fi, parking.* ⊟*AE, MC, V.*

$$★   🏨 **Casa de las Flores.** A favorite with those traveling for business as well as pleasure, this B&B is charismatic and inviting, with lovely art and wonderful food. Owners Stan and José, from the United States and Mexico, respectively, enjoy directing their guests to the best shops and markets for purchasing handicrafts. Guests meet and socialize by the fireplace in the cozy living room and out in the magical garden. Pros: Yummy, inventive breakfasts made by the owner; the inn is filled with local folk art and a brief tour is common; one computer for checking e-mail, no charge. Cons: Some might consider the garden fussy, or overwhelming ⊠*Calle Santos Degollado 175, Tlaquepaque,* 🕾*33/3659–3186* ⊕*www.casadelasflores.com* 📞*7 rooms* ♿*In-room: no a/c (some), no TV (some), Wi-Fi (some). In-hotel: laundry service, public Internet, public Wi-Fi, parking (no fee)* ⊟*MC, V* ⦿*BP.*

$$ 🏨 **Quinta Don José.** This B&B one block from Tlaquepaque's main plaza and shopping area feels more like a small hotel. Natural lighting and room size vary, so look at a few before you choose one. Suites face the pool, and are spacious but a bit dark. There's remarkable tile work in the master suite. Hearty breakfasts, with eggs made to order, are served in an inner courtyard, and good pizza is produced in the brick oven during the evening meal in the onsite Italian restaurant (closed Monday). Inexpensive area tours are offered here, too. Pros: Centrally located in downtown Tlaquepaque, friendly staff speaks excellent English, free coffee and fruit in reception area, free phone calls worldwide, free Wi-Fi. Cons: More hotelish (which is fine unless you're craving a B&B), freezing-cold swimming pool. ⊠*Calle Reforma 139, Tlaquepaque,* 🕾*33/3635–7522, 01800/700–2223 in Mexico, 866/629–3753 in U.S. and Canada* ⊕*www.quintadonjose.com* 📞*8 rooms, 7 suites* ♿*In-hotel: bar, pool, laundry service, public Wi-Fi, airport shuttle* ⊟*AE, MC, V* ⦿*BP.*

$$ 🏨 **La Villa del Ensueño.** Even with the 10-minute walk from Tlaquepaque's center, this intimate B&B is near the town's shops. The restored 19th-

century hacienda has thick, white adobe walls, exposed-beam ceilings, and plants in huge unglazed pots. Smokers should request a room with private balcony, as smoking isn't allowed inside. Pro: Restaurant in the works. Con: Only junior suites have bathtubs. ⊠*Florida 305,* ☎*33/3635–8792* ⊕*www. villadelensueno.com* ➾*16 rooms, 4 suites* ⟁*In-room: refrigerator (some), dial-up, Wi-Fi (some). In-hotel: restaurant, bar, pools, parking (no fee), no-smoking rooms* ⊟*AE, MC, V* ⌑O⌑*BP.*

> ### JALISCO'S HOLY WAR
>
> When ultra-right-wing president Plutarco Elías Calles effectively criminalized Catholicism in 1926, Jalisco-area Catholics launched an armed rebellion against the government. During the bitter *La Cristiada* war, many priests were executed. In recent years dozens of *Cristero* martyrs have been canonized by the Vatican, a great source of pride for Guadalajara's Catholics.

ZONA MINERVA

$$ ⌑Crowne Plaza Guadalajara.** Gardens encircling the pool add a bit of nature to this family-friendly hotel. A mix of antiques and reproductions fills the public spaces. Rooms have very little in the way of decor, but they do offer marble baths with small tub, hair dryer, iron and ironing board, and natural lighting; those in the tower have city views. (Ask for a room near the back; those near the playground can be noisy.) Plaza Club room rates include a buffet breakfast. The top-floor restaurant, Jacarandas (a real '60s throwback with white tablecloths, red carpet with gold stars, red leatherette booths, and brass chandeliers), has the best panoramic view in Guadalajara. Pros: Free coffee in rooms, 24-hour business center. Cons: Uninspired room decor, not all rooms have Wi-Fi. ⊠*Av. López Mateos Sur 2500, Col. Ciudad del Sol, Zapopan,* ☎*33/3634–1034, 01800/009–9900* ⊕*www.cpguadalajara. com.mx* ➾*297 rooms, 5 suites* ⟁*In-room: Wi-Fi (some). In-hotel: 2 restaurants, bar, room service, pool, gym, executive floor, public Wi-Fi, laundry service, parking (fee), no-smoking rooms* ⊟*AE, DC, MC, V* ⌑O⌑*EP.*

$$–$$$ **Fiesta Americana.** The dramatic glass facade of this high-rise faces
★ the Minerva Fountain and Los Arcos monument. Four glass-enclosed elevators ascend dizzyingly above a 14-story atrium lobby to the guest rooms, which have dignified, modern furnishings, small marble bathrooms with bathtub, and, for the most part, arresting views (rooms 1211 through 1217 have the very best). The lobby bar has live music every night. Executive floor rooms come with breakfast, and there's a business center. Pros: Portable room heaters available at no charge, ample parking, nice bathroom amenities, AAA discount. Cons: Some rooms have unattractive views of roof and generators, no swimming pool. ⊠*Av. Aurelio Aceves 225, Zona Minerva,* ☎*33/3818–1400, 800-fiesta1 in Mexico* ⊕*www.fiestamericana.com.mx* ➾*387 rooms, 4 suites* ⟁*In-room: Wi-Fi. In-hotel: restaurant, bar, gym, public internet, concierge, no-smoking rooms* ⊟*AE, DC, MC, V.*

$$ ★ **Hotel Plaza Diana.** At this modest hotel two blocks from the Minerva Fountain the standard-size rooms have white walls and bright, patterned fabrics. One suite even has a sauna. Stay on the upper floors

9

in the rear for the quietest rooms. Rooms are smallish and windows don't open, but each has its own small sitting area and two TVs. The large, open restaurant specializes in Argentine-style cuts of beef and there's a piano in the adjacent lounge. The huge, rectangular, indoor pool is good for swimming laps. Pros: Heated indoor pool, inexpensive Internet, free airport shuttle. Cons: Basic rooms, small gym. ⊠ *Ave. Agustín Yáñez 2760, Zona Minerva,* ☎ *33/3540–9700, 01800/024–1001 in Mexico* ⊕ *www.hoteldiana.com.mx* ⟿ *127 rooms, 24 suites* △ *In room: safe. In-hotel: restaurant, room service, bar, pool, gym, airport shuttle* ⊟ *AE, DC, MC, V* ꣼ *EP.*

$$$$ ⊞ **Quinta Real.** Stone-and-brick walls, colonial arches, and objets d'art ★ fill this luxury hotel's public areas. Suites are plush, though on the small side, with classy, elegant neocolonial-style furnishings and faux fireplaces. Junior suites are only slightly more expensive than master suites. Master suites have a separate seating area with love seat and marble-top desk. It's a small price upgrade to get the Gran Class suite with round Jacuzzi tub and CD player. Guests can get in-room spa treatments from one of two nearby spas. The wood-floored gym boasts LifeFitness and FlexDeck brand equipment and has plasma-screen TVs, cold towels, water in a small fridge, and bouncy music. Pros: No charge for in-room dial-up; original oil paintings; forced-air heating (many Guadalajara hotels aren't heated); stately, quiet grounds. Cons: Pricey, no on-site spa. ⊠ *Av. México 2727, at Av. López Mateos Norte, Zona Minerva,* ☎ *33/3669–0600, 01800/500–4000 in Mexico* ⊕ *www.quinta real.com* ⟿ *76 suites* △ *In-room: safe, dial-up. In-hotel: restaurant, bar, pool, concierge, gym, public Wi-Fi, no-smoking rooms, laundry service* ⊟ *AE, D, MC, V.*

NIGHTLIFE

With the exception of a few well-established night spots like La Mae-stranza, downtown Guadalajara is mostly asleep by 11 PM. The existing nightlife centers around Avenida Vallarta, favored by the well-to-do, under-30 set; Avenida Patria (full of bars for teenagers and young adults who party until early in the morning on weekend nights); and the some-what seedy Plaza del Sol. Bars in these spots usually close by 3 AM. Dance clubs may charge a $15–$20 cover, and many are open on Fri-day and Saturday nights only. Dress up for nightclubs; highly subjective admission policies hinge on who you know or how you look. The local music scene centers around Peña Cuicacalli and the Hard Rock Cafe.

Guadalajara has a decent arts and culture scene. You can catch the Uni-versity of Guadalajara's Ballet Folclórico on Sunday morning at Teatro Diana. International exhibitions are sometimes shown at the Instituto Cultural Cabañas or the Arts Museum of Zapopan.

BARS Open since 1921, **La Fuente** (⊠ *Calle Pino Suarez, Centro Histórico* ☎ *No phone*) draws business types, intellectuals, and blue-collar work-ers, all seeking cheap drinks, animated conversation, and live music. Arrive early to avoid crowds, a din, and a thick carpet of cigarette smoke over the tables. Restaurant by day, Guadalajara hot spot by ★ night, **I Latina** (⊠ *Av. Inglaterra at López Mateos* ☎ *33/3647–7774*) is where a cool international crowd has cocktails.

For some local color, stop at **La Maestranza** (⊠*Calle Maestranza 179, CentroHistórico* ☎*33/3613–5878*), a renovated 1940s cantina full of bullfighting memorabilia. After 9 PM Tuesday through Sunday, patrons cluster around the small stage at **La Peña Cuicacalli** (⊠*Av. Niños Héroes 1988, at Suarez traffic circle, Centro Histórico* ☎*No phone*). There's *rock en español* on Tuesday and folk music from Mexico, Latin America, and Spain other nights.

TIP

For the latest listings, grab a *Público* newspaper on Friday and pull out the weekly Ocio cultural guide.

DANCE CLUBS **El Gran Mexicano** (⊠*Av. Mariano Otero 5850, at the Periférico, Col. Jardines Ixtepete, Zapopan* ☎*33/3180–4012 or 33/3180–4013*) is the place to listen to or dance to some very typical Mexican music, including mariachi and banda groups. Cover is $10 per person; it's open on Friday and Saturday only between 9 PM and 3 AM.

Salón Astoria (⊠ *Prisciliano Sánchez 345, Centro* ☎*33/3614–6570*) opens lots earlier than most clubs and offers live tropical tunes until about 4 AM. The dance hall opens Thursdays and Sundays at 6 PM and Friday and Saturday at 8. Cover charge is just $3 for the ladies and $4 for gents.

Salón Veracruz (⊠*Calle Manzano 486, behind Hotel Misión Carlton, Centro Histórico* ☎*33/3613–4422*) is a spartan, old-style dance hall where a 15-piece band keeps hoofers moving to *cumbia*, merengue, and the waltz-like *danzón*. It's closed Monday and Tuesday.

SPORTS & THE OUTDOORS

BULLFIGHTS *Corridas* (bullfights) are generally held Sunday at 4:30 from October to December (usually just twice a month) at **Plaza Nuevo Progreso** (⊠*Calle M. Pirineos 1930 and Calz. Independencia Norte, Zona Huentitán* ☎*33/3637–9982 or 33/3651–8506*). Tickets are $10–$80; bleacher seats far from the action on the *sol* (sunny) side are much cheaper than more-comfortable up-close seats on the *sombra* (shady) side.

These "rodeos" of elegant equestrian maneuvers and rope tricks are the epitome of upper-class rural Mexican culture. Men in tight, elegant suits with wide-brimmed felt hats perform *suertes* in which they subdue young bulls or jump from one galloping horse to another in *el paso de la muerte* (the pass of death). Teams of women in flowing dresses perform audacious (yet less dangerous) synchronized movements on horseback. Mariachi or brass bands play between acts. Charreadas run year-round at the **Lienzo Charros de Jalisco** (⊠*Av. Dr. R. Michel 577, Centro Histórico* ☎*33/3619–3232*), next to Parque Agua Azul, usually Sunday at noon. Admission is $3–$5.

SHOPPING

Guadalajara is shopping central for people from all over Nayarit, Jalisco, and surrounding states. The labyrinthine Mercado Libertad is one of Latin America's largest markets; modern malls are gathering spots with restaurants and theaters. Tlaquepaque and Tonalá have the most extensive selection of Mexican art and handicrafts (mainly pottery). In Tlaquepaque, stroll along Independencia and Juárez streets for dozens of artsy shops. In less touristy Tonalá most shops and factories are spread out, with the exception of a concentration of shops on Avenida de los Tonaltecas, the main drag into town. On Thursday and Sunday, bargain-price merchandise is sold at a terrific street market there packed with vendors from 8 to 4.

CRAFTS &   Better known as Mercado San Juan
FOLK ARTS   de Dios, **Mercado Libertad** (⊠ *Calz.*
★   *Independencia Sur; use pedestrian bridge from Plaza Tapatía's south side, Centro Histórico*) has shops that are organized thematically on three expansive floors. Be wary of fakes in the jewelry stores. Most shops are open Monday–Saturday 10–8, and 10–3 on Sunday.

> **ROOT FOR THE HOME TEAM**
>
> *Futbol* (soccer) is a national obsession. Guadalajara's two main teams nurse a healthy rivalry—as do their fans. Atlas appeals more to the middle and upper classes; working-class Tapatíos and students prefer Las Chivas. In fact the Chivas seem to be the working-class heroes of much of Mexico. Both teams play at Guadalajara's **Estadio Jalisco** (☎ *33/3637–0301*) on weekends or Wednesday night January–May and July–December. Tickets are $5–$45.

★ **Tonalá crafts market** (⊠ *Av. Tonaltecas, north of Av. Tonalá, Tonalá*) is *the* place for Mexican arts and crafts. Vendors set up ceramics, carved wood, candles, glassware, furniture, metal crafts, and more each Thursday and Sunday (roughly 9–5). Look for *vajilla* (ceramic dining sets), but note that the more high-end ceramic offerings are at government-sponsored Casa de los Artesanos down the street. Antiquers come out of the woodwork every Sunday 10–5 to sell their antique European flatware and Mexican pottery at **El Trocadero** (⊠ *Av. Mexico at Av. Chapultepec, Zona Minerva*) market in the antiques district.

MALLS   Sprawling, tri-level **La Gran Plaza** (⊠ *Av. Vallarta 3959, Zona Minerva* ☎ *33/3122–3004*) has nearly 330 shops and a big cinema. The food court is Guadalajara's best. Among the most memorable stores, Eréndira Contis (☎ *33/3123–1254*), on the top floor, has exceptional jewelry and modern Mexican art and crafts. Guadalajara's first mall, **Plaza del Sol** (⊠ *Av. López Mateos Sur 2375, at Mariano Otero, Zona Minerva* ☎ *33/3121–5950*) has 270 commercial spaces scattered around an outdoor atrium and wacky sculpture-fountains by Alejandro Colunga. It's got everything the more modern malls have in a more low-key environment.

TEQUILA

56 km (35 mi) northwest of Guadalajara.

For an in-depth look at how Mexico's most famous liquor is derived from the spiny blue agave plant that grows in fields alongside the highway, stop by this tidy village. Head west from Guadalajara along

Avenida Vallarta for about 25 minutes until you reach the toll road junction (Puerto Vallarta Cuota). Choose the toll road (faster, safer, and about $10) or the free road (*libre*) toward Puerto Vallarta. Or catch a bus to Tequila from the Antigua Central Camionera (Old Central Bus Station), northeast of the Parque Agua Azul on Avenida Dr. R. Michel, between Calle Los Angeles and Calle 5 de Febrero.

> **CAUTION**
>
> Mercado Libertad has silver at great prices, but not everything that glitters there is certifiably silver. A safer, albeit pricier, bet are the shops along Avenida República in downtown Guadalajara, where there are more than 400 jewelers.

Buses marked Amatitán–Tequila are easy to spot from the entrance on Calle Los Angeles.

WHAT TO SEE

The **Sauza Museum** (⊠ *Calle Albino Rojas 22* ☎ *374/742–0247*) has memorabilia from the Sauza family, a tequila-making dynasty second only to the Cuervos. The museum opens Monday–Friday 10–2 ($1).

Another option is the Tequila Express, a daylong train ride with mariachis, a distillery tour, food, and plenty of tequila. There's no stop in the town of Tequila itself, but this is a great way to soak up Jalisco's tequila-making region. Most hotels offer or can refer you to such tours.

Opened in 1795, the **José Cuervo Distillery** (⊠ *Calle José Cuervo 73* ☎ *374/742–2442*) is the world's oldest tequila distillery. Every day, 150 tons of agave hearts are processed into 80,000 liters of tequila here. Hard-hat tours are offered daily every hour from 10 to 4. The tours at noon are normally in English, but English-speakers can often be accommodated at other times. The basic tour, which includes sips of tequila en route, costs $10. It's $15 for tours with an additional three tasting at tour's end or $24 adding special reserve tequilas. Tours including round-trip transportation can be arranged through the Camino Real hotel, in Guadalajara. Theirs is a good deal, including three tequila tastings and a complimentary margarita and free time for lunch for about $25. Call 33/3134–2444 at least a day in advance to make arrangements.

TEUCHITLÁN

50 km (28 mi) west of Guadalajara.

For decades, residents in this sleepy village of sugarcane farmers had a name for the funny-looking mounds in the hills above town, but they never considered the Guachimontones to be more than a convenient source of rocks for local construction. Then in the early 1970s an American archaeologist asserted that the mounds were the remnants of a long-vanished, 2,000-year-old state. It took Phil Weigand nearly three decades to convince authorities in far-off Mexico City that he wasn't crazy. Before he was allowed to start excavating and restoring this monumental site in the late 1990s, plenty more houses and roads were produced with Guachimonton rock—and countless tombs were looted of priceless art.

The spot is most distinctive for its sophisticated concentric architecture—a circular pyramid surrounded by a ring of flat ground, surrounded by a series of smaller platforms arranged in a circle. The "Teuchitlán Tradition," as the concentric circle structures are called, is unique in world architecture. Weigand believes the formations suggest the existence of a pre-Hispanic state in the region, whereas it was previously held that only socially disorganized nomads inhabited the region at the time. Similar ruins are spread throughout the foothills of the extinct Tequila Volcano, but this is the biggest site yet detected.

> ### DEDICATED TO ITS CRAFT
>
> Like Tlaquepaque, neighboring **Tonalá** was in the crafts business long before the Spanish conquistadors arrived. Independent and industrious, less-touristy Tonalá remains dedicated to traditional pursuits: brilliant blown glass, gold jewelry, and goofy piñatas. But it's the exquisitely stylized *petatillo*-style ceramics that's the town's best-known handcraft. The distinctively Mexican earthenware is decorated with placid-looking birds and beasts and glazed in subtle tans and blues. Thursday and Sunday markets are the source of terrific bargains.

To get to Teuchitlán from Guadalajara, drive west out along Avenida Vallarta for 25 minutes to the toll road junction to Puerto Vallarta: choose the free road 70 (*libre*) toward Vallarta. Head west along Route 15 for a couple of miles, then turn left onto Route 70 and continue until you reach the town of Tala. One-and-a-half kilometers (1 mi) past the sugar mill, turn right onto Route 27. Teuchitlán is 15 minutes from the last junction. The ruins are up a dirt road from town—just ask for directions when you arrive. There's a small museum off the main square. Plans to build greater infrastructure around the site continue. If you visit during the dry season, you may score a look at a dig or restoration project.

LAKE CHAPALA

Lake Chapala is Mexico's largest natural lake and just an hour's drive south of Guadalajara. Surrounded by jagged hills and serene towns, it is a favorite Tapatío getaway and a haven for thousands of North American retirees.

The area's main town, Chapala, is flooded with weekend visitors and the pier is packed shoulder-to-shoulder most Sundays. Neighboring Ajijic, 8 km (5 mi) west, has narrow cobblestone streets and vibrantly colored buildings. Its mild climate and gentle pace has attracted a large colony of English-speaking expats, including many artists.

CHAPALA
45 km (28 mi) south of Guadalajara.

When elitist president Porfirio Díaz bought a retreat in lakeside Chapala in 1904, his aristocratic pals followed suit. Today, some of these residences on the shore of Mexico's largest natural lake have been converted to cozy lodges, many geared to families. About an hour south of downtown Guadalajara, the diminutive town is a retreat for the middle and upper classes, although there aren't as many restaurants, shops, and cafés as one might expect.

Three blocks north of the promenade, the plaza at the corner of López Cotilla is a relaxing spot to read a paper or succumb to sweets from surrounding shops. The Iglesia de San Francisco (built in 1528), easily recognized by its blue neon crosses on twin steeples, is two blocks south of the plaza.

On weekends the town is paralyzed by Mexican families who flock to the shores of the (for now, at least) rejuvenated lake. Vendors sell refreshments and souvenirs, while lakeside watering holes fill to capacity.

WHERE TO EAT

$ ✕**Cozumel.** Ajijic residents regularly drive to Chapala on Wednesday and Friday for live mariachi music (7 to 9 PM) and inexpensive, well-prepared specials, which includes, in addition to a main course, a margarita cocktail, dessert, coffee, and a digestive after-dinner drink called "el beso." Wednesday is chicken cordon bleu night and Friday it's surf-n-turf; on other days, choose from trout, breaded shrimp, and other seafood and international dishes. Reservations are essential for Friday and sometimes for Wednesday night. ⊠*Paseo Corona 22–A* ☎*376/765–4606* ▤*MC, V* ✆*Closed Mon.*

$ ✕**Mariscos Guicho's.** Bright orange walls and checkerboard tablecloths lend the best of the waterfront seafood joints an authentic Mexican flair. Dig into savory caviar tostadas, frogs' legs, garlic shrimp, and spicy seafood soup. ⊠*Paseo Ramón Corona 20* ☎*376/765–3232* ▤*No credit cards* ✆*Closed Tues.*

WHERE TO STAY

$ ⊡**Hotel Villa Montecarlo.** The hotel's simple, clean rooms are in three-story contiguous units, all with patios or terraces. Built on a Mediterranean-style villa that is nearly 100 years old, the property has extensive, well-maintained grounds with several eating and play areas. One of the two swimming pools (the biggest in the area) is filled with natural thermal water; it's drained regularly and usually only open on weekends and holidays. Popular with Mexican families, the hotel has frequent discounts and packages. Twenty bucks upgrades you from a standard room to a suite with larger terrace or balcony, kitchenette, and king bed. Pros: Huge pools and extensive grounds; outdoor dining under enormous, flowering laurel de la india tree. Con: Can be noisy with student groups. ⊠*Av. Hidalgo 296, about 1 km (½ mi) west of Av. Madero,* ☎*376/765–2216 or 376/765–2120* ↵*46 rooms, 2 suites* ⚶*In-hotel: restaurant, bar, tennis courts, pools, laundry service, parking (no fee)* ▤*AE, MC, V.*

$ 🔲 **Lake Chapala Inn.** Now that the lake is back to its original size (the
★ 1990s saw it shrink to an unattractive shadow of its former self due
to lack of rainfall and overuse of supplying rivers), this European-style
inn is an especially appealing place to stay. Three of the four rooms in
this restored mansion face the shore; all have high ceilings and white-
washed oak furniture. Rates include an English-style breakfast (with a
Continental breakfast on Sunday). Pros: Deep green, solar-heated lap
pool; English-speaking host; big sunny reading room. Cons: Dated,
70s-style furniture; square, tiled bathtubs not conducive to comfortable soaks. ⊠*Paseo Ramón Corona 23,* ☎*376/765–4786* ⊕ *www.
mexonline.com/chapalainn.htm* 🔁*4 rooms* ♿*In-room: no a/c, Wi-Fi.
In-hotel: restaurant, pool, laundry service, public Wi-Fi*🖃*No credit
cards* 🍽*BP.*

AJIJIC
8 km (5 mi) west of Chapala.

Ajijic has narrow cobblestone streets, vibrantly colored buildings, and
a gentle pace—with the exception of the very trafficky main highway
through the town's southern end. The foreign influence is unmistak-
able: English is widely (though not exclusively) spoken and license
plates come from far-flung places like British Columbia and Texas.

The Plaza Principal (aka El Jardín) is a tree- and flower-filled central
square at the corner of Avenidas Colón and Hidalgo. In late November
the plaza and its surrounding streets fill for the saint's nine-day fiesta of
the town's patron, St. Andrew. From the plaza, walk down Calle Morelos (the continuation of Avenida Colón) toward the lake and peruse the
boutiques on Ajijic's main shopping strip. (There are also many galleries and shops east of Morelos, on Avenida 16 de Septiembre and Calle
Constitución.) Turn left onto Avenida 16 de Septiembre or Avenida
Constitución for art galleries and studios. Northeast of the plaza, along
the highway, activity centers around the soccer field, which doubles as
a venue for bullfights and concerts.

WHERE TO EAT
$ ✕**La Bodega de Ajijic.** Eat in a covered patio overlooking a grassy lawn
and a small pool at this low-key restaurant. The menu has Italian and
Mexican dishes, which are a bit small and overpriced. Still, service is
friendly, and there's live music—ranging from Mexican pop and rock
to jazz, guitar, and harp—most nights. ⊠*Av. 16 de Septiembre 124*
☎*376/766–1002* 🖃*MC, V.*

$$ ✕**Johanna's.** Come to this intimate bit of Bavaria on the lake for Ger-
man cuisine like sausages and goose or duck pâté. Main dishes come
with soup or salad, applesauce, and cooked red cabbage. For dessert
indulge in plum strudel or blackberry-topped torte. ⊠*Carretera Cha-
pala-Jocotepec, Km 6.5* ☎*376/766–0437* 🖃*No credit cards* �−*No
dinner Sun.; closed Mon.*

$ ✕**Salvador's.** An old mainstay that's showing its years, this cafeteria-
like eatery is a popular expat hangout. There's a well-kept salad bar
and specialties from both sides of the border. On Friday and Saturday
people flock here for the fish-and-chips lunch special. Reasonable break-

fasts are offered daily after 7:30 AM, some include juice and coffee along with main dish for $3–$4. ☒*Carretera Chapala-Jocotepec Oriente 58* ☎*376/766–2301* ☐*No credit cards.* ⊘*No dinner Sun.*

WHERE TO STAY

$ ⬚**Casa Blanca.** The "white house" brings a hint of the East in the form of gracious gardens and tinkling fountains. Rooms are cheerful and tastefully decorated, if compact. There's just one smaller room at the cheaper price. The other rooms are still not large; most have a king bed, microwave, coffeemaker, and pleasant, shared outdoor patio. Despite their diminutive size, rooms are decorated in pretty blond furnishings with pleasingly clean lines. Each room has plenty of free drinking water. The on-site Internet center offers inexpensive access to guests and others. Pros: Charming and inexpensive, free Wi-Fi, centrally located near lake and shopping. Con: Small rooms. ☒*Calle 16 de septiembre #29, Centro* ☎*376/766–4440, 800/436–0759 from the U.S. or Canada* ⊕*www.casablancaajijic.com* ⇨ *8 rooms* ⬚*In-room: kitchen (some), Wi-Fi. In-hotel: public Internet, public Wi-Fi, airport shuttle* ☐*AE, MC, V* �ⓞ⊘⬚.

$-$$ ⬚**La Nueva Posada.** The gardens framed in bougainvillea define this
★ inviting inn. Rooms are large, with carpets, high ceilings, and local crafts. Villas share a courtyard and have tile kitchenettes. The bar has jazz or Caribbean music most weekend evenings. In the garden restaurant ($), strands of tiny white lights set the mood for an evening meal. Pros: Unique and lively décor, airy rooms, onsite restaurant with entertainment. Con: Small room TV. ☒*Calle Donato Guerra 9,* ☎*376/766–1344* ⊕*www.mexconnect.com/MEX/rest/nueva/posada. html* ⇨*19 rooms, 4 villas* ⬚*In-hotel: restaurant, bar, pool, laundry service* ☐*MC, V* �ⓞ*BP.*

SPORTS & THE OUTDOORS

The **Rojas family** (☒*Paseo Del Lago and Camino Real, 4 blocks east of Los Artistas B&B* ☎*376/766–4261*) has been leading horseback trips for more than 30 years. A ride along the lakeshore or in the surrounding hills costs around $7 an hour.

HEALING WATERS

☾ San Juan Cosalá, 2 km (1 mi) west of Ajijic, is known for its natural thermal-water spas along Lago de Chapala. **Hotel Balneario San Juan Cosalá** (☒*Calle La Paz Oriente 420, at Carretera Chapala–Jocotepec, Km 13*☎☎*387/761–0302* ⊕*www. hotelspacosala.com*) has a spa offering massage at reasonable prices. The water park offers a picnic area as well as several large swimming pools and two wading pools; admission is $13.

9

Gay Puerto Vallarta

WORD OF MOUTH

"Puerto Vallarta is *the* gay destination in Mexico, sort of like a Mexican Ft. Lauderdale or Miami."

–MikeT

"[PV is] as quiet or as happening as you want it to be. You could stay close to town at a big resort hotel like the Westin (*very* nice), or you could stay at a hotel in town, near or even right on the gay beach."

–robertino

PUERTO VALLARTA IS A GAY old town. Men check each other out over drinks and suntan oil at Blue Chairs, dangle from parachutes above Los Muertos beach, buff themselves out at South Side gyms. Rainbow boys (and girls) spend a day sailing on vessels flying the multicolored flag of love and then dance 'til morning in one of the city's oversexed discos. Mexico's most popular gay destination draws crowds of "Dorothy's friends" from both sides of the Río Grande, and from the Old World as well.

The Romantic Zone is the hub for rainbow bars and sophisticated, gay-friendly restaurants. Here, many foreigners have—after falling in love with Puerto Vallarta's beaches, jungly green mountains, and friendly people—relocated to PV to fulfill their ultimate fantasy in the form of bistro, bar, or B&B. International savvy (and backing) teamed up with Mexican sensibilities have produced a number of successful gay businesses.

Clubbing may be the favorite pastime in the Romantic Zone, but there's more than one way to cruise Vallarta. Gay boat tours keep the libations flowing throughout the day, and horses head for the hills for bird's-eye views of the beach.

DAYTIME ACTIVITIES

PV has something for every energy level. You can chill on the beach, get active by joining gay-oriented horse-riding tours or sailing expeditions, or spend the day at a secluded spot on the Cuale River.

BEACHES & RESORTS

The undisputed yet unassuming king of daytime beach action is **Blue Chairs** (⊠*South end of Los Muertos Beach, Col. E. Zapata* ☎*322/222– 5040 or 866/514–7969 toll-free in U.S. and Canada*). Shaded by the bright azure umbrellas that distinguish the restaurant/bar/hotel, local boys from the 'hood mingle with asphalt cowboys from the Midwest. Waiters range from snarky queens to cherubic heteros. This is PV's most popular gay beach scene, a magnet for first-timers as well as those sneaking away from social obligations in Guadalajara.

CRUISES

Boana Tours (⊠ *Casa Boana, Calle Amapas 325, Col. E. Zapata* ☎*322/223–4289* ⊕*www.boana.net*) offers a gay cruise for up to 20 passengers aboard a 36-foot sailboat. The tour ($75 per person) runs 9 to 5 and leaves from Marina Vallarta. Since this is basically a chartered cruise, guests can swim and snorkel and hang out on the South

Shore beach of the group's choice. Food and drink on the boat are included, but drinks and eats on the beach are not. Although groups can charter it any time of year, the usual run is Monday through Friday between October and May, for up to 12 people.

Affiliated with Blue Chairs, **Diana's Tours** (☎322/222–1510 or 866/514–7969 in U.S (for reservations) ⊕www.dianastours.com) is a Thursday booze and beach cruise (most Fridays also in high season) popular with lesbians and gays. Straights are also welcome, but minors are not. Go for the swimming, snorkeling, and lunch on the beach at Las Animas or another area beach, or for the unlimited national-brand beers and mixed drinks. Most of the time is spent on the boat. It's easiest to reserve tickets ($75) online using PayPal. There's also a three-hour Monday night sunset cruise with, you guessed it, unlimited booze, as well as wine, cheese, and snacks.

> ### TOTAL RELAXATION
>
> If you must break a sweat on your vacation, the best way is while experiencing a *temazcal*, an ancient Indian sweat lodge ceremony at **Terra Noble** (⊠ *Av. Tulipanes 595, Fracc. Lomas de Terra Noble* ☎ *322/222–5400 or 322/223–3530* ⊕ *www.terranoble. com*). The spa also has therapeutic massage, body treatments, and facials.

SPORTS & OUTDOORS

HORSEBACK RIDING

Four-hour (including transportation), $40 horse-riding adventures with **Boana Tours** (⊠ *Torre Malibú, Carretera a Mismaloya* ☎322/222–0999 ⊕*www.boana.net*) include round-trip transportation to its ranch outside the city, several hours on the horse, a light lunch, and two drinks. Guests can take a swim in the river before returning to PV. Most of the year there are two tours, at 9:30 AM and 2:30 PM, every day but Sunday.

10

AFTER DARK

Puerto Vallarta's club scene may seem tame compared to that of San Francisco or New York, but it's Mexico's most notorious. Guys and dolls begin their nocturnal perambulations at martini and piano bars and chummy pubs before heading to late-night drag shows, dance clubs, and strip joints.

BARS

★ Lesbian-owned, lovingly run **Apaches** (⊠ *Olas Altas 439, Col. E. Zapata* ☎322/222–5235) is Vallarta's original martini bar. The single row of sidewalk tables fills up soon after the 5 PM opening, as that's the start of the two-hour happy hour. Popular with straights, lesbians, and gay men warming up for later-evening activities, the narrow bar has added an equally slender adjoining bistro serving bar food and snacks.

★ In addition to its famous beach scene, **Blue Chairs** (⊠*South end of Los Muertos Beach, Col. E. Zapata* ☎*322/222–5040*) has the popular **Blue Sunset Rooftop Bar**, which is the perfect place to watch the sun set. Nightly late-afternoon and evening entertainment ranges from "Blue Balls" Bingo to the biweekly

> **KEEP 'EM COMING**
>
> Not that we're encouraging massive alcohol consumption, but you can spend all night at "happy hour." Hit the first at 4 in the afternoon and rotate throughout gay bars and clubs until 4 AM the next day.

drag show and the Saturday night "Blue Hombre Review." The place has good snacks, and a small swimming pool. Monday is karaoke night, beginning at 8 PM.

We've heard **Frida** (⊠*Lázaro Cárdenas 361, between Insurgentes and Aguacate Col. E. Zapata* ☎*No phone*) described as "the gay Cheers of Mexico." It's a friendly neighborhood cantina where you'll meet middle-aged or older queens, many Mexicans, fewer foreigners, and maybe even some straights. Show up a few times for $1 beers (served daily between 1 and 7 PM) and everyone is sure to know your name.

As popular with straights as it is with PV's rainbow crowd, **Kit Kat** (⊠*Calle Púlpito 120, Col. E. Zapata* ☎*322/223–0093*) has a huge list of fun martinis and other classy cocktails. The small space combines South Beach retro with a Zen-like simplicity. The food's good, too, and they have drag shows at least two weekends a month in high season, at which times reservations are de rigueur.

The air is sometimes smoky in tightly sealed **Garbo** (⊠*Púlpito 142, Col. E. Zapata* ☎*322/223–5753*), open daily 6 PM to 2 AM. The small, highly refrigerated piano and jazz bar has a nice varied menu of sophisticated drinks, good tunes (live music nightly except Tuesday in high season, less often the rest of the year), and waiters that regularly check on your welfare. On the downside, the beer is pricey, and mixed drinks are even more so.

★ The charming **La Noche** (⊠*Lázaro Cárdenas 257, Col. E. Zapata* ☎*322/222–3364*) martini lounge has red walls and a huge, eye-catching chandelier. Gringo-owned, it attracts a crowd of 20- to 40-year-olds (a mix of foreigners and Mexicans), who bring their CDs to play: electronica and house are the favorites. Speaking of which, the house makes excellent cocktails, and not too expensive, either.

DANCE & STRIP CLUBS

Billing itself as "The Study of Man," **Anthropology** (⊠*Calle Morelos 101, near Calle Encino below Ignacio L. Vallarta street bridge, Centro* ☎*322/221–5013*) has nightly strip shows beginning around 11 PM and yup, they take it all off. The management has no rules about customers, shall we say, "interacting" with the strippers during their nearly nonstop parades, and some customers complain of nonstop solicitations. There's a cover of about $5, and the club is open nightly after 9 PM. There's a late-night happy hour from 1 to 4 AM.

Club Paco Paco/The Ranch (✉ *Lázaro Cárdenas 258, Col. E. Zapata* ☎ *322/ 222–1899*) were the gay club pioneers of Vallarta, although they have now lost their alpha-dog status. One cover charge gets you into both. The main draw has never been the high-school-auditorium decor but the crowd; the female impersonators miming pop songs aren't too bad either. Back at the Ranch, strippers are the draw: policemen, firefighters, construction-worker types baring . . . almost all. Paco Paco's biggest selling point is that it outlasts the other gay clubs: it opens at 1 in the afternoon and doesn't close until 6 AM. The $5 cover gets you one national-label well drink.

> **TRAILBLAZER LIZ**
>
> According to a 2001 article in *Passport* magazine, many gay men moved to PV in actress Elizabeth Taylor's wake. After filming *The Night of the Iguana* in 1963, Ms. Taylor established a home here, and many of her gay friends from the movie crew followed suit.

★ Another club that focuses on the after-hours crowd is **Mañana** (✉ *Venustiano Carranza 290* ☎ *322/222–7772* ⊕ *www.clubmanana.com*). Come for the nightly strip show at 11:30, the theme parties (full-moon party, cowboy Mardi Gras, or "queen for a day")—which usually run about $12 per person—or the many other whacky activities. If you feel like swimming in the pool in middle of the bar, strip down to your underwear; the staff will give you a towel when you're done showing (or cooling) off. Things don't wind down until 6 AM or so, unless the authorities are on one of their occasional crack-down moods, enforcing the 4 AM curfew.

WHERE TO STAY

Gay hotels offer entertainment that allows you to party on-site without having to worry about getting "home." In addition to the hotels listed here, which are the crème de la crème of Vallarta, hotels like Los Cuatro Vientos, in el Centro, and Quinta María Cortez above Playa Conchas Chinas (⇨ *Chapter 2*) are gay-friendly.

■ **TIP →** Gayguide Vallarta (⊕ www.gayguidevallarta.com) has lots of listings for long- and short-term condo rentals.

$$–$$$ 🏨 **Blue Chairs.** Guys stay here not for the plain rooms but for all that Blue Chairs offers. Horseback riding, drag and strip shows, theme nights, events, parties, booze cruises, and beach cruising all begin—and often end—right here. **Pros:** *The* place to hang, nonstop evening activities, right on the gay beach, significant low season and online discounts. **Cons:** Unexciting rooms, lackadaisical service by beachside waiters. ✉ *Los Muertos Beach, Col. E. Zapata,* ☎ *322/222–5040, 866/514–7969 from Canada and U.S.* 🛏 *24 rooms, 16 suites* ♿ *In-room: kitchen (some). In-hotel: 2 restaurants, bars, pool, concierge* ⊟ *AE, MC, V* ⚐ *EP.*

WORK UP A SWEAT

There's more to a gay Vallarta vacation than drinking and dancing. Before baring your bod at the beach, burn off those extra calories at one of PV's many gyms.

On the South Side, gay-friendly **Acqua Day Spa and Gym** (✉ Constitución 450 ☎ 322/223–5270) has a sauna and steam room in addition to free weights and machines, massage, body treatments, and more. It's $12 per day and closed Sundays.

Serious muscle men and women head for **Gold's Gym** (✉ Calle Pablo Picasso s/n, Plaza Las Glorias, Zona Hotelera ☎ 322/225–6671) with aerobics, yoga, and Pilates as well as a sauna, steam, climbing wall, and hot tub. Child care is available. $10 per day. For women only, **Total Fitness Gym** (✉ Calle Timón 1, at marina, Marina Vallarta ☎ 322/221–0770) is a sparkly clean gym with a sauna as well as lots of classes: yoga, spinning, meditation, step, dance, salsa, jazz, aerobics, and Pilates. $14 daily fee.

$$$ ★ 🏨**Casa Cupula.** This multistory, up-to-date boutique hotel has a variety of rooms and prices that fluctuate by season. It's just a 15-minute walk down to the beach and the Romantic Zone (but the return trip is uphill). Most of the guest rooms have balconies with wonderful views of the sea and of layers of houses up and down the surrounding hills. Suites have kitchenettes, washer-dryers, and a separate bedroom. All the rooms are classy, restrained, and distinctly masculine. The airy shared dining room–lounge is comfortable and welcoming; the rooftop terrace with infinity dipping pool is lovely. Gays, lesbians, their dogs, and straight friends are welcome. **Pros:** Reasonably priced airport transfers, free Wi-Fi, oh-so-comfy beds and pillows. **Cons:** Aerobically challenging location, strict cancellation policy ✉ Callejon de la Igualdad 129, Col. Amapas, ☎ 322/223–2484, 866/352–2511 in U.S. and Canada ⊕ www.casacupula.com ➪ 9 rooms, 5 suites ⚿ In-room: safe, kitchen (some), refrigerator (some), DVD (some), dial-up, Wi-Fi. In-hotel: restaurant, room service, bar, pools, no elevator, laundry service, concierge, parking (no fee), no kids under 18, some pets allowed ⊟ AE, MC, V ☉ Closed Aug. and Sept. �CP

$ 🏨**Mercurio.** The rooms here are plain, but there's nonetheless much to be said for this small, motel-like place surrounding a swimming pool. First, it has a fabulous location—although not on the beach—in the heart of the Zona Romántica, PV's gay headquarters. The reasonable price leaves money left over for shopping and cruising. **Pros:** Excellent gay-central location, free Wi-Fi, all rooms have a small fridge. **Cons:** Small rooms, ho-hum motel-like furnishings ✉ Calle Francisco Rodriguez 168, Col. E. Zapata, ☎ 322/222–4793 ⊕ www.hotel-mercurio. com ➪ 28 rooms ⚿ In-room: no phone, safe, refrigerator, kitchen (some), Wi-Fi. In-hotel: bar, pool, no elevator, laundry service, concierge, public Internet, public Wi-Fi ⊟ AE, D, DC, MC, V ⏆ BP.

$$ 🏨**Villa David.** The public spaces and rooms here meld traditional Mexican architecture with more modern elements and lots of tile. The owners take good care of their gay (male) guests, and don't allow straights or lesbians to book rooms. A trio of little Pomeranians have the run of the place, but they're friendly. The clothing-optional guesthouse is securely tucked behind old walls in Gringo Gulch, a straight neighborhood made famous by Liz and Richard. Views of the town and bay are outstanding from the rooftop aerie, and some of the rooms have great views, too. **Pros:** Gay-only policy suits some folks; clothing-optional, heated swimming pool. **Cons:** Outside the gay Zona Romantica; some of the wicker furniture in public spaces is fussy or uncomfortable ⊠*Calle Galeana 348, Centro,* ☎*322/223–0315 or 877/832–3315 (reservations)* ⊕*www.villadavidpv.com* ⇔*10 rooms* ⚲*In-room: DVD, Wi-Fi. In-hotel: pool, no elevator, public Internet* ⊟*MC, V* ⍟|*BP.*

UNDERSTANDING PUERTO VALLARTA

PUERTO VALLARTA AT A GLANCE

FAST FACTS

Nickname: Foreigners call it PV, or Vallarta, but it has no real nickname. A *vallartense* (person from Puerto Vallarta), however, is known as a *pata salada* (salty foot).

State: PV is in the state of Jalisco, whose capital is Guadalajara.

Population: 220,368

Population density: 142.03 people per square km

Population growth rate 1990–2000: 65.74%

Literacy rate: 95.78%

Religion: Catholic 90%; Protestant/Evangelical 8.5%; other/no religion 1.5%

Type of government: Federal republic; municipality has a democratically elected city council and mayor

Language: Spanish is the official language and spoken by nearly everyone. Many people speak intermediate to fluent-level English; the few people who speak indigenous languages are Cora- and Huichol-speaking people from remote areas of Jalisco and Nayarit.

"I was taken in by the bravado and the sounds of Mexico ... not so much the music, but the spirit."
–Herb Alpert (musician)

"In its male aspect, in its public, its city aspect, Mexico is an arch-transvestite, a tragic buffoon. Dogs bark and babies cry when Mother Mexico walks abroad in the light of day. The policeman, the Marxist mayor— Mother Mexico doesn't even bother to shave her mustachios. Swords and rifles and spurs and bags of money chink and clatter beneath her skirts. A chain of martyred priests dangles from her waist, for she is an austere, pious lady. Ay, how much—clutching her jangling bosoms; spilling cigars— how much she has suffered."
–Richard Rodriguez

GEOGRAPHY & ENVIRONMENT

Latitude: 20°N (same as Cancún, Mexico; Port-au-Prince, Haiti; Khartoum, Sudan; Hanoi, Vietnam; Calcutta, India)

Longitude: 105° W (same as Regina, Saskatchewan; Denver, Colorado; El Paso, Texas)

Elevation: 40 meters (131 feet) above sea level

Land area: 1,972,550 square km (761,605 square mi)

Terrain: River basin backed by Sierra Madre foothills

Natural hazards: Hurricanes, tidal surges causing inundation of beachfront properties

Environmental issues: Destruction of natural areas due to migration and tourism

ECONOMY

Currency: Mexican peso

Exchange rate: 10.32 pesos = $1

Life Expectancy: 75 years

Per capita income: $7,310

Workers receiving minimum wage or less: 9.5%

Major industries: Tourism, commerce, construction, agriculture.

"I have said that Mexico does not stop at its border, that wherever there is a Mexican, there is Mexico," he said. "And, for this reason, the government action on behalf of our countrymen is guided by principles, for the defense and protection of their rights."– Felipe Calderón

DID YOU KNOW?

Two of the four quadrants in Puerto Vallarta's official seal symbolize the tourism industry: a sailfish represents sportfishing; the hands welcome tourists.

International law limits the production of tequila to specific regions of Mexico; most are in Jalisco (with specific regions also in Michoacán, Nayarit, Guanajuato, and Tamaulipas states).

HISTORY

PRE-COLUMBIAN MEXICO

The first nomadic hunters crossed the Bering Straight during the Late Pleistocene Era, some 30,000 or 40,000 years ago, fanning out and finding niches in the varied landscape of North America. In the hot and arid "Great Chichimeca," as the vast area that included the Sonora and Chihuahua deserts and the Great Plains of the United States was known, lived far-flung tribes whose circumstances favored a nomadic lifestyle. Even the unassailable Aztecs were unable to dominate this harsh wilderness and its resilient people.

Mesoamerica, the name given posthumously to the great civilizations of mainland Mexico, spanned as far south of the Great Chichimeca as Honduras and El Salvador. Here, trade routes were established, strategic alliances were formed through warfare or marriage, and enormous temples and palaces were erected on the backs of men, without the aid of beasts of burden or the wheel. Some cultures mysteriously disappeared, others were conquered but not absorbed.

It was in northern Mesoamerica that the continent's first major metropolis, Teotihuacán—which predated the Aztec capital of Tenochtitlán by more than half a century—was built. The gleaming city with beautifully decorated pyramids, palaces, homes, and administrative buildings covered miles and administered to some 175,000 souls; it was abandoned for unknown reasons around AD 700. On the Yucatán Peninsula, great and powerful Maya cities rose up, but like Teotihuacán were abandoned one by one, seemingly at the height of civilization.

During the rise and fall of these great cities, small, loosely organized bands of individuals occupied Mesoamerica's western Pacific coast. By 1200 BC, the culture that archaeologists call Capacha occupied river valleys north and south of what would later be named Bahía de Banderas. From well-positioned settlements, they planted gardens and took advantage of animal and mineral resources from the sea and the surrounding foothills.

These cultures—centered primarily in the present-day states of Nayarit, Jalisco, and Colima—built no large, permanent structures and left few clues about their society. Some of the most compelling evidence comes from artifacts found in tombs. Unlike their more advanced neighbors, the Pacific coast people housed these burial chambers not in magnificent pyramids but in the bottom of vertical shafts deep within the earth. Lifelike dog sculptures were sometimes left to help their deceased owners cross to the other side; servants, too, were buried with their masters for the same purpose. Realistically depicted figures involved in myriad rituals of daily and ceremonial life, most of them excavated only since the 1970s, have given more clues about pre-Hispanic civilizations of Western Mexico.

Only so much information can be gleaned, however, especially since the majority of tombs were looted before archaeological research began. North and south of Banderas Bay, the Aztatlán people seem to have established themselves primarily in river valleys between Tomatlán, in southern Jalisco, and northern Nayarit. In addition to creating utilitarian and ceremonial pottery, they appear to have been skilled in at least rudimentary metallurgy. Aside from the Purépecha of Michoacán, to whom the Aztatlán (or Aztlán) are related, no other Mesoamerican societies were skilled in making or using metal of any kind.

The Colonial Period

History favors those who write it, and the soldier-priest-scribe who documented the discovery of Banderas Bay in 1525 gave it a decidedly European spin. According to Padre Tello, four years after the

Spanish demolished the Aztec capital at Tenochtitlán, about 100 Spanish troops met 10,000 to 20,000 Aztatlán at Punta de Mita, the bay's northernmost point. Then, by Tello's fantastic account, the sun's sudden illumination of a Spanish battle standard (a large pennant) bearing the image of the Virgin of the Immaculate Conception caused the armed indigenous peoples to give up without a fight. When they lay their colorful battle flags at the feet of Francisco Cortés de Buenaventura, the Spanish commander named the site Bahía de Banderas, or Bay of Flags.

Subsequent adventurers and explorers rediscovered and used the region around the bay, but it wasn't colonized until three centuries later. The name Bahía de Banderas is seen on maps from the 1600s, although whalers in the 1800s called it Humpback Bay, after their principal prey. Boats were built on the beach in today's Mismaloya for a missionary expedition to Baja California, and the long, deep bay was used as a pit stop on other long sailing voyages.

To a lesser extent, Banderas Bay was a place of refuge and refueling for pirates. Around the end of the 16th century, Sir Francis Drake laid in wait here for the Manila galleon—sailing south along the coast laden with wares from the Orient. He sent the booty to his patron, Queen Elizabeth of England.

The Formative Years

Although adventurers made use of the area's magnificent bay, Puerto Vallarta's story started inland and made its way to the coast. Mining in this part of the Sierra Madre wasn't as profitable as in Zacatecas and Guanajuato, but there was plenty of gold and silver to draw the Spaniards' attention. At the vanguard of Spanish exploration in 1530, the infamous conquistador Nuño Beltrán de Guzmán arrived in the region with a contingent of Spanish soldiers and indigenous allies.

During his tenure in Nueva Galicia (which included today's Jalisco, Zacatecas, and Durango states), de Guzmán siezed land that was settled by native peoples and parceled out *encomiendas* (huge grants of land) to lucky *encomendados* (landholders) in return for loyalty and favors to the Crown. The landholders were entitled to the land and everything on it: the birds of the trees; beasts of the forest; and the unlucky indigenous people who lived there, who were consequently enslaved. De Guzmán's behavior was so outrageous that by 1536 he had been stripped of authority and sent to prison.

In exchange for their forced labor, the native population received the "protection" of the encomendado, meaning food and shelter, that they had enjoyed previously without any help from the Spanish. Abuse was inevitable, and many overworked natives died of famine. Epidemics of smallpox, diphtheria, scarlet fever, influenza, measles, and other imported diseases had a disastrous effect. The region's native population was reduced by about 90% within the first 100 years of Spanish occupation.

By the early 17th century, gold and silver were being mined throughout the region; there were bases of operation at San Sebastián del Oeste, Cuale, and Talpa. After the War for Independence (1810–21), Mexican entrepreneurs began to extract gold, silver, and zinc previously claimed by the Spanish. In the mid-1800s, the coast around today's Vallarta was under the jurisdiction of the mountain municipalities.

Independence from Spain brought little contentment to average people, who were as disenfranchised and poor as ever. A prime topic of the day among the moneyed elite was the growing conflict between Liberals and Conservatives. Liberals, like the lawyer Benito Juárez, favored curtailing the Church's vast power. When the Liberals prevailed and Juárez became Mexico's first indigenous president (he was a Zapotec from Oaxaca), a host of controversial reforms were enacted. Those regarding separation of church and state had immediate and lasting effects.

Settlers on the Bay

The power struggles of the first half of the 19th century had little real impact on relatively unpopulated coastal areas like Banderas Bay. In 1849, a few men from the fishing hamlet of Yelapa camped out at the mouth of the Cuale River, in present-day Puerto Vallarta. A few years later, young Guadalupe Sánchez, his wife, and a few friends were the first official settlers. This entrepreneur made his money by importing salt, vital for extracting mineral from rock. From this business grew the tiny town Las Peñas de Santa María de Guadalupe.

When silver prices dipped between the two World Wars, some of the mountain-based miners returned to their farming roots, relocating to the productive lands of the Ameca River basin (today, Nuevo Vallarta) at the southern border of Nayarit. The fecund land between the mountains and the bay produced ample corn crops, and the growing town of Las Peñas—renamed Puerto Vallarta in honor of a former Jalisco governor—became the seat of its own municipality in 1918.

Development came slowly. By the 1930s there was limited electricity; a small airstrip was built in the 1950s, when Mexicana Airlines initiated the first flights and electricity was finally available around the clock. Retaining the close-knit society and values brought down from the mining towns, each family seemed to know the others' joys and failures. They sat outside their adobe homes to discuss the latest gossip and the international news of the day.

THE MODERN ERA

Honoring a promise made to the Mexican government by John F. Kennedy, President Richard Nixon flew into an improved PV airport in 1970 to sign a treaty settling boundary disputes surrounding the Rio Grande, meeting with his Mexican counterpart, Gustavo Díaz Ordaz. Upon asking for an armored car, he was cheerfully told that the convertible that had been arranged would do just fine. After riding parade-style along the roadway lined with cheering citizens and burros garlanded in flowers, the American leader is said to have asked why, if he was a Republican, the road was lined with donkeys. To which his host sensibly responded, "Well, where in the world would we get all those elephants?"

It took about 500 years for Puerto Vallarta to transition from discovery to major destination, but the city is making up for lost time. "When I was a child here, in the 1950s, Puerto Vallarta was like a big family," the town's official chronicler, the late don Carlos Munguía, said. "When I married, in 1964, there were about 12,000 people." By the early '70s the population had jumped to 35,000 and continued to grow steadily.

Today the greater Puerto Vallarta area has some 220,368, a significant number of them expat Americans and Canadians who vacationed here and never left. The metropolitan area has three universities and a vast marina harboring yachts, tour boats, and the Mexican navy. In 2005 the harbor was expanded to accommodate three cruise ships; the overflow has to anchor offshore. While many folks lament the loss of the good old days before tourism took off, some things haven't changed: Most *vallartenses* (Puerto Vallarta natives) are still intimately acquainted with their neighbors and the man or woman who owns the corner taco stand, which is likely to have been there for years, maybe even generations.

CHRONOLOGY

ca. 350 BC   Oldest evidence of civilization—a ceramic piece from Ixtapa (northwest of Puerto Vallarta)—dates to this time

ca. 1100   Indigenous Aztatlán people dominate region from present-day Sinaloa to Colima states; create first-known settlement in area

1525   First Spanish–Indian confrontation in the region, at Punta de Mita. By Spanish accounts, 100 Spanish soldiers prevailed over tens of thousands armed native peoples. Bahía de Banderas (Bay of Flags) was named for the battle flags of the indigenous army that were (or so claimed the Spanish) thrown down in defeat

1587   Pirate Thomas Cavendish attacks Punta de Mita, looting pearls gathered from Mismaloya and the Marietas Islands

1664   Mismaloya serves as a shipyard for vessels bound for exploration and conquest of Baja California

1849   Yelapa fishermen are said to have found excellent fishing at the mouth of the Cuale River, making them the first unofficial settlers

1851   Puerto Vallarta founded, under the name Las Peñas de Santa María de Guadalupe, by the salt merchant Guadalupe Sánchez

1918   The small but growing seaside town becomes county seat and is renamed Puerto Vallarta in honor of former Jalisco State governor Ignacio Luis Vallarta (1871–75)

1922   Yellow fever kills some 150 people

1925   Flood and landslides during a great storm form narrow Cuale Island in the middle of the Cuale River in downtown PV

1931   Puerto Vallarta gets electricity (7–10 PM only)

1951   Reporters covering centennial celebrations—marked with a 21-gun naval salute and a wealthy wedding—capture the small town charm, exposing this isolated coastal gem to their countrymen

1963   Hollywood film *The Night of the Iguana*, directed by John Huston and starring Richard Burton and Ava Gardner, puts PV on the world map, due to the much-publicized affair between Burton and Elizabeth Taylor (who was not in the movie) during the filming here

1970   Vallarta builds a new airport, and improves the electrical and highway systems for Richard Nixon's official visit with President Díaz Ordaz

2000   Census reports the city's population as 159,080

2005   Population rapidly increases to 220,368 in greater metropolitan area

2006   Ground is broken for the 385-slip luxury-yacht marina at La Cruz de Huanacaxtle, north of Bucerías, continuing the trend of converting quiet fishing villages into big-bucks vacation destinations

CHRONOLOGY

2007   The "Riviera Nayarit," referring to the real estate between San Blas and Nuevo Vallarta, is officially launched as a newly branded destination.

2008   On May 31, Puerto Vallarta celebrates its 40th anniversary as a full-fledged city.

GOVERNMENT & ECONOMY

Government & Politics

Mexico is a federal republic with three branches of government—executive, judiciary, and legislative; the latter comprised by a senate and house of deputies (house of representatives). The basis for today's government is the 1917 Constitution, which, when ratified and implemented several years after that date, signaled the end of the Mexican Revolution.

The Revolution, at the dawn of the 20th century, was the combined, if disjointed, effort of various groups with almost polar opposite ideals and reasons for revolt. Campaigning under the slogan "No reelection!" the wealthy and influential northerner Francisco I. Madero's driving desire was to end the 33-year presidency/dictatorship of General Porfirio Diaz. Madero's goals were mainly ideological and intellectual. In the south, the poor, disenfranchised, and mainly indigenous population rallied around the charismatic Emiliano Zapata, who crusaded relentlessly for land reform in his native state of Morelos. Lack of cohesive leadership and goals made the revolt drag on for a decade, resulting in some 2 million deaths—including many civilians.

From the ashes of postwar chaos rose the political party known by its acronym, PRI (Partido Revolucionario Institucional). Adopting the green, red, and white of the Mexican flag, the Institutional Revolutionary Party quickly became the national party of Mexico.

As the decades rolled by, opposition parties were allowed in the legislature in small numbers, mainly to provide an illusion of legitimacy. Outgoing PRI presidents hand-selected their successors and left office with piles of the nation's cash and magnificent properties. And why not, as federal law protects ex-presidents from prosecution?

Modern presidents have been no exception to the pattern of corruption. Well-respected during his term, president (and Harvard-educated economist) Carlos Salinas de Gortari (term: 1988–94) increased his personal fortune while leaving Mexico in financial ruin. Mexico's economy had been on a downward spiral for decades, and Salinas's imprudent fiscal policies pushed the country to the breaking point (⇨ Economy).

Other issues, too, forced the normally fatalistic Mexicans to become increasingly unhappy with the status quo. Mexico City mayor Cuauhtémoc Cárdenas lost the 1988 election due to obvious election fraud. Fighting for social justice, the Zapatista Liberation Army (EZLN) staged a sudden and dramatic uprising in Chiapas State, while lesser rebellions threatened in Guerrero and Oaxaca. Popular presidential candidate Luis Donaldo Colosio was murdered in 1994. It was increasingly difficult to ignore the nation's financial, political, and social crises.

Salinas's successor, Ernesto Zedillo Ponce de León (term: 1994–2000), was left to deal with a massive devaluation of the country's currency and the resulting across-the-board financial hardship for the Mexican people. Middle-class people awoke just weeks after the president's inauguration to find their salaries cut by 40% and their mortgages and car payments increased by roughly the same amount.

Although generally following the mandate of his political party, Zedillo did institute important changes. Instead of hand-selecting his successor in the time-honored tradition, the former banker and education minister established the first presidential primary election. This departure from the norm inspired cautious optimism in previously apathetic voters. Blatantly illegal election maneuvers like voter intimidation and ballot-box stuffing in the countryside were monitored and curtailed.

The election in 2000 of opposition-party candidate Vicente Fox Quesada, and the peaceful transition to power that followed, left the country in a state of shock: more than 70 years of one-party rule was over. Even the winning party, PAN (Partido de Acción Nacional, or National Action Party), could scarcely believe the results.

By his own account, President Vicente Fox (term: 2000–2006) fell far short of such election promises as 7% economic growth per year; however, his historic tenure of office has changed the country. He enjoyed an approval rating averaging nearly 60% during his six-year term, and earned the admiration of his countrymen for his sincere interest in the working poor.

Mexico's 2006 presidential election was nothing if not controversial. The front runner was Andrés Manuel López Obrador, a huge hit with the poor. Representing the left-of-center PRD (Partido de la Revolución Democrática, or Party of Democratic Revolution), the former mayor of Mexico City lost the election by less than 1% to PAN's candidate, Felipe Calderón. Charges of fraud and even meddling by the United States were rampant, and López Obrador initially refused to concede defeat, setting up a "parallel government" and holding massive rallies in downtown Mexico City.

President Calderón got off to a rocky start, amid mass confusion and resentment and a weak mandate from the Mexican people. Still, he's started out with a show of force, especially tackling the twin demons of drug trafficking and corruption. His other most important challenges will be expanding trade-creating jobs, and improving living conditions for millions of underprivileged children and adults.

Following the national template, Puerto Vallarta and Jalisco State have traditionally voted PRI, and the majority of legislators still represent the tri-color party, as does the mayor of Puerto Vallarta. The last two governors (since 1994) have belonged to the business-oriented PAN, including the incumbent, Francisco Javier Ramírez Acuña. Mirroring the national trend, greater transparency is seen in local and state politics.

Economy

The U.S. is far and away Mexico's largest trading partner. Trade with its northern neighbor has grown significantly in the past decade, increasing from a surplus of $14,549 million in 1997 to more than $74,257 at the start of 2008. Trade with Canada, its second biggest trading partner, represents less than five percent of Mexican trade.

Trade statistics in the past had been significantly smaller. Traditionally inward-looking, the government party, PRI, was forced to expand Mexico's static and tightly controlled economy under President Miguel de la Madrid (1982–88) after a necessary but painful devaluation of the peso in 1982. Successor Carlos Salinas de Gortari continued to open the Mexican market, signing the North American Free Trade Agreement (NAFTA) with the United States and Canada in 1994.

However, Salinas and the PRI ignored the country's obvious signs of economic distress. Salinas's blatant corruption and failed economic programs left his successor, Ernesto Zedillo, with a 40% currency devaluation just weeks after taking office, followed by a bank bailout of more than $90 billion.

Zedillo's prudent economic policies slowly got the country back on track. And his handling of the opposition party's triumph in the 2000 presidential election—after 71 years of uninterrupted PRI rule—kept Mexico from erupting into political and economic chaos.

Today Mexico fluctuates between the largest and second-largest economy—and consistently has the highest per-capita income—in Latin America. Conversely, the unemployment rate, 3.6% (April 2006), is the lowest in Latin America. In January 2007 Mexico's inflation rate was 3.981%, one of the lowest rates in 37 years.

It's not all highs and glory, however. The 490,000 new jobs created during President Fox's administration is about one-tenth of what's needed to keep the country employed. Many millions of Mexicans—including a significant number from Jalisco State—work illegally in the United States, where they might easily earn 10 times or more the minimum wage of their own country, which is less than US$5 a day. According to *The New York Times,* remittances from these workers totaled some $24 billion in 2006.

Another of Mexico's leading industries is tourism. The last period Mexican tourism authorities have statistics for, January–March 2008, showed international tourism up 8.1% over the same period in 2007. According to Bank of Mexico figures, in 2007, international visitors spent US$11,547,000, a 6.8% increase over 2006. The number of cruise ship passengers entering Mexico was down12.2%, however.

Claudia Velázquez, Director of Marketing Research for the real estate consulting firm Softec, reported that in 2007 the Puerto Vallarta had the highest sales in the nation of "tourist-related" properties (time shares and second homes). Eighty percent of beach properties sold were purchased by foreigners, primarily Canadians and Americans, at an average price of $350,000.

PEOPLE & SOCIETY

Ethnic Groups

The population of Puerto Vallarta is overwhelmingly of mextizo (mixed native American and Spanish descent). According to the 2000 census, fewer than 1% of Jalisco residents speak an indigenous language. Compare that to nearby states: Michoacán with 3.6%, Guerrero with about 14% and Oaxaca, where more than a third of the inhabitants converse in a native language. Those indigenous people who do live in Jalisco State are small groups of Purépecha (also called Tarascans), in the south. The Purépecha were among the very few groups not conquered by the powerful Aztec nation that controlled much of Mesoamerica at the time of the Spanish conquest.

Although not large in number, the indigenous groups most associated with Nayarit and Jalisco states are the Cora and their relatives, the Huichol. Isolated in mountain and valley hamlets and individual *rancherías* (tiny farms) deep in the Sierra Madre, both have maintained to a large extent their own customs and culture. According to the CDI (Comisión Nacional Para el Desarrollo de los Pueblos Indígenas, or National Commission for the Development of Native Peoples), there are about 24,390 Cora in Durango, Zacatecas, and Nayarit states, and some 43,929 Huichol, mainly in Jalisco and Nayarit. Nearly 70% of the culturally related groups speak their native language and about half of the households have electricity.

In 1947 a group of prominent vallartenses was returning along twisty mountain roads from an excursion to Mexico City. When the driver lost control and the open-sided bus plunged toward the abyss, death seemed certain. But a large rock halted the bus's progress, and "*Los Favorecidos*" ("The Lucky Ones"), as they came to be known, returned to Puerto Vallarta virtually unharmed. Their untrammeled gestures of thanks to the town's patron saint, the Virgin of Guadalupe, set the precedent for this animated religious procession. Today, all Puerto Vallartans consider themselves to be Los Favorecidos, and thus universally blessed. This optimism and good cheer are two vital components of the local persona. For those of us fortunate enough to visit—for a short vacation or half a year—that angelic magnetism is a big part of the pull.

Religion

Mexico is about 89% Catholic; Puerto Vallarta is 90% Catholic. The Catholic population is overwhelmingly dedicated to the Virgin of Guadalupe, the patron saint of Puerto Vallarta, and of Mexico. Most of the non-Catholic 10% of the population have been converted in the last 50 years to Protestant and Evangelical Christianity.

Despite its strong religious character, Mexico has strict anticlerical laws inaugurated by president Benito Juárez and codified in the 1917 Constitution, which still governs the country. Dozens of laws limit religious participation in civil life. A church wedding is not recognized, churches and church land are public property, and Mass may not be held in public. Ministers, priests, and nuns may not vote or wear their vestments in public.

It's no surprise that these and other strict laws outraged the Church and devout Catholics when the Constitution was ratified. The ensuing Cristero Revolt (1926–29) led to tens of thousands of deaths and the assassination of then-President Alvaro Obregón by a religious fanatic. The headquarters for the revolt was staunchly Catholic and traditionalist Guadalajara, the capital of Jalisco State.

Many of the religious laws are not strictly enforced, however. No one dared to deny charismatic John Paul II the right to hold open-air Masses when the hugely popular pope visited in the 1980s and '90s. And because of the need, foreign priests are permitted to work in Mexico despite a law that bans this.

Family, friends, and having a good time are central to Mexican life, and the Catholic liturgical calendar obliges with many excuses to party. In Puerto Vallarta the biggest fiesta of the year honors the Virgin of Guadalupe. Consecutive visions of *la virgen morena* (the dark-skinned virgin), as she is affectionately called, are said to have appeared to Juan Diego, a Chichimec peasant, soon after the Spanish conquest of Mexico. Asked by a bishop to provide proof of the Lady's visit (on Tepeyac Hill, north of present-day Mexico City), Juan Diego is said to have collected in his cloak a shower of roses that the apparition provided. During transport, however, the bundle of roses disappeared to be replaced by an image of the saint herself. Report of the supposed miracle greatly helped the invaders to convert the pantheistic native population.

The bishop, the pope, and soon the majority of Mexicans were convinced of the miracle. The cloak, with the image still clearly visible, hangs above the altar in one of several important churches built at Tepeyac Hill, now called La Villa de Guadalupe. The site of the Virgin's reported 1531 visit was near a temple to the Aztec earth goddess Tonantzín.

The Feast Day of the Virgin of Guadalupe is Puerto Vallarta's most important religious holiday. During the weeks leading to the Mass held in her honor on December 12, area congregations, civic leaders, and businesses—including restaurants and hotels—join in colorful processions from their place of business to the downtown cathedral.

Dress

In deference to the tropical heat, vallartenses dress comfortably and casually, yet not indifferently. Young girls wear the latest fashions, with bellies—of all shapes and sizes—bared, while matrons favor comfortable, cool shifts and skirts. Men wear suits (with or without ties) or slacks and guayaberas. Businesswomen wear suits or classy outfits, panty hose, and high heels with elegant aplomb, always managing to look cool and crisp, while their north-of-the-border counterparts sport red faces, swollen ankles . . . and swoon at the mere mention of panty hose.

Mexican men don't walk around shirtless except at the beach or pool, and women don a cover-up at least. While increasingly stylish and modern, Mexicans tend to dress modestly. It's only in the last generation or two that women have felt comfortable wearing bathing suits, and many—especially those from smaller towns—still swim in shorts and T-shirts.

In downtown PV, cobblestone streets make walking in heels difficult, although Mexican women seem to pull it off. The addition of potholes and uneven sidewalks make sensible walking shoes or sandals preferable for most occasions. Popular on PV streets is the comfortable women's "San Miguel shoe," which comes in many styles and colors.

Etiquette

Mexicans are extremely polite people. The proverb "You catch more flies with honey than with vinegar" might have been invented here. Mexicans wait to be invited into a home, even by relatives. Business meetings begin with small talk and inquiries about family and mutual friends. Even phone conversations take a while to get to the point.

Ask a business acquaintance the name of the person who will be leading a meeting, and he might respond "*Su servidor*" (Your servant), referring to himself. Business letters often conclude "I remain your faithful servant."

Some of these formulaic phrases should be taken with a big grain of sea salt.

When talking about his home, a Puerto Vallartan might say *"Your* home (meaning *his* home) is at 333 Juárez Street."* This form of *"mi casa es su casa"* can be used equally with a great friend or a first-time acquaintance.

Resist the impulse to pay an unsolicited visit. Unspecific invitations to "come visit some time," which are, in most cases, made just to be polite, should be ignored unless a summons to a specific event is made.

Even when extremely annoyed or angry, Mexicans tend to maintain calm and decorum, using hyperbole or veiled sarcasm to display their displeasure. Foreign travelers throwing tantrums because of late tour buses or poor service must seem like creatures from another planet to Mexicans, who would usually endure most any inconvenience rather than create a scene.

This tendency of Mexicans to keep their thoughts to themselves can lead to frustration and confusion for foreigners. "When will the bus come?" a traveler might inquire regarding a bus that is 15 minutes late. *"Ahorita viene"* is the tour leader's inevitable answer. While the literal translation of this phrase is "It will be right here," the meaning in its cultural context is something like: "It will get here when it gets here. I have no control over the matter, but certainly cannot tell you that." Mexicans are experts at reading— and speaking—between the lines.

Language

The Mexican lexicon is full of examples of exceeding reticence and politeness. Some of these phrases leave other Spanish speakers rolling their eyes or rolling in the aisles with mirth. For example, instead of saying *"¿Cómo?"* ("What?") when something is not heard or understood, Mexicans say *"¿Mande?,"* an extremely old-fashioned, formal command meaning "Order me."

Most Mexicans use the terms *"Me da vergüenza"* and *"Me da pena"* interchangeably. To a Spaniard, the former means "I am embarrassed" or "I am ashamed"; the latter, "I'm in pain" or "It hurts me."

Another idiosyncrasy of Mexican Spanish is the use of the diminutive suffix *"–ita."* In Spain this word ending is mainly used to indicate a thing's small size or delicate nature. In Mexico this add-on is so common that words without it seem almost brusque, rude, or indicating lack of love or concern. Few people call their grandmother *abuela,* for example: *abuelita* (dear or little grandmother) is almost universal. One might ask for a *cervecita* instead of a *cerveza* to convey the desire not to impose on another person or put them out. A tour guide mentions that *propinitas* (small tips) are accepted when she is actually hoping for a big, fat tip. It's just another example of the national obsession with dancing delicately around life's baser truths and demands.

In his epic examination of the Mexican national character, *The Labyrinth of Solitude,* Nobel prize–winning essayist Octavio Paz describes the Mexican like this: "His language is full of reticences, of metaphors and allusions, of unfinished phrases, while his silence is full of tints, folds, thunderheads, sudden rainbows, indecipherable threats." Which demonstrates that while the national tendency might be toward disguising true meanings, Mexican speech can be brilliant and filled with imagery.

The Magic of Mexico

To say that Mexico is a magical place means more than it's a place of great natural beauty and fabulous experiences. Cities like Catemaco, in Veracruz, have a reputation for their *brujos* and *brujas* (male and female witches, respectively) and herbal healers (*curanderos/curanderas*). But Mexicans use these services even in modern Mexico City and Guadalajara, and tourist towns like Puerto

Vallarta, although they don't always advertise it. Some might resort to using a curandera to reverse *mal de ojo*, the evil eye, thought to be responsible for a range of unpleasant symptoms, circumstances, disease, or even death.

A *limpia*, or cleansing, is the traditional cure for the evil eye. The healer usually passes a raw chicken or turkey egg over the sufferer to draw out the bad spirit. Green plants like basil, or branches from certain trees can also be used, drawing the greenery over the head, front, and back to decontaminate the victim. Prayer is an essential ingredient.

Some cures are of a more practical nature. Mexican herbalists, like their colleagues around the world, use tree bark, nuts, berries, roots, and leaves to treat everything from dandruff to cancer. Epazote, or wormseed, is a distinctly flavored plant whose leaves are used in cooking. As its English name implies, its medicinal task is to treat parasites.

Most folk wisdom seems to draw from both fact and, if not fiction, at least superstition. Breezes and winds are thought to produce a host of negative reactions: from colds and cramps to far more drastic ailments like paralysis. Some people prefer sweating in a car or bus to rolling down the window and being hit by the wind, especially since mixing hot and cold is something else to be avoided. Even worldly athletes may refuse a cold drink after a hot run. Sudden shock is thought by some to cause lasting problems.

Although it doesn't take a leap of faith to believe that herbal remedies cure disease and grandma's advice was right on, some of the stuff sold in shops is a bit "harder to swallow." It's difficult to imagine, for example, that the sky-blue potion in a pint-size bottle will bring you good luck, or the lilac-color one can stop people from gossiping about you. Those that double as floor polish seem especially suspect.

Whether magic and prophesy are real or imagined, they sometimes have concrete results. Spanish conquistador Hernán Cortés arrived on the east coast of present-day Mexico in 1519, which correlated to the year "One Reed" of the Aztec calendar. A few centuries prior to Cortés's arrival, the benevolent god-king Quetzalcoatl had, according to legend, departed the same coast on a raft of snakes, vowing to return in the year One Reed to reclaim his throne.

News of Cortés—a metal-wearing god-man accompanied by strange creatures (horses and dogs) and carrying lightning (cannons and firearms)—traveled quickly to the Aztec capital. The Emperor Moctezuma was nervous about Quetzalcoatl's return and his reaction to the culture of war and sacrifice the Aztecs had created. In his desire to placate the returning god, Moctezuma ignored the advice of trusted advisers and literally opened the door for the complete destruction of the Aztec empire.

Machismo & La Malinche

Mexican machismo is a complicated concept fit for entire books of study. It's more than *piropos* (flirtatious or suggestive, and sometimes poetic, comments) or drinking beer for days at a time with the boys. According to essayist Octavio Paz (1914–98), the Mexican's machismo is in fact defensive rather than offensive: a kind of immunity to being hurt or humiliated by the outside world. Several great thinkers, including Paz, have suggested that this stoicism dates back to the Spanish conquest. Taking indigenous women as slaves or concubines, Spanish invaders left the girls' and women's husbands, fathers, and brothers outraged, yet powerless to intervene.

According to this psychological scenario, Mexican men take lovers in order to reject their wives before being snubbed themselves. Scorned and humiliated by her husband, a woman may then lavish her love and attention on her sons, who idolize their perfect mothers but grow up to emulate their fathers, perpetuating the cycle.

If the icon of the perfect woman is the Virgin Mary, the faithless woman who epitomizes female perfidy is La Malinche. Born Malinztín and christened Doña Marina by the Spanish, La Malinche was a real woman who played a fascinating role in the conquest of Mexico. As a young woman of possibly noble birth, Malinztín was sold into slavery and later given as a gift to the Spanish. She became a valued interpreter for Hernán Cortés thanks to her ability to speak three languages: her native Mayan tongue; Nahuatl, language of the Aztecs; and (later) Spanish. Her keen mind helped the Spanish strategize; as Cortés's mistress, she bore him a son. Although it was her own people who originally sold her into slavery, La Malinche has become the national symbol for female infidelity and betrayal.

La Vida Loca

Living the good life in Mexico—specifically in and around Banderas Bay—seems to get easier year by year, but it's getting pricey as well. Americans and Canadians are by far the biggest groups of expats. In addition to those who have relocated to make Mexico their home, many more foreigners have part-time retirement or vacation homes here. Those who realized their dreams of moving to Mexico a decade or more ago are sitting pretty, as the cost of land and houses soars. A two-bedroom property in a gated community by the sea begins at around $350,000, and the cost is climbing. You could get more modest digs for several times less; at the upper end of the spectrum, the sky's the limit. Construction prices keep going up, too, as builders realize how deep are the pockets of foreign investors.

The sheer number of foreigners living in Puerto Vallarta facilitates adventures that were much more taxing a decade or two ago, like building a home or finding an English-speaking realtor or lawyer. Contractors and shopkeepers are used to dealing with gringos; most speak good to excellent English. The town is rich with English-language publications and opportunities for foreigners to meet up for events or volunteer work.

THE NATURAL WORLD

Geography

On the same latitude as the Hawaiian Islands, Puerto Vallarta sits at the center point of C-shape Banderas Bay. Spurs from the Sierra Cacoma run down to the sea, forming a landscape of numerous valleys. This highly fractured mountain range is just one of many smaller ranges within the Sierra Madre—which runs south from the Rockies to South America. Sierra Cacoma sits at the juncture of several major systems that head south toward Oaxaca State. Forming a distinct but related system is the volcanic or transversal volcanic axis that runs east to west across the country—and the globe. Comprising part of the so-called Ring of Fire, this transverse chain of mountains includes some of the world's most active volcanoes. Both Volcán de Fuego, southeast of Puerto Vallarta in Colima State, and the giant Popocateptl, near the Gulf of Mexico, are currently active. Visible from Puerto Vallarta are the more intimate Sierra Vallejo and the Sierra Caule ranges, to the north and south respectively.

Heading down to the sea from these highlands are a number of important rivers, including the Ameca and the Mascota, which join forces not far from the coast at a place called Las Juntas (the joining). The Ameca is a large river whose mouth forms the boundary between Jalisco and Nayarit states. The valley floor is naturally boggy in some areas, but suitable for growing corn, sugarcane, and other crops elsewhere. The Cuale River empties into the ocean at Puerto Vallarta, dividing the city center in two. In addition to many rivers the area is blessed with seasonal and permanent streams and springs.

Banderas Bay, or Bahía de Banderas, is Mexico's largest bay, at 42 km (26 mi) tip to tip. The northern point, Punta de Mita, is in Nayarit state. Towns at the southern extreme of the bay, at Cabo Corrientes, are accessible only by boat or dirt roads. Cabo Corrientes (Cape Currents) is named for the frequently strong offshore currents. The mountains backing the Costalegre are part of the Sierra Madre Occidental range. The hilly region of eroded plains has two main river systems: the San Nicolás and Cuitzmala.

Several hundred miles east of Banderas Bay, Guadalajara—capital of Jalisco State—occupies the west end of 5,400-foot Atemajac Valley, which is surrounded by mountains. Just south of Guadalajara, Lake Chapala is Mexico's largest natural lake. It is fed by the Lerma–Santiago system, which, crossing the mountains, feeds other rivers and streams that empty into the Pacific.

Flora

The western flanks of the Sierra Madre and foothills leading down to the sea are characterized by tropical deciduous forest. At the higher levels are expanses of pine-oak forest. Many species of pines thrive in these woods, mixed in with *encinos* and *robles,* two different categories of oak; within each are many separate species. Walnut trees and oyamel, a type of fir, are the mainstays of the lower arroyos, or river basins. Along the coastal fringe magnificent *huanacaxtle,* also called *parota* (in English, monkey pod or elephant ear tree), mingle with equally huge and impressive mango as well as kapok, cedar, tropical almond, tamarind, flamboyant, and willow. The brazilwood tree is resistant to insects and therefore ideal for making furniture. *Matapalo,* or strangler fig, are common in this landscape. As its name hints, these fast-growing trees embrace others in a death grip; once the matopalo is established, the host tree eventually dies.

Colima palms, known locally as *guaycoyul,* produce small round nuts smashed for oil or sometimes fed to domestic animals. Mango, avocado, citrus, and guava are found in the wild; these and a huge number of cultivated crops thrive in the region. Imported trees and bushes often seen surrounding homes and small farms include Indian laurel, bamboo, and bougainvillea.

The coastal fringe north of San Blas (in Nayarit) is surprisingly characterized by savannas. Guinea grass makes fine animal fodder for horses and cows. Lanky coconut trees line roads and beaches. These have many uses and are sometimes planted in groves. The watery "milk" is a refreshing drink, and the meat of the coconut, although high in saturated fat, can be eaten or used in many types of candy. Another drink, *agua da tuba,* is made from the heart of the palm; the trunk is used in certain types of construction. Mangroves thrive in saltwater estuaries, providing an ecosystem for crabs and crustaceans as well as migratory and local birds.

South of Banderas Bay, thorn forest predominates along the coastal strip, backed by tropical deciduous forest. Leguminous trees like the tabachin, with its bright orange flowers, have long dangling seed pods used by indigenous people as rattles. Other prominent area residents are the acacias, hardy trees with fluffy puff-balls of light yellow blooms. Many species of cactus thrive in the dry forest, which is home to more than 1,100 species of vascular plants. The *nopal,* or prickly pear cactus abounds; local people remove the spines of the cactus pads and grill them, or use them in healthful salads. The fruit of the prickly pear, called *tuna,* is used to make a refreshing drink, *agua de tuna.* In this region, especially around Chamela and Cuixmala, about 16% of the plant species are endemic.

Fauna

Mammals in the area are few. Hunting, deforestation, and the encroachment of humans have diminished many once-abundant species. In the mountains far from humankind, endangered margay, jaguar, and ocelot hunt their prey, which includes spider monkeys, deer, and peccaries. More commonly seen in a wide range of habitats are skunks, raccoons, rabbits, and coyote. The coatimundi is an endearing little animal that lives in family groups, often near streambeds. Inquisitive and alert, they resemble tall, slender prairie dogs. Along with tanklike, slow-moving armadillo, the sandy-brown coatimundi is among the animals you're most likely to spot without venturing too deep within the forest. Local people call the coatimundi both *tejón* and *pisote,* and often keep them as pets.

Poisonous snakes in the area include the Mexican rattlesnake and the fer-de-lance. Locals call the latter *cuatro narices* (four noses) because it appears to have four nostrils. It's also called *nauyaca;* the bite of this viper can be deadly. There are more than a dozen species of coral snakes with bands of black, yellow, and red in different patterns. False corals imitate this color scheme to fool their predators, but unless you're an expert in the subject, it's probably best not to try to figure out which is which.

Of interest to most visitors are the region's birds and sea creatures both resident and migratory. The most famous of the migratory marine species is the humpback whale for which Banderas Bay was once named. Called *ballena jorobada,* or "humpback" whale, these leviathans grow to 17 meters (51 feet) and weigh 40 to 50 tons and travel in pods, feeding on krill and tiny fish. During a given year the females in area waters may be either mating or giving birth. During their amazing annual migration of thousands of miles from the Bering Sea, the hardy creatures may lose some 10,000 pounds. Hunted nearly to extinction in the 1900s, humpbacks remain an endangered species.

A few Bryde whales make their way to Banderas Bay and other protected waters near the end of the humpback season, as do some killer whales (orca) and false killer whales. Bottlenose, spinner, and pantropic spotted dolphins are present pretty much year-round. These acrobats love to bow surf just under the water's surface and to leap into the air. Another spectacular leaper is the velvety-black manta ray, which can grow to 9 meters (30 feet) wide. Shy but lovely spotted eagle rays hover close to the ocean floor, where they feed on crustaceans and mollusks. Nutrient-rich Pacific waters provide sustenance for a wide range of other sea creatures as well. Among the most eye-catching are the graceful king angelfish and the iridescent bumphead parrotfish, striped Indo-Pacific sargeants and Moorish idols, and the funny-looking guinea fowl puffer and its close relative, the equally unusual black-blotched porcupine fish.

The varied landscape of Nayarit and Jalisco states provides a tapestry of habitats—shoreline, rivers, marshes, lagoons, and mangroves—for some 350 species of birds. In the mangroves, standouts are the great blue heron, mangrove cuckoo, and vireo. Ocean and shore birds include red-billed tropic birds as well as various species of heron, egret, gulls, and frigatebirds. Military macaws patrol the thorn forests, and songbirds of all stripes live in the pine-oak forests. About 40% of the birds in the Costalegre region are migratory. Among the residents are the yellow-headed parrot and the Mexican wood nymph, both threatened species.

Environmental Issues

The biggest threat to the region is deforestation of the tropical dry forest. Slash-and-burn techniques are used to prepare virgin forest for agriculture and pasturing of animals. Like tropical forest everywhere, this practice has a very harmful and nonproductive effect, as the thin soil fails to produce after the mulch-producing trees and shrubs have been stripped.

Although the tropical dry forest (also called tropical thorn forest) has only been easily accessible to settlement since

a coast highway opened in 1972, they are now being deforested due to the increasing tourism and human population. Controlled ecotourism offers a potential solution, although failed projects in the area have significantly altered or drained salt marshes and mangrove swamps.

Like similar ecosystems along Mexico's Pacific coast from southern Sonora to Chiapas, the dry forest is an extremely important ecosystem. It represents one of the richest in Mexico and also one with the highest level of endemism (plant and animal species found nowhere else). Several species of hardwood trees, including the Pacific coast mahogany and Mexican kingwood, are being over-harvested for use in the building trade. The former is endangered and the latter, threatened.

South of Puerto Vallarta in the Costalegre are two adjacent forest reserves that together form the 32,617-acre **Chamela–Cuixmala Biosphere Reserve.** Co-owned and managed by nonprofit agencies, private companies, and Mexico's National University, UNAM, the reserve protects nine major vegetation types, including the tropical dry forest, tropical deciduous, and semi-deciduous forests. A riparian environment is associated with the north bank of the Cuixmala River. Within the reserve there are approximately 72 species considered at risk for extinction including the American crocodile and several species of sea turtles.

Hojonay Biosphere Reserve was established by the Hojonay nonprofit organization to preserve the jaguar of the Sierra de Vallejo range and its habitat. The 157,060-acre reserve is in the foothills and mountains behind La Cruz de Huanacaxtle and San Francisco, in Nayarit State.

At the present time there are no tours or casual access to either reserve, which serve as a buffer against development and a refuge for wildlife.

BOOKS & MOVIES

Books

Those interested in Mexican culture and society have a wealth of books from which to choose. *The Mexicans: A Personal Portrait of a People,* by Patrick Oster, is a brilliant nonfiction study of Mexican persona and personality. Like Patrick Oster, Alan Riding, author of *Distant Neighbors: A Portrait of the Mexicans,* was a journalist for many years in Mexico City whose insight, investigative journalism skills, and cogent writing skills produced an insightful look into the Mexican mind and culture.

Written by poet, essayist, and statesman Octavio Paz, *The Labyrinth of Solitude,* is classic, required reading for those who love Mexico or want to know it better. *The True Story of the Conquest of Mexico,* by Bernal Diaz de Castillo, is a fascinating account of the conquest by one of Cortés's own soldiers.

There are few recommended books specifically about Puerto Vallarta. These are available mainly in PV.

La Magia de Puerto Vallarta, by Marilú Suárez-Murias, is a bilingual (English and Spanish) coffee-table book discussing beaches, history, people, and places of Puerto Vallarta. The information is interesting, but the photographs are terribly grainy. For a lighthearted look at life in PV through the eyes of an expat, read *Puerto Vallarta on 49 Brain Cells a Day* and *Refried Brains,* both by Gil Gevins. Along these same lines is Gringos in Paradise, by Barry Golson, which evolved out of an assignment for AARP magazine and provides a lighthearted look at building the author's dream house in Sayulita, Nayarit. Those interested in Huichol art and culture might read *People of the Peyote: Huichol Indian History, Religion and Survival,* by Stacy Shaefer and Peter Furst. If you can get past the first couple of chapters, it's smoother sailing. Also by Stacy Shaefer is *To Think With a Good Heart: Wixarica Women, Weavers and Shamans.*

Movies

The Night of the Iguana (1964), directed by John Huston, is the movie that alerted the world to Puerto Vallarta's existence. Set on the beach and bluffs of Mismaloya, the haunting movie with the jungle-beat soundtrack combines great directing with an excellent cast: Richard Burton as a cast-out preacher-turned-tour-guide, Sue Lyons and Deborah Kerr as his clients, and Ava Gardner as the sexy but lonely proprietress of the group's idyllic Mexican getaway. There's no better mood-setter for a trip to Vallarta.

Like Water for Chocolate (Como Agua Para Chocolate) (1992) is a magic-realism glance into rural Mexico during the Mexican Revolution. This visual banquet will make your mouth water for the rose-petal quail and other recipes that the female lead, Tita, prepares. It's based on the novel of the same name by Laura Esquivel, which is equally wonderful. Academy Award winner The *Treasure of the Sierra Madre* (1948), with Humphrey Bogart, is a classic with great mountain scenery. For more fantastic scenery and a great town fiesta, see *The Magnificent Seven,* (1960) starring Yul Brenner and Eli Wallach. Set in Mexico City with Pierce Brosnan as a failing hit man, *The Matador* (2005) has some good scenes of the Camino Real in Mexico City, a great bullfighting sequence, and is a good drama.

SPANISH VOCABULARY

	ENGLISH	SPANISH	PRONUNCIATION
BASICS			
	Yes/no	Sí/no	see/no
	Please	Por favor	pore fah-**vore**
	May I?	¿Me permite?	may pair-**mee**-tay
	Thank you (very much)	(Muchas) gracias	(**moo**-chas **grah**-see-as)
	You're welcome	De nada	day **nah**-dah
	Excuse me	Con permiso	con pair-**mee**-so
	Pardon me	¿Perdón?	pair-**dohn**
	Could you tell me?	¿Podría decirme?	po-dree-ah deh-**seer**-meh
	I'm sorry	Lo siento	lo see-**en**-toh
	Good morning!	¡Buenos días!	**bway**-nohs **dee**-ahs
	Good afternoon!	¡Buenas tardes!	**bway**-nahs **tar**-dess
	Good evening!	¡Buenas noches!	**bway**-nahs **no**-chess
	Goodbye!	¡Adiós!/¡Hasta luego!	ah-dee-**ohss**/**ah** -stah **lwe**-go
	Mr./Mrs.	Señor/Señora	sen-**yor**/sen-**yohr**-ah
	Miss	Señorita	sen-yo-**ree**-tah
	Pleased to meet you	Mucho gusto	**moo**-cho **goose**-toh
	How are you?	¿Cómo está usted?	**ko**-mo es-**tah** oo-**sted**
	Very well, thank you.	Muy bien, gracias.	**moo**-ee bee-**en**, **grah**-see-as
	And you?	¿Y usted?	ee oos-**ted**
	Hello (on the telephone)	Diga	**dee**-gah
NUMBERS			
	1	un, uno	oon, **oo**-no
	2	dos	dos
	3	tres	tress
	4	cuatro	**kwah**-tro
	5	cinco	**sink**-oh

ENGLISH	SPANISH	PRONUNCIATION
6	seis	saice
7	siete	see-**et**-eh
8	ocho	**o**-cho
9	nueve	new-**eh**-vey
10	diez	dee-**es**
11	once	**ohn**-seh
12	doce	**doh**-seh
13	trece	**treh**-seh
14	catorce	ka-**tohr**-seh
15	quince	**keen**-seh
16	dieciséis	dee-**es**-ee-**saice**
17	diecisiete	dee-**es**-ee-see-**et**-eh
18	dieciocho	dee-**es**-ee-**o**-cho
19	diecinueve	**dee**-**es**-ee-new-**ev**-eh
20	veinte	**vain**-teh
21	veinte y uno/veintiuno	**vain**-te-**oo**-noh
30	treinta	**train**-tah
32	treinta y dos	train-tay-**dohs**
40	cuarenta	kwah-**ren**-tah
43	cuarenta y tres	kwah-**ren**-tay-**tress**
50	cincuenta	seen-**kwen**-tah
54	cincuenta y cuatro	seen-**kwen**-tay **kwah**-tro
60	sesenta	sess-**en**-tah
65	sesenta y cinco	sess-**en**-tay **seen**-ko
70	setenta	set-**en**-tah
76	setenta y seis	set-**en**-tay **saice**
80	ochenta	oh-**chen**-tah
87	ochenta y siete	oh-**chen**-tay see-**yet**-eh
90	noventa	no-**ven**-tah
98	noventa y ocho	no-**ven**-tah-**o**-choh
100	cien	see-**en**

ENGLISH	SPANISH	PRONUNCIATION
101	ciento uno	see-**en**-toh **oo**-noh
200	doscientos	doh-see-**en**-tohss
500	quinientos	keen-**yen**-tohss
700	setecientos	set-eh-see-**en**-tohss
900	novecientos	no-veh-see-**en**-tohss
1,000	mil	meel
2,000	dos mil	dohs meel
1,000,000	un millón	oon meel-**yohn**

COLORS

black	negro	**neh**-groh
blue	azul	ah-**sool**
brown	café	kah-**feh**
green	verde	**ver**-deh
pink	rosa	**ro**-sah
purple	morado	mo-**rah**-doh
orange	naranja	na-**rahn**-hah
red	rojo	**roh**-hoh
white	blanco	**blahn**-koh
yellow	amarillo	ah-mah-**ree**-yoh

DAYS OF THE WEEK

Sunday	domingo	doe-**meen**-goh
Monday	lunes	**loo**-ness
Tuesday	martes	**mahr**-tess
Wednesday	miércoles	me-**air**-koh-less
Thursday	jueves	hoo-**ev**-ess
Friday	viernes	vee-**air**-ness
Saturday	sábado	**sah**-bah-doh

MONTHS

January	enero	eh-**neh**-roh
February	febrero	feh-**breh**-roh
March	marzo	**mahr**-soh

ENGLISH	SPANISH	PRONUNCIATION
April	abril	ah-**breel**
May	mayo	**my**-oh
June	junio	**hoo**-nee-oh
July	julio	**hoo**-lee-yoh
August	agosto	ah-**ghost**-toh
September	septiembre	sep-tee-**em**-breh
October	octubre	oak-**too**-breh
November	noviembre	no-vee-**em**-breh
December	diciembre	dee-see-**em**-breh

USEFUL PHRASES

Do you speak English?	¿Habla usted inglés?	**ah**-blah oos-**ted** in-**glehs**
I don't speak Spanish	No hablo español	no **ah**-bloh es-pahn-**yol**
I don't understand (you)	No entiendo	no en-tee-**en**-doh
I understand (you)	Entiendo	en-tee-**en**-doh
I don't know	No sé	no seh
I am American/ British	Soy americano (americana)/ inglés(a)	soy ah-meh-ree-**kah**-no (ah-meh-ree-**kah**-nah)/in-**glehs(ah)**
What's your name?	¿Cómo se llama usted?	koh-mo seh **yah**-mah oos-**ted**
My name is . . .	Me llamo . . .	may **yah**-moh
What time is it?	¿Qué hora es?	keh **o**-rah es
It is one, two, three . . . o'clock.	Es la una./Son las dos, tres . . .	es la **oo**-nah/sohnahs dohs, tress
Yes, please/No, thank you	Sí, por favor/No, gracias	**see** pohr fah-**vor**/no **grah**-see-us
How?	¿Cómo?	**koh**-mo
When?	¿Cuándo?	**kwahn**-doh
This/Next week	Esta semana/ la semana que entra	**es**-teh seh-**mah**- nah/ lah seh-**mah**-nah keh **en**-trah
This/Next month	Este mes/el próximo mes	**es**-teh mehs/el **proke**-see-mo mehs

ENGLISH	SPANISH	PRONUNCIATION
This/Next year	Este año/el año que viene	**es**-teh **ahn**-yo/el **ahn**-yo keh vee-**yen**-ay
Yesterday/today/tomorrow	Ayer/hoy/mañana	ah-**yehr**/oy/mahn-**yah**-nah
This morning/afternoon	Esta mañana/ tarde	**es**-tah mahn-**yah**- nah/**tar**-deh
Tonight	Esta noche	**es**-tah **no**-cheh
What?	¿Qué?	keh
What is it?	¿Qué es esto?	keh es **es**-toh
Why?	¿Por qué?	pore **keh**
Who?	¿Quién?	kee-**yen**
Where is . . . ?	¿Dónde está . . . ?	**dohn**-deh es-**tah**
the train station?	la estación del tren?	la es-tah-see-on del trehn
the subway station?	la estación del tren subterráneo?	la es-ta-see-**on** del trehn la es-ta-see-**on** soob-teh-**rrahn**-eh-oh
the bus stop?	la parada del autobus?	la pah-**rah**-dah del ow-toh-**boos**
the post office?	la oficina de correos?	la oh-fee-**see**- nah deh koh-**rreh**-os
the bank?	el banco?	el **bahn**-koh
the hotel?	el hotel?	el oh-**tel**
the store?	la tienda?	la tee-**en**-dah
the cashier?	la caja?	la **kah**-hah
the museum?	el museo?	el moo-**seh**-oh
the hospital?	el hospital?	el ohss-pee-**tal**
the elevator?	el ascensor?	el ah-**sen**-sohr
the bathroom?	el baño?	el **bahn**-yoh
Here/there	Aquí/allá	ah-**key**/ah-**yah**
Open/closed	Abierto/cerrado	ah-bee-**er**-toh/ ser-**ah**-doh
Left/right	Izquierda/derecha	iss-key-**er**-dah/ dare-**eh**-chah
Straight ahead	Derecho	dare-**eh**-choh

ENGLISH	SPANISH	PRONUNCIATION
Is it near/far?	¿Está cerca/lejos?	es-**tah sehr**-kah/ **leh**-hoss
I'd like . . .	Quisiera . . .	kee-see-ehr-ah
a room	un cuarto/una habitación	oon **kwahr**-toh/ **oo**-nah ah-bee- tah-see-**on**
the key	la llave	lah **yah**-veh
a newspaper	un periódico	oon pehr-ee-**oh**- dee-koh
a stamp	un sello de correo	oon **seh**-yo deh korr-ee-oh
I'd like to buy . . .	Quisiera comprar . . .	kee-see-**ehr**-ah kohm-**prahr**
cigarettes	cigarrillos	ce-ga-**ree**-yohs
matches	cerillos	ser-**ee**-ohs
a dictionary	un diccionario	oon deek-see-oh- **nah**-ree-oh
soap	jabón	hah-**bohn**
sunglasses	gafas de sol	**ga**-fahs deh sohl
suntan lotion	Loción bronceadora	loh-see-**ohn** brohn- seh-ah-**do**-rah
a map	un mapa	oon **mah**-pah
a magazine	una revista	**oon**-ah reh-**veess**-tah
paper	papel	pah-**pel**
envelopes	sobres	**so**-brehs
a postcard	una tarjeta postal	**oon**-ah tar-**het**-ah post-**ahl**
How much is it?	¿Cuánto cuesta?	**kwahn**-toh **kwes**-tah
It's expensive/	Está caro/barato	es-**tah kah**-roh/
cheap		bah-**rah**-toh
A little/a lot	Un poquito/ mucho	oon poh-**kee**-toh/ **moo**-choh
More/less	Más/menos	mahss/**men**-ohss
Enough/too	Suficiente/	soo-fee-see-**en**-teh/
much/too little	demasiado/ muy poco	deh-mah-see-**ah**- doh/ **moo**-ee **poh**-koh

ENGLISH	SPANISH	PRONUNCIATION
Telephone	Teléfono	tel-**ef**-oh-no
Telegram	Telegrama	teh-leh-**grah**-mah
I am ill	Estoy enfermo(a)	es-**toy** en-**fehr**- moh(mah)
Please call a	Por favor llame a	pohr fah-**vor ya**-meh
doctor	un medico	ah oon **med**-ee-koh

ON THE ROAD

Avenue	Avenida	ah-ven-**ee**-dah
Broad, tree-lined boulevard	Bulevar	boo-leh-**var**
Fertile plain	Vega	**veh**-gah
Highway	Carretera	car-reh-**ter**-ah
Mountain pass	Puerto	poo-**ehr**-toh
Street	Calle	**cah**-yeh
Waterfront promenade	Rambla	**rahm**-blah
Wharf	Embarcadero	em-bar-cah-**deh**-ro

IN TOWN

Cathedral	Catedral	cah-teh-**dral**
Church	Templo/Iglesia	**tem**-plo/ee-**glehs**- see-ah
City hall	Casa de gobierno	kah-sah deh go-bee-**ehr**-no
Door, gate	Puerta portón	poo-**ehr**-tah por-**ton**
Entrance/exit	Entrada/salida	en-**trah**-dah/sah-**lee**-dah
Inn, rustic bar, or restaurant	Taverna	tah-**vehr**-nah
Main square	Plaza principal	plah-thah prin- see-**pahl**

DINING OUT

Can you	¿Puede	**pweh**-deh rreh-koh-
recommend a good	recomendarme un	mehn-**dahr**-me oon
restaurant?	buen restaurante?	bwehn rrehs-tow- **rahn**-teh?

ENGLISH	SPANISH	PRONUNCIATION
Where is it located?	¿Dónde está situado?	**dohn**-deh ehs-**tah** see-**twah**-doh?
Do I need reservations?	¿Se necesita una reservación?	seh neh-seh-**see**-tah **oo**-nah rreh-sehr- bah-**syohn**?
I'd like to reserve a	Quisiera reservar	kee-**syeh**-rah rreh-
table . . .	una mesa . . .	sehr-**bahr oo**-nah **meh**-sah . . .
for two people.	para dos personas.	**pah**-rah dohs pehr- **soh**-nahs
for this evening.	para esta noche.	**pah**-rah **ehs**-tah **noh**-cheh
for 8:00 p.m.	para las ocho de la noche.	**pah**-rah lahs **oh**-choh deh lah **noh**-cheh
A bottle of . . .	Una botella de . . .	**oo**-nah bo-**teh**- yah deh
A cup of . . .	Una taza de . . .	**oo**-nah **tah**-thah deh
A glass of . . .	Un vaso de . . .	oon **vah**-so deh
Ashtray	Un cenicero	oon sen-ee-**seh**-roh
Bill/check	La cuenta	lah **kwen**-tah
Bread	El pan	el pahn
Breakfast	El desayuno	el deh-sah-**yoon**-oh
Butter	La mantequilla	lah man-teh-**key**-yah
Cheers!	¡Salud!	sah-**lood**
Cocktail	Un aperitivo	oon ah-pehr-ee-**tee**-voh
Dinner	La cena	lah **seh**-nah
Dish	Un plato	oon **plah**-toh
Menu of the day	Menú del día	meh-**noo** del **dee**-ah
Enjoy!	¡Buen provecho!	bwehn pro-**veh**-cho
Fixed-price menu	Menú fijo o turistico	meh-**noo** **fee**-hoh oh too-**ree**-stee-coh
Fork	El tenedor	el ten-eh-**dor**
Is the tip included?	¿Está incluida la propina?	es-**tah** in-cloo-**ee**-dah lah pro-**pee**-nah

ENGLISH	SPANISH	PRONUNCIATION
Knife	El cuchillo	el koo-**chee**-yo
Large portion of savory snacks	Raciónes	rah-see-**oh**-nehs
Lunch	La comida	lah koh-**mee**-dah
Menu	La carta, el menú	lah **cart**-ah, el meh-**noo**
Napkin	La servilleta	lah sehr-vee-**yet**-ah
Pepper	La pimienta	lah pee-me-**en**-tah
Please give me	Por favor déme	pore fah-**vor deh**-meh
Salt	La sal	lah sahl
Savory snacks	Tapas	**tah**-pahs
Spoon	Una cuchara	**oo**-nah koo-**chah**-rah
Sugar	El azúcar	el ah-**thu**-kar
Waiter!/Waitress!	¡Por favor Señor/Señorita!	pohr fah-**vor** sen- **yor**/sen-yor-**ee**-tah

Travel Smart
Puerto Vallarta

WORD OF MOUTH

Puerto Vallarta is extremely welcoming and friendly. Some parts of town are more local, where only Spanish is spoken. But in tourist shops and restaurants someone will always speak at least some English or even be fluent. One thing you might want to do is pick up a Spanish phrase book. People really warm up when you make an attempt.

—Suze

GETTING HERE & AROUND

▌BY AIR

Flights with stopovers in Mexico City tend to take the entire day. There are nonstop flights from a few U.S. cities, including Los Angeles (Alaska Air), San Francisco (United), Seattle (Alaska Air), Phoenix (US Airways), Houston (Continental), Dallas (American), Denver (Frontier Air, United), and Kansas City, MO (Frontier Air).

Air Canada has nonstop flights from Toronto, and connecting flights (via Toronto) from all major cities. Avolar is a Tijuana-based airline with reasonable fares. It flies to Colima, Colima (near the Costalegre), Tepic in Nayarit, and Guadalajara. You can fly to Manzanillo, just south of the Costalegre, via many airlines with a stop in Mexico City.

If you plan to include Guadalajara in your itinerary, consider an open-jaw flight to Puerto Vallarta with a return from Guadalajara (or vice versa). There's almost no difference in price, even when factoring in bus fare.

Flying times are about 2¾ hours from Houston, 3 hours from Los Angeles, 3½ hours from Denver, 4 hours from Chicago, and 8 hours from New York.

Airline & Airport Links **Airline and Airport Links.com** (⊕www.airlineandairportlinks.com).

Airlines **Aeroméxico** (☎800/237-6639 in U.S. and Canada, 01800/021-4010 in Mexico, 322/221-1204 in PV ⊕www.aeromexico.com). **Air Canada** (☎888/247-2262 in Canada or the U.S., 322/221-1823 in PV ⊕www.aircanada.com). **Alaska Airlines** (☎800/252-7522 or 206/433-3100, 01800/426-0333 in Mexico, 322/221-1350 in PV ⊕www.alaskaair.com). **American Airlines** (☎800/433-7300, 01800/904-6000 in Mexico, 322/221-1799 in PV ⊕www.aa.com). **U.S. Airways** (☎800/622-1015 in U.S., 01800/235-9292 in Mexico, 322/221-1333 in PV ⊕www.

usairways.com). **Avolar** (☎01800/2128-6527 in Mexico or 888/328-6527 in U.S. ⊕www.avolar.com.mx). **Continental Airlines** (☎800/523-3273 for U.S. and Mexico reservations, 800/231-0856 for international reservations, 01800/900-5000 in Mexico, 322/221-1025 in PV ⊕www.continental.com). **Frontier** (☎800/432-1359 in U.S. ⊕www.frontierairlines.com). **Mexicana** (☎800/531-7921 in U.S., 866/281-3049 in Canada, 01800/801-2010 in Mexico, 322/221-1823 in PV ⊕www.mexicana.com).

Airline Security Issues **Transportation Security Administration** (⊕www.tsa.gov)

AIRPORTS

The main gateway, and where many PV-bound travelers change planes, is Mexico City's large, modern Aeropuerto Internacional Benito Juárez (airport code: MEX), infamous for pickpocketing and taxi scams; watch your stuff.

Puerto Vallarta's small international Aeropuerto Internacional Gustavo Díaz Ordáz is (PVR) 7½ km (4½ mi) north of downtown.

Airport Information **Aeropuerto Internacional Benito Juárez** (MEX ⊕www.aicm.com.mx). **Aeropuerto Internacional Gustavo Díaz Ordáz** (PVR ⊕ vallarta.aeropuertosgap.com.mx).

GROUND TRANSPORTATION

Vans provide transportation from the airport to PV hotels; there's a zone system with different prices for the Zona Hotelera Sur, downtown PV, and so on. Outside the luggage collection area, vendors shout for your attention. It's a confusing scene. Purchase the taxi vouchers sold at these stands inside the terminal, but make sure to avoid the timeshare vendors which trap you in their vans for a high-pressure sales pitch en route to your hotel. Also, don't leave your luggage unattended while making transportation arrangements.

Before you purchase your ticket, look for a taxi-zone map (it should be posted on or by the ticket stand), and make sure your taxi ticket is properly zoned; if you need a ticket only to Zone 3, don't pay for a ticket to Zone 4 or 5. Taxis or vans to the Costalegre resorts between PV and Manzanillo are generally arranged through the resort. If not, taxis charge about $19 (200 pesos) an hour—more if you're traveling beyond Jalisco State lines.

▐ BY BUS

LONG-DISTANCE SERVICE

PV's Central Camionero, or Central Bus Station, is 1 km (½ mi) north of the airport, halfway between Nuevo Vallarta and downtown.

First-class Mexican buses (known as *primera clase*) are generally timely and comfortable, air-conditioned coaches with bathrooms, movies, and reclining seats—sometimes with seat belts. Deluxe (*de lujo* or *ejecutivo*) buses offer the same and usually have refreshments. Second-class (*segunda clase*) buses are used mainly for travel to smaller, secondary routes.

A lower-class bus ride can be interesting if you're not in a hurry and want to experience local culture; these buses make frequent stops and keep less strictly to their timetables. Often they will wait until they fill up to leave, regardless of the scheduled time of departure. Fares are up to 15%–30% cheaper than first-class buses. The days of pigs and chickens among your busmates are largely in the past. ▐ TIP→ **Unless you're writing a novel or your memoir, there's no reason to ride a second-class bus if a first-class or better is available.** Daytime trips are safer.

Bring snacks, socks, and a sweater—the air-conditioning on first-class buses is often set on high—and toilet paper, as restrooms might not have any. Smoking is prohibited on all buses.

Estrella Blanca goes from Mexico City to Manzanillo, Mazatlán, Monterrey, Nuevo Laredo, and other central, Pacific coast, and northern-border points. ETN has the most luxurious service—with exclusively first-class buses that have roomy, totally reclining seats—to Guadalajara, Mexico City, Barra de Navidad, Chamela, and Manzanillo. Primera Plus connects Mexico City with Manzanillo and Puerto Vallarta along with other central and western cities.

TAP serves Mexico City, Guadalajara, Puerto Vallarta, Tepic, and Mazatlán. Basic service, including some buses with marginal or no air-conditioning, is the norm on Transportes Cihuatlán, which connects the Bahía de Banderas and PV with southern Jalisco towns such as Barra de Navidad.

Tickets for first-class or better—unlike tickets for the other classes—can be reserved in advance; this is advisable during peak periods, although the most popular routes have buses on the hour. You can make reservations for many, though not all, of the first-class bus lines, through the Ticketbus central reservations agency. Rates average 45–67 pesos per hour of travel, depending on the level of luxury. Plan to pay in pesos, although most of the deluxe bus services accept Visa and MasterCard.

Bus Contacts Central Camionero (✉ Puerto Vallarta–Tepic Hwy., Km 9, Las Mojoneras ☎ 322/290–1008). **Estrella Blanca** (☎ 01800/507–5500 toll-free in Mexico, 322/290–1001 in Puerto Vallarta ⊕ www.estrellablanca.com.mx). **ETN** (☎ 01800/800–0386 toll-free in Mexico, 322/290–0996, 322/290–0997 in PV ⊕ www.etn.com.mx). **Primera Plus** (☎ 322/290–0715 in PV). **Transportes Cihuatlán** (☎ 322/290–0994 in PV). **Transporte del Pacifico (TAP)** (☎ 322/290–0119, 322/290–0993 in PV).

CITY BUSES

City buses (4.5 pesos) serve downtown, the Zona Hotelera Norte, and Marina Vallarta. Bus stops—marked by blue-and-white signs—are every two or three long blocks along the highway (Carretera Aeropuerto) and in downtown Puerto Vallarta. Green buses to Playa Mismaloya and Boca de Tomatlán (5.5 pesos) run about every 15 minutes from the corner of Avenida Insurgentes and Basilio Badillo downtown.

Gray ATM buses serving Nuevo Vallarta and Bucerías (20 pesos), Punta de Mita (30 pesos), and Sayulita (50 pesos) depart from just two places: Plaza las Glorias, in front of the HSBC bank, and Wal-Mart, both of which are along Carretera Aeropuerto between downtown and the Zona Hotelera.

■TIP→ It's rare for inspectors to check tickets, but just when you've let yours flutter to the floor, a figure of authority is bound to appear. So hang on to your ticket and hat: PV bus drivers race from one stoplight to the next in jerky bursts of speed.

There's no problem with theft on city buses aside from perhaps an occasional pickpocket that might be at work anywhere in the world.

■ BY CAR

Driving in PV can be unpleasant, but the main problem is parking. From December through April—peak season—traffic clogs the narrow downtown streets, and negotiating the steep hills in Old Vallarta (sometimes you have to drive in reverse to let another car pass) can be frightening. Avoid rush hour (7–9 AM and 6–8 PM) and when schools let out (2–3 PM). Travel with a companion and a good road map or atlas. Always lock your car, and never leave valuable items in the body of the car. The trunk is generally safe, although any thief can crack one open if he chooses.

■TIP→ It's absolutely essential that you carry Mexican auto insurance for liability, even if you have full coverage for collision, damages, and theft. If you injure anyone in an accident, you could well be jailed—whether it was your fault or not—unless you have insurance.

GASOLINE

Pemex (the government petroleum monopoly) franchises all of Mexico's gas stations, which you'll find at most junctions and in cities and towns. Gas is measured in liters, and stations usually don't accept U.S. or Canadian credit cards or dollars, but this is beginning to change. Fuel prices tend to be about the same as in the United States.

Premium unleaded gas (called *premium,* the red pump) and regular unleaded gas (*magna,* the green pump) are available nationwide, but it's still best to fill up whenever you can and not let your tank get below half full. Fuel quality is generally lower than that in the United States, but it has improved enough so that your car will run acceptably.

Attendants pump the gas for you and may also wash your windshield and check your oil and tire air pressure. A small tip is customary (from just a few pesos to 5 or 10). Keep a close eye on the gas meter to make sure the attendant is starting it at "0" and that you're charged the correct price.

PARKING

A circle with a diagonal line superimposed on the letter *E* (for *estacionamiento*) means "no parking." Illegally parked cars are usually either towed or have wheel blocks placed on the tires, which can require a trip to the traffic-police headquarters for payment of a fine.

When in doubt, park in a lot rather than on the street; your car will probably be safer there anyway. There are parking lots in PV at Parque Hidalgo (Av. México at Langarica, Col. 5 de Diciembre), in El

Centro (at Av. Juárez at Calle 31 de Octubre and another at Leona Vicario), just north of the Cuale River at el malecón and Calle A. Rodríguez, and in the Zona Romántica at Parque Lázaro Cárdenas. Fees are reasonable—as little as $4 for a day up to $1 or more an hour, depending on where you are. Sometimes you park your own car; more often, you hand the keys to an attendant.

ROAD CONDITIONS

Several well-kept toll roads head into and out of major cities like Guadalajara—most of them four lanes wide. However, these *carreteras* (major highways) don't go too far into the countryside. *Cuota* means toll road; *libre* means no toll, and such roads are often two lanes and not as well-maintained.

Roads leading to, or in, Nayarit and Jalisco include highways connecting Nogales and Mazatlán; Guadalajara and Tepic; and Mexico City, Morelia, and Guadalajara. However, tolls as high as $40 one-way can make using these thoroughfares expensive.

In rural areas roads are sometimes poor; other times the two-lane, blacktop roads are perfectly fine. Be extra cautious during the rainy season, when rock slides and potholes are a problem.

Watch out for animals, especially untethered horses, cattle, and dogs, and for dangerous, unrailed curves. *Topes* (speed bumps) are ubiquitous; slow down when approaching any town or village and look for signs saying TOPES or VIBRADORES. Police officers often issue tickets to those speeding through populated areas.

Generally, driving times are longer than for comparable distances in the United States. Allow extra time for unforeseen occurrences as well as for traffic, particularly truck traffic.

ROADSIDE EMERGENCIES

To help motorists on major highways, the Mexican Tourism Ministry operates a fleet of more than 250 pickup trucks, known as the Angeles Verdes, or Green Angels, easily reachable by phone throughout Mexico by simply dialing 078. (If this number doesn't work—occasionally the case—call the Mexico Tourism Hotline at 01800/903–9200 toll-free.) The bilingual drivers provide mechanical help, first aid, radio-telephone communication, basic supplies and small parts, towing, tourist information, and protection.

Services are free, and spare parts, fuel, and lubricants are provided at cost. Tips are always appreciated (figure a minimum of $5–$10 for big jobs and $3–$5 for minor repairs). The Green Angels patrol the major highways twice daily 8–8 (usually later on holiday weekends). If you break down, pull off the road as far as possible, lift the hood of your car, hail a passing vehicle, and ask the driver to notify the patrol. Most drivers will be quite helpful.

Emergency Services **Angeles Verdes**
(☎078, 01800/903–9200 toll-free in Mexico).

RULES OF THE ROAD

When you sign up for Mexican car insurance, you may receive a booklet on Mexican rules of the road. It really is a good idea to read it to familiarize yourself with not only laws but also customs that differ from those of your home country. For instance: if an oncoming vehicle flicks its lights at you in daytime, slow down: it could mean trouble ahead; when approaching a narrow bridge, the first vehicle to flash its lights has right of way; right on red is not allowed; one-way traffic is indicated by an arrow; two-way, by a double-pointed arrow. (Other road signs follow the widespread system of international symbols.)

⚠ On the highway, using your left turn signal to turn left is dangerous. Mexican drivers—especially truck drivers—use their left turn signal on the highway to signal the vehicle behind that it's safe to pass. Conversely they rarely use their signal to actually make a turn. Foreigners signaling a left turn off the highway into a driveway or onto a side road have been killed by cars or trucks behind that mistook their turn signal for a signal to pass. To turn left from a highway when cars are behind you, it's best to pull over to the right and make the left turn when no cars are approaching, to avoid disaster.

Mileage and speed limits are given in kilometers: 100 kph and 80 kph (62 mph and 50 mph, respectively) are the most common maximums on the highway. A few of the toll roads allow 110 kph (68 mph). However, speed limits can change from curve to curve, so watch the signs carefully. In cities and small towns, observe the posted speed limits, which can be as low as 20 kph (12 mph).

Seat belts are required by law throughout Mexico. Drunk driving laws are fairly harsh in Mexico, and if you're caught you may go to jail immediately. It's difficult to say what the blood-alcohol limit is since everyone we asked gave a different answer, which means each case is probably handled in a discretionary manner. The best way to avoid any problems is simply to not drink and drive.

If you're stopped for speeding, the officer is supposed to take your license and hold it until you pay the fine at the local police station. But the officer will usually prefer a *mordida* (small bribe). Just take out a couple hundred pesos, hold it out discreetly while asking politely if the officer can "pay the fine for you." Conversely, a few cops might resent the offer of a bribe, but it's still common practice.

If you decide to dispute a charge that seems preposterous, do so with a smile, and tell the officer that you would like to talk to the police captain when you get to the station. The officer usually will let you go rather than go to the station.

SAFETY ON THE ROAD

Never drive at night in remote and rural areas. *Bandidos* are one concern, but so are potholes, free-roaming animals, cars with no working lights, road-hogging trucks, and difficulty in getting assistance. It's best to use toll roads whenever possible; although costly, they're safer, too.

Driving in Mexico can be nerve-wracking for novices, with people sometimes paying little attention to marked lanes. Most drivers pay attention to safety rules, but be vigilant. Drunk driving skyrockets on holiday weekends.

A police officer may pull you over for something you didn't do; unfortunately a common scam. If you're pulled over for any reason, be polite—displays of anger will only make matters worse. Although efforts are being made to fight corruption, it's still a fact of life in Mexico, and for many people, it's worth the $10 to $100 it costs to get their license back to be on their way quickly. (The amount requested varies depending on what the officer assumes you can pay—the year, make, and model of the car you drive being one determining factor.) Others persevere long enough to be let off with a warning only. The key to success, in this case, is a combination of calm and patience.

RENTAL CARS

Mexico manufactures Chrysler, Ford, General Motors, Honda, Nissan, and Volkswagen vehicles. With the exception of Volkswagen, you can get the same kind of midsize and luxury cars in Mexico that you can rent in the United States and Canada. Economy usually refers to a Volkswagen Beetle or a Chevy Aveo or Joy, which may or may not come with air-conditioning or automatic transmission.

It can really pay to shop around: in Puerto Vallarta, rates for a compact car with air-conditioning, manual transmission, and unlimited mileage range from $18 a day and $120 a week to $50 or even $60 a day and $300–$400 a week. Full-coverage insurance varies greatly depending on whether it includes a deductible, but averages $25 a day. As a rule, stick with the major companies because they tend to be more reliable.

You can also hire a car with a driver (who generally doubles as a tour guide) through your hotel. The going rate is about $22–$25 an hour within town. Limousine service runs about $65 an hour and up, with a three- to five-hour minimum.

In Mexico the minimum driving age is 18, but most rental-car agencies have a surcharge for drivers under 25. Your own country's driver's license is perfectly acceptable.

Surcharges for additional drivers are around $5 per day plus tax. Children's car seats run about the same, but not all companies have them.

CAR-RENTAL INSURANCE

You must carry Mexican auto insurance, at the very least liability as well coverage against physical damage to the vehicle and theft at your discretion, depending on what, if anything, your own auto insurance (or credit card, if you use it to rent a car) includes. For rental cars, all insurance will all be dealt with through the rental company.

Major Rental Agencies **Alamo** (☎800/522–9696 ⊕www.alamo.com). **Avis** (☎800/331–1084 ⊕www.avis.com). **Budget** (☎800/472–3325 ⊕www.budget.com). **Hertz** (☎800/654–3001 ⊕www.hertz.com). **National Car Rental** (☎800/227–7368 ⊕www.nationalcar.com).

▌ BY CRUISE SHIP

Companies with cruises to the Pacific Coast include Carnival, Cunard, Celerity Cruises, Holland America, Princess, Norwegian, and Royal Caribbean. Most depart from Los Angeles, Long Beach, or San Diego and head to Los Cabos or Mazatlán, Puerto Vallarta, Manzanillo, Ixtapa/Zihuatanejo, and/or Acapulco;

some trips originate in Vancouver or San Francisco.

Cruise Lines **Carnival Cruise Line** (☎305/599–2600 or 800/227–6482 ⊕www.carnival.com). **Celebrity Cruises** (☎800/647–2251 ⊕www.celebrity.com). **Cunard Line** (☎661/753–1000 or 800/728–6273 ⊕www.cunard.com). **Holland America Line** (☎206/281–3535 or 877/932–4259 ⊕www.hollandamerica.com). **Norwegian Cruise Line** (☎305/436–4000 or 800/327–7030 ⊕www.ncl.com). **Princess Cruises** (☎661/753–0000 or 800/774–6237 ⊕www.princess.com). **Royal Caribbean International** (☎305/539–6000 or 800/327–6700 ⊕www.royalcaribbean.com).

▌ BY TAXI

PV taxis aren't metered, and instead charge by zones. Most of the larger hotels have rate sheets, and taxi drivers should produce them upon request. Tipping isn't necessary unless the driver helps you with your bags, in which case a few pesos are appropriate.

The minimum fare is 30 pesos (about $3), but if you don't ask, you'll probably be overcharged. Negotiate a price in advance for out-of-town and hourly services as well; many drivers will start by asking how much you want to pay or how much others have charged you to get a sense of your street-smarts. The usual hourly rate at press time is $19 (200 pesos) per hour. In all cases, if you are unsure of what a fare should be, ask your hotel's front-desk personnel.

The ride from downtown to the airport or to Marina Vallarta costs $10, it's $19 to Nuevo Vallarta, and $24 to Bucerías. From downtown south to Mismaloya it's about $4 to the hotels of the Zona Hotelera Sur, $8 to Mismaloya, and $13 to Boca de Tomatlán. You can easily hail a cab on the street. Radio Taxi PV provides 24-hour service.

Taxi Company **Radio Taxi PV** (☎322/225–0716).

ESSENTIALS

▌COMMUNICATIONS

INTERNET

Internet cafés have sprung up all over Puerto Vallarta and even small surrounding towns and villages, making e-mail by far the easiest way to get in touch with people back home. At PV Café you can enjoy a sandwich or a salad and coffee while downloading digital photos, sending a fax, or surfing the Web (35 pesos per hour).

At less-comfortable PV Net (computers lower than eye level promote slouching), which is open 24 hours a day, 365 days a year, you obtain an access code and use your minutes each time you visit; the cost for Internet access is 20 pesos per hour, offers monthly and weekly rates, and has a room at the back just for the kids and teens. For laptop connections you can pay by the day, week, or month.

If you're bringing a laptop with you, check with the manufacturer's technical support line to see what service and/or repair affiliates they have in the areas you plan to visit. Carry a spare battery to save yourself the expense and headache of having to hunt down a replacement on the spot. Memory sticks and other accessories are usually more expensive in Mexico than in the U.S. or Europe, but are available in megastores such as Sam's Club and Office Depot.

The younger generation of Mexicans are computer savvy and there are some excellent repair wizards and technicians to help you with problems; many are bilingual.

Contacts Cybercafes (⊕www.cybercafes. com) lists over 4,000 Internet cafés worldwide. **PV Café** (✉Calle Olas Altas 250, Olas Altas ☎322/222–0092). **PV Net** (✉Blvd. Francisco M. Ascencio 1692, across from Sheraton Buganvilias, Zona Hotelera Norte ☎322/223–1127).

PHONES

The area code for PV (and the northern Costalegre) and Nuevo Vallarta is 322; San Francisco has both 311 and 329 area codes, otherwise between Bucerías and San Francisco it's 329. Lo De Marcos and Rincón de Guayabitos: 327. The Costalegre from around Rancho Cuixmala to San Patricio–Melaque and Barra de Navidad has a 315 area code.

The country code for Mexico is 52. When calling a Mexico number from abroad, dial any necessary international access code, then the country code, and then all of the numbers listed for the entry. When calling a cell phone in Mexico dial 01152 (access and country codes) and then 1 and then the number.

Toll-free numbers in Mexico start with an 800 prefix. These numbers, however, are billed as local calls if you call one from a private phone. To reach them, you need to dial 01 before the number. In this guide, Mexico-only toll-free numbers appear as follows: 01800/123–4567. The toll-free numbers listed simply 800/123–4567 are U.S. or Canadian numbers, and generally work north of the border only (though some calling cards will allow you to dial them from Mexico, charging you minutes as for a toll call). Numbers listed as 001800/123–4567 are toll-free U.S. numbers; if you're calling from Mexico, you'll be charged for an international call.

INTERNATIONAL CALLS

To make an international call, dial 00 before the country code, area code, and number. The country code for the United States and Canada is 1. Avoid phones near tourist areas that advertise in English (e.g., "Call the U.S. or Canada here!"). They charge an outrageous fee per minute. If in doubt, dial the operator and ask for rates. AT&T, MCI, and Sprint calling cards are useful, although

LOCAL DO'S & TABOOS

CUSTOMS OF THE COUNTRY

In the United States and elsewhere in the world, being direct, efficient, and succinct is highly valued. But Mexican communication tends to be more subtle, and the direct style of Americans, Canadians, and Europeans is often perceived as curt and aggressive. Mexicans are extremely polite, so losing your temper over delays or complaining loudly will get you branded as rude and make people less inclined to help you. Remember that things move slowly here, and that there's little stigma attached to being late; be gracious about this and other local customs and attitudes.

You'll probably notice that local friends, relatives, and significant others show a fair amount of physical affection with each other, but you should be more retiring with people you don't know well.

GREETINGS

Learning basic phrases in Spanish such as "*por favor*" (please) and "*gracias*" (thank you) will make a big difference in how people respond to you. Also, being deferential to those who are older than you will earn you lots of points, as does addressing people as señor, señora, or señorita.

Also, saying "*Desculpe*" before asking a question of someone is a polite way of saying "Excuse me" before launching into a request for information or directions. Similarly, asking "*¿Habla inglés?*" is more polite than assuming every Mexican you meet speaks English.

SIGHTSEEING

In Puerto Vallarta, it is acceptable to wear shorts in houses of worship, but do avoid being blatantly immodest. Bathing suits and immodest clothing are also inappropriate for shopping and sightseeing in general. Except at beach and fishing communities, Mexican men do not generally wear shorts, even in extremely hot weather. This rule is generally ignored by both Mexican and foreign men on vacation here and at other beach resorts.

OUT ON THE TOWN

Mexicans call waiters "*joven*" (literally, "young man") no matter how old they are (it's the equivalent of the word "maid" being used for the old woman who cleans rooms). Call a female waitress *señorita* ("miss") or *señora* ("ma'am"). Ask for "*la cuenta, por favor*" ("the check, please") when you want the bill; it's considered rude to bring it before the customer asks for it. Mexicans tend to dress nicely for a night out, but in tourist areas, dress codes are mainly upheld only at the more sophisticated discoteques. Some restaurants have separate smoking sections, but in smaller establishments people may smoke with abandon anywhere.

DOING BUSINESS

Personal relationships always come first here, so developing rapport and trust is essential. A handshake and personal greeting is appropriate along with a friendly inquiry about family, especially if you have met the family. In established business relationships, don't be surprised if you're greeted with a kiss on the cheek or a hug. Always be respectful toward colleagues in public and keep confrontations private.

Meetings may or may not start on time, but you should be patient. When invited to dinner at the home of a client or associate, it's not necessary to bring a gift; however, sending a thank-you note afterward scores points.

Your offers to pick up the tab at business lunches or dinners will be greatly appreciated but will probably be declined; as a guest in their country, most Mexicans will want to treat you to the meal. Be prepared to exchange business cards, and feel free to offer yours first. Professional attire tends to be on the conservative side. Mexicans are extremely well-groomed, so you'll do well if you follow suit.

infrequently hotels block access to their service numbers.

CALLS WITHIN MEXICO

Directory assistance is 040 nationwide. For assistance in English, dial 090 first for an international operator; tell the operator in what city, state, and country you require directory assistance, and he or she will connect you.

A *caseta de larga distancia* is a long-distance/overseas telephone service usually operated out of a store such as a *papelería* (stationery store), pharmacy, restaurant, or other small business; look for the phone symbol on the door. Casetas may cost more to use than pay phones, but you tend to be shielded from street noise, as you get your own little cabin. They also have the benefit of not forcing you to buy a prepaid phone card with a specific denomination—you pay in cash according to the calls you make. Tell the person on duty the number you'd like to call, and she or he will give you a rate and dial for you. Rates seem to vary widely, so shop around. Overall, they're higher than those of pay phones.

PHONE CARDS

Using a prepaid phone card is by far the most convenient way to call long distance within Mexico or abroad. Look for a phone *booth* away from traffic noise; these phones are tucked behind three sides of plexiglass, but street noise can make hearing difficult. If you're calling long distance within Mexico, dial 01 before the area code and number. For local calls, just dial the seven-digit number; no other prefix is necessary. If calling abroad, buy the 100-peso card, the largest denomination available.

PAY PHONES

Most pay phones only accept prepaid cards, called Ladatel cards, sold in 30-, 50-, or 100-peso denominations at newsstands, pharmacies, or grocery stores. These Ladatel phones are all over the place—on street corners, in bus stations, and so on.

Older, coin-only pay phones are rarely encountered, those you do find are often broken or have poor connections. Still other phones have two unmarked slots, one for a Ladatel (a Spanish acronym for "long-distance direct dialing") card and the other for a credit card. These are primarily for Mexican bank cards, but some accept Visa or MasterCard, though *not* U.S. phone credit cards.

To use a Ladatel card, simply insert it in the appropriate slot with the computer chip insignia forward and right-side up, and dial. Credit is deleted from the card as you use it, and your balance is displayed on a small screen on the phone. You'll be charged about 1 peso per minute for local calls, 4 pesos per minute for national long-distance, and 5 pesos for calls to the United States or Canada. Most pay phones display a price list and dialing instructions.

MOBILE PHONES

If you have a multiband phone (some countries use different frequencies from those used in the United States) and your service provider uses the world-standard GSM network (as do T-Mobile, Cingular, and Verizon), you can probably use your phone abroad. Roaming fees can be steep, however: 99¢ a minute is considered reasonable. And you normally pay the toll charges for incoming and outgoing calls. It's almost always cheaper to send a text message (or at least to receive one, which is sometimes substantially cheaper than to send).

If you just want to make local calls, consider buying a new SIM card (note that your provider may have to unlock your phone for you to use a different SIM card) and a prepaid service plan in the destination. You'll then have a local number and can make local calls at local rates. If your trip is extensive, you could also simply buy a new cell phone in your destination, as the initial cost will be offset over time.

■TIP➔ **If you travel internationally frequently, save one of your old mobile phones or buy a cheap one on the Internet; ask your cell phone company to unlock it for you, and take it with you as a travel phone, buying a new SIM card with pay-as-you-go service in each destination.**

There are now many companies that rent cell phones (with or without SIM cards) for the duration of your trip. You get the phone, charger, and carrying case in the mail and return them in the mailer. EZ Wireless charges $22 per week for equipment (phone, charger, adapter) and $1.99/minute for incoming calls, a whopping $2.50 per minute for outgoing. Daystar rents cell phones at $6 per day, with incoming calls at 22¢ a minute and outgoing at $1.20.

Contacts Daystar (☎888/908–4100 ⊕www.daystarwireless.com) **EZ Wireless** (☎866/939–9473 ⊕www.rentacellularphone. com).

▌CUSTOMS & DUTIES

Upon entering Mexico, you'll be given a baggage declaration form and asked to itemize what you're bringing into the country. You are allowed to bring in 3 liters of spirits or wine for personal use; 400 cigarettes, 25 cigars, or 200 grams of tobacco; a reasonable amount of perfume for personal use; one video camera and one regular camera and 12 rolls of film for each; and gift items not to exceed a total of $300. If driving across the U.S. border, gift items must not exceed $50.

You aren't allowed to bring firearms, ammunition, meat, vegetables, plants, fruit, or flowers into the country. You can bring in one of each of the following items without paying taxes: a cell phone, a beeper, a radio or tape recorder, a musical instrument, a laptop computer, and portable copier or printer. Compact discs

and/or audio cassettes are limited to 20 total and DVDs to five.

Mexico also allows you to bring one cat or dog, if you have two things: (1) a pet health certificate signed by a registered veterinarian in the United States and issued not more than 72 hours before the animal enters Mexico; and (2) a pet vaccination certificate showing that the animal has been treated (as applicable) for rabies, hepatitis, distemper, and leptospirosis.

For more information or information on bringing other animals or more than one type of animal, contact the Mexican consulate, which has branches in many major American cities as well as border towns. To find the consulate nearest you, check the Ministry of Foreign Affairs Web site ⇨go to the "Servicios Consulares" option).

Information in Mexico Mexican Embassy (☎202/728–1600 ⊕www.embassyofmexico. org).**Ministry of Foreign Affairs** (⊕ portal.sre. gob.mx/eua).

U.S. Information U.S. Customs and Border Protection (⊕www.cbp.gov).

▌ELECTRICITY

For U.S. and Canadian travelers, electrical converters aren't necessary because Mexico operates on the 60-cycle, 120-volt system; however, many Mexican outlets have not been updated to accommodate three-prong and polarized plugs (those with one larger prong), so to be safe bring an adapter.

Blackouts and brownouts—often lasting an hour or so—are not unheard of, particularly during the rainy season, so bring a surge protector.

Consider making a small investment in a universal adapter, which has several types of plugs in one lightweight, compact unit.

▮ EMERGENCIES

If you get into a scrape with the law, you can call your nearest consulate; U.S. citizens can also call the Overseas Citizens Services Center in the United States. The Mexican Ministry of Tourism has Infotur, a 24-hour toll-free hotline.

Consulate & Embassy **United States Consul** (⊠ Local 4, Int. 17, 2nd fl., Centro Comercial Paradise Plaza, Nuevo Vallarta, Puerto Vallarta ☎ 322/222–0069). **U.S. Embassy** (⊠ Paseo de la Reforma 305, Col. Cuauhtémoc, Mexico City ☎ 55/5080–2000 ⊕ mexico.usembassy.gov).

General Emergency Contacts **General Emergency (Police, Transit, Fire)** (☎ 060 or 066). **Infotur** (☎ 01800/903–9200 toll-free in Mexico). **U.S. Overseas Citizens Services Center** (☎ 888/407–4747 or 202/501–4444 ⊕ www.travel.state.gov).

▮ HEALTH

According to the CDC, there's a limited risk of malaria, dengue fever, and other insect-carried or parasite-caused illnesses in certain areas of Mexico (largely but not exclusively rural and tropical coastal areas). In most urban or easily accessible areas you need not worry. If, however, you're traveling to remote areas or simply prefer to err on the side of caution, check with the CDC's International Travelers' Hotline. Malaria and dengue are both carried by mosquitoes; in areas where these illnesses are prevalent, use insect-repellant coiling, clothing, and sprays/lotion. Also consider taking antimalarial pills if you're doing serious adventure activities in tropical and subtropical areas.

Make sure polio and diphtheria–tetanus shots are up to date well before your trip. Hepatitis A and typhoid are transmitted through unclean food or water. Gamma-globulin shots prevent hepatitis; an inoculation is available for typhoid, although it's not 100% effective.

A little *turista*, or traveler's diarrhea, is to be expected when you plop down in a foreign culture, but to minimize risks, avoid questionable-looking street stands; and if you're not sure of a restaurant's standards, pass up *ceviche*, raw fish cured in lemon juice, and don't eat any raw vegetables that haven't been, or can't be, peeled (e.g., lettuce and raw chili peppers).

Drink only bottled water or water that has been boiled for at least 10 minutes, even when you're brushing your teeth. *Agua mineral* or *agua con gas* means mineral or carbonated water, and *agua purificada* means purified water. Hotels with water-purification systems will post signs to that effect in the rooms; even then, be wary.

Despite these warnings, keep in mind that Puerto Vallarta, Nuevo Vallarta, and the Costalegre have virtually no industry beyond tourism and are unlikely to kill the geese that lay their golden egg. Some people choose to bend the rules about eating at street stands and fresh fruits and chopped lettuce or cabbage, as there's no guarantee that you won't get sick at a five-star resort and have a delicious, healthful meal at a shack by the sea. If fish or seafood smells or tastes bad, send it back and ask for something different.

Don't fret about ice: tourist-oriented hotels and restaurants, and even most of those geared toward the locals, used purified water for ice, drinks, and washing vegetables. Many alleged cases of food poisoning are due instead to hangovers or excessive drinking in the strong sun. But whenever you're in doubt, ask questions about the origins of food and water and if you feel unsure, err on the side of safety.

Mild cases of turista may respond to Imodium (known generically as loperamide), Lomotil, or Pepto-Bismol (not as strong), all of which you can buy over the counter; keep in mind, though, that these drugs can complicate more serious illnesses. You'll need to replace fluids, so drink plenty of purified water or tea; chamomile tea (*te de manzanilla*) is a good folk remedy, and it's readily available in restaurants throughout Mexico.

In severe cases, rehydrate yourself with Gatorade or a salt-sugar solution (½ teaspoon salt and 4 tablespoons sugar per quart of water). If your fever and diarrhea last longer than a day or two, see a doctor—you may have picked up a parasite or disease that requires prescription medication.

Mosquitoes are most prevalent during the rainy season, when it's best to be cautious and use mosquito repellent daily, even in the city; if you're in jungly or wet places and lack strong repellent, consider covering up well or going indoors at dusk (called the "mosquito hour" by locals).

An excellent brand of *repelente de insectos* (insect repellent) called Autan is readily available; do not use it on children under age two. Repellents that are not at least 10% DEET or picaridin are not effective here. If you're hiking in the jungle or boggy areas, wear repellent and long pants and sleeves; if you're camping in the jungle, use a mosquito net and invest in a package of *espirales contra mosquitos,* mosquito coils, which are sold in *ferreterías* or *tlalpalerías* (hardware stores).

OTHER ISSUES

Caution is advised when venturing out in the Mexican sun. Sunbathers lulled by a slightly overcast sky or the sea breezes can be burned badly in just 20 minutes. To avoid overexposure, use strong sunscreens, sit under a shade umbrella, and avoid the peak sun hours of noon to 2 PM. Sunscreen, including many American brands, can be found in pharmacies, supermarkets, and resort gift shops.

Health Information **National Centers for Disease Control & Prevention** (CDC ☎877/394-8747 international travelers' health line ⊕www.cdc.gov/travel). **World Health Organization** (WHO ⊕www.who.int).

MEDICAL CARE

Cornerstone Hospital accepts various types of foreign health insurance and traveler's insurance and is American owned. The other recommended, privately owned hospital is Hospital San Javier Marina. Although most small towns have at least a clinic, most travelers would be more comfortable traveling to the major hospitals than using these clinics.

Farmacias (pharmacies) are the most convenient place for such common medicines as *aspirina* (aspirin) or *jarabe para la tos* (cough syrup). You'll be able to find many U.S. brands (e.g., Tylenol, Pepto-Bismol, etc.), but don't plan on buying your favorite prescription or nonprescription sleep aid, for example. The same brands and even drugs aren't always available. The Sanborns chain stores also have pharmacies as do the Cornerstone and San Javier Marina hospitals.

Pharmacies are usually open daily 9 AM to 10 PM; on Sunday and in some small towns they may close several hours earlier. In neighborhoods or smaller towns where there are no 24-hour drug stores, local pharmacies take turns staying open 24 hours so that there's usually at least one open on any given night—it's called the *farmacia de turno.* Information about late-night pharmacies is published in the daily newspaper, but the staff at your hotel should be able to help you find an all-night place.

Hospitals & Clinics **Cornerstone Hospital** (⊠Av. Los Tules 136, next to Plaza Caracol, Zona Hotelera ☎322/226-3700 ⊕www.hospitalcornerstone.com). **Hospital San Javier Marina** (⊠Blvd. Francisco M. Ascencio 2760, at María Montessori, Zona Hotelera Norte ☎322/226-1010).

Pharmacy **Farmacia CMQ** (⊠Calle Basilio Badillo 365 ☎322/222-2941 ⊕www.cmq.com.mx).

MEDICAL INSURANCE & ASSISTANCE

Consider buying trip insurance with medical-only coverage. Neither Medicare nor some private insurers cover medical expenses anywhere outside of the United States. Medical-only policies typically reimburse you for medical care (excluding that related to pre-existing conditions) and hospitalization abroad, and provide for evacuation. You still have to pay the bills and await reimbursement from the insurer, though.

Another option is to sign up with a medical-evacuation assistance company. Membership gets you doctor referrals, emergency evacuation or repatriation, 24-hour hotlines for medical consultation, and other assistance. International SOS Assistance Emergency and AirMed International provide evacuation services and medical referrals. MedjetAssist offers medical evacuation.

Medical Assistance Companies AirMed International (⊕ www.airmed.com).**International SOS Assistance Emergency** (⊕ www.intsos.com)**MedjetAssist** (⊕ www.medjetassist.com).

Medical-Only Insurers International Medical Group (☎ 800/628–4664 ⊕ www.imglobal.com).**International SOS** (⊕ www.internationalsos.com).**Wallach & Company** (☎ 800/237–6615 or 540/687–3166 ⊕ www.wallach.com).

▌HOURS OF OPERATION

Banks are generally open weekdays 9 to 3. In Puerto Vallarta most are open until 4, and some of the larger banks keep a few branches open Saturday from 9 or 10 to 1 or 2:30; however, the extended hours are often for deposits or check cashing only. HSBC is the one chain that stays open for longer hours; on weekdays they are open 8 to 7 and on Saturday from 8 to 3. Government offices are usually open to the public weekdays 9 to 3; along with banks and most private offices, they're closed on national holidays.

Gas stations are normally open 7 AM–10 PM daily. Those near major thoroughfares stay open 24 hours, including most holidays.

Stores are generally open weekdays and Saturday from 9 or 10 AM to 5 or 7 PM; in resort areas, those stores geared to tourists may stay open until 9 or 10 at night, all day on Saturday; some are open on Sunday as well, but it's good to call ahead before making a special trip. Some more traditional shops close for a two-hour lunch break, roughly 2–4. Airport shops are open seven days a week.

HOLIDAYS

Banks and government offices close on January 1, February 5 (Constitution Day), March 21 (Benito Juárez's birthday), May 1 (Labor Day), September 16 (Independence Day), November 20 (Revolution Day), and December 25. They may also close on unofficial holidays, such as Day of the Dead (November 1–2), Virgin of Guadalupe Day (December 12), and during Holy Week (the days leading to Easter Sunday). Government offices usually have reduced hours and staff from Christmas through New Year's Day.

▌MAIL

The Mexican postal system is notoriously slow and unreliable; never send packages through the postal service or expect to receive them, as they may be stolen. (For emergencies, use a courier service.) If you're an American Express cardholder, you may be able to receive packages at a branch office, but check beforehand with customer service to find out whether this client mail service is available at your destination.

Post offices (*oficinas de correos*) are found in even the smallest villages. International postal service is all airmail, but even so your letter will take anywhere from 10 days to six weeks to arrive. Service within Mexico can be equally slow.

It costs 10.5 pesos (about 95¢) to send a postcard or letter weighing under 20 grams to the United States or Canada; it's 13 pesos ($1.17) to Europe and 14.5 pesos ($1.30) to Australia and New Zealand.

Contacts **American Express** (⊕ www. americanexpress.com/travel).

Correos (⊠ Calle Mina 188, El Centro ☎ 322/222–1888).

SHIPPING PACKAGES

Federal Express, DHL, Estafeta, and United Parcel Service are available in major cities and many resort areas (though PV doesn't have a FedEx office). It's best to send all packages using one of these services. These companies offer office or hotel pickup with 24-hour advance notice (sometimes less, depending on when you call) and are very reliable. FedEx's Web site is especially easy to navigate. From Puerto Vallarta to large U.S. cities, for example, the minimum charge is around $30 for an envelope weighing about ½ pound.

Express Services DHL (⊠ Blvd. Federico M. Ascencio 1834, across from the SheratonCol. Olímpica ☎ 322/222–4720 or 322/222–4620 ⊕ www.dhl.com). **Estafeta** (⊠ Blvd. Federico M. Ascencio 1834, across from Mega grocery store, Col. Olímpica ☎ 322/223–1700 or 322/223–2898 ⊕ www.estafeta.com). **Mail Boxes Etc.** (⊠ Edifício Andrea Mar Local 7, Blvd. Francisco M. Ascencio 2180, Zona Hotelera Norte (Col. Versalles) ⊹ Across from Hotel Los Tules ☎ 322/224–9434).

▌ MONEY

Prices in this book are quoted most often in U.S. dollars. We'd prefer to list costs in pesos, but because the value of the currency fluctuates, what costs 90 pesos today might cost 120 pesos in six months.

A stay in one of Puerto Vallarta's top hotels can cost more than $250, but if you aren't wedded to standard creature comforts, you can spend as little as $50 a day on room, board, and local transportation. Lodgings are less expensive in the less-developed spots north and south of Puerto Vallarta as well as the charming but unsophisticated mountain towns like San Sebastián del Oeste.

You can get away with a tab of $50 for two at a wonderful restaurant (although it's also easy to pay much more). The good news is that there are hotels and eateries for every budget, and inexpensive doesn't necessarily mean bargain basement. This guide will clue you in to some excellent places to stay, eat, and play for extremely reasonable prices.

ITEM	AVERAGE COST
Cup of Coffee	80¢ to $1.50
Glass of Wine	$3.50–$8
Bottle of Beer	$2–$3
Sandwich	$1.50–$2.50
One-Mile Taxi Ride	$3
Museum Admission	free

Prices throughout this guide are given for adults. Substantially reduced fees are almost always available for children, students, and senior citizens.

ATMS & BANKS

Your own bank will probably charge a fee for using ATMs abroad; the foreign bank you use may also charge a fee. You'll usually get a better rate of exchange at an ATM, however, than you will at a currency-exchange office or at a teller window. And extracting funds as you need them is a safer option than carrying around a large amount of cash.

ATMs (*cajeros automáticos*) are widely available, with Cirrus and Plus the most frequently found networks. However, the transaction fees charged by your bank can be up to $5 a pop; before you leave home, ask your bank about fees for withdrawing money in Mexico.

Many Mexican ATMs cannot accept PINs with more than four digits. If yours is longer, change your PIN to four digits before you leave home. If your PIN is fine yet your transaction still can't be completed, chances are that the computer lines are busy or that the machine has run out of money or is being serviced. Don't give up.

For cash advances, plan to use Visa or MasterCard, as many Mexican ATMs don't accept American Express. Large banks with reliable ATMs include Banamex, HSBC, BBVA Bancomer, Santander Serfín, and Scotiabank Inverlat. *(For information about avoiding ATM robberies, see Safety.) Travelers must have their passport in order to change traveler's checks.*

Banks **Banamex** (✉ Calle Juárez, at Calle Zaragoza, Centro ☎ 322/226–6110 ✉ Calle Emiliano Zapata 175, Pitillal ☎ 322/224–8115 ✉ Paseo de los Cocoteros s/n, Paradise Plaza, Nuevo Vallarta ☎ 322/297–0688). **Banorte** (✉ Paseo Díaz Ordaz 690 at Calle L. Vicario, Centro ☎ 322/222–4040 ✉ Calle Olas Altas 246, at Calle Basilio Badillo, E. Zapata ☎ 322/223–0481 ✉ Blvd. Francisco Medina Ascencio 500, Zona Hotelera Norte ☎ 322/224–9744).

CREDIT CARDS

Throughout this guide, the following abbreviations are used: **AE**, American Express; **D**, Discover; **DC**, Diners Club; **MC**, MasterCard; and **V**, Visa.

Credit cards are accepted in Puerto Vallarta and at major hotels and restaurants in outlying areas. Smaller, less expensive restaurants and shops tend to take only cash. In general, credit cards aren't accepted in small towns and villages, except in some hotels. The most widely accepted cards are MasterCard and Visa.

When shopping, you can often get better prices if you pay with cash, particularly in small shops. But you'll receive wholesale exchange rates when you make purchases with credit cards. These exchange rates are usually better than those that banks give you for changing money. The decision to pay cash or to use a credit card might depend on whether the establishment in which you are making a purchase finds bargaining for prices acceptable, and whether you want the safety net of your card's purchase protection. To avoid fraud or errors, it's wise to make sure that "pesos" is clearly marked on all credit-card receipts.

Before you leave for Mexico, contact your credit-card company to get lost-card phone numbers that work in Mexico; the standard toll-free numbers often don't work abroad. Carry these numbers separately from your wallet so you'll have them if you need to call to report lost or stolen cards. American Express, MasterCard, and Visa note the international number for card-replacement calls on the back of their cards.

CURRENCY & EXCHANGE

Mexican currency comes in denominations of 20-, 50-, 100-, 200-, and 500-peso bills. Coins come in denominations of 1, 2, 5, 10, and 20 pesos, and 10, 20, and 50 centavos. (Ten and 20-centavo coins are only rarely seen.) Many of the coins and bills are very similar, so check carefully.

U.S. dollar bills (but not coins) are widely accepted in tourist-oriented shops and restaurants in Puerto Vallarta. Pay in pesos where possible, however, for better prices. Although in larger hotels U.S. dollars are welcome as tips, it's generally better to tip in pesos so that service personnel aren't stuck going to the bank to exchange currency.

At this writing, the exchange rate was 10.44 pesos to the U.S. dollar. ATM transaction fees may be higher abroad than at home, but ATM exchange rates are the best because they're based on wholesale rates offered only by major banks. And if you take out a fair amount of cash per withdrawal, the transaction fee becomes less of a strike against the exchange rate (in percentage terms). However, most ATMs allow only up to $300 per transaction. Banks and *casas de cambio* (money-exchange bureaus) have the second-best exchange rates. The difference from one place to another is usually only a few pesos.

Some banks change money on weekdays only until 1 or 3 PM (though they stay open until 4 or 5 or later). Casas de cambio generally stay open until 6 or later and often operate on weekends; they usually have competitive rates and much shorter lines. Some hotels exchange money, but they help themselves to a bigger commission than banks for providing you this convenience.

You can do well at most airport exchange booths, though not as well as at the ATMs. You'll do even worse at bus stations, in hotels, in restaurants, or in stores.

When changing money, count your bills before leaving the window of the bank or casa de cambio, and don't accept any partially torn or taped-together notes: you won't be able to use them anywhere. Also, many shop and restaurant owners are unable to make change for large bills. Enough of these encounters may compel you to request *billetes chicos* (small bills) when you exchange money. It's wise to have a cache of smaller bills and coins to use at these more humble establishments to avoid having to wait around while the merchant runs off to seek change.

PACKING

High-style sportswear, cotton slacks and walking shorts, and plenty of colorful sundresses are the palette of clothing you'll see in PV. Bring lightweight sportswear, bathing suits, and cover-ups for the beach. In addition to shorts, pack at least a pair or two of lightweight long pants.

Men may want to bring a lightweight suit or slacks and blazers for fancier restaurants (although very few have dress codes). For women, dresses of cotton, linen, or other lightweight, breathable fabrics are recommended. Puerto Vallarta restaurants are extremely tolerant of casual dress, but it never hurts to exceed expectations.

The sun can be fierce; bring a sun hat and sunscreen for the beach and for sightseeing. You'll need a sweater or jacket to cope with hotel and restaurant air-conditioning, which can be glacial, and for occasional cool spells. A lightweight jacket is a necessity in winter, and pack an umbrella for summer or unexpected rainstorms.

Bring along tissue packs in case you hit a place where the toilet paper has run out. You'll find familiar toiletries and hygiene products, as well as condoms, in shops in PV and in most rural areas.

PASSPORTS & VISAS

U.S. citizens of all ages traveling from Mexico need to present a valid U.S. passport; a passport card (being introduced for travel between the United States and Canada, Mexico, the Caribbean, and Berumda); or a government-issued photo ID, such as a driver's license, along with proof of citizenship, such as a birth certificate upon returning to the States. Also accepted are Western Hemisphere Travel Initiative—compliant documents, including trusted traveler cards and U.S. Military IDs and with military travel orders.

All visitors must get a tourist card. If you're arriving by plane from the United States or Canada, the standard tourist card will be given to you on the plane. They're also available through travel agents and Mexican consulates, and at the border if you're entering by land.

■TIP➔You're given a portion of the tourist card form upon entering Mexico. Keep track of this documentation throughout your trip: you will need it when you depart. You'll be asked to hand it, your ticket, and your passport to airline representatives at the gate when boarding for departure.

A tourist card costs about $20. The fee is generally tacked onto the price of your airline ticket; if you enter by land or boat you'll have to pay the fee separately. You're exempt from the fee if you enter by sea and stay less than 72 hours, or by land and do not stray past the 26- to 30-km (16- to 18-mi) checkpoint into the country's interior.

Tourist cards and visas are valid from 30 to 180 days, at the discretion of the immigration officer at your point of entry (90 days for Australians). Americans, Canadians, New Zealanders, and the British may request up to 180 days for a tourist card or visa extension; Australians are allowed up to 90 days. The extension fee is about $20, and the process can easily take up an entire day. There's no guarantee that you'll get the extension you're requesting. If you're planning an extended stay, plead with the immigration official for the maximum allowed days at the time of entry. It will save you time and money later.

■TIP➔Mexico has some of the strictest policies about children entering the country. Minors traveling with one parent need notarized permission from the absent parent. And all children, including infants, must have proof of citizenship (the same as adults; *see above*) for travel to Mexico.

If you're a single parent traveling with children up to age 18, you must have a notarized letter from the other parent stating that the child has his or her permission to leave his or her home country. The child must be carrying the original letter—not a facsimile or scanned copy—as well as proof of the parent/child relationship (usually a birth certificate or court document), and an original custody decree, if applicable. If the other parent is deceased or the child has only one legal parent, a notarized statement saying so must be obtained as proof. In addition, you must fill out a tourist card for each child over the age of 10 traveling with you.

Info **Mexican Embassy** (☎202/728–1600 ⊕www.embassyofmexico.org/eng .

U.S. Passport Information **U.S. Department of State** (☎877/487–2778 ⊕ travel.state. gov/passport).

■ RESTROOMS

Expect to find reasonably clean flushing toilets and cold running water at public restrooms in the major tourist destinations and attractions; toilet paper, soap, hot water, and paper towels aren't always available, though. Keep a packet of tissues with you at all times.

At many markets, bus stations, and the like you usually have to pay 5 pesos to use the facilities.

■TIP➔Remember that unless otherwise indicated you should put your used toilet paper in the wastebasket next to the toilet; many plumbing systems in Mexico still can't handle accumulations of toilet paper.

Gas stations have public bathrooms—some tidy and others not so tidy. You're better off popping into a restaurant, buying a little something, and using its restroom, which will probably be simple but clean and adequately equipped.

Find a Loo **The Bathroom Diaries** (⊕www. thebathroomdiaries.com) is flush with unsanitized info on restrooms the world over—each one located, reviewed, and rated.

▌ SAFETY

Horror stories about highway assaults, pickpocketing, and bus robberies by armed bandits don't really apply to the area around Puerto Vallarta. Despite recent growth, PV retains a small-town attitude where crime isn't much of a problem. Of course, pickpocketing can be a concern, and precaution is in order here as elsewhere. Store only enough money in your wallet or bag to cover the day's spending. And don't flash big wads of money or leave valuables like cameras unattended. Leave your passport and other valuables you don't need in your hotel's safe.

Bear in mind that reporting a crime to the police is often a frustrating experience unless you speak excellent Spanish and have a great deal of patience. If you're victimized, contact your local consulate or your embassy in Mexico City.

One of the most serious threats to your safety is local drivers. Although pedestrians have the right of way, drivers disregard this law. And more often than not, drivers who hit pedestrians drive away as fast as they can without stopping, to avoid jail. Many Mexican drivers don't carry auto insurance, so you'll have to shoulder your own medical expenses. Pedestrians should be extremely cautious of all traffic, especially city bus drivers, who often drive with truly reckless abandon.

If you're on your own, consider using only your first initial and last name when registering at your hotel. Solo travelers, or women traveling with other women rather than men, may be subjected to *piropos* (flirtatious compliments). Piropos are one thing, but more aggressive harassment is another. If the situation seems to be getting out of hand, don't hesitate to ask someone for help. If you express outrage, you should find no shortage of willing defenders.

General Information & Warnings **Transportation Security Administration** (TSA ⊕www. tsa.gov)**U.S. Department of State** (⊕www. travel.state.gov).

▌ TAXES

Mexico charges an airport departure tax of US$18 or the peso equivalent for international and domestic flights. This tax is usually included in the price of your ticket, but check to be certain. Traveler's checks and credit cards aren't accepted at the airport as payment for this, but U.S. dollars are. Jalisco and Nayarit charge a 2% tax on accommodations, the funds from which are being used for tourism promotion.

Puerto Vallarta and environs have a value-added tax of 15%, called IVA (*impuesto al valor agregado*). It's often waived for cash purchases, or it's incorporated into the price. When comparing hotel prices, it's important to know if yours includes or excludes IVA and any service charge. Other taxes and charges apply for phone calls made from your hotel room.

▌ TIME

Puerto Vallarta, Guadalajara, and the rest of Jalisco State fall into Central Standard Time (the same as Mexico City). Nayarit and other parts of the northwest coast are on Mountain Standard Time.

The fact that the state of Nayarit (including Nuevo Vallarta and points north) are in a different time zone from Puerto Vallarta and points east and south leads to confusion. And to add to this confusion, Mexico does observe daylight savings time, but not on the same schedule as the United States.

▌TIP→ Businesses in Nuevo Vallarta and many tourism-related businesses in Bucerías run on Jalisco time.

Since tourism in these towns has always been linked to that of Puerto Vallarta, hotels in the two areas almost always run on Jalisco time to avoid having their clients miss planes when returning home. When asking the time, checking hours of operation, or making dinner reservations, double check whether the place runs on *hora de Jalisco* (Jalisco time) or *hora de Nayarit*.

▌TIPPING

When tipping in Mexico, remember that the minimum wage—which is what maids, bellmen, and others in the tourism industry earn—is just under $5 a day. Waiters and bellmen in international chain hotels think in dollars and know, for example, that in the United States porters are tipped about $2 a bag; they tend to expect the equivalent.

TIPPING GUIDELINES FOR PUERTO VALLARTA	
Bartender	10% to 15% of the bill
Bellhop	10 to 30 pesos (roughly $1 to $3) per bag, depending on the level of the hotel
Hotel Concierge	30 pesos or more, if he or she performs a service for you
Hotel Doorman	10 to 20 pesos if he helps you get a cab
Hotel Maid	10 to 30 pesos a day (either daily or at the end of your stay); make sure the maid gets it, and not the guy who checks the mini-bar prior to your departure
Hotel Room-Service Waiter	10 to 20 pesos per delivery, even if a service charge has been added
Porter/Skycap at Airport	10 pesos per bag
Restroom Attendant	5 to 10 pesos
Taxi Driver	cab drivers aren't normally tipped; give them 5 to 10 pesos if they help with your bags
Tour Guide	10% of the cost of the tour

TIPPING GUIDELINES FOR PUERTO VALLARTA	
Valet Parking Attendant	10 to 20 pesos but only when you get your car
Waiter	10% to 15%; nothing additional if a service charge is added to the bill

▌TOURS

SPANISH-LANGUAGE STUDY

Attending a language institute is an ideal way not only to learn Mexican Spanish but also to acquaint yourself with the customs and the people. For total immersion, most schools offer boarding with a family, but there's generally flexibility in terms of the type of lodgings and the length of your stay.

AmeriSpan Unlimited, based in the United States, specializes in medical and business Spanish; see the Web site for student blogs. The Academia Hispano Americana offers a variety of language-study options as well as weekly cooking classes. Many programs offer courses in Latin American studies and culture, as well as language.

Contacts Academia Hispano Americana (☎415/152–0349 (Mexico) ⊕www.aha speakspanish.com). **AmeriSpan Unlimited** (☎800/879–6640, 215/751–1100 in U.S. ⊕). **Centro de Estudios para Extranjeros** (☎33/3616–4399 in Guadalajara, 322/223–2082 in PV ⊕www.cepe.udg.mx).

▌TRIP INSURANCE

Comprehensive trip insurance is valuable if you're booking a very expensive or complicated trip (particularly to an isolated region) or if you're booking far in advance. Comprehensive policies typically cover trip-cancellation and interruption, letting you cancel or cut your trip short because of a personal emergency, illness, or, in some cases, acts of terrorism in your destination. Such policies also cover evacuation and medical care.

(For trips abroad you should at least have medical-only coverage; for more information, see Health, above). Some also cover you for trip delays because of bad weather or mechanical problems as well as for lost or delayed baggage.

Another type of coverage to look for is financial default—that is, when your trip is disrupted because a tour operator, airline, or cruise line goes out of business. Generally you must buy this when you book your trip or shortly thereafter, and it's only available to you if your operator isn't on a list of excluded companies.

Always read the fine print of your policy to make sure that you are covered for the risks that are of most concern to you. Compare several policies to make sure you're getting the best price and range of coverage available.

Insurance Comparison Sites Insure My Trip. com (☎800/487–4722 ⊕www.insuremytrip. com). **Square Mouth.com** (☎800/240–0369 or 727/490–5803 ⊕www.squaremouth.com).

Comprehensive Travel Insurers Access America (☎866/729–6021 ⊕www. accessamerica.com) **AIG Travel Guard** (☎800/826–4919 ⊕www.travelguard.com) **CSA Travel Protection** (☎800/873–9855 ⊕www.csatravelprotection.com) **HTH Worldwide** (☎610/254–8700 ⊕www.hthworldwide. com)**Travelex Insurance** (☎888/228–9792 ⊕www.travelex-insurance.com)**Travel Insured International** (☎800/243–3174 ⊕www. travelinsured.com).

■TIP➔ OK. You know you can save a bundle on trips to warm-weather destinations by traveling in rainy season. But there's also a chance that a severe storm will disrupt your plans. The solution? Look for hotels and resorts that offer storm/hurricane guarantees. Although they rarely allow refunds, most guarantees do let you rebook later if a storm strikes.

■ VISITOR INFORMATION

The Mexican Ministry of Tourism has Infotur, a 24-hour toll-free hotline, and a Web site with general info about the tourism industry. There's info about PV and the state of Jalisco, too (as well as the other states of the republic), but the English translation is very poor. The Mexico Tourism Board has branches in New York, Chicago, Los Angeles, Houston, Miami, Montréal, Toronto, and Vancouver; the official page has information about popular destinations, but again, information is pedestrian.

For information before you visit, try the Puerto Vallarta Tourism Board & Convention and Visitors Bureau. You can also stop in for maps and other information once you're in town. Other convenient sources of information are the Municipal Tourist Office, right on the Plaza Principal. It's open weekdays 8–4.

The friendly folks at the Jalisco State Tourism Office, open weekdays 9–5, are helpful with information about PV and destinations throughout the state, including mountain towns like Mascota and Talpán. For information about Nuevo Vallarta and southern Nayarit, contact the Nayarit State Tourism Office.

Contacts Mexican Ministry of Tourism (☎800/446–3942 Infotur in U.S., 01800/903–9200 in Mexico ⊕www.sectur.gob.mx). **Mexican Tourism Board (U.S. & Canada)** (☎800/446–3942 [44-MEXICO] in U.S. and Canada ⊕www.visitmexico.com). **Puerto Vallarta Tourism Board & Convention and Visitors Bureau** (✉Local 18 Planta Baja, Zona Comercial Hotel Canto del Sol Zona Hotelera, Las Glorias ☎322/224–1175, 888/384-6822 in U.S., 01800/719–3276 in Mexico ⊕www. visitpuertovallarta.com). **Municipal Tourist Office** (✉Av. Independencia 123, Centro ☎322/223–2500 Ext. 131). **Jalisco State Tourism Office** (✉Plaza Marina shopping center, Local 144, Planta Alta, Marina Vallarta ☎322/221–2676). **Bay of Banderas/Nuevo Vallarta Tourism Office** (✉Paseo de los

Cocoteros at Blvd. Nuevo Vallarta, between Gran Velas and Maribal hotels ☎322/297–1006 or 322/297–0180).

ONLINE RESOURCES

The best of the private enterprise Web sites is Virtual Vallarta, , which has tons of good info and short articles about life in PV. Bucerías and Punta Mita have their own Web sites, as does the Costalegre region as a whole.

Excellent English-language sites for general history, travel information, facts, and news stories about Mexico are: the United States' Library of Congress well-organized, albeit dated, Mexico pages; Mexico Online; and Mexico Connect. Mexico Guru has news about PV and nearby destinations, and interactive maps.

The nonprofit site Ancient Mexico has information about Western Mexico as well as more comprehensive information about the Maya and Aztecs.

Contacts Ancient Mexico (⊕ www.ancient-mexico.com).**Bucerías** (⊕ www.buceriasmexico. com).**Costalegre** (⊕ www.costalegre.ca). **Mexico Connect** (⊕ www.mexconnect.com). **Mexico Guru** (⊕ www.mexicoguru.com). **Mexico Online** (⊕ www.mexonline.com).**Punta Mita** (⊕ www.puntamita.com). **United States Library of Congress** (⊕ lcweb2.loc.gov/frd/ cs/mxtoc.html and ⊕ www.loc.gov/rr/ international/hispanic/mexico/mexico.html). **Virtual Vallarta** (⊕ www.virtualvallarta.com).

INDEX

Photo Credits: Cover Photo, (Tequila, Jalisco). Patrick Frilet/hemis.fr. 5, Eric Wessman/viestiphoto. com. **Chapter 1: Experience Puerto Vallarta:** 11, Danita Delimont/Alamy. 12, Jane Onstott. 13, Mary Magruder/viestiphoto.com. 14, Walter Bibikow/viestiphoto.com. 15 (left), Puerto Vallarta Tourism Board. 15 (right), Ken Welsh/age fotostock. 16, Ken Ross/viestiphoto.com. 17 (left), Ken Ross/viesti photo.com. 17 (right), Walter Bibikow/viestiphoto.com. 18, Terrance Klassen/age fotostock. 19 (left), Puerto Vallarta Tourism Board. 19 (right), Walter Bibikow/viestiphoto.com. 20, Ken Ross/viesiphoto. com. **Chapter 2: Where to Stay:** 21, El Tamarindo Golf Resort. 42, El Careyes Beach Resort. 43 (left and right), Four Seasons Resort, Punta Mita. 44, Four Seasons Resort, Punta Mita. 46, Grand Velas. 48, Ken Ross/viestiphoto.com. **Chapter 3: Where to Eat:** 61, Ken Ross/viestiphoto.com. 79, Lisa Candela. 80 (all), Ken Ross/viestiphoto.com. 81 (top), Jane Onstott. 81 (center), Mark's Restaurant. 81 (bottom), Ken Ross/viestiphoto.com. 82 (top and bottom), Ken Ross/viestiphotocom. 83, Ken Ross/ viestiphoto.com. **Chapter 4: Beaches:** 93, Corbis. **Chapter 5: Shopping:** 113, Ken Ross/viestiphoto.com. 126, Ken Ross/viestiphoto.com. 127 (top), Ken Ross/viestiphoto.com. 127 (bottom), Walter Bibikow/ viestiphoto.com. 128, Ken Ross/viestiphoto.com. 127 (top right), Ken Ross/viestiphoto.com. 125 (top left, bottom left and bottom right), Jane Onstott. 127 (center right), José Zelaya Gallery: artedelpueblo. com. 130 (top, bottom left, center left, bottom right), Ken Ross/viestiphoto.com. 137 (center right), Jane Onstott. **Chapter 6: After Dark:** 137, Jeff Greenberg/Alamy. 142, Russell Gordon/viestiphoto.com. 143 (all), Russell Gordon/viestiphoto.com. 144, Ken Ross/viestiphoto.com. 145 (top and bottom), Ken Ross/viestiphoto.com. 151, David Sanger Photography/Alamy. **Chapter 7: Adventure:** 153, Bruce Herman/Mexico Tourism Board. **Chapter 8: Culture:** 175, Fideicomiso Turismo de Puerto Vallarta (FIDE-TUR). **Chapter 9: Overnight Excursions:** 185, Bruce Herman/Mexico Tourism Board. 186 (top), Corbis. 186 (bottom), Ken Ross/viestiphoto.com. 187, Colonial Arts, San Francisco. 215, Ken Ross/viesti photo.com. 216 (top left, bottom left, and bottom right), Ken Ross/viestiphoto.com. 216 (top right), C Squared Studios/Photodisc. 217, Jeff Greenberg/Alamy. 218, Ken Welsh/age fotostock. 219 (top), Pablo de Aguinaco/Mexico Tourism Board. 219 (bottom), Bruce Herman/Mexico Tourism Board. **Chapter 10: Gay Puerto Vallarta:** 233, Marka/age fotostock.

NOTES

NOTES

NOTES

NOTES

NOTES

NOTES

NOTES

NOTES

ABOUT OUR WRITER

Jane Onstott was primed for adventure travel in her late teens, when she wandered Central America for six months after being stood up at the Tegucigalpa airport up by an inattentive suitor. She has since survived a near plunge into a gorge in the highlands of Mexico, a knife-wielding robber in Madrid, and a financial shipwreck on one of the more remote Galapagos Islands. The last led to a position as director of communications and information at the Charles Darwin Research Station on the island of Santa Cruz, where she lectured on the ecology of Ecuador's unique Galapagos archipelago.

Jane's trip to rural Honduras, taken before she turned 20, became an unofficial total-language-immersion course, paving the way for a love of the Spanish language and of Hispanic culture. She studied for a year at la Universidad Complutense de Madrid, in Spain, and graduated from San Diego State University with a B.A. in Spanish language and literature.

But at age 17 this adventurer's first foray outside the United States—Southern California's concrete jungle—was to a small village in the tropical forest just a few hours north of Puerto Vallarta. The stick-and-thatch house where she stayed has since been replaced by a more modern one of cement and bright stucco, but the warm hearts of its owners have changed little in the ensuing three decades. Mexico is Jane's favorite country, and Puerto Vallarta and the surrounding coast, one of her more frequent destinations, whether traveling for business or pleasure.

In the 1990s Jane spent several years studying painting, sculpting, and the fine art of loafing in Oaxaca—ancient capital of the Zapotec nation—where she was inspired by landscape, the people, and the culture. Today Jane continues to edit and write mainly about travel and mostly about Mexico. She has a home in San Diego county, a short hop north of the border—and of the Tijuana airport.